Introduction to Housing

Introduction to Housing

Edited by

John L. Merrill
University of Wisconsin

Sue R. Crull
Iowa State University

Kenneth R. Tremblay, Jr.
Colorado State University

Loraine L. Tyler
State University of New York, Oneonta

Andrew T. Carswell
University of Georgia

PEARSON

Prentice
Hall

Upper Saddle River, New Jersey 07458

housingeducators.org

Library of Congress Cataloging-in-Publication Data

Introduction to housing / edited by John L. Merrill ... [et al.].
   p. cm.
  Includes bibliographical references and index.
  ISBN 0-13-119042-3
  1. Housing. I. Merrill, John L.
  HD7287.I74 2006
  363.5--dc22   2005017813

Director of Development: *Vernon R. Anthony*
Senior Editor: *Eileen McClay*
Editorial Assistant: *Yvette Schlarman*
Managing Editor: *Mary Carnis*
Production Editor: *Judy Ludowitz Carlisle Publishers Services*
Production Liaison: *Janice Stangel*
Director of Manufactring and Production: *Bruce Johnson*
Manufacturing Manager: *Ilene Sanford*
Manufacturing Buyer: *Cathleen Petersen*
Creative Director: *Cheryl Asherman*
Cover Design Coordinator: *Miguel Ortiz*
Executive Marketing Manager: *Ryan DeGrote*
Senior Marketing Coordinator: *Elizabeth Farrell*
Marketing Assistant: *Les Roberts*
Cover Design: *Miguel Ortiz*
Cover Image: *Corbis (Royalty-Free)*

Pearson Education LTD.   Pearson Education Australia PTY, Limited
Pearson Education Singapore, Pte. Ltd   Pearson Education North Asia Ltd
Pearson Education, Canada, Ltd   Pearson Educacíon de Mexico, S.A. de C.V.
Pearson Education–Japan   Pearson Education Malaysia, Pte. Ltd

PEARSON
Prentice
Hall

10 9 8 7 6 5 4 3 2 1
ISBN: 0-13-119042-3

Contents

Preface   vii
Acknowledgment   xv

Chapter   1   **A Short History of Housing
in America**   1
John L. Merrill

Chapter   2   **Influences on Housing Choice
and Behaviors**   25
*Julia O. Beamish, Rosemary Carucci Goss,
and JoAnn Emmel*

Chapter   3   **Home Environments and Health**   55
*Kathleen R. Parrott, Jorge H. Atiles,
and Michael P. Vogel*

Chapter   4   **The Housing Industry**   87
Andrew T. Carswell and Anne L. Sweaney

Chapter   5   **Housing and Community**   113
*Loraine L. Tyler, Nancy C. Higgitt,
and Carla C. Earhart*

Chapter   6   **Federal Government Housing
Policies**   139
Carol B. Roskey and Mary Sue Green

Chapter   7   **Interior Space Planning**   167
Jean A. Memken and Starr Gobtop

Chapter 8   Universal Design in Housing   191
             Sandra C. Hartje, Kenneth R. Tremblay, Jr.,
             and Craig Birdsong

Chapter 9   Housing Affordability   225
             Christine C. Cook, Carmen D. Steggell,
             Andrea Suarez, and Becky L. Yust

Chapter 10 Homeownership   257
             Sue R. Crull, Marilyn J. Bruin,
             and Thessalenuere Hinnant-Bernard

Chapter 11 Sustainable Buildings
             and Communities   291
             Leona K. Hawks, Kerry F. Case,
             and Jane D. Reagor

Chapter 12 Housing Challenges for
             the Twenty-first Century   327
             Andrew T. Carswell, John L. Merrill, Anne L.
             Sweaney, and Kenneth R. Tremblay, Jr.

Index   337

Preface

The study of housing makes many people think of studying architecture, specifically the structures in which most of us live. However, the study of housing is much more than a study of the design and construction of residential structures. It also involves human habitation through the interplay of design and economic, social, cultural, and policy factors and how our housing, in turn, affects our behavior and our culture.

Housing's complexity as a field of inquiry is reflected in the variety of disciplines that touch on housing. For example, housing plays a major role in our economy, as economists use "housing starts" as a measure of the economy's health. Real estate, a subfield of business administration, studies housing markets and how they function as well as housing finance mechanisms. The latter is also a concern of their business colleagues studying banking and finance.

Because of its strong connection to the local and national economy, housing is an important part of public policy. At the local and regional level, urban planners view housing from a land use planning perspective. In many communities housing is the predominant land use and drives regulatory issues such as zoning, as well as utility and road building decisions.

Architects, interior designers, and landscape architects all focus attention on housing's physical development. They are supported by structural, mechanical, electrical, civil, and other engineers who develop modern housing's equipment and materials.

Sociologists, anthropologists, and psychologists look at the impact specific housing aspects have on its inhabitants and how people make housing decisions. For example, geographers look at the way climate and culture have affected housing's evolution over time, and architectural historians look at the evolution of housing forms over time, although they usually emphasize formal styles and ornamentation.

While scholars in many fields of study contribute to our knowledge of housing, relatively few would classify themselves as housing scholars. Furthermore, few of these scholars attempt to look at housing systematically as a critical component of our society.

WHY STUDY HOUSING?

Housing Is Much More than Shelter

Ask a homeless person why housing is important and you are likely to get a variety of answers, including the provision of shelter from the cold and rain. In fact, shelter is frequently used as a synonym for housing. Unlike other animals we do not have thick fur or feathers or other adaptive characteristics that allow us to withstand weather extremes. Humans actually have a very narrow tolerance for temperature change. If our body cools, even a little, hypothermia sets in, which can easily result in death if we are not rescued. Heat stroke and other health problems can occur in warm climates if we go for long periods without shelter.

A more specific physical housing need pertains to sleep. Hunter (1999) pointed out that, unlike humans, sharks do not sleep at all, and horses sleep standing up. To retain our sanity and health, however, we need to sleep and do so in a nearly horizontal position. Even though we may doze off in chairs, our bodies are most relaxed while lying down. Having a home in which to lie down undisturbed is important to our survival.

Our homeless informant would probably identify other problems he or she encounters as well. Personal safety and security for their possessions would likely be among them. If you are sleeping in a public place, the chances of being attacked or robbed are much greater than they would be inside a home with locked doors. The homeless need to constantly keep all their possessions with them to be sure they are not taken and to protect them from the weather.

A house also provides you with an address. Although easy to take for granted, people need to be able to contact you if you are looking for work or a place to live. Similarly, without a permanent address, enrolling children in school can be difficult and also may cause delays when you are applying for a job, housing, or social services.

Homelessness appears to have a very negative impact on the large number of children who experience it. One study found that a majority of homeless children functioned at the bottom of their age group in verbal skills and were likely to exhibit emotional and behavioral problems (Hart-Shegos, 1999).

Housing Is a Critical Part of Household Budgets

Housing is the largest expense in most household budgets. According to the 2002 consumer expenditure survey from the U.S. Department of Labor (2003), housing-related expenses accounted for 32.9 percent of consumer expenditures, including rent or house payments as well as utilities such as heating fuel, electricity, water, and sewer. The next highest item was transportation at 19.3 percent.

Housing also creates wealth for American households, particularly middle- and lower-income households (Kennickell, 2003). At least two thirds of U.S. households own their own homes. Technically, most homeowners do not own their home free and clear, but have a mortgage loan that they are repaying. However, if the house increases in value after purchase that added value belongs to the homeowner.

Social and Psychological Housing Functions

In addition to its economic importance, housing provides important psychological and social functions. People who buy homes are seeking much more than shelter. They are also looking to express their values and aspirations. The home becomes an important part of many people's identities. They may select an older house that connects them with traditions that they value and a sense of continuity with the past, or a condominium in an urban high rise that supports an active cultural life and limits yard care requirements. Others may choose a rural home that helps the owners connect with nature and gain an added sense of retreating from their work world, while others want to build their own home so they can express their own design ideas and feel comfortable with the structure's quality and form. Yet other people value knowing and interacting with neighbors and may choose to live in an intentional community arrangement such as cooperative housing or cohousing. In almost all cases, people hope to gain much more than refuge from the weather when they select a home.

Once people move in the home it remains a vehicle for self-expression. Americans spend billions of dollars each year improving their homes. They install elaborate landscaping and spend hours tending it. They change furnishings, colors, and flooring of various rooms not only when the previous items are worn out but also when the owners are inspired to change the look of their homes.

One's home is clearly a symbol of one's status in the community. The phrase "moving up in society" can clearly mean more than moving up the social ladder. It means moving up in terms of the house and neighborhood where one lives. For centuries, housing has been a way to show wealth and status. In addition to the size, ornamentation, and design of one's house, the neighborhood matters as well. Most communities have a neighborhood where the elite live. In recent years some such communities have tried to set minimum lot and house sizes, but these have come under public scrutiny as blatantly "exclusionary"—attempts to ensure that the neighborhood would remain an enclave for high-status persons.

In a landmark legal case, the New Jersey Supreme Court ruled on two occasions that the township of Mt. Laurel was guilty of such exclusionary zoning by allowing only single-family detached houses and industrial uses in the township, thus excluding lower-income households (Hughes & Van Doren, 1990). The Mt. Laurel outcome, that all developing municipalities in New Jersey must provide their "fair share" of the region's affordable housing needs, means they are subject to lawsuits if an affordable housing plan is not in place. While the court's ruling has been controversial, Mt. Laurel has come to symbolize rules and regulations that attempt to limit a neighborhood's population to match some arbitrary image based on income or other criteria.

Housing has a number of other social-psychological benefits as well. The term *home,* which is often used interchangeably with house, suggests housing's social dimension. While dictionaries list them as synonyms, the definition of house starts with the word *structure* while the definition of home starts with the word *family* (*Webster's New Collegiate Dictionary,* 1979). One social science researcher identified 85 different possible meanings of home (Hayward, 1982) by asking a sample of householders living in urban apartments and in small Massachusetts towns to sort these possible meanings into clusters. The results stress housing dimensions we have not yet explored.

> *A place where you belong*—one cluster of meanings emphasized feelings of connectedness with the people who shared the house.
>
> *A place of refuge*—another cluster emphasized the home as a place you can relax from the pressures of the outside world.
>
> *A place of permanence*—a source of continuity amidst the constant change that most people experience in life.
>
> *A home base*—the place where you begin and end your day and where you do core activities such as sleeping, bathing, and changing clothes.

In reviewing all the ways we are affected by housing, both as individuals and a society, it is surprising that so many of us take housing for granted or, at best, look at it in small pieces. The chapters that follow will look at a number of housing aspects to provide a fuller sense of its complexity and dimensions.

A PREVIEW OF THE CHAPTERS AHEAD

While the study of housing is much more than the study of houses, a look at the history of North American housing in terms of its form and function seems to be a good place to start. Chapter 1 considers the architectural styles that have influenced today's homes, including styles that represented the high fashion of their day and others that were modest but also common. These houses are examined by historical period and include a few details about society changes that were associated with the styles of various periods. As with all of this book's content, entire books have been written about the history of houses. Due to space limitations, only the main topics have been covered. Some books primarily focus on the architecture, while others focus on the cultural implications. We have consulted both and sought out areas of consistency.

This Preface has briefly alluded to some of housing's social-psychological aspects. Chapter 2 delves into this area more deeply, examining factors that influence how we choose and use our homes. Chapter 3 explores another human side of housing by introducing a number of health issues associated with housing. It reviews the potential for health problems from the products used in constructing our homes, the way we build our homes, and our behavior in the homes. The authors also discuss some of the most common strategies for minimizing these home environmental health concerns.

Housing is a large industry. Chapter 4 explores the complexity and scale of the industry's major components, including a discussion of the home building and remodeling industry. It also introduces the roles of developers, bankers, and real estate brokers.

Chapter 5 discusses the neighborhood setting's impact on our homes. This chapter explores community concepts with regard to place-based (physical) and people-based (social) housing issues, examines various definitions of neighborhood and community, reviews social aspects of communities and neighborhoods, and considers some elements of residential satisfaction and dissatisfaction with homes and physical surroundings.

The federal government's role in housing has varied since the depression of the 1930s, particularly in providing housing for people not well served by the private housing market. Chapter 6 discusses the government's changing roles on the development of housing by reviewing government housing programs from their first appearance during the 1930s to the present with an emphasis on current programs. Programs are divided into five themes: quality of housing, homeownership, renter assistance, affordability, and fair housing.

Chapter 7 introduces one aspect of interior design work—space planning. Determining the way rooms are related to each other and how they match the occupants' activities are critical to efficiently utilize space. This chapter introduces a conceptual framework for space planning and a number of concepts designers use in developing house floor plans. Space planning is especially important as we work to provide safe, comfortable, and usable homes for everyone regardless of abilities or disabilities. Chapter 8 looks at the federal laws and regulations designed to ensure that persons with various physical limitations are provided with usable housing. These led to the universal design movement and its goal of creating house designs to meet all persons' needs. Through careful design of exterior and interior spaces, universal design benefits people through all life stages. The chapter discusses universal design and provides illustrations of its housing applications.

Perhaps the most pervasive housing issue of our times is the lack of an adequate supply of affordable housing for low- and moderate-income households. Chapter 9 examines several dimensions of the affordable housing picture. The authors examine spiraling housing costs and the role that local and federal policies play in housing prices. The affordable housing shortage stems from issues related to both housing's supply and demand. Strategies are advanced to reduce housing costs and to increase the resources available to low- and moderate-income households. A brief discussion of homelessness is also included. Chapter 10 focuses on homeownership issues. As most American households own their own homes, this chapter's purpose is to familiarize you with the basic concepts of housing finance and the process of buying and maintaining a home. Special attention is given to the advantages and disadvantages of homeownership as well as to predatory lending.

Chapter 11 explores sustainability, a concept expected to play an increasing role in housing in the years to come. Sustainability refers to the use of renewable construction materials, and also includes durability, energy efficiency, and healthy environments. The authors explore these issues at the individual house level and at the community level.

Chapter 12 completes the text by discussing a number of housing challenges our society will face in the coming decades. Some of the challenges will have been alluded to in previous chapters, while others will be new to the chapter.

REFERENCES

Hart-Shegos, E. (1999). Homelessness and its effect on children. *Family Housing Fund,* Minneapolis, MN, 7–9.

Hayward, D. G. (1982). The meanings of home. *Human Ecology Forum, 13*(Fall), 3–6.

Hughes, M. A., & Van Doren, P. M. (1990). Social policy through land reform: New Jersey's Mount Laurel controversy. *Political Science Quarterly, 105,* 97–111.

Hunter, C. (1999). *Ranches, rowhouses and railroad flats. American homes: How they shape our landscape and neighborhoods.* New York: W. W. Norton.

Kennickell, A. B. (2003). *A rolling tide: Changes in the distribution of wealth in the U.S. 1989-2001.* Washington, DC: Federal Reserve Board.

U.S. Department of Labor. (2003). *Consumer expenditure survey, 2002.* Washington, DC: U.S. Department of Labor.

Webster's New Collegiate Dictionary. (1979). Springfield, MA: G. and C. Merriam Co.

Acknowledgment

This book is a public service of the Housing and Education Research Association (HERA). HERA, an international association that consists of scholars in housing education and research, promotes excellence in the planning, development, delivery, and service of decent, safe, sanitary, affordable, ecologically sound, and appropriately designed housing for all people. HERA members recognize and understand the relationship between individual, family, and community well-being and the holistic housing environment. HERA is a major forum for professional dialogue among educators, researchers, and policymakers in the housing field through its annual meeting and its journal, *Housing and Society.* Members of HERA wrote, edited, and reviewed the text, and have all agreed that any royalties or fees accruing from their work should be used by the association to further housing education and research. For more information about HERA and to access consumer housing resources, please visit www.housingeducators.org.

We would like to thank the following reviewers and acknowledge their dedication to the field of housing and the Housing Education and Research Association.

Katherine Allen	University of Florida
William Angell	University of Minnesota
Lucy Delgadillo	Utah State University
JoAnn Emmel	Virginia Polytechnic Institute and State University
Victoria Feinberg	California State University, Northridge
Victoria Gribschaw	Seton Hill University
Sandra Hartje	Seattle Pacific University
Sarah Kirby	North Carolina State University
Joseph Laquatra	Cornell University

Sharon Laux	University of Missouri
Joan McFadden	Ball State University
Jean Memken	Illinois State University
Shirley Niemeyer	University of Nebraska
Joseph Ponessa	Rutgers University
Joyce Rasdall	Western Kentucky University
Jane Reagor	University of Tennessee, Chattanooga
Anne Sweaney	University of Georgia
B. J. White	Kansas State University
Joseph Wysocki	U.S. Department of Agriculture
Ann Ziebarth	University of Minnesota

CHAPTER 1

A Short History of Housing in America

John L. Merrill
John L. Merrill is Professor Emeritus, School of Human Ecology,
University of Wisconsin, Madison, WI.

North American homes have changed over time. This chapter focuses primarily on issues and home styles that directly impact today's single-family homes. Since a sizable proportion of the U.S. population lives in rental housing—often multifamily housing—rental housing's evolution is also discussed. The chapter is organized as a series of predominantly single-family housing styles associated with major cultural or technological changes. The chapter uses both line drawings and photographs to help visualize the various styles. The line drawings highlight the distinctive features associated with a specific style, while the photos show homes that feature particular styles. Readers who are interested in a more in-depth exploration of housing styles should consult one of the housing style guides, such as McAlester and McAlester's (1984) *A Field Guide to American Homes.*

VERNACULAR HOUSES

Architectural historians generally study houses by developing a classification of styles based on ornament and form (Ennals & Holdsworth, 1998; Jakle, Bastian, & Meyer, 1989). The vast majority of housing constructed in North America is generally ignored in this focus on style. Yet, these houses say much about the meaning and function of American housing since European settlement. Architectural historians sometimes refer to these homes as vernacular, or in some cases folk housing. According to McAlester and McAlester (1984), folk houses are primarily built by the occupants for shelter and with little concern for the currently popular styles of the homes of the wealthy.

Rapoport (1969) distinguished two stages of vernacular architecture. The first type, traditional, is based on a local model and uses local materials and construction techniques. The second type, modern, is more typical of vernacular architecture today in that it uses

1

readily available materials, not necessarily of local origins, and traditional construction techniques. It is based on a variety of models that are shared in written and pictorial form.

Many of the early European settlers came to North America from densely populated countries where only the wealthy owned land. The prospect of owning homes and their own land led many to endure the hardships of coming to the new world (Hunter, 1999). While homeownership was still the goal of most Americans, it was unattainable for a large portion of the population. As a consequence, our modern image of a single-family home occupied by parents and children was rarely seen in colonial times. Homeowners often rented rooms to help pay for their homes. In fact, most early rental housing consisted of rented rooms or even entire homes and was not a distinct housing type (Hunter, 1999).

In the early stages of North American colonization, most homes were of Rapoport's traditional type. While colonists could envision the homes they had lived in when in Europe, they had to adapt these concepts to utilize the immediately available materials. Like the homes they left behind, their North American homes centered around a large fireplace which offered heat, light, and served as the center of many family activities including food preparation (Ennals & Holdsworth, 1998). Since glass had to be imported, windows were used sparingly and were usually small in size.

Early settlers spent much of their time raising food, which meant clearing and cultivating land. With survival at stake, the house was primarily shelter from weather and danger. Homes built by the household members were typically small. Even though many European homes were made of stone, North America's more severe climate, frost, and condensation created problems with stone construction. Since wood was more plentiful in America and had better insulating qualities, it soon became the material of choice (Ennals & Holdsworth, 1998).

HALL AND PARLOR COTTAGES

Several sources described the Hall and Parlor home as one of the early forms of housing. According to Wright (1981), the oldest remaining frame home in North America, the Fairbanks House in Dedham, Massachusetts, is a Hall and Parlor cottage, originally described as a small receiving hall with stairs leading up to the loft sleeping space. However, Hall and Parlor cottages are not always this elaborate. The early versions had no chimneys; therefore, the attic space was left open to let smoke exit through roof openings. Their roofs are steep because

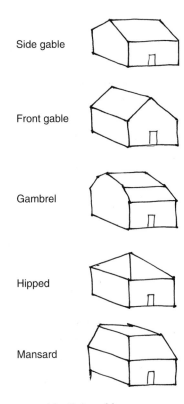

Side gable

Front gable

Gambrel

Hipped

Mansard

Figure 1.1   Common residential roof forms

the European dwellings that inspired them had thatched roofs (McAlester & McAlester, 1984). Hall and Parlor homes generally have gabled roofs with the sloped sides parallel to the front door. The gable, a roof type for homes, has two sloped sides joined at a peak or ridge and supported at either end by a triangular extension of the end wall. Gables are either referred to as side gables if the slope parallels the street or front of the house, or as front gables if the slopes are perpendicular to the front. Figure 1.1 shows a variety of roof forms.

When chimneys became popular in the northern United States, they were generally placed in the center of the house to make the most efficient use of heat. However, in the southern colonies, they were at the ends of the house since energy conservation was not an issue (Jakle et al., 1989). The hall was the public and work area while the parlor was reserved for family sleeping; later, lofts were added for the householder man and wife (Ennals & Holdsworth, 1998). Families often included six persons or more, and often included servants and apprentices. For religious reasons it was considered important to share space and be constantly busy. Privacy was not valued, so private bedrooms were rare (Wright, 1981). Jakle et al. (1989) noted that early colonial homes were often viewed as temporary and were consciously designed to conform to popular taste so they would sell easily when it was time to move.

The Cape Cod cottage, one variant of the Hall and Parlor design, has had recurring popularity, as shown in Figures 1.2 and 1.3. While

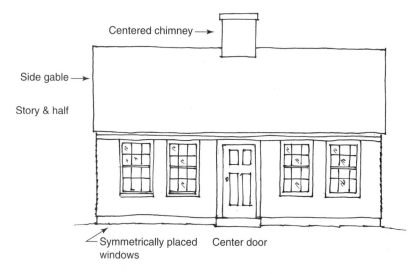

Figure 1.2   Drawing of a Cape Cod style cottage

Figure 1.3   Photo of a Cape Cod style cottage

Cape Cod :
- Side gable roof
- 1½ story
- centered front door
- symmetrically placed windows
- dormers

the style dates back to the seventeenth century, it was most popular in the late eighteenth century and enjoyed a major revival in the mid-twentieth century. Like the Hall and Parlor cottage, it is a story and a half with a side gable and centered front door. Revivals of this design often include dormers facing the front and symmetrically placed windows (Jakle et al., 1989). Dormers are gables perpendicular to the main gable that provide extra room under a roof and usually include windows.

GEORGIAN STYLE HOMES

Merchants and farmers were eventually prosperous enough to hire others to build their homes. These people paid more attention to aesthetics, dividing the interior of their homes into separate areas for different uses (Ennals & Holdsworth, 1998). These more prosperous homeowners could also afford to be fashionable. One style, which took on an early importance and has been one of the most persistent residential styles in much of North America, is known as Georgian, as shown in Figures 1.4 and 1.5. Georgian style, inspired by classical Greek and Roman design, arrived from England around 1700 and remained the primary style in the English colonies until the early nineteenth century. Windows are large and placed symmetrically

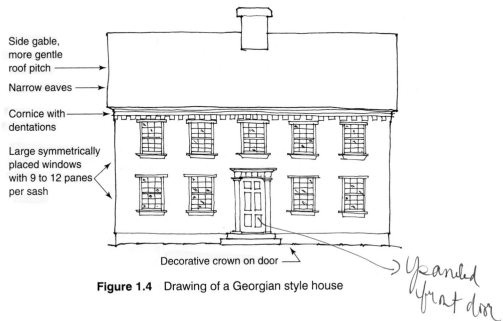

Side gable, more gentle roof pitch ⟶

Narrow eaves ⟶

Cornice with dentations ⟶

Large symmetrically placed windows with 9 to 12 panes per sash

Decorative crown on door ⟶

⟶ paneled front door

Figure 1.4 Drawing of a Georgian style house

half-round
Palladian
windows

Figure 1.5   Photo of a Georgian style house

with 9 to 12 panes in each sash of the typical double-hung window. Entry doors are paneled and capped by decorative crowns. The eaves are narrow and often include a decorative cornice typically with rectangular toothlike notches. The roof pitch is less steep than in earlier homes. In most cases Georgian homes have side gable style roofs (McAlester & McAlester, 1984). The style, revived in the first half of the twentieth century and referred to as Colonial, also had a major influence in the house styles of the latter half of the twentieth century (McAlester & McAlester, 1984).

GREEK REVIVAL STYLE HOMES

In the early nineteenth century the ideal home was a single-family detached homestead surrounded by a garden. According to Wright (1981), houses and gardens were favorite subjects for needlework samplers produced by girls and women alike. The home's importance in the new democracy was argued by teachers, ministers, and poets. The nation was also in search of its own identity and symbols. Many people were attracted to the ancient Greeks, who had invented democracy, and to the simplicity and rational style of ancient Greek architecture (Smiens, 1999).

Greek Revival, as the style was known, became the dominant architectural style immediately following the Georgian style and remained dominant until shortly before the Civil War (McAlester & McAlester, 1984). Greek Revival buildings are characterized by roofs

front-facing gable

Side gable, shallow pitched roof

Large elaborate cornice

Roof

Simpler symmetrical windows

Prominent porch with elaborate columns

Figure 1.6 Drawing of a Greek Revival style house

Figure 1.7 Photo of a Greek Revival style house

that have less slope than Georgian style buildings, as shown in Figures 1.6 and 1.7. Greek Revival homes often include a front-facing gable and a roof cornice that generally continues around the house at the base of the gable end wall (McAlester & McAlester, 1984). The cornice is a decorative border that runs at the top of a wall. The cornice band of Greek Revival homes is wider than that of previous styles. In fact, it is wide enough that it sometimes includes small windows set into the flat part of the cornice.

Most Greek Revival homes have porches associated with the front entry that are often the full width of the building's front facade. The porches are supported by large columns modeled after the columns of Greek temples. Windows are symmetrical as they are in Georgian homes, with window sashes typically divided into six sections. The formerly popular half-round Palladian windows disappeared and were replaced by simpler window details. The Southern plantation mansion is perhaps the most easily recognized example of Greek Revival architecture. However, more modest urban homes located in the Northeast and Midwest are also examples (McAlester & McAlester, 1984).

Even though the ideal continued to be the single-family home in a country setting, only about half of the adult males were landowners at the end of the eighteenth century. Slaves constituted 20 percent of the adult male population, while 20 percent were servants or tenant farmers, and 10 percent were apprentices (Wright, 1981). Furthermore, speculators bought up large tracts of land in the cities, making it difficult for new migrants to realize homeownership even if they were skilled tradespeople such as carpenters (Wright, 1981).

GOTHIC REVIVAL STYLE HOMES

The 1840s saw conscious competition between various styles of house design, spurred by the introduction of house design books developed by architects. Alexander Jackson Davis published the first of these so-called pattern books in 1838. Andrew Jackson Downing, one of the most renowned of these early pattern book authors, published *Country Cottages* in 1842. These early pattern books not only included floor plans and perspective drawings but contained extensive narrative intended to educate the public about what the authors considered good design (Smiens, 1999). In Downing's case, he was making the argument for the picturesque. Whereas Greek Revival houses were generally white, Downing advocated muted colors that blended with nature, and proposed irregular shapes that fit better with natural forms. The early picturesque style, also known as Gothic Revival, is characterized by steeply pitched roofs with decorative trim on the gable ends, as shown in Figures 1.8 and 1.9. Houses in this style often have doubled windows with sharply arched tops, as well as dormers (Smiens, 1999). While the Gothic Revival style itself was not a long-lived fashion, it was the beginning of a major shift to the picturesque approach to house design that dominated the last half of the nineteenth century.

Steeply
pitched front
gabled roof

Decorative
facia

Doubled windows
with arched tops

Figure 1.8 Drawing of a Gothic Revival style house

Oriel window

Figure 1.9 Photo of a Gothic Revival style house

9

THE IMPACT OF INDUSTRIALIZATION ON HOUSE DESIGN

Several mid-nineteenth century technological advances had a major design impact on the homes that followed, such as the introduction of stud frame construction in the Chicago area in approximately 1830 (McAlester & McAlester, 1984). Prior to its introduction most homes used timber frame, also known as post and beam, construction where large timber posts were mated to equally large beams using hand-crafted mortise and tenon joints, as shown in Figure 1.10. A mortice notch and hole in the post and the end of the beam cut away to form a tenon that fit tightly into the mortice hole, and the joint was secured with wooden pegs. Because creating these joints required both a high level of skill and a great deal of time, it was typical to keep the number of such joints to a minimum, which in turn meant that the number of outside corners were kept to a minimum. Therefore, the shapes of houses were fairly simple (Hunter, 1999).

The development of commercial sawmills capable of inexpensively producing vast quantities of sawn boards and the invention of a nail-making machine led to stud wall or light frame construction. A stud wall consists of a number of studs, usually two inches by four inches in cross-section (2" × 4"), nailed together by similar pieces at the top and the bottom of the wall, known as plates. The

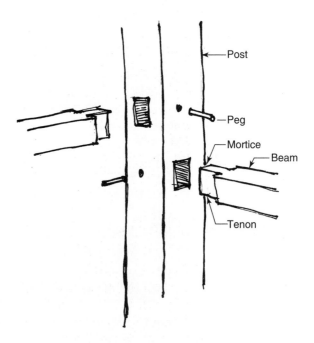

Figure 1.10   Mortise and tenon-timber framing

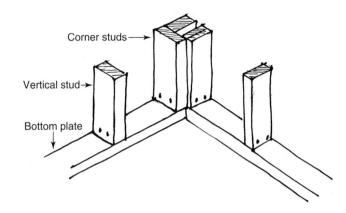

Figure 1.11   Stud wall framing

studs are placed about 16 inches apart in the wall frame and, when combined, provide sufficient strength to support the structure, as shown in Figure 1.11. Corners are no problem with stud wall construction, as an extra 2" × 4" accomplishes the job. Similarly, angled walls are easily formed so that the box shape typical of timber frame construction is no longer a constraint on design (Hunter, 1999).

The cast iron stove, another innovation, first appeared in the 1830s. Prior to its appearance, massive fireplaces were the principle source of heat, and their placement often dominated the home's design. Metal stoves, in contrast, required much smaller chimneys that could be located out of view and thus had less impact on design. Central heating, which became common in the 1880s, required only one chimney and, as a result, allowed even more flexibility in floor plans (McAlester & McAlester, 1984).

The final innovation was the widespread network of railroads that permitted shipment of lumber and millwork (architectural trim and decorative elements) across the country. By 1890 there were over 163,500 miles of railroad tracks in the United States, a 75 percent increase from just 10 years earlier (Hoge, 1988).

VICTORIAN ERA HOME STYLES

The design freedom allowed by these technological advances and the focus on the picturesque in design led to a style that is widely recognized as Victorian. While *Victorian* often refers to these late nineteenth-century houses, the name was only recently applied and refers to the period during the reign of Queen Victoria of England in which these houses were built.

At the time this style was referred to as the modern suburban home (Smiens, 1999), and echoed Andrew Jackson Downing's ideas that the house should have an organic form and a suburban setting with trees and gardens surrounding it. Such features were promoted by both pattern books and land developers. The developers, noting that workers could use railways to commute from these suburban areas to jobs in the cities, marketed suburban homes by identifying the problems of the cities and encouraging householders to think of their families' welfare. In a time when progress and self-improvement were strong popular cultural themes, moving to the wholesome suburbs was also a sign of achieving middle class status (Wright, 1981).

Victorian era homes are characterized by complex exterior forms and roof lines including multiple gables, towers and bay windows, wide porches, and a variety of siding types all designed to add aesthetic interest (Jakle et al., 1989). The workmanship and elaborately detailed millwork we now admire were, in fact, factory-produced and relatively inexpensive at the time (Wright, 1981). Architectural historians identify a number of styles that were used at the time including Eastlake, Shingle and Stick, and Queen Anne (Smiens, 1999). However, Queen Anne is probably most associated today with Victorian era design. The design is eclectic, characterized by the use of elements of an array of previous styles, as shown in Figures 1.12 and 1.13. The exteriors and the interiors of these homes

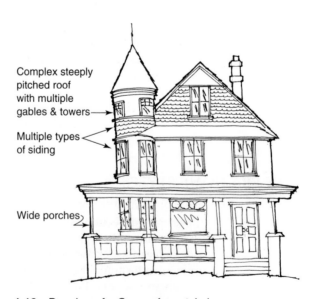

Complex steeply
pitched roof
with multiple
gables & towers→

Multiple types
of siding

Wide porches

Figure 1.12   Drawing of a Queen Ann style house

Figure 1.13 Photo of a Queen Anne style house

are heavily ornamented with elaborate woodwork and multiple special purpose spaces. In addition, the wives were expected to add additional decoration of all sorts, including various types of handwork (Smiens, 1999).

While developers widely promoted the modern suburban home, families without the income to move remained in the cities, often living in crowded tenements. Large numbers of immigrants were among these city dwellers. Because they were often unskilled and did not speak English they had no choice but to live in ethnic ghettos and work in factories or small businesses that hired by the day (Wright, 1981). At first the surging urban population was housed by dividing up existing homes and by adding extra stories or additions. By the 1860s, new purpose-built tenement housing was available in the cities. These structures, which were often five to six stories high with four narrow apartments on each floor, allowed 20 to 24 families housing on a lot that had previously housed only one family (Hunter, 1999). The toilets were either in the back yard or basement and were not connected to sewer systems so they frequently overflowed (Hunter, 1999). Gradually reformers concerned about the squalid conditions of such housing brought about changes. Their most effective arguments often were based on the self-interest of the middle class. This crowded, unsanitary housing was easily linked to disease that could be spread through products such as clothing sewn by the tenement residents (Wright, 1981).

However, not all families who could afford to escape to the suburbs did so. Some preferred the new multifamily structures being built for the well-to-do. Prior to the advent of these structures the term *apartment* had not been used to describe a type of housing (Hunter, 1999). These new multistory buildings were frequently referred to as apartment hotels since they provided not only living space but also services such as laundries and dining rooms (Wright, 1981). Hunter (1999) attributed the advent of apartment buildings largely to the development of reliable passenger elevators in the 1870s, which allowed convenient access to much taller buildings than had previously been possible. By 1878 Boston had at least 108 apartment hotels serving its upper income residents (Wright, 1981).

However, even the luxury apartments were criticized, in part because they flew in the face of the prevailing beliefs about the benefits of single-family homes and the dangers of city life. Some worried the closeness and shared facilities might spark promiscuity in the luxury apartments as well as the tenements. Apartments were also different from single-family homes of the period in that bedrooms were on the same floor as the entry hall and living room. The possibility of strangers looking into one's bedroom was considered indecent (Wright, 1981).

BUNGALOW STYLE HOMES

At the turn of the twentieth century, critics were decrying the excesses of the so-called Victorian style homes. Smiens, in a quote from the 1904 *Craftsman* magazine, stated that "the nineteenth century may be known for many things in the future but it cannot well escape one uncomfortable name, that of the Century of Ugliness" (Smiens, 1999, p. 11). This fury led to a simplicity in design, both of the interior and the exterior.

At this same time, the field of home economics was emerging. Its practitioners advocated for hygienic kitchens and bathrooms, and along with public health officials warned against dust-catching woodwork and decorations as well as paints that masked dirt and dust (Hunter, 1999). Decreasing family sizes also led to smaller houses. Between 1800 and 1900, the average number of children born to white women that survived birth dropped from 7.0 to 3.5. More specifically, at the end of the nineteenth century, the size of a comparably priced house in 1905 had dropped from the 2,000 to 2,500 square feet that had been typical of the 1880s to between 1,000 and 1,500 square feet (Hunter, 1999).

Bungalow, a term for these smaller, simpler home designs of the early twentieth century, derived from the British name for a small low-roofed cottage used for shelter along Indian highways (Jakle et al., 1989). In North America, it referred to a relatively small structure of one or one and a half stories, often set on a high basement, as shown in Figures 1.14 and 1.15. The buildings most commonly referred to as Bungalows today are also known as Craftsman style homes. They generally have low-pitched roofs with wide eaves that are not boxed in so that the rafter ends are exposed. The roofs are either front-facing or side-facing gables. Porches are included under the main roof and often have large taper columns supporting

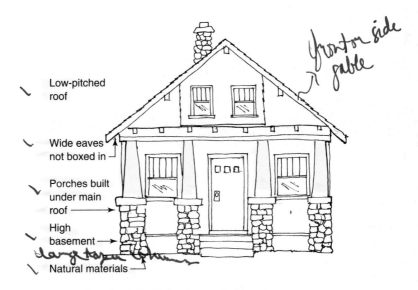

front or side gable

Low-pitched roof

Wide eaves not boxed in

Porches built under main roof

High basement

large taper columns

Natural materials

Figure 1.14   Drawing of a Bungalow style house

Figure 1.15   Photo of a Bungalow style house

them. The side-gable version often employs large dormers. Natural materials and colors are favored. One typically enters the home directly into the living room rather than a hall (Jakle et al., 1989; McAlester & McAlester, 1984).

Prairie style, another early twentieth-century style, is often credited to the Midwest-based architect Frank Lloyd Wright. Unlike the Bungalow style, Prairie style homes usually are two stories in height, and usually have very low-pitched hipped roofs with wide overhangs (a hipped roof has sloping sides facing in all directions; in other words, it is pyramidal in form). The detailing and window massing all provide a strong horizontal emphasis, as shown in Figures 1.16 and 1.17. Local builders throughout the country

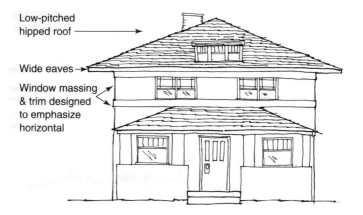

Figure 1.16   Drawing of a vernacular Prairie style house

Figure 1.17   Photo of a vernacular Prairie style house

developed their own versions of the Prairie style based on widely available pattern book designs.

THE ECLECTIC STYLES OF THE 1920S

After World War I, architects displayed a renewed interest in reviving traditional styles. McAlester and McAlester (1984) referred to this as the "eclectic period." They explained that it started in the late nineteenth century as European-trained architects built detailed replicas of European styles for their wealthy clients. The development of brick veneer and stucco construction techniques allowed these styles to be appropriated by builders of more modest homes. While the eclectic period included many styles, two particularly distinctive and widely used ones for modest homes were the Tudor style and Dutch Colonial.

Tudor style is loosely based on late medieval designs. The North American version is characterized by steeply pitched roofs with front-facing gables, often with cross gables and minimal eave overhangs, as shown in Figure 1.18. Decorative, false half timbering is also used, particularly on gable ends. Windows are usually tall, multipaned, and set in groups. Chimneys are often prominent and topped with decorative chimney pots (McAlester & McAlester, 1984).

Figure 1.18 Photo of a Tudor style house

Figure 1.19   Photo of a Dutch Colonial style house

Dutch Colonial is based on the homes of early European settlers in the mid-Atlantic states. Its most distinctive feature is its gambrel roof, as shown in Figure 1.19. This style of roof has changes of slope; the top section has a very low slope, while the bottom part has a much steeper slope and often flares at the very bottom.

THE POST WORLD WAR II HOUSING BOOM

The depression of the 1930s, followed by the effects of World War II, created a pent-up demand for housing which inspired the advent of large subdivisions with mass-produced homes. The pioneers in this housing production approach were the Levitt family, who acquired thousands of acres of farmland on Long Island, New York, and between 1947 and 1950 built 17,400 homes. The homes were smaller than Bungalows and were built on larger lots than traditional urban lots. This allowed the long side of the home to face the street while providing space for an automobile on the side of the house (Hunter, 1999). Construction benefited from some of the assembly line techniques refined during the war with one crew building the basement, another framing the walls, and another installing the roof, for example. The designs were typically based on the earlier Cape Cod style.

In the 1950s, as automobiles became widely available, houses needed to accommodate them. The larger lots and the automobile

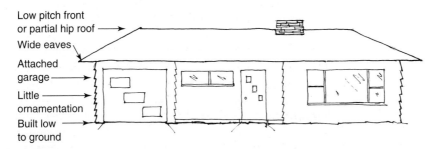

Figure 1.20   Drawing of a Ranch style house

Figure 1.21   Photo of a Ranch style house

inspired what came to be known as Ranch style. These homes, originally inspired by western ranch homes, are generally on one level and include an attached garage. The Ranch style spread rapidly across the country from California (Jakle et al., 1989).

Ranch style homes differ from Bungalows in that they are set much lower to the ground with little if any exposed basement. They are also sprawling in form and were sometimes even referred to as ramblers. They generally have side-facing gables with low slopes and wide eaves as shown in Figures 1.20 and 1.21. There is little ornamentation on the facades. As with Bungalows, the public spaces flow into each other without doors. Ranch style homes often include glass sliding doors that open to a patio or garden (Jakle et al., 1989).

Rental housing also changed following the war. The tenement housing of the inner cities was deteriorating and continued to be a source of social concern. At the same time the international architectural styles which featured high-rise structures set in parklike settings became popular. These two forces came together in urban renewal programs which led to massive removal of older dilapidated housing and the development of high-rise apartment structures to take their place. Unfortunately, high-rise living created problems for families and slums. In spite of the physical deterioration and crowding, they offered advantages in terms of providing community support. High-rise apartment structures built as public housing to replace the slums quickly became unsafe. Perhaps the most notorious example was Pruitt-Igoe in St. Louis, Missouri. Completed in 1955, this project initially received design awards. Seventeen years later, the project was demolished after the buildings were racked by vandalism and violence (Hunter, 1999).

While high-rise apartment buildings went out of favor as low-income family housing, they continue to be built for senior housing and for families with sufficient incomes to make them workable. However, where space is available two- to four-story apartments are most common. These apartments, often built as part of large developments, frequently feature club houses, swimming pools, and other amenities not available in comparable single-family homes.

In terms of architectural style, the Ranch style and its variants continue to be popular. No other single style has emerged to replace it. Rather, designers combine elements of previous styles to develop new variants. Changes now seem to be less in terms of overall style and more in terms of construction and detail. A continual stream of alternative building techniques have been introduced to save energy, use less labor, use fewer expensive materials, and be more environmentally sustainable.

FACTORY-BUILT HOUSING

One stream of alternative building techniques that deserves particular attention is factory-produced housing. Precut homes from Sears and other suppliers were available at the beginning of the twentieth century. While the pieces were produced in factories, all the assembly took place on site and was similar to that of a conventional house of the period. However, after World War II the federal government supported a number of experiments in producing housing in factories. They were intended to take advantage of assembly line techniques and equipment that had been important in the war effort (Hunter, 1999). Sidebar 1.1 details more about mail order homes.

Sidebar 1.1
Homes by Mail

"$100 set of plans free. Let us be your architect without cost to you." This line came from the 1908 Sears, Roebuck and Company catalog, which added homes to the products sold through its mail order catalogs (Thornton, 2002). In the early twentieth century practically anything was available by mail. Catalogs from the Montgomery Ward Company; Sears, Roebuck and Company; and others offered a vast array of merchandise including automobiles, windmills, dog-powered butter churns, and pump organs.

Sears offered its houses through its *Book of Modern Homes,* which first appeared in 1908 and contained 44 different houses ranging in price from $495 to $4,115. According to Thornton (2002, p. 2), "A few weeks after the order was placed two boxcars containing 30,000 pieces of house would arrive at the nearest train depot. A 75 page leather bound instruction book with the homeowner's name embossed in gold on the cover gave precise directions on how to assemble the 30,000 pieces." Sears bragged that all you needed was a hammer and nails to put up the frame of the house.

The *Book of Modern Homes* not only praised the quality of its products, but extolled the virtues of homeownership and the social, moral, and domestic security it provided (Smeins, 1999). While many of the precut houses Sears sold were modest in size and amenities, the 370 different styles it offered during the first half of the twentieth century included large homes and houses relatively complex in design (Thornton, 2002).

Contrary to the stereotype of manufactured homes being of lower quality, Sears bragged that it used only the finest quality materials. Consequently, many of the approximately 75,000 homes it sold are still standing and highly valued by their owners (Thornton, 2002). In general, it is difficult to identify a Sears' home, as they had similar designs to those by architects and builders of the times. In many cases, furthermore, they have been modified over the years, making recognition even more difficult. For more information go to the Sears Archive at *www.searsmodernhomes.com.*

One of these experiments produced the Lustron Home. This home was produced entirely of steel and featured porcelain enamel exterior siding panels, interior wall panels, and roof tiles, as shown in Figure 1.22. The home used the latest in technology including clothes washers built in under the kitchen sink (Thornton, 1998–2004; 2002). Unfortunately, costs were higher than anticipated both to produce the components and to assemble the home on site. The company went out of business just four years after opening its doors. Before closing the company, however, it had produced 3,000 homes and distributed them throughout the Midwest. Many are still standing today and are recognizable by their unique appearance.

Figure 1.22   Photo of a Lustron house

Another form of factory-produced housing was the trailer home built for war workers. These were built on a steel chassis with wheels so they could be moved from place to place. Over the years the quality of factory-built homes has improved and is closely monitored to comply with federal standards. The size of what became known as the mobile home also increased so that units were difficult to move once placed on their initial home site. In 1994 approximately 240 factories across the United States were producing mobile homes (Krigger, 1994). Now referred to as manufactured homes, they constitute approximately 7 percent of U.S. homes. In the early 1990s one in six homes in Wyoming, South Carolina, and New Mexico were manufactured homes (U.S. Census Bureau, 1994).

In addition to manufactured homes, other factories produce modular homes and panelized homes that are not mounted on a chassis and not intended to be moved once delivered to the site. Modular homes are produced in sections that are assembled on site, as are some manufactured homes. Panelized homes are produced in two-dimensional wall sections that are combined on site. Panelized homes look virtually identical to site-built housing and can often be custom designed.

CONCLUSION

This brief history of North American housing introduced many of the housing styles that influenced the look of the houses we see around us today, and provided insights into some of the social and technical changes that occurred over the last three centuries. One of the threads that runs through this history is the importance of housing to families and to society over a long period of time. Housing has clearly been much more than shelter from the elements.

REFERENCES

Ennals, P., & Holdsworth, D. (1998). *Homeplace: The making of the Canadian dwelling over three centuries.* Toronto, Canada: University of Toronto Press.

Hoge, C., Sr. (1988). *The first hundred years are the toughest: What we can learn from the century of competition between Sears and Wards.* Berkeley, CA: Ten Speed Press.

Hunter, C. (1999). *Ranches, rowhouses and railroad flats. American homes: How they shape our landscape and neighborhoods.* New York: W. W. Norton.

Jakle, J. A., Bastian, R. W., & Meyer, D. K. (1989). *Common housing in America's small towns, the Atlantic Seaboard to the Mississippi Valley.* Athens, GA: University of Georgia Press.

Krigger, J. T. (1994). *Your mobile home: Energy and repair guide for manufactured housing* (3rd ed.). Helena, MT: Saturn Resource Management.

McAlester, V., & McAlester, L. (1984). *A field guide to American homes.* New York: Alfred A. Knopf.

Rapoport, A. (1969). *House form and culture.* Inglewood Cliffs, NJ: Prentice Hall.

Smiens, L. E. (1999). *Building an American identity: Pattern book homes and communities 1870–1900.* Walnut Creek, CA: Alta Mira Press.

Thornton, R. (2002). *The houses that Sears built: Everything you wanted to know about Sears catalog homes.* Alton, IL: Gentle Beam Publications.

Thornton, R. (1998–2004). *Lustron homes: Part 1.* Available at *www.oldhouseweb.com.*

U.S. Census Bureau. (1994). *Statistical brief: Mobile homes.* Washington, DC: U.S. Department of Commerce, SB/94-10.

Wright, G. (1981). *Building the dream: A social history of housing in America.* New York: Random House.

CHAPTER

2

Influences on Housing Choice and Behaviors

Julia O. Beamish, Rosemary Carucci Goss, and JoAnn Emmel
Julia O. Beamish and Rosemary Carucci Goss are Professors and JoAnn Emmel is Associate Professor, Department of Apparel, Housing, and Resource Management, Virginia Polytechnic Institute and State University, Blacksburg, VA.

Although choosing a place to live may initially seem like a fairly simple decision, many factors enter into the decision process. Will it be a two-bedroom apartment, an old house in need of repairs, or an estate home with acreage for horses? Each of these choices might be appropriate for a certain individual, but not all are appropriate for the same person at the same point in life. Age, income, and household size might make the apartment appropriate for a young couple just getting started, while the estate home might be too expensive and require too much work. As consumers of housing we are influenced by social, cultural, and economic factors as we make decisions and select housing. Once we choose a home we become users of space, and certain behaviors evolve as we interact with the home. We react and respond to various aspects of our dwelling like seating arrangements, room use, and personalization that allow us to be comfortable and claim the space as our home. This chapter examines housing choice from both the consumer and user perspectives.

HOUSING AND HUMAN ECOLOGY

Housing choice can be viewed from many disciplines—marketing, construction, planning, economics, and design—to name just a few. For the purpose of this chapter, we will view housing from an ecological model adapted from human ecology. Human ecology focuses on the interaction and interdependence of humans with the environment (Bubolz & Sontag, 1993). Housing, as viewed from the ecological model shown in Figure 2.1, is examined as the built environment and how it interacts with the natural environment, the social-cultural environment, and the person or self. The model is diagramed as a series of spheres that surround the individual self. Although the diagram seems to create sharp boundaries for the spheres, they are probably more fluid with some things impacting

25

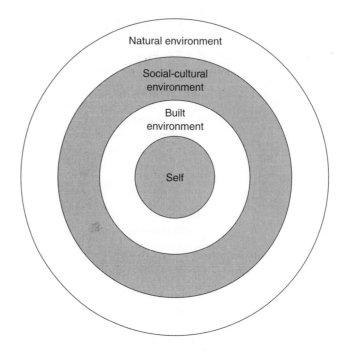

Figure 2.1 Human ecology model

our "self" directly and others influencing us through the filter of another sphere.

The natural environment includes land, water, air, and other natural resources. Examples of how the natural environment interacts with housing could include zoning, land development, city planning, and "green" or environmentally friendly housing. Although the natural environment influences and impacts housing choice and the dwellings we choose impact the environment, these topics will not be a major emphasis of this chapter.

The social-cultural environment includes the impact of society and culture on our housing choices. Concepts related to this environmental sphere include demographics, lifestyles, values and norms, and their impact on housing choice. Various aspects of this sphere help shape the communities, neighborhoods, and actual housing units in which we choose to live.

The built environment (defined here as the housing unit) is a mid-level sphere that bridges the impact of the natural and social environments on the "self." The influence of spatial relationships and the personalization of the home environment are concepts that might fall into this sphere of study.

The final dimension of the ecological model is that of self—the individual, family, or household that occupies the dwelling. The individual certainly impacts the built environment, the social-cultural environment, and the natural environment and in turn is impacted by each dimension. In the housing literature, Winston Churchill has frequently been quoted as saying, "We shape our buildings; thereafter they shape us."

Housing Needs

Shelter is a basic commodity that all people need for survival. However, housing addresses a number of other needs as well. Nygren (1989) reported that in 1939 the American Public Health Association's Committee on the Hygiene of Housing identified four human needs that should be addressed by the housing environment: (1) fundamental physiological needs, (2) fundamental psychological needs, (3) protection against contagions, and (4) protection against accidents.

In 1942 Abraham Maslow presented a theoretical structure on human needs to a psychoanalytic society (Maslow, 1970). The theory, often referred to as the Hierarchy of Human Needs, helps to explain human motivation and has been adapted by many disciplines including housing. According to this framework, humans are trying to satisfy five levels of needs, as shown in Figure 2.2. The lower level needs must be satisfied before higher level needs can be addressed. Physiological needs, the lowest level, are needs that must be met for human survival: food, protection from the elements, and maintenance of body temperature. Basic shelter is essential for humans in most climates and geographical areas. The second level is security and safety needs, which reflect a need to

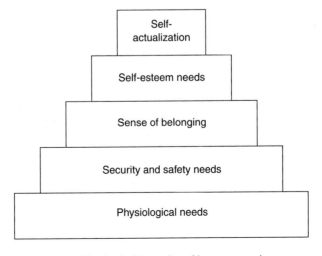

Figure 2.2   Maslow's hierarchy of human needs

23

protect oneself and control one's life. Housing can help meet these needs by offering a healthful space that is free of hazards. The third level is social needs or a sense of belonging. Family socialization in the home environment is an important focus of this level of needs. The fourth level is self-esteem or ego needs. In the United States, housing is often an expression of one's image of self. The final level is self-actualization, which occurs when a person is able to meet his or her fullest potential. The home can provide a setting for creative expression. Several authors have used Maslow's framework to describe the role of housing in supporting human life (Lindamood & Hanna, 1979; Newmark & Thompson, 1977).

Other authors have enumerated several other key roles that housing provides to individuals, families, and households. Montgomery (1966) identified seven human needs that are fulfilled by the home environment: protection from man and nature, need for a sense of place or rootedness, need for a wholesome self-concept, need to relate to others, need for social and psychological stimulation, creative or transcendental needs, and the need to fulfill values. Each of these needs can be viewed as transcending the layers of the human ecology model, as shown in Figure 2.3. The need for protection from man and nature interacts with the self to the built and natural environment. The need for a wholesome self-concept, the

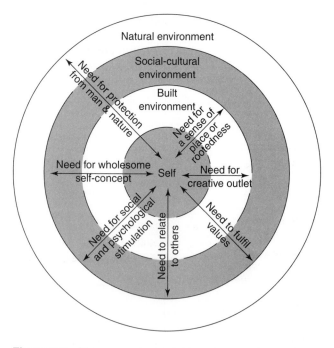

Figure 2.3   Human ecology and housing needs

need for social and psychological stimulation, the need to fulfill values, and the need to relate to others reflect the interactions among self, the built environment, and the social-cultural environment. The need for a sense of place and the need for a creative outlet are most closely associated with the person or self and the built environment.

Many housing choices are available to U.S. consumers. A variety of locations, structure types, sizes, styles, materials, and construction types provide many unique living environments. Most of these housing choices could fulfill the human housing needs previously discussed. How do households choose between the array of available housing choices? What influences their preference and final choice of housing? How and why does a match between a household and a house occur? Are our behaviors influenced by the home we live in? This chapter will explore the answers to these questions in two major sections: lifestyle and housing choice, and behaviors in the home environment.

LIFESTYLE AND HOUSING CHOICE

The conceptual framework used in this section on lifestyle and housing choice first identifies factors that impact lifestyle (household characteristics, social class, and housing values). Then, lifestyle and housing norms are shown to influence housing choice, as shown in Figure 2.4.

As presented in this framework, lifestyle is influenced by household characteristics, including age of household members, household

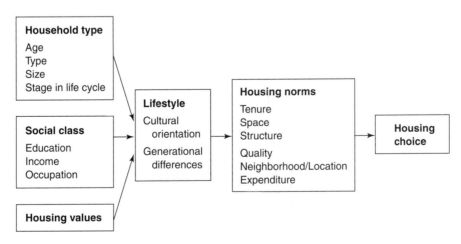

Figure 2.4 Conceptual framework for influences on housing choice
(*Source:* Reprinted with permission by the Housing Education and Research Association)

type, size of household, and stage in the life cycle. Social class is another category of factors that influences lifestyle. Traditionally social class has been determined by income, education, and occupation. Finally, lifestyle is impacted by the values of key household members. Values, internalized standards which materially affect the way a person will react when confronted with a situation permitting more than one decision, guide consumers in making decisions (Montgomery, 1966). A number of values specific to housing choice exist. Household characteristics, social class, and housing values are discussed in more detail throughout the next sections.

Lifestyle is an individual's whole way of living. It does not refer to the style of one's furnishings or one's automobile, but rather is a style of living. One's interests, opinions, activities, and attitudes all reflect lifestyle. In the conceptual model, lifestyle is classified by cultural orientation and generational differences.

The conceptual framework then shows how housing choice is influenced by lifestyle through the filter of housing norms. Morris and Winter (1978) discussed housing norms extensively and identified six housing norms present in the United States. Three of these norms (tenure, space, and structure type) are essential in determining most Americans' housing choice today: the single-family detached house that is owned by the occupants and has adequate sleeping space for all household members. The three other norms (quality, neighborhood, and expenditures) have more varied outcomes depending on the lifestyle factors influencing the household.

Finally, the conceptual framework indicates that a housing choice emerges from a combination of all of these factors. In the next several sections, each of the concepts presented in the framework will be explained in more detail.

Household Characteristics

An individual's or family's lifestyle is impacted by their household characteristics, such as age, type, size, and stage in the life cycle. Depending upon these household characteristics, very different decisions may be made related to lifestyle, norms, and housing choice. The more we know about how these characteristics relate to certain populations, the better we can understand such choices.

Demographers and other social scientists often categorize information about individuals and households to broadly explain how a population lives. In the United States, several sources are frequently used to provide demographic information. The American Census of Population and Housing, conducted by the U.S. Census Bureau every 10 years on years ending in 0 (zero), reapportions the U.S. House of Representatives and serves as an important planning tool for governments to use in allocating resources. The Census was started in 1890, and a more detailed housing section was added in 1940 to provide an ongoing comparison of the housing stock. The Census is updated annually through the Current Population Survey (CPS), which uses a sample of the population to provide more timely information about households.

The American Housing Survey (AHS), used frequently by housing researchers and planners, is collected on a biannual basis and uses the housing unit for its sample, thus providing information about the nation's housing stock. The survey returns to the same house each time it is collected, and new housing units are added to reflect recent additions to the housing stock.

The U.S. Census Bureau defines a *household* as a group of individuals who are living together in a housing unit. Some households may be temporary, such as college roommates or people sharing housing. Other households may be nonmarried couples. A *family* is a specific type of household in which the members are related by blood, marriage, or adoption. Although a majority of American households are classified as families (68 percent in 2002), a growing number of nonrelated persons live in the same household (U.S. Census Bureau, 2002). As these household types change, housing norms may also be changing because the current cultural norm is based on families rather than on households. Let us now take a closer look at the four ways we characterize households: age, type, household size, and stage in the life cycle.

Age. Age is an important way to categorize the population and can be useful in tracking population segments. Current population statistics identify a very large age group, the Baby Boomers, who were born between 1946 and 1964. As this group moves toward retirement, they could have a definite impact on housing availability and design. A demographic echo of the Baby Boomer generation is the Echo Boomer or Millennial generation, who were born after 1977. This generation is already having a major impact on the economy and will continue to do so, as their parents have done. It is also evident that our population of older adults (those 65 and over) is growing, and the fastest growing segment is made up of people over 85 years of age. More about age and lifestyle is presented in the section on generational differences.

Type. The Census categorizes family households into three categories: married-couple families; female householder families, no husband present; and male householder families, no wife present. *Householder* is used to designate the adult in the household, formerly termed the household head. For nonfamily households, the categories are female householder and male householder. Census data from the last three decades have shown an increase in the number of single-parent families and nonfamily households. A very large portion of nonfamily households is made up of people living alone (82 percent) (U.S. Census Bureau, 2002).

Household Size.   In 2002 the average U.S. family size was 3.86 members. This average varied among race and ethnic origin, with Hispanic families being the largest on average. The size of the family or household has a great influence on the number of bedrooms that may be required in housing choices.

Stages in the Life Cycle.   The concept of life cycle can be applied to the transformation (maturation, generation, and decline) of any living organism or organization (O'Rand & Krecker, 1990). Housing literature has often viewed life cycle in the context of the family and referred to it as *family life cycle.* The term is a way to group the influences of householder age and the presence and age of children in an effort to identify patterns that will explain resource allocation. Since the middle of the twentieth century, numerous researchers have identified stages that families go through during their lifetime. Early models had seven (Glick, 1947) and eight stages (Duvall, 1957), while later models expanded the number to encompass more variations (Hohn, 1987). The earlier models focused on nuclear families with marriages that remained intact throughout the couple's lives. The stages usually gave minimal consideration to the period before marriage and after retirement or widowhood. These models are perhaps less reflective of today's households, which are made up of people who stay single or childless longer, who may divorce one or more times during their lifetime, and who because of longevity remain in the aging family stage longer. The stages according to Duvall (1957) are:

- **Single stage:** under 35, no children
- **Couple stage:** married, no children
- **Childbearing family stage:** married, birth of first child
- **Preschool family stage:** married, young children
- **School-age family stage:** married, older children
- **Launching family stage:** married, oldest child has left home
- **Middle-age family stage:** head over 45, no children at home, empty nest
- **Aging family stage:** retirement to death

The complexity of current family and household living arrangements indicate that a simple linear stage approach to family development may not be effective in today's society. In reality, it probably was not very applicable to families in the eighteenth and nineteenth centuries, either (O'Rand & Krecker, 1990). Current patterns include delayed marriage, cohabitation, divorce, remarriages, blended families, multigenerational families, same-sex unions, and singleness.

However, the stage approach does have some implications for housing choices. Since the family life cycle stages present normative expectations for family life, housing norms often parallel this cycle. For example, a young single person will probably expect to rent an apartment, but a married couple with a child will expect to buy a house. A move to a larger house might coincide with the arrival of more children and the space needs of older children. Some retired couples will move into smaller housing units once their children have left home.

Social Class

Another factor affecting lifestyle is social class or socioeconomic status. Social scientists use *social class* and *socioeconomic status* to describe a cluster of demographic characteristics including income, occupation, and education. People in different socioeconomic classes may have different expectations for personal and family behavior as well as housing preferences and choices. Michelson (1976, p. 112) identified five levels of social class:

- **Lower class:** low income; often no steady job or one subject to the whims of the employer; little education
- **Working class:** regular blue-collar employment
- **Lower middle class:** regular white-collar employment, usually for others; moderate salary at most
- **Upper middle class:** high amount of education; comfortable salary or fees; sometimes self-employed but skills are transferable regardless
- **Upper class:** great personal wealth either at present or within the family at some past date; at least moderate education; occupation, if any, is respectable

These levels represent a generalization with many variations and distinctions possible within each level. These categories reflect a suitable stereotype of social structure for an Industrial Age, with laborers, management, and owners comprising the top four levels. As our society moves more deeply into the Technology Age, these class distinctions may not hold true. Modest levels of education and nontraditional occupations may lead to large amounts of wealth, while some occupations requiring extensive education may not lead to the highest paying jobs.

Although we generally believe that the United States is a socially mobile society, examples indicate that not everyone can move easily from one class segment to another. Escaping poverty and welfare has been especially difficult for some households who lack education and employment opportunities.

Income.   By 2002 the median U.S. income for a four-person household had grown to $42,409 (U.S. Census Bureau, 2002). Income can vary greatly, however, between household groups. The average income level of married-couple families was significantly higher than the income of single-parent families, and among these single-parent families, female-headed families had an average income significantly lower than male-headed families. Households with heads in the 45–54 age range had the highest median income, while the lowest median income was among households with heads over 65. Income differences also exist among racial groups. Asians and Pacific Islanders had the highest median income, while African Americans had the lowest median income.

The association between income and housing is evident, because income is a key indication of what a household is able to pay for housing. By 2003 households with incomes above the median had homeownership rates of approximately 83.7 percent, while those with incomes below the median had ownership rates of 52.1 percent (U.S. Census Bureau, 2003).

Occupation.   There are many occupation classifications. The CPS identified 11 major occupation categories (U.S. Census Bureau, 2001). The highest paying occupations were classified as Professional Specialists, followed closely by Executives, Administrative, and Managerial occupations. The lowest paying jobs for men and women were Farming, Forestry, and Fishing occupations; Handlers, Equipment Cleaners, Helpers, and Laborers; and Service Workers. With its direct relationship to income, occupation can be a very important factor in determining the type of housing a household can afford.

Education.   In the United States education is viewed as a way to increase one's income and social status. Education can prepare individuals for specialized jobs, and provide for a well-rounded and knowledgeable public. Both men and women experience a steady rise in income with increased education (U.S. Census Bureau, 2001), which will make consumers better able to become homeowners. In contrast, lack of education, leading to lower-paying jobs, can constrain groups within society from becoming homeowners.

Housing Values

In the early stages of housing research, housing values were considered important concepts to explain the preferences and choices of people selecting housing. The major frameworks for housing values were developed by Cutler (1947) and Beyer, Mackesey, and Montgomery (1955). Cutler identified 10 housing values: beauty, comfort, convenience, location, health, personal interests, privacy, safety, friendship activities, and economy. A house that was inexpensive and efficient to operate might reflect the economy value, while a house with private bedrooms for each family member might reflect the privacy value.

Beyer et al. (1955) developed a list of nine housing values based on the work of Cutler (1947) and Williams (1951): economy, family centrism, physical health, aesthetics, leisure, equality, freedom, mental health, and social prestige. Subsequent research suggested a hierarchy clustered around four main values: economy, family (including physical and mental health, and family centrism), personal (aesthetics, leisure, and equality), and social prestige. Beyer et al. (1955) described the four value clusters as follows:

> *Economy*—Families in this cluster emphasize the economic uses of goods and services. They base choices on selling price and what they consider sound business judgment. They are conservative and take only calculated risks.
>
> *Family*—This cluster emphasizes factors that hold the family together and improve family relationships. They are alert to influences that affect family members' physical and mental well-being.
>
> *Personal*—Families in this cluster take a personal view of their physical and social environment. They are more individualistic and desire independence and self-expression.
>
> *Social prestige*—Families in this category are considered upwardly mobile and view housing in terms of its effect on their social standing.

Lifestyles

For years housing researchers have discussed the impact of housing values and norms on the selection of a family's dwelling. However, today a family's lifestyle may have the greatest impact on its housing choice. Lifestyles, as presented in Figure 2.3, are influenced by various aspects of household characteristics, social class, and housing values. The concept of lifestyle combines these factors to help explain more specific housing choices. Not every 40-year-old couple who is married, without children, and earning $100,000 per year makes the same housing choice, because different lifestyles suggest different housing situations that fit their way of living. The more characteristics households have in common, the more likely they are to have similar lifestyles and to make similar housing choices.

There are many different types of lifestyles: active, sedentary; suburban, metropolitan; traditional, contemporary. Bell (1968) described three different urban lifestyles: careerism (in which it is important to be close to work and have conveniences that would lessen the time spent away from the office); familism (in which the emphasis is on space for family activities and time to be involved with the family); and consumerism (in which the focus is on having the newest goods and services). Most individuals and families combine characteristics of various lifestyles to produce their own unique lifestyle.

Cultural Orientation.   Another way of viewing how housing preferences are influenced is by looking at a population's cultural orientation. Ray (1997) suggested that Americans live in three emerging subcultures of meaning and value. Most of the population is either traditionalist (29 percent) or modernist (47 percent). Traditionalists believe in a nostalgic image of small towns and strong churches that defines the "Good Old American Way," while modernists place high value on personal success, consumerism, materialism, and technological rationality. However, a new movement called cultural creatives (one in four Americans) really blossomed in the 1960s with the civil rights, women's rights, social justice, and ecology movements. Cultural creatives tend to be affluent, well-educated, and on the cutting-edge of social change. Six of ten are women. They tend to be information junkies who read more and watch less TV. As housing consumers they tend to buy existing houses and remodel to suit their needs. They want to be hidden by trees and do not like "display" homes. They prefer established neighborhoods and like lots of privacy both inside and out. Style is not important, as long as it is authentic. They like eclectic interior design with original art and crafts, walls of books, and nooks.

The concepts behind cultural creatives can be found in the work of Brooks (2000), who coined the term *Bobos* or bourgeois bohemians to describe hippies who grew up to become part of the mainstream business world. Florida (2002) took this description a step further by saying that this new "creative class," which represents about 30 percent of the U.S. workforce, is fast becoming a major influence on the remainder of the population by setting consumer trends in such areas as housing. The creative class values creativity, individuality, diversity, and merit, but does not flaunt its wealth.

These "reverse snobs" believe in spending their money conscientiously on well-designed functional items. Kitchens and baths (at least the right kind of kitchens and baths) are high on the list of acceptable expenditures for this group according to Hart (2004). They reject trophy kitchens for ones that include professional equipment and are filled with details. They are attracted to natural, rustic, organic, unique, craftsmanlike, and sensible products (Brooks, 2000). The emergence of the cultural creatives or creative class appears to have evolved enough over the past decade that they will have a significant impact on housing in the decades to come.

Generational Differences. Certainly no lifestyle discussion would be complete without discussing the impact of the generations or age cohorts that strongly influence today's lifestyles. An age cohort is a group of individuals who were born around the same time and experienced many of the same historical events at a similar age. Writers do not agree on what to call the generations any more than they agree on the time spans for each generation (Dent, 1998; Mitchell, 1995; Strauss & Howe, 1997; Zemke, Raines, & Filipczak, 2000). For example, demographers usually define the Baby Boom generation as those born between 1946 and 1964. However, writers have used birth dates that range from 1936–1964. For the purpose of this chapter we have defined the generational groups as Millennials or Echo Boomers (born 1977 or after), Generation Xers (born between 1965 and 1976), Baby Boomers (born between 1946 and 1964), and Seniors (born before 1946). Each generation has been influenced dramatically by defining moments such as events, music, heroes, and common history called generational markers.

Millennials or Echo Boomers, as they are often called, are the most culturally diverse group, as well as those most comfortable with diversity. Eventually, this group will be larger than the Baby Boomers. As they have been growing up, they have been influenced by school violence, the 9-11 terrorist attacks, and the wars that followed. They are confident, computer savvy, and get along well with Baby Boomers and Seniors. They are likely to live in suburban apartments or downtown lofts that they share with roommates.

The *Challenger* explosion, AIDS, computers, and single-parent households were some of the significant generational markers for the *Gen* X generation. Gen Xers, often called the Baby Bust Generation because there are just over 50 million of them, are practical, pragmatic, and value skills over education. They reject the workaholic values of Baby Boomers and want a job that also allows "a life." You may find them living downtown in apartments and condominiums or in townhouses or "starter homes" in the suburbs.

Baby Boomers, the largest of the generations—almost 80 million strong, were influenced by such generational markers as man landing on the moon, Vietnam, the civil rights movement, and Woodstock. Television played a key role in helping to widen the generation gap between Boomers and their Senior parents. Boomers are often described as optimistic, rule-breaking, option-driven idealists who look for personal gratification. Because they are comfortable with debt and enjoy their affluence they have continued to buy newer, bigger, and more elegant housing with more features and amenities. Some Boomers, because of their desire for self-expression, have chosen to move to New Urbanism communities. They may also choose this type of housing as they age rather than a traditional retirement community because a Baby Boomer never wants to think he or she is aging.

The *Seniors* can be described as three different groups in terms of life influences—the Silent Generation born between 1932 and 1945 who were influenced by Sputnik and the Mickey Mouse Club; the World War II Generation who were born between 1917 and 1931 and were influenced by World War II; and the Depression Era Generation born before 1917 and impacted by the depression. Although they had different generational markers, they have similar values. They are conservative, conforming, patriotic, and believe in teamwork, hard work, authority, and sacrifice. Seniors may live in homes they have lived in for years, or they may be downsizing to a smaller home that is new or located in a retirement location.

Structural alternatives will vary as the generations move through various stages in the life cycle, but each generation puts its own stamp on how that structure fits with their lifestyle. Figure 2.5 illustrates some general characteristics of each of the generations.

Housing Norms

As individuals and families evaluate and make decisions about their housing, they are guided by norms. According to this chapter's conceptual framework, *housing norms* act as a filter for the lifestyle influences on housing choices. The *American Heritage Dictionary* (Berube, Neeley, & DeVinne, 1982, p. 848) defined a norm as "a standard, model, or pattern regarded as typical for a specific group." Housing norms, like other norms, are culturally defined standards for behavior. Each society establishes what it considers desirable behavior related to housing people and most members of that society strive to meet or conform to this behavior.

Norms are transmitted from one generation to another through families, mass media, and public interaction. Most people live their lives aspiring to certain housing norms, and the inability to achieve

Seniors	Boomers	Gen Xers	Millennials
Great Depression and WWI	Vietnam War; civil and women's rights	Broken homes	School shootings
Politically and financially conservative	Most affluent; greatest spenders	Participate less in sports; more interested in visual arts	Opinionated consumers
Play by the rules	Redefined roles	More comfortable with diversity	More racially and ethnically diverse
Loyal to workplace	Workaholics	Comfortable with computers and Internet	Grew up with computers
Save, then buy	Buy with credit card	Cautious spenders	Buy with parent's money
Dedicated	Personal gratification	Independent	Confident and social
Home they have lived in for years or downsized home for retirement	Move-up suburban home that says "I've made it"	Suburban townhouse or small starter home	Suburban or downtown apartment

Figure 2.5   Influences and characteristics of the generations (*Source:* Reprinted with permission by the Housing Education and Research Association)

these norms is usually the result of constraints rather than different desires or attitudes (Lindamood & Hanna, 1979).

In their theoretical framework, Morris and Winter (1978) identified six U.S. housing norms—tenure, space, structure type, quality, neighborhood location, and expenditures. Most Americans aspire to fulfill the first three housing norms in the form of a single-family home that is owned by the occupants, and contains an adequate number of bedrooms or sleeping areas for all household members. The last three housing norms are much more dependent upon the lifestyle and status of the household, and will vary more widely among American households. As we examine housing norms today, we may see that some of these norms have changed somewhat over the years to meet the needs of today's population.

Tenure.   Tenure norms relate to owning or renting housing, and the "American Dream" includes the desire to own one's dwelling. Although many Americans rent a residence, most say they plan to buy when they can. Owning land is a democratic freedom we enjoy and one that many early settlers sought when they moved to the United States. By providing tax incentives and financing programs, the U.S. government reflects this tenure norm and encourages homeownership (Lindamood & Hanna, 1979).

In 2003 U.S. homeownership reached a record high of 68.3 percent (Joint Center for Housing Studies, 2004). This increase was enhanced by the lowest mortgage interest rates in three decades. Homeownership is highest in the Midwest at 73.1 percent and lowest in the West at 62.5 percent. The homeownership rate for married couples with families (83.1 percent) far exceeds the ownership rate of single-parent families: 49 percent for female-headed households and 58 percent for male-headed households (U.S. Census Bureau, 2002). Despite the growth in homeownership, rising home prices have made it increasingly difficult for marginal borrowers in some parts of the nation to save enough money to buy a home.

First-time homebuyers have been a substantial part of the new growth in ownership. Included in this group are many low-income buyers who have been able to take advantage of the low interest rates, and first-time homebuyers who have used creative mortgage loan programs from private lenders as well as from state and federally sponsored programs. In 2001 minorities represented 32 percent of the first-time homebuyers, up from 19 percent in 1993 (Joint Center for Housing Studies, 2001).

Not all households share or can attain the norm of homeownership. Experts predict that 30 percent of all households will still rent in 2010. Many low-income households rent because they cannot afford to buy, but an increasing number of people of all ages, including those with high incomes, see renting as an attractive alternative to owning because of the focus on providing lifestyle amenities (Joint Center for Housing Studies, 1999). In 1999, when people were asked why they rented, 28 percent did so out of choice; 40 percent reported that homeownership was not a priority (Ridder, 2000).

Minorities (42 percent) make up a large segment of the renter population, and this proportion is expected to increase to 50 percent in 2020 (Joint Center for Housing Studies, 2002). Although most renters live in multi-unit structures, one third of the rental units are single-family homes (Joint Center for Housing Studies, 2003).

Space.   The amount and type of space that families desire and need are influenced by cultural space norms and are important aspects of selecting a residence. Different lifestyles may require or establish a desire for certain types of space, whereas the family's size, composition, and stage in the life cycle may most directly influence the amount of space needed. As you read real estate ads, take note of how the space divisions of a home are described. Two dwellings that have the same square footage may differ in how that space is divided.

Overcrowding examines the person per room ratio. One accepted guideline establishes crowding as more than two persons per room (American Public Health Association, 1971), while the U.S. Census Bureau defines it as more than one person per room. During the 1990s, crowding once again became a housing issue, mostly among foreign-born residents (Joint Center for Housing Studies, 2004).

Different cultures have different norms about the sexes and ages of individuals who share a sleeping room. When U.S. families evaluate space in a house they consider the number of bedrooms and how they are distributed among household members. For most U.S. households, norms about sleeping spaces are still fairly well defined. Of the many schedules developed for dividing bedrooms, the most complete one is the Standard of Normative Need developed by Morris (1972) and Gladhart (1973). This schedule (Morris & Winter, 1978, p. 98) specified that ideally no more than two people should share a bedroom, and that a bedroom is needed for:

1. The parental couple (or single parent),
2. Each child age 18 or over,
3. Each pair of same-sex children (with at least one child between the ages of 9 and 17) whose ages differ by four years or less,
4. Each pair of children of any sex, both under age 9, whose ages do not differ by more than four years, and
5. Each additional adult or couple.

For many U.S. households, overcrowding and lack of space are not as critical because of smaller families and larger homes. The median square footage of a new home increased from 1,535 square feet in 1975 to 2,302 square feet in 2003 (U.S. Census Bureau, 2003). Homes with 2,400 square feet or more increased from 11 percent to 37 percent of the new homes built. The percentage of new homes with four or more bedrooms increased from 21 percent to 36 percent (U.S. Census Bureau, 2002).

The types of spaces desired by homebuyers and included in new homes have also changed. More homebuyers are looking for larger kitchens, open multipurpose areas, additional bedrooms and bathrooms, and more space overall. Many are even willing to give up amenities and lot size to acquire more housing space, but this willingness varies with age and life cycle. For instance, at retirement people often care less about space and more about amenities.

Structure Type.   The type of dwelling we choose is influenced by structural norms. Within the United States today the predominant housing structure is the single-family detached home, which has traditionally been the housing of choice of most households. The desire to live in this type of structure is very strong, and in a 1996 survey 82 percent of the homebuyers preferred a single-family home further from work and shopping rather than a similarly priced townhouse near employment or city activities (National Association of Home Builders, 1998).

In recent years, however, alternative housing types and ownership forms have increased in popularity. Townhomes, condominiums, and other multifamily structures have developed great appeal for retirees, young professionals, and the more mobile segments of the population because of their amenities, security, low maintenance, and ease of occupancy. Approximately 38 percent of U.S. households live in apartments, and many do so out of choice.

Manufactured housing is seldom included in the category of single-family detached homes, although it actually meets that definition. Often communities restrict the placement of manufactured homes in traditional neighborhoods. As an alternative housing type, manufactured housing accounts for 8.3 percent of all owner-occupied units and 3.6 percent of renter-occupied units. The South has the highest percentage of manufactured homes in the country (American Housing Survey, 2001).

Quality.   Quality norms take into account acceptable structural quality as well as amenities associated with the home. The National Housing Act of 1949 set the goal of a decent home in a suitable environment for every American. As individuals evaluate housing for quality, each may have a different idea of what is considered good or poor quality. In the 1940s the primary focus was on three attributes: plumbing facilities, general state of repair, and the relationship between the size of the home and the number of people. The U.S. Census Bureau judges quality based upon such features as an equipped kitchen, central heating, complete indoor plumbing, and soundness of structure. In 1940, 45.2 percent of American homes lacked some or all plumbing (Weicher, 1977). Since the 1950s problems related to physical qualities such as plumbing, heating/cooling, and overcrowding have decreased substantially in the United States.

Avoiding structural inadequacies, however, may still be very difficult for very low-income families, especially large families who many times sacrifice quality to obtain the space they need. In 1995 some 1.1 million very low-income homeowners still lived in substandard housing (Joint Center for Housing Studies, 1999).

importance of home inspections

Households of all income levels need to be aware of environmental issues that impact their health and the safety of their home. Some common concerns include the presence of lead paint, radon, and asbestos as well as problems with indoor air and water quality. Home inspections and/or testing may be performed to identify such problems (Parrott, 1997).

Along with an increase in structural quality, the level of amenities desired and expected by households has also increased. Many U.S. households are now able to attain a standard for levels of amenities unrealized in earlier years. As one example, homes with 2.5 or more baths increased from 20 percent to 55 percent during 1975–2002 (Joint Center for Housing Studies, 2002). Other amenities once considered extras that are now standard in new homes are dishwashers, microwave ovens, and garages.

Neighborhood/Location.   Real estate agents state that the three most important considerations when buying a home are location, location, and location. By this they mean that the most important determinant of a home's price is not its size or quality of construction, but its location. Neighborhood norms prescribe that we not only choose a safe and attractive area in which to live, but also a neighborhood that is appropriate to a household's social and economic status.

"Clean Living" consideration →

Neighborhoods can be defined by many characteristics or factors, such as wealth or social class. Today we also see lifestyle as a factor in neighborhood development and selection. If you are an avid golfer you may wish to live in a country club setting. Retirees may desire retirement communities that provide activities suited to their new lifestyle.

In the United States we see a shifting of populations from one type of neighborhood to another, based in part on economics. Because of a better economy and aggressive homebuyer programs, former inner city dwellers are able to move into suburban homes left behind by those who have moved to less populated areas surrounding the cities. However, many cities are seeing a reversal in this trend and are experiencing an increase in population resulting from a mix of new immigrants, empty nesters, and young people seeking a vibrant lifestyle offered in many downtown locations.

Expenditures.   The amount of money a household spends on housing is typically related to income and wealth, but housing norms also expect individuals to spend according to that wealth and lifestyle. For example, society would not look favorably upon a family neglecting the necessities of life to live in a home beyond its

7

means, nor would it be expected to see a person of extreme wealth living in a substandard dwelling.

Housing affordability continues to be a problem for a large number of Americans, both in terms of the initial cost of purchasing or renting a dwelling and the long-term cost of energy, utilities, and maintenance. The rising cost of housing has increased the housing expense burden for many households, and the number of affordable housing units continues to dwindle. By 2002 the national median price of a new home was $194,400 and that of an existing home was $172,600 (Realtor Magazine Online, 2003). Other housing-related expenses also place a burden on American households. In addition to mortgage payments and rents, approximately 16 percent of the average U.S. household's spending goes to shelter-related expenses and an additional 6 percent to utilities (Mogelonsky, 1996).

Housing expenditures have had the biggest impact on renters and people with very low incomes. In most major metropolitan areas, overall rents outpaced inflation. Nationally, renter households generally spent 26.7 percent of their income on housing in 2002, and 14.3 million, nearly 1 in 7 American households, spent more than 50 percent of their income on housing (Joint Center on Housing Studies, 2003).

BEHAVIORS IN THE HOME ENVIRONMENT

The framework presented thus far has primarily focused on housing choice as a factor of societal norms and lifestyle choices. Now we move on to discuss how we live in our homes once we have moved in.

desire for ownership, so one can "do what they want" in their space, environment, etc.

Living in a home results in complex interactions between the inhabitants and their immediate environment. Many of these are basic responses to spatial stimuli that seem to be a part of our biological and psychological make-up. Others are learned responses that incorporate our cultural background. These interactions include our reactions to spaces and our involvement with other people in those spaces. They reflect our feelings about the things we select and display in our home, as well as our feelings about the house as a home.

Lewin (1935) proposed that our behavior is a function of both the environment and the person. This general understanding of the relationship between people and their environments has led to several areas of study related to environment-behavior studies. This overarching framework of behavior being influenced by the conditions and design of the home has many implications for understanding how our home environments affect us.

Spatial Relationships

We react to each other through spatial arrangements whenever we interact with one another. The spatial reactions may affect how we feel about our interactions and what type of interactions we have. The way furniture is arranged or the place we sit may have an impact on our behavior with others.

Proximics.   One of the basic concepts related to spatial behavior is proximics. After studying and observing people's behavior in several settings and cultures, Hall (1966), an anthropologist, coined the term *proximics* to describe the way people unconsciously arrange and structure spatial distances with others. He identified four proximic zones related to our sensory experiences to explain the spatial impact on people's behavior.

- **Intimate:** This distance ranges from the skin to 18". This closeness is reserved for people we know well. Viewing another person at this distance is unfocused and other senses impact this situation, such as smell and feeling heat from the other person.
- **Personal:** This distance is from 18" to 4'. Each person is able to see and hear the other, without experiencing his or her body heat. This tends to be the distance that we are comfortable talking to one another and it is a good guide to use in planning seating arrangements where people will have one-on-one conversations.
- **Social:** This distance is from 4' to 12'. This distance is good for conversations among several people. Voices are raised in order to be heard. People can see each other but not at a close range. Comfortable seating arrangements for several people involve a 10'–12' conversation area.
- **Public:** Because this distance is beyond 12' it is difficult to have one-on-one conversations and we tend to think of this as a "presentation" distance. One person is addressing others. The speaker's voice is raised and having good eye contact is difficult because of this distance.

Hall concluded that different cultures define these zones differently. For example, Arab cultures have narrower distances for these zones and have personal conversations in what North Americans would consider the intimate zone.

Personal Space.   Sommer (1969) recognized personal space as a key component in understanding people's behavior in a space. Personal space is a spatial area that a person maintains around himself or herself, similar to what Hall called the personal zone. Sommer considered the personal space distance—18" to 3'—an extension of the self. It is often referred to as an "invisible space bubble" that we carry around with us. This spatial distancing affects our interactions with other people and objects, and might be more accurately called an "interaction distance" (Bechtel, 1997).

The distance may vary depending on participants' relationship, gender, and cultural background as well as the type of interaction. Sommer experimented with determining this space and looking at the "fight or flight" behavior in conjunction with this concept. Generally a person tries to maintain his or her personal space and if someone invades the space, then the person is threatened and will pull back in order to maintain the personal distance. People may then actually leave the setting or confront the intruder. If the purpose of the interaction is understood, then the situation is less threatening and an interaction may occur.

Think about more than 1 person in a kitchen

Although much of the personal space research has been conducted in public spaces, there are applications to the home. Family relationships affect personal space. Couples in good relationships have closer interaction distances. Adolescents and their parents tend to have larger interaction distances than younger children and their parents (Bechtel, 1997).

Seating.   Our sense of personal space affects the placement and arrangement of furniture. Sommer (1969) found that comfortable seating arrangements for talking with a friend are side-by-side and at a right angle. This put them within a comfortable interaction distance and allowed them to have occasional eye contact. The arrangement also made it easier to cooperate on activities because they could share materials. Placing seating at a right angle in a social space in the home would seem to encourage conversation.

Sommer (1969) also found that seating face-to-face across a table was chosen more often for competitive activities. Further, leaders tend to emerge or locate themselves at the head of a rectangular table; eye contact with others seated at the table reinforces the leader's role. The image of the traditional family with Dad or Mom at the head of the dining table has some basis in environment-behavior studies.

Privacy.   Privacy is considered the control of access to oneself. We need privacy for some personal activities, but privacy might also help us recover from the stress of being with others. In our homes

typsy. privacy
re. placement
of bedroom
in floor plan

Consider
placement
of closets
as sound
buffer)

we plan for some private areas, particularly our bathrooms and sleeping spaces. Other private spaces might be a study or home office where it might be important to have no interruptions in order to concentrate. Susanka (2001) talked about having an "away room" that can be used for quiet time by any family member.

In these private areas access to self is controlled by using walls and doors to close off the space. It is important to have this visual and auditory privacy, although some homes and multifamily housing need extra sound insulation to achieve auditory privacy. In some settings we may achieve privacy by simply avoiding eye contact.

Crowding.   Crowding in housing is usually associated with social density; namely, too many people in a housing unit (Bechtel, 1997). It is generally considered to be evident if sleeping arrangements have not met the space norms discussed previously, or if there is more than one person occupying each room in the house. In environment-behavior studies, crowding is seen as intrusions on our personal space. We are often in settings that seem crowded. Waiting in line, shopping, and attending a party or football game might create settings where people are close together and their personal space is invaded. Feeling so "crowded" that it results in negative consequences often depends on a mediating circumstance, such as the event or the duration of the crowding experience. We usually adapt to these temporary situations in various ways. While in line we face the next person's back and do not make eye contact. Seating in theaters allows acceptable personal space when seated. But living with constant crowding in our homes may lead to stressful situations.

Gruell (1993) cautioned that the home interior design can affect our feelings of crowding. She investigated the arrangement of closed and open floor plans on different types of behaviors and interactions and found that perceived crowding occurred at lower density levels in open plan housing than in semi-open or closed plans when low social interaction is desired. Some division of spaces, such as a separate kitchen, dining, and living area, were needed in families with small children to support low social interaction and goal-directed behaviors such as paying bills. The ability to have some control of interaction (privacy) is needed for some activities and a semi-open plan may provide this in a small house.

Sociofugal and Sociopetal Arrangements.   One of the first theories in environment-behavior studies was Osmond's (1957) model of sociofugal and sociopetal spaces to encourage or discourage interaction. Sociofugal spaces are open spaces with very large volume, high ceilings, and bright lighting that discourage interaction,

Sociopetal settings encourage interactions. They are smaller in scale with low lighting and ceilings. Typical home environments would be categorized as sociopetal settings, although some very large-scaled rooms with high ceilings may seem overpowering and actually discourage social interaction.

Sociofugal and sociopetal seating can also encourage interaction. People in seats that face each other will interact more than people who sit in seats with their backs to one another. In our homes we usually want sociopetal seating where the residents sit facing or at an angle to one another. However, in waiting areas at doctors' offices or airports we might appreciate seating that is back-to-back so we can avoid unwanted interactions.

Resident entrances in multifamily housing could also be arranged in a sociopetal or sociofugal arrangement. Residents that open their doors and face another unit might be more likely to become acquainted with their neighbors than those whose entrances all face the same way. Seeing and knowing your neighbor can be an important step in protecting the space from intruders.

Territoriality.   Territoriality is associated with behaviors where we mark and protect our spaces and possessions. We often cite animal behaviors as a justification of our territorial behavior, and some evidence reinforces that view. Studies on humans have found similar behaviors (Bechtel, 1997). We mark our spaces by building fences, putting signs on our doors, placing objects to "hold our place," and tend to guard these spaces. We may notice if someone is in our yard or has taken "our" seat at the dinner table.

Territoriality is an important concept in how we use and arrange our homes. Bedrooms are often one person's territory, but if rooms are shared the territorial space might be just a part of the room. Certain other rooms that we might think are shared are really the province of one person. Is it Mom's kitchen? Dad's study? The kid's basement? Sometimes there are upset feelings if another person goes into the space and rearranges it or moves things around.

Newman (1972) built on ideas of territoriality in designing multifamily housing to be "defensible space." He promoted design that would encourage residents to observe and claim the community space so that they would defend it against crime. Sociopetal designs were encouraged. He suggested that residents should be able to view exterior spaces from the inside of their homes. Lighting and landscaping that encourage people to leave their apartments are important to building community. Neighborhood Crime Watch programs have been developed based on the idea of extending our sense of territory beyond our home's interior walls.

Personalizing Space

Possessions are an important part of the way we mark our space. We collect and display many items over our lifetimes and we often use them to define and claim a space. Workers personalize work spaces by placing photographs and plants in their office or cubicle to make their space feel like their own, and people place their coat in a chair to hold a seat.

Possessions are also important in our homes and may be used to claim a space or area: Dad's chair, Mom's desk, or Kristen's television. We also use possessions for display. These items could be a single special item, a collection of similar items, or just knick-knacks that we pick up at various times. Displaying items tends to express something about us. It has been noted that these displays can be a form of dominance and some can fall into the category of conspicuous consumption or "showing off" how much we have (Bechtel, 1997).

Possessions can also hold meaning in and of themselves. It may recall a special memory or remind us of an important person. Items that hold this importance may need to go with us as we move from one house to another. One girl's family who moved frequently due to the father's military career indicated that she did not feel that she was at home in a new space until the piano with a specific collection of items on top was in its proper place. Older people who move from their family home into a smaller apartment or assisted living facility often go through a process of determining which of their possessions are important to keep in order to feel that they are home.

Symbols of Self. Marcus (1997) wrote about the home's importance as a symbol of who we are, as borne out by the lifestyle orientation of this chapter. The house itself has been selected because its location, size, design, and arrangement fulfill our lifestyle and image of who we are. The process continues in the home as we select furnishings and accessories that express our style and reflect our self to the outside world.

CONCLUSION

Many housing choices are available for American households today, which make it possible for households to seek housing that matches their lifestyles. Many of the variations planned in housing today highlight lifestyle choices. Community amenities such as walking trails, swimming pools, golf courses, or marinas might encourage active lifestyles. Often services such as childcare, cleaners, and business centers are being located in developments to support working lives. The homes themselves have lifestyle features such as office areas, learning centers, media rooms, large bedrooms and baths, and kitchens equipped with commercial cooking appliances. Builders and developers try to differentiate their homes to attract buyers and residents. Presenting normative housing that meets unique lifestyle requirements will continue to be a challenge to designers and planners.

Everyone's lifestyle is somewhat unique. However, basic factors such as demographic (age and household size) and socioeconomic (income and education) characteristics help shape lifestyle. Values and interests also help to characterize the lifestyles of individuals and families. The classifications that identify lifestyles are complex and designed to assist in marketing products. The very nature of lifestyles suggests that they are subject to change over time. Interests, life cycle stages, incomes, and occupations will vary throughout our lives. Housing choices also will vary and change. We may start our adult lives in small apartments that give us freedom and autonomy. After we marry and have children, a house in a suburban neighborhood may be the perfect place to raise children. Soon we have a larger house and once the children have left home we return to a smaller home, but this time amenities support security, recreation, and personal interests.

The norms that we have for housing help shape our choices within the society in which we live. In the United States we strive for a quality-built, single-family, detached house in a good neighborhood that we own and pay for with less than 30 percent of our income. Although the normative description gives us an image of a house, it does not paint a complete picture. Understanding our lifestyles allows us to refine choices and select housing with the features that express who we are and what makes a shelter a home. The causal, two-story contemporary house with a stone fireplace and south-facing windows might really express that back-to-nature lifestyle, while the high-rise condominium with views of the city could fit the urban, professional lifestyle. Arranging the social spaces for conversation, designating the study for Dad, and personalizing our rooms with objects that have meaning for us are all ways we use the house and have it become our home. Selecting and living in a house is a process of knowing who we are and how our house can express ourselves.

REFERENCES

American Housing Survey. (2001). *American housing survey.* Washington, DC: U.S. Census Bureau.

American Public Health Association. (1971). *Housing: Basic health principles and recommended ordinance.* Washington, DC: APHA.

Bechtel, R. B. (1997). *Environment and behavior: An introduction.* Thousand Oaks, CA: Sage Publications.

Bell, W. (1968). The city, the suburb, and a theory of social choice. In S. Greer, D. L. Mcelrath, D. W. Minar, & P. Prleans (Eds.), *The new urbanization.* New York: St. Martin's Press.

Berube, M. S., Neely, D. J., & DeVinne, P. B. (Eds.). (1982). *The American heritage dictionary* (Second College Ed.). Boston: Houghton Mifflin Company.

Beyer, G. H., Mackesey, T. W., & Montgomery, J. E. (1955). *Houses are for people.* Ithaca, NY: Cornell University, Housing Research Center, Research Publication No. 3.

Brooks, D. (2000). *Bobos in paradise: The new upper class and how they got there.* New York: Simon & Schuster.

Bubolz, M. M., & Sontag, M. S. (1993). Human ecology theory. In P. G. Boss, W. J. Doherty, R. LaRossa, W. R. Schumm, & S. K. Steinments (Eds.), *Sourcebook of family theories and methods: A contextual approach* (pp. 419–451). New York: Plenum Press.

Cutler, V. F. (1947). *Personal and family values in the choice of a home.* Ithaca, NY: Cornell University, Agricultural Experiment Station, Bulletin No. 840.

Dent, H. (1998). *The roaring 2000s.* New York: Simon & Schuster.

Duvall, E. M. (1957). *Family development.* Philadelphia: J. B. Lippincott.

Florida, R. L. (2002). *The rise of the creative class: And how it's transforming work, leisure, community and everyday life.* New York: Basic Books.

Gladhart, P. M. (1973). *Family housing adjustment and the theory of residential mobility: A temporal analysis of family residential histories.* Unpublished doctoral dissertation, Cornell University, Ithaca, NY.

Glick, P. C. (1947). The family life cycle. *American Sociological Review, 12,* 164–174.

Gruell, N. L. (1993). *Effects of open-plan housing on perceived household crowding among families with children.* Unpublished doctoral dissertation, Virginia Tech, Blacksburg, VA.

Hall, E. T. (1966). *The hidden dimension.* Garden City, NJ: Doubleday.

Hart, L. (2004, January). Marketing to the 'Bobos'—a new breed. *Kitchen & Bath Design News,* 30–31.

Hohn, C. (1987). The family life cycle: Needed extension of the concept. In J. P. Bongaarts, T. K. Burch, & K. W. Wachter (Eds.), *Family demography: Methods and their application* (pp. 65–80). New York: Oxford University Press.

Joint Center for Housing Studies of Harvard University. (1999). *The state of the nation's housing 1999.* Cambridge, MA: Harvard University.

Joint Center for Housing Studies of Harvard University. (2001). *The state of the nation's housing 2001.* Cambridge, MA: Harvard University.

Joint Center for Housing Studies of Harvard University. (2002). *The state of the nation's housing 2002.* Cambridge, MA: Harvard University.

Joint Center for Housing Studies of Harvard University. (2003). *The state of the nation's housing 2003.* Cambridge, MA: Harvard University.

Joint Center for Housing Studies of Harvard University. (2004). *The state of the nation's housing 2004.* Cambridge, MA: Harvard University.

Lewin, K. (1935). *Dynamic theory of personality.* New York: McGraw-Hill.

Lindamood, S., & Hanna, S. (1979). *Housing, society and consumers.* St. Paul, MN: West Publishing Company.

Marcus, C. C. (1997). *House as a mirror of self.* Berkeley, CA: Conari Press.

Maslow, A. (1970). *Motivation and personality.* New York: Harper & Row.

Michelson, W. (1976). *Man and his urban environment.* Reading, MA: Addison-Wesley.

Mitchell, S. (1995). *The official guide to the generations.* Ithaca, NY: New Strategist Publications.

Mogelonsky, M. (1996, January). America's hottest markets. *American Demographics, 18*(1), 20–31.

Montgomery, J. (1966). *Family housing values: Meaning and implications.* Unpublished manuscript, Florida State University, Tallahassee, FL.

Morris, E. W. (1972). *Departure from a normatively prescribed state as an independent variable: An analysis of housing space norms.* Working paper No. 5 in the series Comparative research on social change and the provision of housing and related services, Cornell University, Ithaca, NY.

Morris, E. W., & Winter, M. (1978). *Housing, family, and society.* New York: John Wiley & Sons.

National Association of Home Builders. (1998). *Housing facts, figures and trends.* Washington, DC: NAHB.

Newman, O. (1972). *Defensible space.* New York: Macmillan.

Newmark, P., & Thompson, J. (1977). *Self, space and shelter.* San Francisco, CA: Canfield Press.

Nygren, M. (1989). Human needs in housing. *Human Ecology Forum, 3*(2), 15–17.

O'Rand, A. M., & Krecker, M. L. (1990). Concepts in the life cycle: Their history, meanings, and uses in the social sciences. *Annual Review of Sociology, 16,* 241–262.

Osmond, H. (1957). Function as the basis of psychiatric ward design. *Mental Hospital, 8,* 23–30.

Parrott, K. (1997). Environmental concerns and housing. *Housing and Society, 24*(3), 47–68.

Ray, P. H. (1997). The emerging culture. *American Demographics, 19*(2), 29–34.

Realtor Magazine Online. (2003, December). *NAR: Housing to stay strong in 2004.* Retrieved February 2, 2004, from *http://realtor.org.*

Ridder, K. (2000, July 15). Apartment rentals become hot housing trend. *Roanoke Times,* pp. A5–A6.

Sommer, R. (1969). *Personal space: The behavioral basis of design.* Englewood Cliffs, NJ: Prentice Hall.

Strauss, W., & Howe, N. (1997). *The fourth turning.* New York: Broadway Books.

Susanka, S. (2001). *The not so big house.* Newtown, CT: Taunton.

U.S. Census Bureau. (2001). *Current population survey.* Washington, DC: U.S. Census Bureau.

U.S. Census Bureau. (2002). *Current population survey.* Washington, DC: U.S. Census Bureau.

U.S. Census Bureau. (2003). *Current population survey.* Washington, DC: U.S. Census Bureau.

Weicher, J. C. (1977). Public policy: Past, present and future. In D. Phares (Ed.), *A decent home and environment: Housing urban America.* Cambridge, MA: Ballinger.

Williams, R. M., Jr. (1951). *American society.* New York: Alfred A. Knopf.

Zemke, R., Raines, C., & Filipczak, B. (2000). *Generations at work.* New York: AMACOM.

Home Environments and Health

Kathleen R. Parrott, Jorge H. Atiles, and Michael P. Vogel
Kathleen R. Parrott is Professor, Department of Apparel, Housing, and
Resource Management, Virginia Polytechnic Institute and State
University, Blacksburg, VA; Jorge H. Atiles is Associate Professor and
Cooperative Extension Associate Director, College of Family and
Consumer Sciences, University of Georgia, Athens, GA; and Michael P.
Vogel is Professor and Housing Specialist, Montana State University
Extension Service, Bozeman, MT.

This chapter presents an overview of the home's impact on the health of the people who live within it. These issues are best studied from a systems approach. The home, as a healthy place to live, is influenced by the larger environment in which it is situated (for example, the climate or building site). Further, the home's microenvironment, including the building structure, heating and cooling equipment, construction materials, and furnishings, are major influences on the health of the home's occupants. Over all this are the home's residents, who influence the home-health system by the choices they make about the home's design, construction, management, and maintenance as well as how they live in the space. In turn, the resident's health is impacted by the various components of the home's environment.

To present this systems view of the home-health interaction, this chapter begins from the outside of the home and works inward. The influences of climate and building site are examined first, followed by building materials and practices, then furnishings, finishes, and household products, and concluding with occupant lifestyle issues. The concept of building practices is defined broadly to include issues of importance to healthy buildings such as ventilation, moisture control, and air and water quality. Lifestyle issues discussed include environmental tobacco smoke, household pests, and pets. While this chapter's content is not exhaustive of all factors influencing people's health in their homes, it does introduce a broad spectrum of issues.

Finally, this chapter's focus is the house, within its macro- and microenvironments, and the *potential* influences on the resident's health. Individual residents vary in their reactions to these influences and in their specific health effects. The chapter does not provide detailed medical information and is not intended to be a diagnostic tool. Rather, this chapter is designed to create an awareness of the possible health effects of various housing choices and decisions, and to suggest alternatives to minimize negative health consequences.

UNDERSTANDING THE HOME ENVIRONMENT-HEALTH INTERACTION

To most, a house is simply an assembly of building materials and furnishings. However, a home, if not properly designed, constructed, and operated, can create health risks to the occupants (Chiras, 2000). Young children and older adults, who have developing or weakening immune systems, respectively, are more susceptible to harmful products in the home than are people of other ages. Much of the research done in the past has focused on effects of contaminants like lead, secondhand smoke, and roach feces on small children. Current emphasis is being placed on how environmental pollutants affect older adults.

People with temporarily or permanently weakened immune systems for other reasons, such as severe allergies or chronic illnesses or people on medications that suppress their immune systems, are also more at risk of suffering the side effects of indoor contaminants. Such people and their families should be especially aware of the issues highlighted in this chapter, as they are of particular importance.

Risk Factors

Sidebar 3.1
Home Environment Health Risk Factors

- Climate
- Building site
- Building materials and practices
- Furnishings, finishes, and household products
- Resident lifestyle

Many factors influence the home environment and the health of those that occupy the building, as shown in sidebar 3-1. Some of the factors are natural such as the radioactive gas radon. Other risk factors are human-caused, created from poor choice of building materials, improper building practices, incorrect installation of mechanical equipment, or lack of timely maintenance (Tremblay & Vogel, 1999). Without careful attention to these factors there is increased risk of health concerns such as:

- Allergies and asthma from excessive *moisture and molds.*
- Irritation to eyes, nose, throat, lungs, and skin; headaches; drowsiness; damage to nervous system, liver, and kidneys; and cancer from *volatile organic compounds (VOCs).*
- Flu-like symptoms, nervous system problems, rapid heart rate, fetus damage, and even death from *combustion gases.*
- Lung cancer from *radon gas* and *asbestos-containing materials.*
- Damage to the nervous system, kidneys, and reproductive system from *lead-based paint, lead-contaminated soils,* and *lead in the drinking water.*
- Blue-baby syndrome (methemoglobinemia) from *nitrate in drinking water.*
- Nervous system damage, headaches, and cancer from *pesticides.*
- Gastrointestinal illnesses from *contamination of ground or surface water* and *faulty septic systems.*

A basic principle of a healthy home is that all things are connected, meaning for each design and construction decision made there is a positive or negative outcome. From the climate where the house is located, to the specific building site, to the thousands of parts and pieces used for the actual construction, all factors have the potential to affect the home and the health of its occupants. Creating and maintaining a healthy home begins with a holistic understanding of how home design, construction, and operational elements interact to create a dynamic system.

The systems approach to home environment-health interaction emphasizes that it is a dynamic relationship. The various system factors can vary, which can increase the risk for health effects. In particular, there is concern about:

- Toxicity of the pollutant or contaminant that has been introduced into the home environment.
- Exposure or dosage, including quantity, length of time, and repetition of exposure.

- Individual susceptibility, which can be influenced by age, general health, previous exposure, and other conditions.
- Cofactors that can increase risk such as smoking or occupational exposure to other pollutants.

These factors illustrate that the health risks are situational and can be greater or lesser for different people in the household.

Risk also involves personal choice. Every day people take personal risks, sometimes of great magnitude, because of the benefit derived despite the risk. Additionally, risks are perceived differently, and one person may fear the outcome of a risky choice that another person does not. A choice must be made to invest time, effort, and resources in reducing a risk, and this is balanced against the expected benefit.

Despite the desire to make a home environmentally healthy, not all environmental hazards can be eliminated. The priority should be to focus on those hazards that present the greatest risk to the resident of a particular home. In addition, the emphasis needs to be on reducing those risks that are perceived as bringing the greatest benefit for the cost and effort invested (Dadd, 1997).

Maintaining a healthy home usually means having an environmentally friendly home as well. Decisions that are good for the health of a home's occupants are generally good for the environment as well. Keeping a home healthy can also make it less polluting and more resource efficient.

Climate Variables

In all climates a basic criterion of home design and construction is to protect occupants from outdoor elements. In doing so, care must be taken to not create an indoor environment that is too tight. Without adequate and managed air exchange, the result can be a home with trapped and elevated levels of pollutants and moisture—an unhealthy environment for occupants. Applying healthy home principles varies from climate to climate. From a building science perspective, U.S. climates are designated in terms of four zones:

- **Cool:** heating-predominant climate
- **Temperate:** heating- and cooling-predominant climate
- **Hot-arid:** cooling-predominant climate
- **Hot-humid:** cooling- and dehumidification-predominant climate

In heating climates the focus is to reduce home heat loss to the cold outdoors. Efficient cold climate homes are typically constructed with greater amounts of insulation and utilize high-performance windows, doors, appliances, and heating systems. Special consideration is also given to preventing unwanted air leakage, while providing healthy air exchange levels. In cooling climates, the emphasis is striving to reduce heat gain and, if necessary, controlling higher levels of relative humidity.

In all climates home design, material selection, and home maintenance are a balancing act of site-specific climate factors that include the following.

- **Solar quantity and quality:** The sun's position in the sky is described by its altitude and azimuth, which vary according to geographical location. Orientation of window openings, roof design, and landscape elements will play a major role in optimizing the sun's benefits, such as solar gain, or in reducing unwanted solar heating in cooling climates.
- **Air temperature:** On a daily and seasonal basis, the air temperature is dependent on the sky's condition. During days of clear skies, solar radiation passes through the atmosphere freely and heats up surfaces and the air. During the night, with clear skies, the heat from the earth's surface passes back through the clear skies causing earth cooling. This diurnal cycle creates a large temperature variation. Climates with generally overcast skies have less variation.
- **Air movements around the home:** Breezes and winds can provide beneficial cooling around the house. However, winds can also create excessive air leakage and heat loss, driving rain, and damage to building materials.
- **Precipitation amounts:** Snowfall, rain, fog, and thunderstorm patterns influence selection of the best building design, style, and type, and the strength requirements of building materials, the level of relative humidity and moisture in the home, and the potential growth of biological pollutants in and around the home.

The Building Site

Constructing a healthy home begins with proper siting of a building (U.S. Department of Energy, 2004). Building site considerations consist of three categories:

- The microclimate—site-specific prevailing climate conditions
- Natural site topographic factors that affect the microclimate
- Human-caused factors

Microclimate.   The performance of every home is influenced by its own microclimate. Microclimate is simply the prevailing weather conditions of a specific building site—solar, air movements, and so forth, as previously discussed. Since the microclimate will affect the energy, durability, and comfort performance of the building, factors such as these should be considered:

- Orientation of window openings to take advantage of solar benefits
- Orientation of building to take advantage of cooling breezes or avoid prevailing winter winds
- Design of the building to reduce exposed surfaces to outside air temperatures
- Selection and installation of building materials to avoid destructive elements of sun, wind, and moisture
- Creation of landscape, architectural, and plant elements such as windbreaks, fences, and earth mounds to direct or divert airflow and precipitation

Natural Site Topographic Factors.   The topography of a site can dramatically influence the daily air temperature, solar exposure, and moisture conditions. Topography defines the land and vegetation character, elevation difference, and water characteristics of the building site. Most people recognize the influence of topography such as experiencing elevation temperature changes, or getting out of a stiff cold wind by hiking on the hillside slope away from the wind.

Topography also influences storm-water run-off (discussed in the next section) and the creation of wetlands on the building site which can cause moisture, mold, and decay problems if not corrected when the house is built. Of any one hazard that is persistent in all climates, water and excessive moisture getting into building materials is the most likely to cause major damage to the building structure and serious health effects to occupants. To minimize water run-off to the building site and keep the structure dry, implement good preventive or corrective building practices as shown in sidebar 3.2. Overall, building site drainage to keep the foundation building materials dry is of particular importance.

Human-Caused Factors.   From a simple look, a building site may appear to be the perfect location for a home. However, before proceeding, any potential building site and the surrounding area should be assessed to determine if hazardous conditions are present that may contaminate the soil and drinking water. While reclaimed industrial areas may be the most obvious areas of suspected hazards, consider the following issues which may affect a chosen building site.

- Brown fields, abandoned, idled, or under-used industrial and commercial facilities (such as a gas station, auto body shop, or dry cleaner).

> **Sidebar 3.2**
> **Water Control**
>
> The following building practices and strategies maximize water control and should be considered during the planning of the home site:
>
> - Properly sized roof overhangs that protect the building's exterior walls from excessive rainfall exposure
> - Gutters and extended downspouts to direct water away from the foundation
> - 5 percent ground slope away from the house foundation in all directions
> - Swales (ditches) used to redirect surface run-off on sloped sites
> - Drainage backfill or board adjacent to foundation to drain water to perforated pipe (placed below level of floor slab), drained to sump pump or outside drain
> - Below grade waterproofing wall barrier such as a membrane or mastic to prevent water entry to foundation
> - Above grade weatherproof materials and proper flashing to resist water entry to building structure
> - Avoid vegetation and landscaping immediately adjacent to the building foundation that may hold water and retain moisture in the building materials
> - Drainage system around the foundation to a storm-water system
> - Membrane over crawl space soil to control moisture
> - Gravel covered with polyethylene membrane beneath floor slab to control moisture
> - Drainage screen between siding and sheathing in the walls in regions subject to wind-blown moisture

- Closed or abandoned dumps and landfills, especially those closed before the regulations of the early 1990s, without proper engineering, monitoring, and guidance.
- Underground fuel/hazardous substance storage tanks left over from service stations and convenience stores, fleet service operators, and local governments; and especially steel tanks, common until the mid-1980s, which are likely to corrode.
- Aboveground fuel/hazardous substance storage tanks, especially if the tank caused spills or leakage onto the ground.
- Agricultural operation, such as a feedlot, machine repair area, or pesticide/fertilizer/fuel storage area.

Before selecting a home or a site to construct a home, it is important to check with the local land use/planning department and conduct research on the site's history to determine its previous uses and if it is safe. Generally, liability for site contamination passes to the current owner.

STORM WATER RUN-OFF

Storm water run-off is water that washes across land into nearby storm drains or directly into bodies of water. Storm water run-off can be a major factor influencing the location and construction of a healthy home (EHS Associates, 2002). Water pollution also often occurs through storm water run-off. Contaminated storm water run-off that flows into storm drains is not treated before being emptied into the nearest body of water. Therefore, no matter where run-off appears to flow initially, the polluted water eventually reaches a water source. Not all water runs off the land, however. Some of it seeps into the groundwater. If contaminated water seeps down it will pollute the groundwater that may feed drinking water wells and cause harm to the users. Therefore, even if people live far from known water sources like oceans, lakes, ponds, rivers, and streams, their actions can still lead to pollution of the water supply. Some common concerns follow.

- **Automotive waste:** Cars and other vehicles can cause water contamination in several ways. Oil drips and fluid spills in driveways and parking areas can be picked up by run-off and carried into water sources. In addition, used oil and antifreeze are sometimes dumped into storm drains or ditches or simply onto the ground. Washing vehicles on paved surfaces like driveways and streets causes potential problems because soapy and dirty water will run off into storm drains and water sources. Vehicles washed on a flat lawn or gravel surface may also cause groundwater contamination.
- **Fertilizers and pesticides:** Many people apply too much fertilizer and pesticide on their lawns and gardens. The extra chemicals have no positive effects on a lawn and increase the risks of water contamination. Spills of pesticides or fertilizers can quickly contaminate groundwater. Treating lawns immediately prior (within 48 hours) to rain will highly contaminate storm water run-off because the products will be picked up by the rain before they can reach plants' root systems. Similarly, excessive watering of lawns after treating with chemicals will interfere with the products' ability to be

effective and may pollute run-off. Using plants native to the area that can grow without much stimulation may be the most water-friendly approach to creating a beautiful lawn.

- **Yard and garden waste:** Grass clippings and leaves are common examples of yard and garden waste. The most potentially harmful treatment of yard waste is to burn it along with household waste or garbage, since burning these wastes could release harmful gases and create air pollution. The ashes from such fires will settle in the ground and can seep down to contaminate surface and groundwater. Composting, the controlled decomposition of organic materials, such as leaves, grass, and food scraps by microorganisms, may be the best approach to handling yard waste. The result of this decomposition process is compost or humus, a crumbly, earthy-smelling, soil-like material which can be used to enrich the soil.

- **Improper landscaping:** A well-designed yard prevents excessive run-off, whereas a poorly designed landscape contributes to pollution problems. Scant landscaping, especially on hilly land, allows storm water to flow at increased rates and results in excess soil erosion. Short grass and lack of vegetation near sources of water is particularly of concern because it increases the ability of run-off to carry pollutants directly into the water. To reduce water pollution and ground erosion, a buffer zone of at least 25 feet of vegetation (grass, shrubs, and trees) should be left adjacent to water sources and should never be fertilized. Also, remember storm water run-off, while typically associated with rain, is produced artificially when people overwater their lawns. Most lawns need only an inch of water per week; excess water simply runs off the land, wasting an important resource. Homes in areas prone to wildfires or forest fires have a special concern when planning erosion-control landscaping. Too many shrubs and trees close to a home can create a fire hazard, so short grasses may be preferable.

- **Roof drainage:** Roof drainage should divert water away from foundation walls, which reduces the potential for interior moisture problems. Appropriate drainage, including the use of gutters, downspouts, and extension hoses, diverts roof water away from the house and driveway and allows it to filter through more permeable grounds such as a soakage trench system. Downspouts that discharge onto paved surfaces cause pollution concerns since they will carry automotive waste and other pollutants into storm drains.

BUILDING MATERIALS AND BUILDING PRACTICES

Whether old or newly constructed, the impact of a home on its occupants' health has much to do with the materials and building practices used during the construction as well as the materials and furnishings added after the original construction (IAQ Indoor Air Quality Resource Center, 2005). To evaluate the impact of building materials and practices on health, there are several areas to consider with respect to construction age and current building practices. Each of these areas will be examined in more detail.

Construction Age

A home's age can tell us much about its potential to affect the occupants' health. Unless the house has undergone utility and material renovations since its original construction, an older home likely consists of hazardous materials, has utilities that do not meet codes, and utilizes inefficient heating and air conditioning equipment that may produce pollutants. Figure 3.1 lists possible hazards of older homes.

CURRENT BUILDING PRACTICES: VENTILATION

Good ventilation, a critical element in a healthy home, is necessary for moisture control as well as to remove airborne chemicals, particles, combustion by-products, and odors (Bower, 1995). Residential ventilation systems are generally designed with the assumption that indoor air is improved by mixing or replacing it with outside air. Although outdoor air is perceived to be fresher, depending on the location of the home this may not always be true. If the outside air is polluted, special ventilation systems may be needed that provide additional air filtration and cleaning.

Planning home ventilation usually focuses on sizing and locating exhaust fans. However, there must also be a way for adequate replacement air to be brought into the home. If not, a dangerous situation—back drafting—can occur. Ventilation systems for a home typically consist of local ventilation for problem areas such as kitchens and bathrooms, and general ventilation for the whole house. Most building codes will specify only minimum ventilation requirements, typically an operable window. For example, the new International Residential Code requirement for bathroom ventilation is:

minimum ventilation for the bathroom is to be a window of at least 3 square feet of which 50% is operable, or a mechanical ventilation

Hazard	Description and Possible Materials
Asbestos-containing materials	Homes built prior to 1980. Found in floor tiles, insulation materials like vermiculite, pipe and boiler wrap, exterior shingle siding. Poses a hazard if friable, damaged, or in poor condition.
Lead-based paint	Exterior and interior paints in homes built prior to 1978, most likely in homes built prior to 1950. Greater hazard if paint is in poor or damaged condition.
Pressure-treated lumber (chromated copper arsenate or CCA, pentachlorophenol, and creosote)	Many exterior construction applications since 1900. Direct skin contact increases hazard. Extremely hazardous if burned.
Combustion gases such as carbon monoxide, nitrogen dioxide, carbon dioxide, and particulates	Any space or water heating equipment (furnace, range/oven, space heater, clothes dryer) that burns gas, oil, wood, coal, or kerosene. If not vented to the outside, or if flue or heat exchanger is not well maintained, a hazard exists. Back drafting hazard is possible.
Lead in water	Pre-1988 homes. Lead found in lead-based solder, brass well pumps and fixtures, and likely in homes with plumbing installed prior to 1930. Increased hazard with corrosive or acidic water.
Radon—naturally occurring radioactive gas	New or old homes. A gas from soil and rock around foundation. Certain areas of the country are designated as high radon risk.
Molds	Can exist in any home. May be present because of high relative humidity (>50%) and/or past flooding or water leaks. Poor home maintenance can contribute to mold growth.
Formaldehyde	Homes insulated with urea formaldehyde foam insulation during late 1970s–early 1980s. May lead to off-gassing of formaldehyde, a toxic volatile organic compound (VOC). Particle board and MDF (medium density fiberboard) used in kitchen cabinets, countertops, and furniture are also sources of formaldehyde.
Underground fuel-oil storage tank	Locations where fuel oil has been a predominant source of heating fuel prior to the 1980s. Leaking tanks can contaminate soil or groundwater.
Drinking water contaminants (such as coliform bacteria, nitrate, or pesticides) in private water systems	Poorly maintained and shallow groundwater wells. Wells too close to septic systems, fuel and chemical storage areas, and agricultural feed lots.

Figure 3.1 Possible hazards of older homes

system of at least 50 cubic feet per minute (CFM) ducted to the outside (International Code Council, 2002).

Although windows can be used to meet ventilation code requirements, reliance on windows for all household ventilation can be a problem. It may not be practical or comfortable to open a window for ventilation on cold or rainy days, and privacy or security may be compromised with an open window. In addition, a single open window may not be enough to provide adequate air circulation to remove moisture. Many professional and industry organizations involved with housing, such as the American Society of Heating, Refrigerating, and Air-conditioning Engineers (ASHRAE), Home Ventilating Institute (HVI), and National Kitchen and Bath Association (NKBA), emphasize that mechanical ventilation is important for a healthy home.

The most effective ventilation system for a home is usually a mechanical system that exhausts air to the outside. Selecting the right fan is important, but only part of the decision. Household ventilation must be considered as a system, including the fan, ducts, air intakes, controls, and installation (U.S. Environmental Protection Agency, 1998).

The simplest ventilation systems use separate, independently operating exhaust fans in each bathroom, the kitchen, and possibly in other areas such as the laundry room or a home workshop. The exhaust fans can operate by a manual switch, an automatic switch such as a humidistat, or be integrated into a light switch.

Many people resist using exhaust fans because of the noise, as a loud fan can be annoying. The noise level of fans is rated in sones, which is a measure of loudness. Generally, a fan rated less than 1.0 to 1.5 sones will be quiet enough to be considered only background noise.

Kitchen Ventilation Fans

The choices in kitchens are usually between a fan mounted above the cook top or range, usually with a hood (updraft), and a proximity system, installed in the cook top or adjacent to the cooking surface (downdraft). Some kitchens may have a ceiling- or wall-mounted exhaust fan, but that is generally not considered as effective as the updraft or downdraft systems. Kitchen ventilation systems are especially critical with gas cooking appliances to control combustion pollutants from gas cooking such as carbon monoxide and water vapor.

Bathroom Ventilation Fans

Bathroom exhaust fans, usually installed near the shower or bathtub, are important to control excess moisture in the home and should be used whenever the shower or tub is in use. Humidistat controls can be used for an automated system. Typically, the bathroom door is undercut to assure replacement air can enter the room.

Whole-House Fans

An exhaust fan mounted in a home's attic can provide ventilation and fresh air to the whole home. Typically, a single large fan pulls air into the house through windows and doors, and then exhausts it through vents in the attic. The air intake is often located in a hall or other central location in the home. This type of ventilation system is mostly used in summer, in climates with hot days and cooler nights. The whole-house fan exhausts heated air from the home and replaces it with cooler night air, providing a slight breeze at the same time.

Fan Size

Exhaust fans are sized in CFM (cubic feet per minute) or L/s (liters per second). These terms both describe the volume of air the fan can move in a period of time. Some ventilation recommendations are given in fan size only, which does not consider the size of the room and the efficiency of the installation. Other ventilation recommendations are made in ACH (air changes per hour), a measure of the number of times per hour a volume of air equivalent to the volume of the room should be exhausted.

The fan size determined by the ACH method is effective fan capacity, or how much air the fan can actually move. Effective fan capacity is not the same as the mechanical size of the fan, and will depend on a number of factors including:

- **Length of duct run from the intake vent to the exhaust vent:** If the duct run is more than about five feet, the size of the fan should increase to compensate for the resistance of a longer duct run.
- **Elbows or bends in the ducts:** If there is more than one elbow or bend in the duct, the size of the fan should increase to compensate for the greater resistance.

Replacement Air

An operating fan exhausts or removes air from the room. This creates a negative pressure in the room, and replacement or make-up air must come from somewhere. If replacement air is not provided, the fan's effectiveness is reduced and the potential for back drafting is increased. For example, a bathroom or kitchen fan is not just exhausting air from that room but from the whole house. Some of the replacement air may come from open windows or people moving in and out of doors. Some replacement air may come from leaks and cracks in the building envelope. However, in well-constructed, energy efficient homes, there are few places for replacement air to leak into the home. If replacement air is not provided, negative pressure can be created in the home.

Back Drafting

Negative pressure inside the home can create problems with the operation of appliances that need to exhaust to the outside such as a gas furnace or water heater. In this situation, called back drafting, dangerous combustion pollutants as well as excess moisture and radon gas can be pulled into the home. A simple solution to back drafting problems, and to providing replacement air, can be opening a window when operating exhaust fans. However, this is not always a practical solution. Other solutions include a fresh air inlet into the home and a whole-house mechanical ventilation system that balances airflow in the home.

Whole-House Ventilation Systems

A whole-house ventilation system is a more complex system that provides controlled, continuous ventilation to a home. Exhaust fan vents in one or more locations throughout the home pull air from the home and exhaust it to the outside. At the same time, fresh air is blown into the home through one or more inlets. The whole-house ventilation system can work through existing ductwork for heating and cooling systems, or be entirely separate.

Some whole-house ventilation systems are known as heat recovery ventilators. In these systems the exhaust air from the home and the fresh air from outside are passed, simultaneously but separately, through a heat exchanger. In the wintertime heat from the house's air is recovered to preheat the fresh, outdoor air. In the summertime heat is removed from the incoming outside air. The net result is increased energy efficiency in the ventilation system. An energy recovery ventilator is a similar system which also dehumidifies the incoming air from outside.

CURRENT BUILDING PRACTICES: MOISTURE CONTROL

Excess moisture presents a potential problem for both a building and its occupants. Excess moisture in building materials leads to structural problems such as peeling paint, rusting metal, and deterioration of joists and framing (Parrott, Kirby, Woodard, Smith, & Wengert, 1996). Damp building materials tend to attract dirt and therefore require more cleaning and maintenance.

Damp spaces make good environments for the growth of many biological pollutants. Bacteria and viruses thrive in moist spaces. Pests, from dust mites to cockroaches, need moisture to thrive. Wet building materials can also harbor mold growth, which leads to further structural damage. Mold can also be a health threat for people living in the home. In addition, mold growing on interior finish materials smells and is ugly.

Varying amounts of water vapor are present in air. The maximum amount of water vapor depends on the temperature. The warmer the air, the more water vapor it will hold. Absolute humidity describes how much water vapor air contains. Relative humidity, expressed as a percent, can be determined by the following formula:

$$\frac{\textit{Amount of water vapor in the air}}{\textit{Maximum amount of water vapor air can hold at a given temperature}} \times 100 = \textit{Relative humidity}$$

Note that the air temperature is important to understanding relative humidity. On a winter's day, when the temperature is 20 degrees Fahrenheit and the humidity is 70 percent, the air will actually contain much less moisture than on a summer's day, when the temperature is 85 degrees Fahrenheit and the humidity is also 70 percent.

Condensation is the opposite of evaporation and occurs when water vapor returns to a liquid state. As air cools it can no longer hold as much water vapor, so the water condenses into a liquid. The temperature at which condensation occurs is referred to as the dew point.

The cycle of water evaporating and condensing in a room can lead to moisture problems. A room where moisture is generated, such as a bathroom, kitchen, or laundry room, tends to have higher humidity. Many activities such as showering and cooking increase the air's temperature as well as its moisture level. However, materials and surfaces in these rooms tend to be cooler than the air, which leads to condensation.

Hidden Condensation

The air temperature inside a room, like the bathroom or kitchen, tends to be higher than the air temperature on the other side of the walls, floor, and ceiling. During the winter, this is especially true of exterior walls and a ceiling with an attic above it. There is a natural tendency for warm air to rise, as warm air is lighter than cool air. Warm, moist air will tend to move upward through walls and ceilings. As the air moves through the wall or ceiling it meets cool surfaces within the wall or ceiling cavity. At some point the dew point temperature is reached and condensation occurs. This hidden condensation, inside walls and attics, can be a particular nightmare for homeowners. As building materials get wetter, deterioration and mold growth can get extensive before the problem is noticed.

Molds and Moisture

There are thousands of varieties of molds. Molds, or fungi, reproduce by spores, which blow out into the air and can be dormant for years. However, given the right conditions of food and moisture, the spores can begin to grow. At any given time there are typically mold spores in the air around us. Molds are a natural part of the ecosystem and play an important role in digesting organic debris. A problem exists, however, when an excess of mold growth exists and the organic matter they are digesting is part of the building structure.

Molds require moisture, oxygen, and food to grow. How much of each element is required will depend on the variety. However, most molds will start growing at a relative humidity of 70 percent or more. Molds can make food out of almost any organic matter including skin cells, shampoo residues, or textile fibers. Cellulosic building materials such as paper, wood, textiles, many types of insulation, carpet, wallpaper, and drywall make an excellent environment for mold growth. The cellulosic materials will absorb moisture, providing the right growth conditions, and the materials themselves provide the food. Molds can grow fast. If cellulosic building materials get wet, mold growth will begin in 24 to 48 hours. Mold growth on the surface of noncellulosic materials can start in the same time period as long as food and moisture are present.

Molds can affect people in different ways. Molds produce chemicals that irritate most people and can cause problems such as headaches, breathing difficulties, and skin, eye, and throat irritation as well as aggravating other health conditions such as asthma. In addition, some people are allergic to specific species of mold. Molds can also sensitize the body so that the person is more susceptible to health effects from exposure. Finally, some molds produce toxins. The likelihood of health issues increases with the amount of exposure to mold as well as the individual's sensitivity (Lankarge, 2003).

Preventing Moisture Problems

Good ventilation is necessary to prevent moisture problems and mold growth in the home. Exhaust ventilation removes excess moisture and prevents condensation. Using exhaust ventilation when showering, bathing, cooking, and doing laundry is important.

Managing and limiting interior moisture sources in the home are also critical to preventing moisture problems. Typical household moisture sources include cooking, bathing, refrigerator drip pans, drying laundry, plants, and plumbing leaks. In new or remodeled homes, new building materials such as lumber, paint, concrete, and drywall can be a major source of moisture for a year or more.

The finish materials in a home can contribute to, or help prevent, moisture problems. After exposure to water and humidity, the more absorbent the materials the longer they will stay damp, which supports mold growth. A hard surface or nonabsorbent material such as glazed tile, solid surfacing, vitreous china, or engineered stone reduces the likelihood of moisture absorption. Sealers applied to absorbent or porous materials such as clay tile, marble, or grout can also reduce moisture absorption. Low-maintenance materials, fixtures, and fittings are also important to preventing mold growth. Materials that are kept clean are less likely to accumulate debris that can support mold growth.

A vapor retarder material such as plastic sheeting can be used in wall construction to block the flow of moist air into wall cavities or attics. Special considerations exist about the placement of a vapor retarder, depending on whether the climate is heating or cooling dominant.

New products are becoming available with various types of antimicrobial finishes or additives. Generally, an antimicrobial finish means that the material is treated with a pesticide of some sort to protect the material or product itself. For example, paints are available with fungicides to protect the paint from mold growth. However, this does not mean that mold will not grow on the paint in a moist environment, if a food source were to accumulate on the painted surface.

CURRENT BUILDING PRACTICES: INDOOR AIR QUALITY

Good indoor air quality makes a space pleasant and healthy for the user. Providing good indoor air quality is a three-step process.

- **Source control:** This refers to minimizing or preventing the sources of indoor air pollution in a room or building. Suggestions for minimizing indoor air pollutants such as radon, combustion pollutants (including carbon monoxide), lead dust, volatile organic compounds (VOCs), and molds are presented throughout this chapter. This is the primary strategy for maintaining good indoor air quality. Refer to the appendix at the end of this chapter for suggestions on how to minimize the sources of air pollution in the home.

- **Ventilation:** This refers to providing adequate air exchange, through natural or mechanical ventilation, to dilute the concentration of indoor air pollutants and assure that the space has a supply of fresh air. Mechanical ventilation was discussed earlier.
- **Air cleaning:** This means, when necessary, using filters or other devices to remove potentially harmful indoor air pollutants.

Air Cleaners

Choosing an air cleaner to improve a home's air quality is a complex task. Choices include various types of mechanical filtration, electrostatic, electronic, ion generating, and absorption systems for air cleaning (U.S. Environmental Protection Agency, 1997). According to the U.S. Environmental Protection Agency (EPA) and the American Lung Association, air cleaners that generate ozone are not recommended for use in occupied spaces such as the home.

Air cleaners can be table top, freestanding, or integrated into heating, cooling, or ventilation systems. In addition to size, efficiency (the ability of the collecting medium to capture contaminants from the airstream) and effectiveness (the ability of the air cleaner to reduce contaminant concentrations in the room's air) must be studied. Cost to purchase and maintain as well as the warranty are among the other considerations.

Air cleaners are effective only on those contaminants that stay airborne long enough to reach the air cleaner. Appropriately selected and well-maintained air cleaners may reduce some contaminants in indoor air, but should not be the primary method to improve air quality. The value of air cleaners in actually improving health is of considerable controversy.

CURRENT BUILDING PRACTICES: MUNICIPAL VERSUS PRIVATE WATER SYSTEMS

Some Americans get their water from a public or municipal water system, whereas others use a private water source to tap directly into the groundwater or possibly surface water. Many people who are on public water systems do not understand that their water may come from groundwater, as would a private well-user's water. Public water sources also include local rivers and lakes. All of these water sources may become contaminated in many ways and, therefore, affect consumers of municipal and private water alike. The differences between private and public water sources come in testing and treating the water.

Water Testing

Water from municipal systems is checked regularly by a local water authority or similar agency for safety according to EPA guidelines, which regulate the presence of over 80 chemicals in public water supplies (U.S. Environmental Protection Agency, 2005). If water supply problems are detected the water must be treated. Therefore, consumers of such water can feel confident that the water coming into their house is safe to drink. However, there is still a potential for in-house pollution.

Consumers who obtain their water from a private source such as their own well, however, are responsible for testing their water since routine EPA tests are not required for private water sources. Tests should be conducted at least every two years by a certified laboratory, and include tests for total coliform bacteria, nitrate, pH, and total dissolved solids. Wells that are more than 20 years old should be tested more frequently. In addition, users of private water supplies have the same concerns as users of public water about the potential for in-house contamination.

Regardless of the source of water, households should be alert for the following signs to determine if their water should be tested:

- Household members regularly complain of gastrointestinal ailments.
- Lead or lead-soldered copper pipes may be present.
- Pipes are corroded or leaking.
- Water stains plumbing fixtures and/or laundry.

In addition to following these guidelines, testing of both private and municipal water should be conducted whenever water changes in taste, smell, color, or clarity, or there is a specific reason to believe that other contaminants such as pesticides or chemicals have entered the water supply.

Wells

All private well users should first ensure that they are properly using and protecting their well; this is the best approach to providing a quality water supply. Three basic principles will help well owners ensure the safety of their well water.

- A well should be sited relatively high in the landscape and as far as possible from animal pens, septic tanks, dumps, and chemical storage areas. In addition, wells should not be located in areas that are prone to flooding.

- The well casing (the plastic or steel pipe that runs the depth of the well) should be sealed with a tight-fitting, vermin-proof cap and extend at least one foot above the ground; and the area between the casing and the sides of the hole should be filled with grout.
- Devices designed to prevent backflow should be attached to the ends of faucets and hoses to prevent water-carrying pollutants from siphoning back into the water supply.

In addition, abandoned wells, if not properly handled, present an opportunity for water contamination. Abandoned wells should be filled, sealed, and plugged. Such precautions will prevent the accidental seepage of pollutants into groundwater as well as the intentional disposal of garbage or chemicals down the well.

Water Treatment

Two facts about water contamination and treatment are commonly misunderstood. First, many potentially harmful water contaminants do not affect the taste or appearance of water. Second, simply boiling water may not make it safer as some contaminants like nitrates actually become more concentrated due to boiling. Unfamiliarity with these facts leads many Americans to assume their water is safe when it could actually have short-term and/or long-term health effects on household members.

Fortunately, Americans are becoming more aware of the potentially hidden dangers in their water, and more products to improve water quality are now available on the market as a result. However, any company claiming to eliminate all contaminants, bacteria, and minerals from water is stretching the truth. Not only is such a task impossible but it is also undesirable—such pure water would be both bland and corrosive. Furthermore, the EPA does not test or register any water treatment systems so claims of such a status are deceptive.

Water treatment systems vary in approach, size, effectiveness, and cost. It is important to match any type of water treatment equipment to the water problem and the pollutant to be removed. Also, the amount of water contaminant may determine the type of treatment system. If more than one type of treatment device is needed the order of installation may be critical.

FURNISHINGS, FINISHES, AND HOUSEHOLD PRODUCTS

Houses, old or new, contain furnishings and finishes with chemicals that can affect the occupants' health. In particular, new items such as carpet, varnished woods, and finished textiles have the potential to affect the home's air quality (Tremblay & Vogel, 1999). Ventilation is important when new furnishings or finishes are introduced into a home. Environmentally friendly products with little or no VOCs reduce the risk.

Some potentially hazardous chemicals are also used in the manufacturing of household cleaning supplies, automotive products, hobby materials, and lawn and garden products that are used in and around the home. If not used and stored properly these materials can evaporate, creating poor air quality, and can contaminate water supplies, posing long-term health risks for occupants.

When selecting household products it is important to read the ingredients label and look for warnings such as flammable, combustible, caution, warning, danger, and use in ventilated area that indicate the presence of hazardous contents. Failure to follow label directions for safe use, storage, and disposal of chemical products creates a hazard in the home. Hazardous materials fall into one or more of four basic categories: corrosive materials, flammable materials, explosive or reactive materials, and toxic materials. For a more detailed assessment of the product, Material Safety Data Sheets (MSDS) are available upon request from the product manufacturer. Many MSDSs are now available on the Internet. Figure 3.2 identifies potentially harmful chemical compounds and products found in homes that should be used with caution. Sidebar 3.3 details additional household chemicals and products that may present problems.

Material	Material Applications
Formaldehyde and other volatile organic compounds (VOCs)	Particle board, cabinets and case goods, upholstered furniture, adhesives, carpet, fabric finishes
Petroleum-based products (may also be VOCs)	Paints and paint thinner, paint strippers, wood finishes, cleaning solvents, automotive products
Aerosol containers	Pressurized products that sometimes contain flammable or poisonous chemicals
Pesticides	Herbicides, fungicides, rodenticides, insecticides, mildewcides

Figure 3.2 Potentially harmful materials

Sidebar 3.3
Household Chemicals and Products

You can help to control home indoor air quality by the choices you make in using household chemicals and products.

- Use the least amount of a product that will get the job done.
- Read labels, follow safety precautions, and contact the manufacturer if you have questions.
- Do not use a potentially hazardous chemical unless necessary.
- Use household chemicals and products only for their intended purpose.
- Choose product packaging that reduces the chance of spills and leaks, and is childproof in case children live in or visit the home.
- Keep household products in original containers so safety information and directions for use are with the product.
- Always use household products in well-ventilated areas.

It is also a good idea to reduce the need for potentially hazardous household chemicals in the first place by practicing preventative maintenance.

- Clean spills and stains quickly.
- Remove food wastes promptly.
- Control excess moisture to reduce the likelihood of problems with mold or household pests.

Safe Storage and Disposal of Chemical Products

Improper storage and disposal of household chemicals such as bleach, paint, cleaning products, and pesticides can raise the risk of indoor air pollution, pose a threat to household members, and create a risk for the eventual contamination of groundwater. Two storage problems are of particular concern. First, nonwaterproof containers do not prevent seepage of chemicals when in contact with water; therefore, only use waterproof containers. Second, chemicals should be stored in areas that are protected from storm water to avoid the risk of leaking and causing pollution.

All household chemicals should be stored in their original containers, which will contain product information including data about safety and accidental poisoning. Storage locations should be well ventilated, away from heat sources, and secure from exploring children. Potentially hazardous products such as VOCs are best stored away from living areas. Storage areas designed to capture leaks and spills are recommended.

The best plan for household chemicals disposal is to only purchase what is needed, or to trade or donate any leftovers, leaving nothing for disposal. If, however, leftover chemicals need disposal, product labels or the MSDS will provide information on safe procedures. Leftover household chemicals should never be disposed by flushing them down the toilet, as this directly inserts chemicals into the water supply. The local waste authority will have guidelines on what can be included with regular household waste and what may require special hazardous waste collections.

RESIDENT LIFESTYLE

Concerns for creating and maintaining a healthy home are well founded, as the choices that people make affect the quality of the air and environment in their homes. This chapter has discussed many factors that influence the home's health. Without careful planning of the house site and design, material selection, and maintenance, the home can become a hazardous place. Once the house is constructed it is the resident's responsibility to minimize environmental hazards. Additional lifestyle choices that affect the health of a home's residents include environmental tobacco smoke, household pests, and family pets.

Environmental Tobacco Smoke

Environmental tobacco smoke (ETS), or secondhand smoke from cigarettes, pipes, or cigars, can have devastating effects on a home and its residents. Tobacco smoke is actually a mixture of gasses and particles and is not easily removed from a home. Both the gaseous component and the particulate component have harmful effects on human health. Secondhand smoke is connected to many health problems. The EPA (1999) estimates that 3,000 nonsmokers die every year from lung cancer because of secondhand smoke. Secondhand smoke also causes other types of cancer, emphysema and other chronic lung diseases, and cardiovascular disease in nonsmokers. Less severe but still important consequences of ETS in nonsmokers are impaired breathing, a lowered immune system, and increased heart rate and blood pressure.

Many of the ETS risks, however, are for children. Tens of thousands of infants and toddlers develop lower respiratory infections such as pneumonia, bronchitis, and bronchiolitis each year from exposure to secondhand smoke, and as many as 10 percent of affected children are hospitalized. Even when serious infections do not result children may suffer from coughing, wheezing, and decreased lung capacity and/or growth. In addition, ETS affects children in other ways. It can cause the buildup of excess fluid in the middle ear, which is the most common reason for surgery in young children. Children with asthma are particularly sensitive to second-hand smoke, as it can cause more frequent or more severe asthma attacks. It is also suspected that secondhand smoke triggers asthma for the first time in many children.

The easy solution to the problem of ETS in a home is to not allow smoking inside the home. Especially if children are present, no one should ever smoke inside a house. If someone insists on smoking inside he or she should ensure that the house is properly ventilated by opening windows or using an exhaust fan. However, it is important to know that no ventilation system can completely remove tobacco smoke from a home. Therefore, even one cigarette smoked in a home will increase the health risks of the people living in the home long after the smell of the smoke has dissipated.

Household Pests

No one wants to have pests, bugs, or critters in the house, but a house is never completely pest-free. It is important to know which bugs are to be expected occasionally in a home and which represent serious health risks and should not be tolerated at all. Roaches and dust mites are probably the most hazardous household pests commonly found in homes. Most of this section, therefore, will be devoted to these two pests. However, any bug that is living in the house rather than accidentally getting in from the outside represents a potential health and safety problem that should be addressed (Healthy Indoor Air for America's Homes, 1996)

Roaches.   First, consider the main problems that roaches can cause inside homes. They can get into food and spoil it. Roach feces cause pollution of the indoor air and can be a major trigger for asthma attacks, especially in children. Four basic principles will help get rid of roaches and protect the home.

- Both food particles and water attract roaches, but if roaches have nothing to eat they will look for somewhere else to live. Therefore, garbage should be sealed or thrown out every night, and neither dirty dishes nor pet food should be left out overnight. Food spills, crumbs, and water leaks should also be cleaned up promptly.
- Roaches can be baited and trapped before they even have a chance to starve. Roach bait is available in premade traps and tubes which should be placed in corners or against walls, out of the reach of children. Low toxicity pesticides such as boric acid may also be useful.
- In attempting to defeat roaches, never use outdoor pesticides inside the home, as they are unsafe in closed-in areas.

- All pesticides should be stored and tightly sealed in their original containers in a cool, dry, locked cabinet, out of the reach of children.

Dust Mites.   Another type of household pest that often causes health problems, dust mites, live all over people's homes—in carpets, upholstered furniture, bedding, and stuffed animals—but cannot be seen by the naked eye. Dust mites thrive in moist places and, wherever they can, feed on dead human skin cells. Many people are allergic to dust mites' feces, and in some people they serve as a trigger for asthma attacks.

One of the easiest places to guard against dust mites is in bedding. Zippered plastic mattress and pillow covers should be used underneath sheets to help protect sleepers from dust mites. In addition, all bedding (sheets, blankets, pillow covers, and mattress pads) should be washed in hot water (130°F) every week to kill any dust mites that might be living on them. Keeping the home's relative humidity level below 50 percent and limiting carpeted areas can help control dust mites.

Pets

Unlike household pests, pets are welcome in many U.S. homes. Overall, home pets can provide companionship and bring many people a sense of joy. However, pets that live indoors can create potential health risks for household members. Therefore, precautions should be taken to minimize these risks and ensure that a pet and its owner can live happily and healthily in a home together.

The health threat posed by pets comes primarily in the form of their dander, which is simply skin flakes from cats, dogs, gerbils, and other furry animals. Therefore, pets without dander, which are typically nonfurry animals, do not pose these health risks. Dander is mainly a concern when it is found in the air, which occurs through routine acts like making a bed and vacuuming. To help reduce the amount of dander in the air, pets should be kept out of carpeted areas, since walking across dander-infested carpets stirs up the dander into the air. In addition, pets should be kept out of bedrooms to make the air in sleeping environments more healthy.

The most frequent problems triggered by pet dander in the air are allergic reactions such as watery or puffy eyes, runny nose, sneezing, nasal congestion, itching, hives, coughing, wheezing, difficulty breathing, headaches, dizziness, and fatigue. However, more serious consequences such as asthma attacks can be brought on by exposure to pet dander. Children who suffer from asthma should not live in a home with pets that have dander.

Pets that live both indoors and outdoors present another possible health threat. They can bring outdoor particles such as pollen inside with them, which can further contaminate the house's indoor air. Similar to pet dander, pollen often causes allergic reactions and is one of the suspected triggers or complicating factors of asthma.

CONCLUSION

A home *can* be a healthy place to live. In order for this to happen, however, its residents need to understand that their actions and choices will affect the quality and health of the indoor environment. The beginning of this chapter presented a systems approach for the study of the home-health interaction. The macroenvironment in which the home is situated as well as the microenvironment within the home was presented as being in a dynamic relationship. The residents, through their choices and decisions about design, construction, management, maintenance, and lifestyle, continuously influence the home's system and thus the health quality of the home's environment. This chapter detailed the opportunities that residents have to make their home an environmentally healthy and friendly place to live.

REFERENCES

Bower, J. (1995). *Understanding ventilation.* Bloomington, IN: Healthy Home Institute.

Chiras, D. D. (2000). *The natural house.* White River, VT: Chelsea Green.

Dadd, D. L. (1997). *Home safe home.* New York: Tarcher/Putnam.

EHS Associates. (2002). *Storm water pollution prevention: Doing your part.* Phoenix, AZ: National Environmental, Safety and Health Training Association.

Healthy Indoor Air for America's Homes. (1996). *Ten indoor air hazards every homeowner should know about.* Bozeman, MT: Montana State University Extension Service.

IAQ Indoor Air Quality Resource Center. (2005). *Health effects of inadequate indoor air.* Retrieved June 20, 2005, from *www.indoor-air.org.*

International Code Council. (2002). *2003 International building code.* Country Club Hill, IL: ICC.

Lankarge, V. (2003). *What every home owner needs to know about mold.* New York: McGraw-Hill.

Parrott, K., Kirby, J., Woodard, J., Smith, J., & Wengert, E. (1996). *How to prevent and remove mildew in relation to the house and household furnishings.* Blacksburg, VA: Virginia Cooperative Extension.

Tremblay, K. R., Jr., & Vogel, M. P. (1999). *Improving air quality in your home.* Fort Collins, CO: Colorado State University Cooperative Extension.

U.S. Department of Energy. (2004). *Whole building design.* Retrieved February 4, 2005, from *www.doe.gov.*

U.S. Environmental Protection Agency. (1997). *The inside story: A guide to indoor air quality.* Washington, DC: EPA.

U.S. Environmental Protection Agency. (1998). *Homeowner's guide to ventilation.* Washington, DC: EPA.

U.S. Environmental Protection Agency. (1999). *Children and secondhand smoke.* Washington, DC: EPA.

U.S. Environmental Protection Agency. (2005). *Ground water and drinking water.* Retrieved June 20, 2005, from *www.epa.gov/safewater.*

RESOURCES

Many information sources exist on home environments and health, and new information is constantly becoming available. It is important to carefully evaluate the source of information for accuracy and reliability. The following Internet sites (current as of 2005) are generally considered good sources of unbiased and accurate information.

American Lung Association: www.lungusa.org

Building Science Corporation—Mold Issues: www. buildingscience.com/resources/mold

Canada Mortgage and Housing Corporation: www.cmhc-schl. gc.ca

Children's Environmental Health Network: www.cehn.org

Energy Star: www.energystar.gov

Environmental Health Center, National Safety Council: www.nsc. org/ehc.htm

Healthy Environments and Consumer Safety, Health Canada: www.hc-sc.gc.ca/hecs-esc/hecs/index.html

Healthy Indoor Air for America's Homes: www.healthyindoorair.org

Help Yourself to a Healthy Home (An Environmental Risk-Assessment Guide for the Home): www.uwex.edu/homeasyst/

Home Ventilating Institute: www.hvi.org

National Center for Environmental Health, Centers for Disease Control: www.cdc.gov/nceh

National Center for Lead-Safe Housing: www.leadsafehousing.org

National Institute of Environmental Health Sciences:
www.niehs. nih.gov

Office of Energy Efficiency, Natural Resources Canada:
www.oee.nrcan.gc.ca

U.S. Environmental Protection Agency: www.epa.gov

Asthma	www.epa.gov/asthma
Indoor air quality	www.epa.gov/iaq
Molds	www.epa.gov/mold/moldresources.html
Waste	www.epa.gov/osw
Water	www.epa.gov/ow

U.S. Green Building Council: www.usgbc.org

Water Quality Association: www.wqa.org

APPENDIX

Healthy Indoor Air for America's Homes, a joint program of the U.S. Department of Agriculture's Cooperative State Research, Education, and Extension Service, and the U.S Environmental Protection Agency provides a variety of practical remedies to indoor air quality problems in the home. Following are a variety of ideas for source control of indoor air pollution, by area of the house.

Living Areas

Paneling, Pressed-Wood Furniture, and Cabinetry—These may release formaldehyde gas. **Remedy:** Ask about formaldehyde content before making a purchase, as some types of pressed-wood products, such as those with phenol resin, emit less formaldehyde. Also, products coated with polyurethane or laminates may reduce formaldehyde emissions. After installation, open windows or provide ventilation. Maintain moderate temperature and humidity.

Carpet—biological pollutants can grow on water-damaged carpet; organic gases are released from new carpet. **Remedy:** Promptly clean as well as dry or remove water-damaged carpet. Ask for low-emitting adhesives, if adhesives are needed. During installation open doors and windows, and use window fans or room air conditioners. Vacuum regularly. Consider area rugs instead of wall-to-wall carpet. Rugs are easier to remove and clean, and the floor below rugs can also be cleaned.

Floor Tiles—Some of these contain asbestos. **Remedy:** Periodically inspect tiles for damage or deterioration. Do not cut, rip, sand, or remove any asbestos-containing materials. If you plan to make changes that might disturb the asbestos, or if materials are more than slightly damaged, professional repair or removal is needed.

Moisture—This encourages biological pollutants including allergens such as mold, mildew, dust mites, and cockroaches. **Remedy:** If possible, eliminate moisture source(s) inside and outside of the building. Install and use exhaust fans. Use a dehumidifier if necessary. Remove molds and mildew by cleaning hard surface materials with detergent and water, then drying completely. Moldy porous materials may have to be thrown away. Extensive mold will require professional assistance. Maintain good fresh air with the use of natural and mechanical air circulation.

Fireplace or Wood Stove—These contain carbon monoxide and combustion pollutants. **Remedy:** Open flue when fireplace or wood stove is in use. Have flue and chimney inspected annually for exhaust back drafting, flue obstructions or cracks, excess creosote, or other damage. Install smoke and carbon monoxide detectors.

Central Air Conditioner—This can contain biological allergens. **Remedy:** If there is a water tray, empty and clean it often. Follow all service and maintenance procedures, including changing the filter and checking to see that the water tray drains properly.

Gas or Kerosene Space Heater—This can contain carbon monoxide and combustion pollutants. **Remedy:** The best recommendation is to never use unvented kerosene or gas space heaters. If an unvented heater must be used, provide fresh air to the room by opening a door to the rest of the house, turning on an exhaust fan, and slightly opening a window.

Tobacco Smoke—This may contain harmful combustion and particulate pollutants including carbon monoxide and combustion by-products. **Remedy:** Do not smoke in your home or permit others to do so, especially near children. If smoking cannot be avoided indoors, open windows or use exhaust fans.

Draperies—New draperies may be treated with a formaldehyde-based finish and emit odors for a short time. **Remedy:** Before hanging, air out draperies to ventilate odors. After hanging, ventilate the area. Maintain moderate temperature and humidity.

Lead-Based Paint—Homes built before 1978 frequently contain lead-based point. **Remedy:** Leave lead-based paint undisturbed if in good condition. Prior to removing paint, test for lead. Do-it-yourself lead test kits are often available from hardware or building supply stores. Do not sand, burn off, or remove lead-based paint yourself;

hire a person with special training for correcting lead-based paint problems.

Animals—Many animals leave allergens such as dander, hair, feathers, or skin in the air. **Remedy:** Keep pets outdoors as often as possible. Clean the entire house regularly; deep clean areas where pets are permitted. Do not allow pets in sleeping areas. Clean pets regularly.

House Dust Mites—Biological allergens from mites can trigger asthma. **Remedy:** Clean the house and vacuum regularly. Wash bedding in hot water above 130°F. Use allergen-proof mattress and pillow covers. Use more hard surface finishes which are less likely to attract and hold dust mites.

Kitchen

Household Cleaners—Unhealthy or irritating vapors may be released from chemicals in cleaning products. **Remedy:** Select nonaerosol and nontoxic products. Use, apply, store, and dispose according to manufacturers' directions. If products are concentrated, properly label the storage container with dilution instructions. Limit the amount of products stored and store in a secure area, inaccessible to children.

Pressed-Wood Cabinets—These cabinets are a source of formaldehyde vapor. **Remedy:** Ask about formaldehyde content before making a purchase. Some types of pressed-wood products, such as those with phenol resin, emit less formaldehyde. Also, products coated with polyurethane or laminates may reduce formaldehyde emissions. Solid wood or metal cabinets are alternatives. After installation, open windows or provide ventilation. Maintain moderate temperature and humidity.

Unvented Gas Stove and Range—These appliances are a source of carbon monoxide and combustion by-products. **Remedy:** Keep appliance burners clean. Periodically have burners adjusted (blue flame tip, not yellow). Install and use an exhaust fan. Never use a gas range or stove to heat your home.

Bathroom

Personal Care Products—Organic gases are released from product chemicals. **Remedy:** Select no or low odor-producing products. Select nonaerosol varieties. Open windows or use an exhaust fan. Follow manufacturers' directions for use and container disposal.

Air Freshener—Organic gases are released from product chemicals. **Remedy:** Open windows or use an exhaust fan instead. If using air fresheners, follow manufacturers' directions.

Bedroom

Humidifier/Vaporizer (cool mist and ultrasonic types)—If not properly maintained, biological allergens including mold can grow in a water reservoir and then be dispersed into air; this can trigger asthma and infectious disease agents (viruses and bacteria). Excess use can lead to household moisture problems. **Remedy:** Clean and sanitize regularly according to manufacturers' directions. Refill with fresh water daily. Use only when necessary.

Moth Repellents—These often contain paradichlorobenzene, a pesticide. **Remedy:** Avoid breathing vapors. Place moth repellents in tightly sealed trunks or other containers and store separately in the attic, garage, or storage closet, away from living areas.

Dry Cleaned Goods—Organic gases are released from chemicals used in the cleaning process. **Remedy:** Bring odors to the attention of your dry cleaner and attempt to air out dry cleaned goods before bringing them indoors. Seek alternatives to dry cleaning such as hand washing.

Smoke and Carbon Monoxide Detectors—Install a smoke detector in the hallway adjacent to or located in each bedroom. If you have gas or other fossil-fuel burning appliances in the house, install carbon monoxide detectors in these locations as well. Combination smoke and carbon monoxide detectors are available. Remember to check the batteries frequently.

Utility Room

Unvented Clothes Dryer—This appliance produces carbon monoxide and combustion by-products (gas dryer), excessive moisture, and can be a fire hazard. **Remedy:** Regularly dispose of lint around and under the dryer. Provide air for gas combustion. Exhaust the dryer directly to the outside.

Gas or Other Fossil-Fuel Furnace/Boiler and Gas Water Heater—These can lead to back drafting of carbon monoxide and combustion pollutants. **Remedy:** Have your heating system and water heater (including gas piping and venting) inspected every year. Make sure there is adequate replacement or make-up air available.

Asbestos Pipe Wrap and Furnace Insulation—This can release asbestos fibers into the air. **Remedy:** Periodically inspect for damage or deterioration. Do not cut, rip, sand, or remove any asbestos-containing materials. If you plan to make changes that might disturb the asbestos, or if materials are more than slightly damaged, professional repair or removal is needed.

Basement

Ground Moisture—Moisture encourages biological allergens like mold and mildew. **Remedy:** Inspect for condensation on walls, standing water on the floor, or sewage leaks. To keep basement dry, prevent outside water sources from entering by installing, inspecting, and maintaining roof gutters and downspouts, not watering close to the foundation, and grading soil away from the home. For standing water, consider installing a sump pump. If moisture has no obvious source, install a dehumidifier or an exhaust fan controlled by humidity levels. Remove and kill mold and mildew growth. Clean and disinfect the basement floor drain regularly.

Radon—This is an invisible, radioactive gas which poses a lung cancer risk. **Remedy:** Test your home for radon: do-it-yourself kits are easy and inexpensive. Have an experienced radon contractor fix your home if your radon level is 4 picoCuries per liter (pCi/L) or higher.

Hobby Products—Organic gases are released from product chemicals such as solvents, paint, glue, and epoxy. **Remedy:** Follow manufacturers' directions for use, ventilation, application, clean-up, and container storage and disposal. Use outdoors when possible. If indoors, open windows or use an exhaust fan. Reseal containers well. Clean tools outside or in well-ventilated areas.

Garage

Car and Small Engine Exhaust—These are sources of carbon monoxide and combustion by-products. **Remedy:** Never leave vehicles, lawn mowers, snowmobiles, and so forth, running in the garage.

Paint, Solvent, and Cleaning Supplies—These may release harmful vapors. **Remedy:** Provide ventilation when using these items. Follow manufacturers' directions. Buy limited quantities. If products contain methylene chloride, such as paint strippers, use outdoors. Reseal containers well. Keep products in original labeled containers. Clean brushes and other materials outside.

Pesticides and Fertilizers—These yard and garden chemicals may be toxic. **Remedy:** Use nonchemical methods when possible. Minimize the need for pesticides by following integrated pest management (IPM) practices. Follow manufacturers' directions for mixing, applying, and storing these products, and use protective clothing. Mix or dilute outdoors. Provide ventilation when using indoors. Store products in original labeled container, outside of the home. Remove shoes and clean hands and clothing to avoid spreading chemicals.

The Housing Industry

Andrew T. Carswell and Anne L. Sweaney
Andrew T. Carswell is Assistant Professor and Anne L. Sweaney is
Professor and Head, Department of Housing and Consumer Economics,
University of Georgia, Athens, GA.

The production, distribution, and allocation of various housing services and resources involve literally dozens of different subindustries that make up the core of the vast housing industry. One of the housing industry's most impressive features is the sheer size of its scope. Roughly 20 percent to 25 percent of the entire U.S. economy can be linked to housing (Colton, 2003). Ironically, however, housing is a locally based product in that it is tied to the land on which it rests and is subject to the local rules and regulations pertaining to it (Lindamood & Hanna, 1979). Housing's local emphasis means local employers, many of whom are small in size and provide valuable services to both their communities and their local economies, produce most of the housing.

The complex and fragmented nature of housing as a consumer good prevents large firms from dominating any particular area of the housing production process, although the building industry has been moving to a more consolidated industry (Frey, 2003). The industry itself is a complex flow of value-added goods and services that are provided in a mostly sequential order. The President's Committee on Urban Housing (1969), sometimes referred to as the Kaiser Committee, was one of the first to provide an organized framework describing the housing industry, placing the distribution of housing goods and services into four distinct sequential phases—preparation, production, distribution, and service. These four phases suggest that a smooth division of labor exists within the housing industry; however, that is not the case. These disparate professions within the housing industry are usually represented by organizations, headquartered in Washington, DC, that lobby members of the U.S. Congress to pass legislation and control regulations that best serve that particular profession's members.

This chapter focuses on some of the largest and most influential subsectors within the housing profession, most specifically those pertaining to real estate development, home building, remodeling, mortgage lending, appraising, and real estate brokering, just to name a few. The subsequent sections of this chapter provide a brief description of the housing trade or profession being profiled, some of the important issues that they face on a regular basis and, whenever possible, the trade organization that represents these particular sectors of the housing industry. An attempt is made to describe the various housing professions according to the phases in which the various housing industry professionals would appear within the life cycle of the average housing consumer.

REAL ESTATE DEVELOPMENT

The real estate development industry has evolved over the past 10 to 15 years. A development boom occurred during the early to mid-1980s partially spurred on by Baby Boom generation spending. However, a comprehensive tax reform enacted by Congress in 1986 coupled with the collapse of the U.S. savings and loan industry in the late 1980s helped to cool housing investment considerably. Events from the early 1990s such as a damaging recession and severe cases of overbuilding in some areas of the country forced the development industry to restructure. Real estate development throughout the mid-1990s continued upward thanks to the rebound of the national economy, which enjoyed a nine-year expansion from 1992 to 2001. Housing development continued unabated thereafter, despite the presence of another mild recession and an increasing presence within communities of "slow growth" political movements designed to slow down the rate of residential development within some suburban and rural communities.

The land on which housing is built is converted from other uses. Developers identify land that they believe can be profitable when resold as housing lots, then gain site control, which means that they either take out an option to purchase the land or buy the land with a closing of the purchase at some future date when they are sure that they will be able to resell the land at a profit. A real estate developer must be willing to take risks as part of his or her profession.

The profession of real estate developer is largely unregulated; many areas do not even require licensing and certification for many aspects of real estate development. However, a developer must follow a number of regulatory guidelines and local laws. For example, a real estate developer must adhere to building codes to ensure minimum safety standards, zoning ordinances that prevent developers from placing incompatible uses next to each other, size requirements to prevent excessive and unnecessary growth within the community, transportation rules that prevent developers from disrupting general traffic flow, historic preservation rules that help maintain a community's character, environmental laws related to endangered species and clean water, and various land subdivision

*Paul s+L
Falls:
Id'd 6 Economic
Drivers in
Kingsville*

regulations that specify (among other things) the fees that must be paid to local governments to compensate for the extra burden placed on existing taxpayers for such things as water and sewer hook-ups and other utility access situations.

Developers must also be able to correctly forecast the market. Judging a particular community's needs as well as the economic forces driving the community's future growth is vital if a developer wants to establish success with a specific project. The successful real estate developer will also seek to obtain investors known as equity partners to share the risk and supplement bank financing. Aside from showing future potential lenders that the development in question has solid financial backing, the presence of equity investors helps the developer get started on some of the necessary early steps of development (after land acquisition), and provides a type of internal control mechanism for developers in the areas of planning, budgeting, and cost control (Epley, Rabianski, & Haney, 2002).

The real estate developer has multiple tasks that occur during the stages of a particular development. A developer will initially propose an idea to fill an area market niche while securing a suitable project site, conducting market surveys, and determining the project's feasibility from a financial perspective. If the project's estimated value is unlikely to cover the costs involved, the developer may then determine that the project is not feasible and divert his or her attention elsewhere. Assuming the proposed development does pass feasibility tests and appears to be needed within the market, however, the developer will then negotiate contracts with a number of industry actors—lenders in order to obtain project financing, local governments to obtain the permits, and general contractors to begin the construction. After the construction phase has begun within a development project, the developer seeks to approve suggested changes made by marketing professionals, resorts to a formal accounting system in order to establish a payroll, and resolves any of the inevitable disputes that may arise within the actual construction of the improvements.

At the completion phase a developer will not only bring in an operating staff to help manage the larger property developments, but will begin to advertise the property in the proper fashion. Once utilities are connected and units are approved for occupancy, the buyers are allowed to move into the units within the development. One of the final development process phases is settling loan obligations with the financial institutions involved (Miles, Berens, & Weiss, 2000). After the loan obligations are settled, a developer may or may not be directly involved in the area of property management.

The Urban Land Institute (ULI), one of the organizations representing the development industry, is located in Washington, DC. ULI's main purpose is not necessarily to lobby members of Congress

14

on issues related to development, but rather to serve as a nonprofit, nonpartisan research and educational institute that provides and disseminates information relevant to the long-term health of the real estate sector. Today, the organization is comprised of nearly 20,000 individuals and organizations, and ULI's membership consists of community builders, neighborhood developers and re-developers, property owners and investors, architects, lawyers, and planners, among other professions. More than 20 percent of the organization's membership works in government, academia, or public-private partnerships. The organization provides its members with a variety of meetings, educational program and certification opportunities, publications relevant to the development trade, and advisory services.

HOME BUILDING PROFESSION

While developers prepare the land for construction, the individual home builder's job is to actually construct the dwelling units on the prepared land. It is estimated that over five million people are employed in the building and construction industry (van Vliet, 1997). By most accounts, homes built in the United States have a superior construction quality to those built in other countries, attesting to both the lofty quality standards imposed on builders within the industry and also the skilled labor force that constructs the units. A majority of U.S. home builders provide single-family housing on a single lot.

The indicator most often used to determine the home building industry's vitality is the *housing start*. A housing start is described as the point at which construction begins, as evidenced by the excavation for the footings or the foundations of a privately owned building containing any housing unit. Given its overall impact on the general economy, the housing start is considered an economic leading indicator in that it can be a good forecasting measure for the economy's long-term health. Aside from the sheer number of builders in the market, the building profession has enormous multiplier effects on the U.S. economy as well (Dubin, 1994).

Figure 4.1 shows the steady growth in housing starts since 1960 for both single-family and multifamily housing units. The U.S. construction industry is highly cyclical in that the level of starts can be adversely affected by even slight changes in the general economy. The downturn in single-family starts in 1980 and 1990 was largely attributed to general recessionary conditions in the United States during that time, which caused slight downturns in the single-family market. In addition, the number of housing starts is not uniform across seasons. During the winter months construction lags in many

*update:

Year	All Starts	1 Unit	2–4 Units	5 or More Units
1960	1,252	995	N/A	N/A
1965	1,473	964	87	423
1970	1,434	813	84	536
1975	1,160	892	65	204
1980	1,292	852	110	331
1985	1,742	1,072	93	576
1990	1,193	895	37	260
1995	1,354	1,076	33	244
2000	1,569	1,231	39	299

2005
2009

Figure 4.1   Annual privately owned U.S. housing starts (in 000's), 1960 to 2000 (*Source:* New privately owned housing units started, U.S. Census Bureau Construction Statistics Division, 2004. Retrieved December 15, 2004, from www.census.gov/const/startsan.pdf)

parts of the country due to frigid and uncooperative weather patterns. By contrast, the summer months are usually considered high production months because of a more favorable climate situation.

Builders must adhere to rules and regulations that are commonplace in many U.S. states and localities. For example, the builder needs to apply for a building permit before actually starting construction on a specific parcel of land. The building permit is usually issued by a government regulatory agency, typically after it has approved the builder's site plan. In some cases, the builder may also be compelled to pay an impact fee if the new construction requires significant expenditures in infrastructure for the affected development. These impact fees may be charged either during the construction phase of a particular development or during the occupancy phase, meaning that payment of such fees is absorbed either by the builder/developer or by the occupant of the newly built home (Crow & Cooley, 1988). In addition, a homeowner may face special assessments by a local municipal government to help pay for area improvements, but typically only if the addition of such improvements can be proven to add value to the properties affected by the action (Epley et al., 2002). Builders also must adhere to various codes and regulations when they begin their construction, which cover every facet of the construction process (including renovations), and are either locally developed or modeled after regional model codes.

While support exists for an International Building Code, the stringency of many building codes is dependent upon the jurisdiction

to which the code applies. Builders must adhere to an energy conservation code, which dictates the energy efficiency requirements
with which a new home must comply. Failure to comply with these
codes will usually result in the rejection of a specific building project by the local community planning office. The builder will then
be allowed time to correct any oversights or mistakes made during
the process in order to make the end product more compliant with
the various codes, oftentimes by working closely with the local
planning office. These mandatory codes ensure a high standard of
construction quality and are updated as construction technology
improves.

Builders go through multiple construction phases that usually
span many months of labor. After the developer has graded and prepared the land, a series of steps typically occur in the normal process
of constructing a custom-built home (B4UBuild.com, 2004). Many
experienced builders will be bonded, which provides insurance to
protect clients from any damage that one of their employees may
cause during the construction stage. After receiving a building permit from local government authorities, the home builder usually receives a draw for subsequent phases of construction that take place
on the property in question. These draws allow for periodic funding
for the builders during the course of the construction period.

While the sequencing of draws during construction lending
varies by lender and community, it usually occurs before a few distinct phases. The first draw generally covers the building of the
foundation such as laying building footings, as well as carpentry labor that includes framing for decks, walls, roof trusses, windows,
and doors. Another subsequent draw covers the financing of such
phases as pouring concrete slabs throughout the garage and basement, and preparing heating and air conditioning, plumbing, and
electrical capabilities. The next draw can cover such components as
roofing and siding, insulation, and drywall application. Another
draw covers the costs related to floor finishes and painting. The
final series of draw payments cover such tangible construction
processes as prime paint, cabinets, doors, tile, and trim work around
the house. Sidebar 4.1 briefly addresses the different phases involved in constructing a single-family property.

The building industry is officially represented by the National Association of Home Builders (NAHB) located in Washington, DC. In
2005 the organization consisted of 220,000 members, making it one
of the largest U.S. special interest trade associations. The traditional
home builder member can be categorized in many different ways.
Custom builders are usually defined as those builders constructing
one-of-a-kind units with a heavy degree of skill and craftsmanship

updated
founded in 1942
2010: 175,000 +
members
(builders & remodelers)   other 43 = mtg. finance / building products &
*   service*
800 state & local associations
NAHB: 7 members constructs 80% of new homes
built each yr.

Sidebar 4.1
Sample Construction Activities for Single-Family Housing

1	Develop plans
2	Get necessary permits
3	Excavate
4	Build foundation
5	Complete framing
6	Lay roofing
7	Backfill
8	Install windows and doors
9	Install siding
10	Complete rough mechanicals
11	Plumbing
12	Electrical
13	HVAC
14	Install insulation
15	Install and finish sheet rock/plaster
16	Install flooring
17	Install trim and cabinetry
18	Apply interior finishes
19	Finish mechanicals
20	Complete landscaping and paving

Source: A sample residential construction schedule, by *B4UBuild.com*, 2004. Retrieved November 29, 2004, from *www.b4ubuild.com /resources/ schedule /6kproj.shtml*.

---

that frequently command a higher price per square foot than other builders. Semi-custom builders can be defined as those builders either constructing one-of-a-kind units with moderate sales price per square foot, or building from standard plans with a wide range of optional features. These builders build on scattered lots or in upscale subdivisions. Contract builders are custom or semi-custom builders who build exclusively on others' land (National Association of Home Builders, 1989). Meanwhile, production builders use the same basic floor plans and the homes are built in sequence, generally signifying that each step of the building process occurs simultaneously on other houses (Guarino, 2003).

Other members of the home building community include those who produce multifamily, or apartment, dwellings in which multiple households can reside. Some multifamily builders even specialize in the production of senior housing or housing for active adults. NAHB members receive many benefits for joining the organization, not the least of which is a periodic newsletter that informs members of the various issues affecting them in their particular market areas. They also have access to the home building industry's technical information resource ToolBase Services, which includes ToolBase News, ToolBase/PATH E-News, and the ToolBase Portal. The ToolBase Portal is the web source for information on innovative home building technologies.

Some of the most recent issues of concern to home builders include managed growth, energy efficient and resource efficient building, and housing affordability. As the amount of developed land becomes scarcer, builders are slowly converting from a "leapfrog"-type development style that contributes to sprawl conditions and extensive infrastructures to one that is more cognizant of the scarcity of resources available now and in the future. As a result, builders are moving toward a "New Urbanist" style, which stresses compact and walkable neighborhoods; a diverse mix of residences, green space, and work centers; and priority given to public buildings and spaces.

REALTORS® AND REAL ESTATE AGENTS

When a person first goes to find a house or residence (whether it is a new or existing home), he or she is most likely to consult a real estate agent, who provides efficient methods of matching the prospective buyer with the right house for that household's particular needs. Helping people buy and sell homes is one of the most important and basic services a real estate agent performs. Agents are expected to be experts in buying and selling property, financing, government programs, and so forth, and that expertise facilitates the transaction, saving clients time, trouble, and money. Real estate professionals need to have a thorough knowledge of such areas as real estate law, local economics, fair housing laws, types of financing, mortgages, and government programs. Although real estate agents' compensation varies according to the area in which they work, most agents receive 6 percent to 7 percent of the house sales price as a commission.

Becoming a real estate broker requires a reasonable amount of training, but offers flexibility that is normally lacking in other professions. All 50 U.S. states have some form of licensing statutes for real estate brokers and salespersons, although the requirements for obtaining a license vary by state. Real estate agents may accompany potential homebuyers to visit a lender, show properties, and also be present during real estate purchase negotiations. Most real estate agents work for a real estate broker or brokerage firm.

Real estate brokers must not only have a sales background, but also must take additional education courses and pass a brokerage examination, which allows the person to legally run his or her own office (Anderson, 2005). Additionally, a salesperson must hold a license for some period before qualifying for a broker's license, normally two years. Finally, after obtaining a license a broker or salesperson must complete the state's continuing education requirement to keep his or her license valid.

Real estate licenses are only valid within the state that issues them, but some states will issue nonresident licenses to brokers who wish to do business within that state (van Vliet, 1997). Working in real estate allows for independence and flexibility, as brokers can affiliate themselves with a large or small firm as a listed salesperson. Also, being listed as an actual employee of a realty firm or an independent contractor can make a difference in the flexibility of hours worked, level of supervision and direction, and income tax withholding (Epley et al., 2002).

Real estate agents are represented nationally by the National Association of REALTORS® (NAR), which is located in Washington, DC. The organization's members have access to NAR's much coveted Multiple Listing Service (MLS), which gives real estate agents and brokers an outlet through which most of the house price information in a particular market exists. NAR members are expected to adhere to a strict code of ethics, which separates them from other real estate agents who are not NAR members. NAR membership flourished by the 1970s, coinciding with the run-up in house prices that was occurring in the United States during this time.

Due to some industry problems regarding ambiguity as to whom an agent specifically represented, many states have passed laws since the early 1980s requiring real estate brokers to disclose whom they officially represent. Also, the Real Estate Settlement Procedures Act (commonly referred to as RESPA) requires the disclosure of settlement costs and prohibits kickbacks to brokers for referrals to affiliated types of services such as title insurance (Brobeck, 1997). Today, NAR proclaims itself to be the largest U.S. trade association, boasting a membership of nearly 850,000 members that are separately members of nearly 1,500 local associations throughout the country. NAR's Government Affairs Division works to develop, advance, and implement the federal legislative objectives of the organization. NAR works with Congress and the Executive Branch to achieve these public policy objectives through policy development and communications, as well as the grass roots advocacy of its membership.

REALTORS® also have deep concerns about some of the current issues that resonate within the housing community. One of these issues involves the growing use and influence of the Internet and the potential effects of such technology on the needs for a third party influencing the real estate transaction. One of the concerns within the traditional REALTOR® community is that putting too much information about a residence online threatens to tilt the playing field too far against traditional real estate agents and toward the low-cost Internet-based start-up companies that have not invested time and money into compiling their own real estate listings. In the process, REALTORS® argue that this practice unfairly cuts the commission rate that they have become accustomed to in a normal residential transaction (Barta & Wilke, 2003).

MORTGAGE LENDING PROFESSION

In order for builders and developers to do their jobs optimally, they need to rely on the mortgage lending community. Banks and other lending institutions provide savings opportunities for first-time homebuyers who hope to accumulate enough funds to put toward a down payment. Lenders also provide builders funds in the form of construction loans, which are normally paid off once construction is completed. From the consumer's standpoint, however, banks and other lending institutions serve a large role in that they provide loans to homebuyers. This loan, called a *mortgage,* is really a form of secured loan in which the new homeowner's real property serves as collateral for the loan in the event of default.

If the borrower has not provided an adequate down payment, the lender may require the borrower to purchase private mortgage insurance (PMI). If a borrower is likely to default on his or her mortgage, the PMI company is then obligated to repay the mortgage company a portion of the remaining mortgage, usually 20 percent. The lender would then likely receive the remainder of any outstanding funds due through a foreclosure sale. During the loan's lifetime, the lender may choose to service a homeowner's mortgage loan by continuing to collect monthly payments, or the lender may sell the mortgage to secondary marketing agencies such as Fannie Mae and Freddie Mac who collect these mortgages and package them into securities to be sold on the open market.

One of the driving forces of the mortgage lending cycle is the level of interest rates. General real estate activity, and specifically mortgage lending, usually expands when the general business cycle is down and credit demand is low. When this happens interest rates are depressed, which allows more borrowers to qualify for a

✳ update ⟶

1972-Jan	7.44	1988-Jan	10.43
1973-Jan	7.44	1989-Jan	10.73
1974-Jan	8.54	1990-Jan	9.90
1975-Jan	9.43	1991-Jan	9.64
1976-Jan	9.02	1992-Jan	8.43
1977-Jan	8.72	1993-Jan	8.02
1978-Jan	9.02	1994-Jan	7.06
1979-Jan	10.39	1995-Jan	9.15
1980-Jan	12.88	1996-Jan	7.03
1981-Jan	14.90	1997-Jan	7.82
1982-Jan	17.40	1998-Jan	6.99
1983-Jan	13.25	1999-Jan	6.79
1984-Jan	13.37	2000-Jan	8.21
1985-Jan	13.08	2001-Jan	7.03
1986-Jan	10.88	2002-Jan	7.00
1987-Jan	9.20		

Handwritten annotations (right margin): 2008 Jan 5.74; 2009 Jan 5.05; 2010 Jan 5.03

Handwritten annotations (below table): 2003-Jan 5.92; 2004-Jan 5.71; 2005-Jan 5.71; 2006 Jan 6.0; 2007 Jan 6.22

Figure 4.2   30-year conventional mortgage rates, 1972–2002 (*Source:* Monthly average commitment rate and points on 30-year fixed-rate mortgages by Freddie Mac, 2004. Retrieved December 14, 2004, from www.freddiemac.com/pmms/pdf/pmms30.pdf)

mortgage. By contrast, when interest rates rise, real estate lending begins to slow down (Dennis, 1989). The inflationary environment during the late 1970s and early 1980s caused interest rates to rise precipitously, topping out at nearly 18.5 percent in October 1981. Figure 4.2 provides an historical context of interest rate levels over a 30-year period.

The 1990s was a period of brisk residential activity, largely because of historically low interest rates. Residential lending activity grew almost fivefold from the period between 1990 to 2002. Figure 4.3 provides evidence of this jump in loan activity, which was undoubtedly spurred on by the favorable interest rate environment.

When potential borrowers approach a lender to obtain mortgage funds, they are likely to be confronted by a complex series of stages in the lending process and a lending industry that is very differentiated, with various types of lenders at their disposal. Most lenders, however, do go through a fairly standard mortgage loan processing

update ?

Year	Number of Loans (millions)
1990	6.59
1991	7.89
1992	12.01
1993	15.38
1994	12.20
1995	11.23
1996	14.81
1997	16.41
1998	24.66
1999	22.91
2000	19.24
2001	27.58
2002	31.24

2003   41.60

Figure 4.3 U.S. residential lending activity, 1990–2002 (*Source:*
Residential lending activity reported by financial institutions covered by HMDA, 1981–2002,
by Federal Financial Institutions Examination Council, n.d. Retrieved December 14, 2004,
from www.ffiec.gov/hmcrpr/hm02table1.pdf)

procedure. The mortgage origination process phases are application, assembly of the loan package, actual loan processing, underwriting and approval, preclosing, and closing. By the application phase, a borrower will usually have already gone through a prequalification phase in which the household determines how large a loan it can qualify for given its current income, savings, and debt load. During application the borrower will actually come into the lending office and complete a mortgage application form. Three days or so after the application is submitted, the lender sends out a Truth-in-Lending disclosure form and a Good Faith Estimate, which approximates and itemizes the amount of closing costs the borrower should expect to face at closing.

Assembling the loan package may be the lender's most intense phase of the loan process. During this phase the lender will order a property appraisal, a credit report, preliminary title work, and any other documents deemed necessary for the completion of the loan package, including a borrower's verification of employment and verification of deposit. During the actual processing stage the lender will address various issues that may arise concerning the paperwork that has already been sent in by the borrower. If there are any problems with the appraisal or credit report, the lender will have to address them during this phase. During the next phase the actual underwriting of the loan takes place. In order for the borrower to be approved at this phase, he or she must demonstrate an ability and willingness to repay the mortgage loan, as well as offer sufficient collateral to secure against the loan. If the mortgage loan is made for more than 80 percent of the house's value, the lender will also submit documentation to a mortgage insurance company for further underwriting to determine whether or not a highly leveraged borrower will be worth the risk for the bank. The preclosing phase will occur after the loan has been approved. The lender must ensure that all contingency provisions have been met, and the borrower's interest rate is locked during this stage. Closing documents are then sent to the title and escrow company, and then a closing date is usually set.

During the closing phase the lender will likely ensure that the proper signatures are obtained from the borrower, and that the remainder of the closing costs are collected from the borrower as well (Sun Nations, 2004). When the borrower takes out the mortgage the lender will also demand that the borrower sign a promissory note, which serves as evidence of the mortgage debt and is the borrower's personal IOU to repay. The actual mortgage document, a standardized document that is used in many states, contains four essential characteristics: (1) a notice that the parties involved are of sound mind; (2) evidence that consideration, or something of value, is given; (3) notification that the mortgage is a certified legal document; and (4) mutual assent that there has been an offer and acceptance. Most mortgages will also require a series of uniform covenants to which the borrower will be expected to adhere, which vary state by state (Epley et al., 2002).

Aside from the complexity of the documentation the borrower needs to complete, the type of lending institution that offers the mortgage varies as well. The most likely source of funding for mortgage loans is the mortgage company, which makes up over half of the single-family loan origination market. Mortgage companies originate mortgage loans for other institutions, and traditionally operate with small amounts of capital and have no deposits. A retail mortgage banker typically makes several single-family home loans, which eventually will be sold to an investor. The second largest single-family mortgage loan originator is the commercial bank, which is federally chartered and offers a host of consumer and industrial loans to the general public. One of the most visible lenders of mortgage funds before the early 1990s was the savings and loan association, which specialized in accepting individual borrowers'

savings deposits and subsequently transferring those monies to individual borrowers who want to either build or buy a home. Savings and loans, or S&Ls, have fallen out of favor, largely because
many in the S&L industry became insolvent due to too many poor
quality loans during the 1980s.

A mutual savings bank is similar to an S&L, except that ownership of the bank is held by its depositors rather than stockholders.
These institutions are mainly centered in the northeastern region of
the country. Finally, credit unions are state or federally chartered organizations who pool their savings and make loans to members.
While credit unions do make mortgage loans to their members, these
organizations specialize more in short-term loans; thus, 30-year
mortgage originations for this sector of the residential loan market
are rare (Epley et al., 2002). There has also been a tremendous rise
in the number of mortgage originations being made by the "subprime" lending industry, which refers to households that do not
quite qualify for "prime" lending rates (i.e., those that are given to
borrowers with blemish-free credit reports).

While there has been a substantial increase in these types of
loans relative to those made in the prime lending arena (Immergluck & Wiles, 1999), sub-prime lending has gained some notoriety
since at least the late 1990s due to some overly aggressive predatory lending that has occurred within the sub-prime industry. Nev-
ertheless, the sub-prime lending industry remains a legitimate home
buying option for many Americans who have been shut out of the
traditional venues for obtaining home loans.

One of the foremost industry groups lobbying on behalf of residential lenders is the Mortgage Bankers Association of America
(MBAA). Comprised of over 2,800 corporate members nationwide
and located in Washington, DC, the organization faces a few major
issues in the coming years, particularly those regarding predatory
lending and disclosure of credit scores. The mortgage lending industry is populated with sub-prime lenders, a group of primary
mortgage lenders who specialize in making loans to low and moderate income groups as well as special populations such as minorities and the elderly. While there are many opportunities for low and
moderate income populations to seek conventional financing opportunities in today's lending climate, still many within this population are shut out of receiving funding either through lack of
knowledge about such opportunities or excessive exposure to
credit, which precludes this group from receiving funding.

These sub-prime lenders operate under little, if any, regulation
in many jurisdictions, and have largely been seen both within and
outside the profession with suspicion. Whereas the sub-prime lending industry is by itself a legitimate profession, there are so-called

predatory lenders which have been known to charge excessive fees and skyrocketing interest rates. MBAA seeks to establish a list of "best practices" for sub-prime lenders while simultaneously fighting state legislative efforts to place burdensome restrictions on all mortgage lending in an effort to thwart predatory lending practices. MBAA also supports legislation which would make mandatory the disclosure of a borrower's credit score, which is a vital component in whether or not a person will receive mortgage funding during the application process. Traditionally, however, the borrower is often left confused as to what constitutes his or her credit score and is given little information on the specific tasks that will be needed to bolster the credit score. Recognizing that increasing this type of disclosure will ultimately lead to greater origination business in the long term, MBAA supports the release of such information to consumers.

APPRAISAL PROFESSION

Before a household makes its ultimate home buying decision, it must be certain of a house's true value. The lender that ultimately makes the loan to the borrowing household usually does so with the understanding that the loan is based on a product in which the bank can recover its value, in the unfortunate event that the borrower defaults on his or her mortgage loan. For that reason, the lending industry has a standard requirement that each borrower pay for an *appraisal,* which is an estimate of the property's value (and the land that it accompanies). The appraisal differs from an assessment, which is a valuation procedure conducted by a government official strictly for taxation purposes.

The appraiser has three different approaches to complete an appraisal: (1) sales comparison approach, (2) cost approach, and (3) income approach. The sales comparison approach is the most common technique used when appraising single-family properties. When using the sales comparison approach the appraiser must base the value of the subject property (the one being considered for purchase) against at least three comparable properties. These comparable properties should resemble the subject property as closely as possible. For each component that differs between the subject and the comparable properties, an adjustment is made to the comparables which will hopefully more adequately reflect the value of the subject property.

The cost approach estimates the current market value of the land and approximates the value of the improvements, all the while using cost data related to the improvements. The principle for utilizing the cost approach is that a rational person will not pay more for a property than the amount at which an equally desirable and useful property can be obtained without an undue delay (Epley et al., 2002). Some common situations in which an appraiser would use the cost approach are for insurance purposes, and when houses are either in a limited market or are so unusual that they have no similar type of houses in the surrounding area (and thus not enough comparable properties to justify using the sales comparison approach).

The income approach is used exclusively for income-producing properties such as apartment dwellings. Property value when using the income approach is created by the benefits that the property derives in the future (in the form of rental payments received).

The appraisal community is represented by the Appraisal Institute, which enforces a code of ethics and standards by which its members must adhere. Located in Chicago, Illinois, the Appraisal Institute has around 18,000 members, many of which are divided into both commercial and residential appraisers. Some of the issues that the appraisal industry faces now and in the near future show that the appraisal profession is both in a constant state of flux and that it sometimes falls into conflict with the lending industry with which it so closely works. The introduction of automated valuation models (AVMs), which are integrative technological models that adequately predict house property values, has pushed the industry in a direction in which the human appraiser may eventually become a rare occurrence.

Though they lack a human appraiser's familiarity with a local real estate market, AVMs have attracted the attention of the mortgage lending industry due to their abilities to shorten the amount of time necessary to complete an appraisal, lower the overall cost of producing an appraisal report, and in some cases even providing a more accurate reading on a home's value than would a human appraiser (Maselli, 2002; Murray, 2002). Another persistent issue that the appraisal industry faces is its continuing need to have independence from interference by those within the lending industry. Although appraisers are meant to provide an unbiased assessment of property value, there is constant lender pressure to come in with appraised values that meet the property values so as not to scuttle the real estate transaction. While this issue has been ongoing for many decades, recent pressures directed at appraisers prompted Congressional hearings on the issue of maintaining protections for the appraisal industry, and further attempts to strengthen a "firewall" between the lending industry and those appraisers who play a supporting role for them (Cocheo, 2004).

REMODELORS

After homebuyers spend some time within their houses, they may need to increase the amount of living space or simply add or modify rooms that the existing structure did not originally have. These individual remodeling decisions are done to fit modern tastes, technologies, and living standards, and are usually completed to accommodate Americans' increasing space demands. Remodeling also allows homeowners an alternative to going through the time-intensive process of seeking another home, and it may also be in the best interests of individuals and families who have established roots within their neighborhoods. Remodeling has taken on significant importance in today's housing environment since the age of the U.S. housing stock has consistently gotten older (Joint Center for Housing Studies, 2001).

The remodeling industry has seen a significant increase in expenditures over the past decade, and the industry has simultaneously undergone much change. In 1999 home improvement spending stood at $180 billion, making it a significant sector of the housing production industry. The overall economic impact is even higher, however, as homeowners spend additional dollars on such things as appliances and furniture for the remodeled or new spaces. Some remodeling jobs are simply "do-it-yourself" jobs that are completed by the homeowners themselves, but popularity for this type of remodeling job has diminished over time (Joint Center for Housing Studies, 2001). Instead, many homeowners choose to seek the services of a remodeling professional.

Overall, over 270,000 residential contractors reported at least some revenue from home improvements and repairs in 1997, and the number of firms has grown considerably since 1987. Nearly 80 percent of the remodeling activity is generated by firms that have annual receipts of less than $500,000, signifying the importance of small contractors within the remodeling industry. Few barriers generally exist to entering the industry, as nearly a third of the states have either no requirements for licensing and certification of remodeling general contractors, or require only as little as a registration fee. A majority of these remodeling contractors are self-employed as well, comprising both general and special trade contractors. Despite the fact that the industry is growing, the failure rate is high for newly established remodeling firms (Joint Center for Housing Studies, 2001).

The remodeling industry is represented by two major organizations: the National Association of the Remodeling Industry (NARI) and NAHB's Remodeling Council. Both organizations are made up of various professionals within the remodeling field; namely, manu-facturers, suppliers, and distributors. NARI does provide a certification program, which provides the remodeling industry with a formalized, yet voluntary, standard of expertise, knowledge, and ethical conduct among professional remodelors. NAHB's Remodeling Council pro-vides many of the same services that NARI provides to its members, but it also has the benefit of utilizing the vast array of resources that are available to the regular builder members within NAHB.

As a result, the Remodeling Council offers an impressive number of education and research programs to its members. Some of the key issues affecting the remodeling industry in the future include the aging of the U.S. population, minority participation in the re-modeling process, and continuing issues of preparing a qualified la-bor force. There have traditionally not been many remodeling expenditures for older Americans, and many expenditures are largely made by households in the 46–55 age group and younger. With the aging of the Baby Boomers and their increasing earnings potential, however, the remodeling industry is seeking to tap into this demographic cohort group more broadly. As a result, remode-lors are trying to emphasize an "aging in place" concept, which al-lows older Americans to undergo remodeling efforts in their current homes to better adapt themselves to a safer and more comfortable lifestyle that accompanies growing older.

Because more and more African Americans and Hispanics are entering into homeownership situations, the remodeling profession will try to attract more business from minorities in the future. Cul-tural differences may require changes in residential space. As the industry is not heavily regulated, professional remodelors will also try to improve their profession's image. Several scandals regarding egregious practices by remodeling contractors persisted throughout the 1970s and 1980s, and resulted in much state and federal legis-lation dealing with ethics and practices (Brobeck, 1997).

RESIDENTIAL PROPERTY MANAGEMENT

Even though much of the residential housing market is comprised of single-family units, a large number of multifamily properties still serve as income-producing properties for investors willing to as-sume the risk. After construction is completed, a builder/developer of multifamily properties would likely utilize a residential property management (RPM) firm to help maintain the multifamily structure and preserve the investment's value, which can easily exceed a mil-lion dollars. Many property management companies require a certain

> **Sidebar 4.2**
> **Roles and Functions of Property Managers**
>
> - Establish tenant relations; maintain tenant retention
> - Collect rent payments
> - Control operating expenses
> - Maintain financial reporting and record keeping
> - Maintain property; plan capital expenditures
> - Perform crisis management
> - Correct security issues
> - Maintain public relations
>
> *Source*: Real estate development: Principles and process (3rd ed.), by M. E. Miles, G. Berens, and M. A. Weiss, 2000, Washington, DC: Urban Land Institute.

amount of personnel to perform certain tasks to ensure that management of the property will be efficient, thus ensuring that profitability will be maximized for the real estate investor. Sidebar 4.2 lists some of the operations that property managers are expected to perform.

Although residential property managers may be affiliated with some of the previously mentioned trade associations, the National Association of Residential Property Managers is an organization devoted to the industry's specific needs. One of the biggest crises facing the residential property management (RPM) industry is a pending shortage of qualified personnel. Employee recruitment and retention seem to be major concerns facing the RPM industry today. This personnel crisis is exacerbated by the fact that there is currently a lack of university and college level courses devoted to the issue of residential property management. The industry is trying to upgrade its image by hiring young, bright, recent college graduates who are willing to learn and become successful in the industry. There are currently some online courses that are available to the public which offer an RPM curriculum, but the value of these programs is unclear to many industry participants.

OTHER PROFESSIONS IN THE HOUSING INDUSTRY

While builders, developers, lenders, and real estate agents assume the highest-profile professions within the housing industry, other industries also play integral supporting roles. As with many other industries, the housing industry relies on insurance within the profession. The two most prevalent insurance forms in the housing realm are property insurance and mortgage insurance. Property insurance providers write policies to homeowners that cover the homeowner's loss in the event of natural disasters or fire. Normally, a single-family residential transaction cannot be closed without the presence of a valid policy in hand. Mortgage insurance, paid by borrowers in the event that they default on their mortgage obligations, is offered through both government and private mortgage lenders. Real estate attorneys also play a vital role both in the housing transaction process and during the residential process. Not only do they assist new homebuyers in navigating through the complex home buying process, but oftentimes they have their own title insurance business to help the borrower obtain legal title to the property being purchased.

Title insurance businesses assume the risk that the real estate title is as stated to ensure legitimacy. Attorneys also assist developers in dealing with public authorities over legal issues regarding zoning or subdivision regulation considerations, and may be involved in the legal aspects of the real estate transaction. Architects provide not only the proper design for a particular housing project, but the effective architect will also provide one that maximizes efficiency within the dwelling, which aids in the property's resale. Nonprofit housing developers, sometimes referred to as community development corporations (CDC), also fill the void of creating affordable housing units for low- and moderate-income communities in times when the federal government reduces funding for construction and renovation of housing for needy populations.

MANUFACTURED HOUSING INDUSTRY

Before discussing the manufactured housing industry it is important to understand the broader context of factory-built, or industrialized, housing. Manufactured homes are just one of several types of industrialized homes, which also include modular homes and panelized homes. What distinguishes these homes from one another and from traditional site-built homes is the amount of construction that is done ahead of time in the factory, as opposed to on the home site. Manufactured homes and site-built homes represent the ends of the continuum; the former are built almost entirely in the factory and the latter incorporate only select factory-made components such as roof or floor trusses. Modular and panelized homes fall in the middle of the continuum. Next to manufactured homes, modular homes are the most complete when they leave the factory. The panelized home industry includes a range of home types such as precut homes and log homes that are partly premade in the factory but are assembled on the home lot ("The Seven Segments," 2002).

Manufactured homes differ from other factory-built housing as well as site-built housing in ways other than just the amount of factory construction. Manufactured homes are the only homes required to meet the national building code of the U.S. Department of Housing and Urban Development (HUD). All other types of housing are built according to state or local building codes. Manufactured homes are also required to be built on a permanent metal chassis to which wheels are attached (Atiles & Vanderford, 2004). By contrast, modular homes are transported on a flatbed truck to the building site and are placed on the foundation by a crane.

The National Manufactured Housing Construction and Safety Standards Act passed by Congress in 1974 and implemented in June 1976 established the HUD Code for manufactured housing. The Code regulates the design, construction, safety, strength, durability, transportability, fire resistance, energy efficiency, and quality of manufactured homes. It also outlines performance standards for the heating, air conditioning, plumbing, thermal, and electrical systems. Additionally, the Act officially changed the name of what had been called a "mobile home" to a "manufactured home" (Suchman, 1995).

Manufactured housing producers are viable players within the housing industry for several reasons. As housing prices increase more people are being priced out of the housing market, dashing their dream of homeownership. Because manufactured housing is generally less expensive than standard site-built housing, it is an increasingly affordable option for many Americans seeking to become first-time homeowners. One recent study found that, on average, manufactured homes' values are less than one third of the values of site-built homes, when important quality variables are controlled (Vanderford, Mimura, & Sweaney, in press). The lower prices of manufactured homes are due, at least in part, to more efficient construction in the factory's controlled environment. Factory construction has other benefits to the consumer such as being quicker than on-site construction and resulting in less moisture damage from exposure during construction. Figure 4.4 shows a variety of factory-built houses.

The manufactured housing industry is represented largely by two organizations: the Manufactured Housing Institute (MHI) and the Manufactured Housing Research Alliance (MHRA). MHI is a non-profit national trade association representing all segments of the manufactured housing industry, including manufactured home producers, retailers, developers, community owners and managers, suppliers, insurers, and financial service providers. According to its mission statement MHI serves as an information outlet and provides

Figure 4.4   Photos of a variety of factory-built houses (*Source:* From "Palm Harbor Homes; Gallery of Homes." Retrieved December 9, 2004, from http://palmharborhomes.com/our_homes/gallery_of_homes/index.asp Used by permission of Palm Harbor Homes, Inc.)

educational opportunities for its members, while also serving as a lobbying organization for the industry's needs before Congress (Manufactured Housing Institute, 2004). Meanwhile, the Manufactured Housing Research Alliance is a nonprofit organization that serves as the industry's product development and research arm. MHRA's mission is to develop new technologies to enhance the value, quality, and performance of the nation's manufactured homes. MHRA strives for new innovations in home design, construction, and installation. With continued assistance from HUD, MHRA continues to improve the image of manufactured housing by increasing the quality of the manufactured housing stock.

For various reasons the manufactured housing industry is presently faced with some obstacles that will continue in the future unless they are adequately addressed. Industry issues include declining sales, the need to provide viable financing alternatives for manufactured home purchasers, poor product image and the lack of widespread consumer acceptance, and barriers to the placement of manufactured housing by state and local governments.

Poor sales have plagued the manufactured housing industry since the late 1990s for three primary reasons. First, there was liberal underwriting in the manufactured housing industry during the mid-1990s which created a large influx of repossessions from homebuyers who really could not afford to purchase a home. Second, increasing consolidation within the industry may be associated with a decline in consumer interest, as producers become less familiar with the areas that they serve and may not be able to target potential consumers as effectively. Third, sales may also have been hurt by the increasingly liberal underwriting standards for site-built housing. In some cases lenders will allow new homebuyers to put down as little as 3 percent on a real estate purchase. Such practices allow borrowers to enter into a home market they have never experienced before and may lure capable buyers away from manufactured housing.

Many of the financing concerns regarding manufactured housing have been ongoing industry problems. For example, most manufactured housing loans are still classified as chattel loans rather than real property loans. Such chattel loans more closely resemble automobile financing than real estate financing and tend to have terms that are less favorable to the borrower (Apgar, Calder, Collin, & Duda, 2002). In most states traditional real estate mortgages are only available to manufactured homebuyers if they are also purchasing their land. A homebuyer also may be required to meet other standards such as placing his or her home on a solid foundation to get a traditional mortgage. Some signs of change exist in the industry, however, as California now allows real estate mortgages for manufactured homes regardless of whether the land is leased or owned (Atiles & Vanderford, 2004). Another concern about financing is that many manufactured housing producers offer financing as well, and some producers have participated in unscrupulous predatory lending practices. Some of the characteristics of such loans are overcharging on interest, flipping, and requiring balloon payments or prepayment penalties. Partly as a result of these questionable lending practices many consumers have not been able to meet their financial obligations, which have caused repossessions to increase at a dramatic rate. According to one estimate, manufactured housing loans default at a rate nearly four times that of conventional home mortgages (Consumers Union, 1998).

Evidence suggests that manufactured home communities display tightly woven social networks (MacTavish & Salamon, 2001). However, in many people's minds, manufactured housing includes a stigma. Consumers, government officials, and leaders in related industries often do not fully understand what manufactured homes are and still refer to them as "mobile homes" or "trailers," names that are reminiscent of the pre-1976 manufactured housing stock. Neighborhood and community residents often do not want manufactured housing placed nearby because of the bad image they have of the housing type and its residents. In addition, many residents of site-built homes fear that placing manufactured homes nearby will negatively impact their property values. This hypothesis has been tested, but research results have been inconclusive. In three North Carolina counties, analysis of property values indicated that manufactured homes had negative effects on values of nearby site-built homes (Wubneh & Shen, 2004). In two Alabama counties, however, there was no evidence that proximity to manufactured homes significantly affected site-built home property values (Hegji & Mitchell, 2000).

Unfortunately, in many areas of the country the stigma of manufactured housing is reinforced by local government actions. Zoning discrimination has existed in some communities, even in areas where other forms of factory-built housing are widely accepted. Inclusionary zoning requirements have helped to alleviate some of these concerns, but much progress is still needed (van Vliet, 1997). Also, pressure to create a uniform standard for installation of manufactured housing led to the creation of upgraded federal standards for manufactured housing. These changes have further tightened the gap between manufactured housing and the more traditional site-built housing, which may help manufactured homes gain popularity and acceptance. Indeed, given its price advantage over conventional housing, manufactured housing placement has become an integral part of some local governments' affordable housing strategies (Apgar et al., 2002).

CONCLUSION

The housing industry is both large and varied. In this chapter we examined the industry's impact on the U.S. economy and the range of professions involved. The housing industry remains quite traditional, although improvements in factory-built housing may change that in the future. You might consider the possibility of finding a job within the housing industry—as a developer, home builder, realtor, mortgage lender, appraiser, remodelor, or residential property manager.

REFERENCES

Anderson, S. (2005). Loans & financing: Know your real estate experts. *MSN House & Home.* Retrieved January 21, 2005, from *http://houseandhome.msn.com/financing/firsttimebuyers0.aspx.*

Apgar, W., Calder, A., Collin, M., & Duda, M. (2002, September). *An examination of manufactured housing as a community- and asset-building strategy* (Report to the Ford Foundation). Cambridge, MA: Harvard Joint Center for Housing Studies.

Atiles, J. H., & Vanderford, S. E. (2004). *Manufactured home buyers education guide.* Unpublished manuscript currently under review, University of Georgia, Athens, GA.

B4UBuild.com. (2004). *A sample residential construction schedule.* Retrieved November 29, 2004, from *www.B4UBuild.com/resources/schedule/6kproj.shtml.*

Barta, P., & Wilke, J. R. (2003, October 24). Realtors' limits on web listings face a federal antitrust inquiry. *Wall Street Journal,* p. A-1.

Brobeck, S. (Ed.). (1997). *Encyclopedia of the consumer movement.* Santa Barbara, CA: ABC-CLIO.

Cocheo, S. (2004). *Appraisers seek independence from "lender pressure."* Washington, DC: American Bankers Association.

Colton, K. (2003). *Housing in the 21st century.* Cambridge, MA: Harvard University Press.

Consumers Union. (1998, February). Dream home . . . or nightmare? *Consumer Reports.* Retrieved June 16, 2004, from *www.consumerreports.org.*

Crow, S. R., & Cooley, J. L. (1988). *Impact fees: Private funding for infrastructure improvements.* Athens, GA: Institute of Community and Area Development.

Dennis, M. W. (1989). *Residential mortgage lending* (2nd ed.). Englewood Cliffs, NJ: Prentice Hall.

Dubin, E. (1994, May). Direct fiscal impacts of residential construction. *Housing Economics.* Washington, DC: National Association of Home Builders.

Epley, D. R., Rabianski, J. S., & Haney, R. L., Jr. (2002). *Real estate decisions.* Cincinnati, OH: Thomson South-Western Publishing.

Frey, E. F. (2003, August). Building industry consolidation. *Housing Economics.* Washington, DC: National Association of Home Builders.

Guarino, J. (2003). What is the difference between a production, semi-custom and a custom builder? *Pioneer Press.* Retrieved November 14, 2004, from *www.pioneerlocal.com/ realestate/newhomesfaq2.html.*

Hegji, C. E., & Mitchell, L. (2000). *The impact of manufactured housing on adjacent site-built residential properties in two Alabama counties* (Technical Report to the Alabama Manufactured Housing Institute). Montgomery, AL: Auburn University.

Immergluck, D., & Wiles, M. (1999, November). *Two steps back: The dual mortgage market, predatory lending and the undoing of community development.* Chicago, IL: Woodstock Institute.

Joint Center for Housing Studies. (2001). *Remodeling homes for changing households.* Cambridge, MA: Harvard Joint Center for Housing Studies.

Lindamood, S., & Hanna, S. D. (1979). *Housing, society and consumers.* St. Paul, MN: West Publishing.

MacTavish, K., & Salamon, S. (2001). Mobile home park on the prairie: A new rural community form. *Rural Sociology, 66,* 487–506.

Manufactured Housing Institute. (2004). *Mission statement.* Retrieved June 15, 2004, from *www.manufacturedhousing.org/lib/showtemp_detail.asp? id=236&cat=search.*

Maselli, P. F. (2002, October 11). *AVMs have to pass the test of time, but they're off to a good start.* New York: American Banker.

Miles, M. E., Berens, G., & Weiss, M. A. (2000). *Real estate development: Principles and process* (3rd ed.). Washington, DC: Urban Land Institute.

Murray, M. (2002, March 25). *AVMs are the talk of the town.* Washington, DC: Real Estate Finance Today.

National Association of Home Builders. (1989). *Single-family builder profit and loss study.* Washington, DC: NAHB.

President's Committee on Urban Housing. (1969). *A decent home.* Washington, DC: U.S. Government Printing Office.

The Seven Segments of Industrialized/Manufactured Housing Today. (2002, August). *Automated Builder, 374,* 14–15.

Suchman, D. R. (1995, March). *Manufactured housing: An affordable alternative* (Working Paper). Washington, DC: The Urban Land Institute.

Sun Nations. (2004). *Overview of the loan application process.* Retrieved June 10, 2004, from *www.sunnations.com/mortgagelibrary/apply_for_a_loan/ loan_timeline.asp.*

van Vliet, W. (Ed.). (1997). *Encyclopedia of housing.* Thousand Oaks, CA: Sage Publications.

Vanderford, S. E., Mimura, Y., & Sweaney, A. L. (in press). A hedonic price comparison of manufactured and site-built homes in the non-MSA United States. *Journal of Real Estate Research, 26.*

Wubneh, M., & Shen, G. (2004). The impact of manufactured housing on adjacent residential property values: A GIS approach based on three North Carolina counties. *Review of Urban and Regional Development Studies, 16,* 56–73.

CHAPTER 5

Housing and Community

Loraine L. Tyler, Nancy C. Higgitt, and Carla C. Earhart
Loraine L. Tyler is Professor Emeritus, Department of Human Ecology,
State University of New York, Oneonta, NY; Nancy C. Higgitt is Associate
Professor, Department of Family Social Sciences, University of Manitoba,
Winnipeg, Canada; and Carla C. Earhart is Professor, Department of
Family and Consumer Sciences, Ball State University, Muncie, IN.

Housing policy analyst Nenno (1996, pp. 172–173) noted that complex relationships exist between housing and communities, observing that "housing is a durable physical product in a neighborhood setting" and also an "ingredient in family satisfaction or dissatisfaction and in a community's sense of well being." The physical context of place is relatively understandable compared to concepts of community. However, issues regarding community can be difficult to explain in useful ways to those who shape policy and provide housing that meets local wants and needs.

This chapter explores concepts of community with regard to place-based (physical) and people-based (social) housing issues. It examines various definitions of neighborhood and community, reviews social aspects of communities and neighborhoods, describes the process of community development as well as some traditional and nontraditional tools and models for physical development, and finally, considers elements of residents' satisfaction and dissatisfaction with their homes and physical surroundings.

Studying neighborhoods and communities is both exciting and challenging. This field crosses a number of disciplines including sociology, psychology, economics, anthropology, geography, urban and rural planning, community development, and housing. Although different disciplines take various approaches to this topic, two general approaches are discussed. The ecological approach considers housing, neighborhoods, and communities as functional entities and examines the interdependence between residents and their surrounding environments as well as the interrelationships among residents. It also relates the community's physical features to the social situations in various neighborhood settings.

The planning approach, in contrast, is concerned with the physical layout of housing, streets, sidewalks, open spaces, and utility lines. Its focus is how the physical environment supports the neighborhood's residents. Those professionals who create new neighborhoods (real estate developers, builders, architects, and city planners) consider neighborhoods as physical constructs in the layout of residential areas. These approaches consider both the social and physical community aspects.

DEFINING NEIGHBORHOOD AND COMMUNITY

The terms *neighborhood* and *community* have many definitions and are often used interchangeably. A simple approach for distinguishing between the two terms is to link neighborhoods with a geographic location and communities with social interaction (Cater & Jones, 1989). However, not all scholars follow this custom. Several definitions are described in the following text.

In a classic article on community, Hillery (1955) reported almost 100 definitions of that term. Most referred to people living in a specific area who share common ties and interact in some way. Mumford (1961) defined *neighborhood* as an area in which people share certain common facilities necessary to domestic life. Twenty years later, Lynch (1981) referred to neighborhood as a local unit in which people are personally acquainted with each other by reason of residential proximity. British geographers Cater and Jones (1989) defined neighborhood as local urban space bounded by the occupants' self-definitions and practices. In contrast, they viewed *community* as a network of social interaction and bonding, usually based on mutual interest. Cater and Jones argued for conceptualizing the two terms as a neighborhood-community equation which they defined as local space that contains friends and associates, supplies many immediate needs, and functions as a microcosmic social system.

According to Canadian researchers Connor and Brink (1999), a neighborhood can be either geographically or socially defined. However, researchers tend to favor geographic definitions because such definitions facilitate their use of census tracts or zip (postal) codes for isolating data. Briggs (1997) called these spatially defined units *statistical neighborhoods*. The strength of this approach is its ease of definition and measurement, while its weakness is that it may not reflect residents' sense of neighborhood. Social definitions incorporate residents' perceptions of their neighborhoods; Briggs referred to these as *functional neighborhoods*. Although this approach respects residents' understandings of their neighborhoods, it makes the neighborhoods difficult to operationally define and measure.

Community Development

The term *community development* is frequently used in different contexts. For example, it may refer to a new neighborhood's physical planning and development. This might be termed *physical community development.* In contrast, community development can refer to enhancing residents' capacities, skills, and resources, usually in an existing neighborhood. This meaning might be termed *social community development.*

HISTORY OF STUDYING NEIGHBORHOODS AND COMMUNITIES FROM A SOCIAL PERSPECTIVE

Anthropologists and urban sociologists have studied communities and neighborhoods with great interest over the last century. As early as 1916 urban sociologist Park published research on human behavior in urban neighborhoods. Using a traditional urban ecological perspective, Park and other sociologists from the University of Chicago studied urban neighborhoods to learn about poverty, social mobility, class relations, and other social processes (Park, 1967; Park & Burgess, 1967). As more people moved from rural areas to cities, many researchers became deeply concerned about the negative effects of urban centers on families. For instance, Wirth (1938), in his study of disorderly aspects of urban neighborhoods, believed that as neighborhoods became denser people would no longer know each other and the social ties that traditionally held people together would disintegrate.

By the end of World War II cities were industrial, urban, and growing rapidly. All these factors helped develop neighborhoods (Auld, 1997). This period saw many interesting studies published. For example, Whyte (1943) studied Italian immigrants in a neighborhood he called Cornerville. Gans (1962) studied an Italian neighborhood in the west end of Boston, Massachusetts, during the 1950s. Liebow (1967) produced a classic study of poor African American men on a street corner in Washington, DC.

Despite the interest in ethnographic accounts of life in these different neighborhoods and communities, social research shifted emphasis from small neighborhood studies to macrotheories of society thanks to advanced statistical methods (Hornburg & Lang, 1997). About the same time the federal governments of the United States and Canada began to address the pressing need for low-cost housing. Policymakers sought to house large numbers of residents without regard for developing healthy, supportive environments. This oversight resulted in large but unsuccessful housing projects such as Robert Taylor Homes in Chicago, Illinois; Pruitt-Igoe in St. Louis, Missouri; and Regent Park in Toronto, Canada.

Toward the end of the twentieth and into the twenty-first century, thanks to the increasing visibility of homeless people and media reports about alarming increases of violent crime, drug use, single women having babies, and welfare dependency in inner-city neighborhoods (Gephart & Brooks-Gunn, 1997), there has been a resurgence of interest in neighborhood and community effects on individuals and families. Current Canadian and U.S. research focuses on the combined effects of individual, family, neighborhood, and community characteristics on the development of children and other community members.

Theoretical Approaches to Studying Social Aspects of Neighborhoods and Communities

Many different theoretical orientations are used to study the social aspects of neighborhoods and communities. For instance, developmental psychologists often study neighborhoods from an ecological perspective. Bronfenbrenner's (1989) ecological model assumes that individuals cannot be studied without considering the multiple ecological systems in which they operate. Park (1967) called his theoretical approach human ecology.

Wirth was the first American to develop an urban theory by isolating several universal social characteristics of the city and then systematically determining the consequences of these factors for the character of urban social life (Macionis & Parrillo, 1998). Wirth (1938) defined the city as a large, dense, permanent settlement with socially and culturally heterogeneous people. He argued that size, density, and heterogeneity interact to produce the unique way of life he termed *urbanism.*

McKnight has been at the forefront of the community building movement approach, which focuses on community assets rather than deficits. According to McKnight, the basic tools for community building include mobilizing people's capacities and skills and mobilizing them in all kinds of groups (Kretzmann & McKnight, 1993).

More recently, psychologists, sociologists, and planners have developed conceptual frameworks that help to explain how or why neighborhood and community characteristics affect people's behavior and life chances (Ellen & Turner, 1997). Although no single causal model fully explains neighborhood and community roles across domains in a person's life, several theories explain their influence on families and children (Jencks & Mayer, 1990), including social contagion, collective socialization, neighborhood resource, and relative deprivation theories.

Social Contagion Theories. Social contagion focuses on children's peers influencing their behavior. For instance, if positive behavior such as graduating from college or a university is modeled in a neighborhood, the chances will increase that other neighborhood children will value education and strive for academic success. However, negative behavior such as poor school attendance or criminal activity may encourage others to follow suit (Connor & Brink, 1999).

Hillary Clinton: "...it takes a village..." approach

Collective Socialization Theories. Collective socialization theories consider the impact of adult role models and informally shared parenting functions by neighborhood residents. Adults can act as positive role models and exert social control on the neighborhood children by monitoring behavior and by being aware of and dealing with potential trouble.

Neighborhood Resource Theories. Neighborhood resource theories emphasize the link between the quality and quantity of resident services. Examples of services include schools, police protection, parks, recreation, and health. Available services should lead to increased opportunities for positive development among neighborhood children.

Nature vs. nurture perspective?

"Trading Places" movie?

All three of these models predict that disadvantaged children will do better when they reside in affluent neighborhoods where they will have access to conforming peers, successful adult models, and abundant resources (Furstenberg & Hughes, 1997; Kohen, Hertzman, & Brooks-Gunn, 1998).

Relative Deprivation Theories. Relative deprivation theories assume that people judge their success or failure by comparing their status to others around them. Thus, children in less-affluent families living among more-affluent neighbors are predicted to feel more deprived than children in less-affluent families living among less-affluent neighbors. Furthermore, if children see themselves at a disadvantage relative to their peers they may be less motivated to try.

Local (e.g., municipal and county) units of government are generally responsible for regulating existing housing as well as the production of new housing. Regulations affecting the existing stock include health and sanitation standards, fire codes, noise ordinances, crowding standards, and others that contribute to the quality of housing and the home environment. New housing production and, often, rehabilitation, adaptive reuse, and neighborhood revitalization projects are governed by local building codes, zoning, and land use regulations.

17

PROCESS OF PHYSICAL COMMUNITY DEVELOPMENT

No uniform planning and land development legislation applies throughout the United States (Galaty, Allaway, & Kyle, 1999). Land use regulations are, for the most part, local regulations. Because these regulations reflect the customs of local inhabitants and physical conditions unique to an area, little uniformity exists. However, the process of community development and the tools used to implement the plans are similar from one community to another.

Planning Commissions

Villages, cities, and other incorporated areas use planning commissions in the community development process. Planning commissions are made up of local residents who recommend to the governing body (such as a city council or county board of commissioners) planning decisions for the entire community (Roske, 1983). Zoning code changes, such as allowing senior citizen housing in an area designated for single-family homes, begin with commission recommendations. Depending on the organizational structure, planning commissions may have limited authority, serving only in an advisory capacity. However, others may have the power to approve or disapprove development plans (Galaty et al., 1999). The effectiveness of planning commissions is dependent on the dedication and competencies of the local residents appointed.

Comprehensive Plan

Community development goals are formulated through a comprehensive plan. This plan, also referred to as a master plan or general plan, is a statement of community development policies as well as a presentation of how those policies are to be implemented. Seeking to ensure that social and economic needs are balanced against environmental and aesthetic concerns, a typical comprehensive plan sets goals for the community's growth and development 5, 10, or 20 years in the future (Galaty et al., 1999; Roske, 1983). Typical topics covered in a comprehensive plan include demographic and economic factors; land use and zoning; housing and neighborhood quality; infrastructure; government services; utilities and facilities; visual, cultural, and environmental factors; open space and recreation; government structure; and visions, goals, and objectives.

The comprehensive plan allocates future land use based on projected growth in population, industry, and commerce as well as on other demographic and economic factors. Future residential land use as well as land usage for schools, factories, hospitals, shopping centers, recreational activity, and other purposes, is considered. Generally, planning commissions made up of appointed members undertake the extensive community study, although citizen participation is often encouraged throughout the process. Following the comprehensive plan's development, community citizens review the plan and provide input before it is adopted. Once the plan is approved, tools such as zoning ordinances and subdivision regulations help authorize the plan's implementation (Roske, 1983).

TOOLS OF PHYSICAL COMMUNITY DEVELOPMENT

Zoning Ordinances

Zoning ordinances can be traced back to 1692, when Boston enacted a land use ordinance confining the location of slaughter houses, tallow chandlers, and other "offensive activities." The New York City Zoning Ordinance in 1916 was the first to include an appeals process, creating the Zoning Board of Appeals. During the twentieth century land use control and city planning processes were combined. In 1922 the federal government enacted a standard State Zoning Enabling Act, by which states could establish legislative powers to promulgate zoning codes (Coon et al., n.d.). Every state now has such enabling legislation. Figure 5.1 illustrates the process of creating and using a zoning ordinance, and the process of appeals.

Based on the interest of promoting residents' health, safety, and welfare, zoning ordinances regulate land use, population density, site requirements, and structural dimensions. Ideally, they are meant to guide the community's future development, not be a straightjacket for the property owner. A zoning ordinance contains three parts: (1) a map showing boundaries of labeled zoning districts, (2) a section of specifically defined and periodically reviewed definitions, and (3) a series of Articles containing the permitted and conditional or special permit uses within each district. The more specific the ordinance the easier it is for a property owner and the Code Enforcement Office to determine adherence and to receive or deny a building permit.

Zoning, which must be enacted in accordance with the comprehensive plan, regulates development by district throughout the municipality. By treating each property within a district equally, zoning regulations preserve the neighborhood's character and protect property values. A zoning classification describes a site's permitted uses within a zoning district; dictates the type of development and placement of buildings; sets limits on type and number of units;

[handwritten margin note: 1. map 2. definitions 3. articles]

[handwritten bottom: 15]

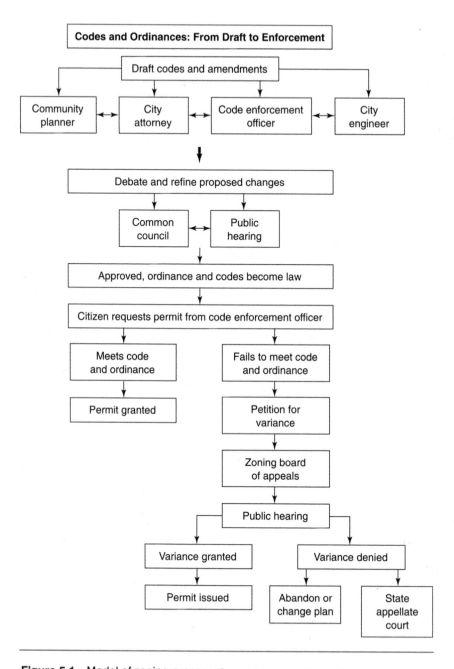

Figure 5.1 Model of zoning process (*Source:* Tyler, 1997, *Housing Resource Guide*)

controls building height, setbacks, and easements; and determines lot density. Figure 5.2 provides examples of typical zoning requirements.

The Articles describe in detail a zone's permitted uses. Zoning districts are classified by the type of development such as residential, industrial, or commercial. Generally, mixed uses are not encouraged. Residential districts are further classified by the type of dwelling unit allowed: single-family, multi-family, or transition. Transition districts allow the conversion of single-family homes to two- and three-family units, thereby allowing a town or city to change over time. The Articles also contain conditional or special permit uses that may meet a desirable need within a neighborhood, but that require more care in planning and implementing. For example, child care centers, professional offices, and mom-pop grocery stores may add to the neighborhood's convenience, but could cause damaging side effects if not carefully controlled (Coon & Damsky, 1989). The Code Enforcement Office, Planning Commission, Zoning Board of Appeals, and/or council of the municipality examine these special uses for development and compliance.

Finally, an ordinance permits nonconforming uses that result from enacting or revising zoning regulations. Nonconforming uses, commonly referred to as grandfathering, are land uses that legally existed before the ordinance's adoption but are no longer legal uses (Coon et al., n.d.). In most ordinances these nonconforming uses

Criteria	Classifications		
Uses Permitted	Single-Family	Multi-Family	Planned Unit Development (PUD)
Maximum Density	20,000 sq. ft/unit	4,000 sq. ft/unit	1,000 sq. ft/unit
Minimum Lot Area	20,000 sq. ft	10,000 sq. ft	2 acres or 1 city block
Minimum Lot Width	100 feet	100 feet	no minimum
Minimum Side Yard Setback	15 feet	10 feet	none
Minimum Front Yard Setback	30 feet	12 feet	none
Minimum Rear Yard Setback	25 feet	20 feet	none
Minimum Lot Coverage	30%	40%	50%
Maximum Building Height	2.5 stories		
Off-Street Parking Spaces	1/unit	2/unit	2/unit

Figure 5.2   Example of typical zoning requirements (Tyler & Earhart, 1997) (*Source:* Reprinted with permission by the Housing Education and Research Association.)

are allowed to continue, but no changes can be made in structure without a variance from the Zoning Board of Appeals.

Appeal Process

Since the first modern zoning ordinance passed in 1916, Zoning Boards of Appeals have acted "to interpret, to perfect, and to insure the validity of zoning" (Coon et al., n.d., p. 3). As early as 1927 the Supreme Court, concerned that zoning regulations limited the property owner's action, created a board of appeals. In the early part of the twentieth century, courts granted Zoning Boards of Appeals (ZBA) discretionary powers to hear specific hardship cases caused by zoning and cases of improper classification, while at the same time maintaining the ordinance's intent and preserving the neighborhood's character. To alleviate the hardship caused by zoning codes, property owners could appeal to the ZBA for relief through variances. Since the board of appeals is administrative and appellate only, it cannot change zoning laws or boundaries; only the local government body can legislate codes. However, it can issue special permits if given powers of original jurisdiction by local ordinance. The board examines the restrictions set forth in individual matters and varies these restrictions if circumstances demand such relief.

A variance is granted whenever practical difficulties or unnecessary hardships prevent carrying out the strict letter of an ordinance. In granting the variance the ordinance's spirit is followed, public safety and welfare are preserved, and substantial justice is done. A use variance allows the property owner to use the property in other ways than those listed in the district. For example, to convert a single-family dwelling unit to a multi-family dwelling unit in a single-family district, the petitioner for a use variance must show that:

1. The land in question cannot yield a reasonable return if used only for the purpose allowed for in that zone.
2. The owner's plight is due to unique circumstances and not to general neighborhood circumstances that may indicate the zoning ordinance itself is unreasonable.
3. The use to be authorized by the variance will not alter the essential character of the locality.
4. The hardship has not been self-created (Coon et al., n.d., p. 8).

In the criteria of reasonable return, unnecessary hardship is not necessarily proven if the property owner suffers financial hardship or if the property in question would sell for more money if another use were permitted. The hardship must not be self-created, but rather due to the unique circumstances of the zoning. The hardship must be such that it applies to only one parcel. If it applies to many parcels in the district, a legislative act to change zoning would be more appropriate.

An area variance is not related to land use, but varies or modifies regulations relating to building use, construction, or alteration. As a practical matter, the permitted use cannot be accomplished because of certain restrictions affecting bulk or density. In granting an area variance, four factors must be considered:

1. Significant economic injury.
2. The magnitude of the variance sought (the greater the deviation, the more likelihood of a severe impact on the neighborhood).
3. Whether the hardship is self-created.
4. If means other than a variance will alleviate the problem.

Suppose an owner wishes to increase the size of residential space from a studio apartment (480 square feet) to a one-bedroom apartment (700 square feet) on an undersized lot. Therefore, an area variance is required before the change can be made. The variance request is filed with the city clerk's office and a nominal fee, typically $50, is charged. Homeowners within 200 feet are notified of the request and date of the public hearing. Official publication is also made in the local news media. Prior to the hearing, ZBA members inspect the site with regard to the magnitude and number of variances requested. Testimony is sought from the owner, concerned residents, professionals (lawyers, engineers, police, and firefighters), and others present at the hearing. The owner provides evidence. In this case the owner testifies that the lot shape is unique in the neighborhood and that the neighborhood's character will not be changed. He also describes the housing unit changes he wishes to make. In order to enlarge the apartment he plans to extend the front of the space, making the front yard smaller (front yard setback). Once the hearing is completed, a decision (by majority vote) must be rendered within 60 days (Tyler & Earhart, 1997, pp. 26–27). In this example, three variances are requested, as outlined in Figure 5.3.

Variance	Code Requirements	Actual Dimension
Density (Sect. 30.32)	16,000 sq. ft (4 units)	10,000 sq. ft
Front yard setback	25 feet	9 feet
Off-street parking	2/unit for residences = 4	2

Figure 5.3 Types of variance requests (Tyler & Earhart, 1997) (*Source:* Reprinted with permission by the Housing Education and Research Association)

The variances granted in this example are stated as follows. Based on testimony presented at the regular meeting of the Zoning Board of Appeals and site visits by ZBA members, variances are granted to allow the expansion of an apartment from a studio apartment (480 square feet) to a one-bedroom apartment (700 square feet) at *street name*. Variances are granted for density, front yard setback, and parking because the shape of the lot is unique in the neighborhood. The character of the neighborhood will not change (Tyler & Earhart, 1997, pp. 26–27).

A special permit allows conditions to be applied to uses already permitted. These permits can be used to control desirable uses such as churches or libraries and less desirable uses such as gasoline stations, both of which can attract large numbers of people and create additional traffic. Zoning boards can issue special permits, or this power can be reserved for the legislative branch.

Subdivision Regulations

Often included as part of the comprehensive plan, subdivision regulations govern the residential development of raw land (Meeks, 1980). Subdivision regulations serve as protection for buyers of new homes and vacant residential lots by assuring them that standards will be upheld because design and construction standards are specified. These regulations also assist communities in planning for public facilities, open space, and traffic control as well as for the funds necessary to meet new residents' demands.

According to Galaty et al. (1999), subdivision regulations usually guide:

- areas to be reserved or dedicated for public use such as parks or schools,
- installation of and easements for public utilities,
- lot and block size, and
- the location, width, and surfacing of streets.

Covenants

In addition to those controls placed on residential land usage by community officials, further restrictions may be present in the form of covenants. Also known as private covenants, protective covenants, or restrictive covenants, these agreements are established by the developer of a residential subdivision or a neighborhood association to restrict the use of their properties, resulting in mutual advantage (Harrison, 2000). This mutual advantage, the desire to maintain the area's aesthetics, protects resale value of the homes in the subdivision and sustains the identity of the development or neighborhood.

While covenant laws vary from state to state, several standard principles have evolved (Harrison, 2000). Most important is that notice must be made of the covenant's existence at the time of purchase, often by making the covenant part of the deed or part of the bylaws for the development. In addition, the only person who can bring action to enforce a covenant is another property owner in the affected area. Also, the restrictions are stated such that residents are prevented from doing something, but cannot be required to take a positive action. Lastly, the covenant must be related to the real estate itself. Figure 5.4 lists sample covenants (Tyler & Earhart, 1997, p. 30).

+ Poulsen Falls examples

1. **Residential Purposes.** No lot shall be used for other than residential purposes. No building shall be erected, altered, placed, or permitted to remain on any lot other than one detached single-family dwelling.

2. **Home Exterior.** Most architectural styles will be acceptable to the committee. In keeping with a harmonious appearance, log houses, geodesic dome houses, barn houses, and earth, underground, or earth berm homes will not be acceptable.

   Acceptable materials include:

   Walls:　Brick, stone varieties native to this area, stucco, wood (cedar, redwood, cypress, or poplar); limited amounts of aluminum and vinyl siding. No pine or plywood may be used.

   Roof:　No roof pitch under 6 1/2′ will be allowed. Roof materials shall be fiberglass, asphalt shingles, slate, or wood shingles. Colors are limited to grays, browns, and other earth tones.

   Colors:　Bright or pastel colors such as yellows, blues, greens, or reds will be acceptable only for trim and other limited uses on a residence.

3. **Exterior Surroundings.** No lot and no dwelling unit shall be permitted to become overgrown, unsightly, or to fall into disrepair. All dwelling units shall at all times be kept in good condition and repair, and adequately painted or otherwise finished in accordance with specifications established by the committee.

   Landscaping: All shrubs, trees, grass, and plantings of every kind shall be kept well maintained, properly cultivated, and free of trash and other unsightly material. Landscaping shall be installed no later than one hundred eighty (180) days following occupancy of or completion of the dwelling unit, whichever occurs first. No trees, while in good condition, shall be cut down, destroyed, or mutilated, except as may be necessary for the construction of a dwelling unit and its appurtenances.

   Driveways and Walks: All driveways and walks must have a surface of concrete, asphalt, bomanite, or brick pavers.

Figure 5.4　Sample covenants (Tyler & Earhart, 1997) (*Source:* Reprinted with permission by the Housing Education and Research Association.)

Pools: Pools must be totally in-ground and within the minimum building lines. All pool equipment must be enclosed in a pump/pool house of an architectural style and material identical to the residence.

Storage and Temporary Structures Storage: No structure of a temporary character, trailer, boat trailer, truck (other than pick-up truck), commercial vehicle, recreational vehicle (RV), camper shell, all terrain vehicle (ATV), camper or camping trailer, basement, tent, shack, garage, barn, or other outbuilding shall be either used or located on any lot, adjacent to any lot, public street, or right-of-way at any time, or used as a residence either temporarily or permanently.

Signs: Once a home dwelling unit is occupied, no sign of any kind shall be displayed to the public view on any lot except one sign of not more than six (6) square feet advertising such lot for sale. Rummage or other sale signs may be placed on any one lot for no more than seven (7) days in a calendar year.

Animals: No animals, livestock, or poultry of any kind shall be raised, bred, or kept on any lot, except that dogs, cats, or other household pets may be kept, provided they are not kept, bred, or maintained for any commercial purpose. Animals shall be confined to the owner's property at all times.

Fencing: The only fencing permitted shall be a privacy fence of not more than six (6) feet in height within the building lines of the rear yard. Dog runs adjacent to the service area of the home but not visible from surrounding dwellings or from the street also will be permitted. No fences will be allowed in the front of any dwelling.

4. **Enforceability.** For a violation, or a breach of any of the covenants, the developer, the committee, and any lot owner, or any of them severally, shall have the right to proceed, at law or in equity, to compel a compliance with the terms hereof or to prevent the violation or breach of any of them.

Figure 5.4   Continued

CRITICS OF PHYSICAL COMMUNITY DEVELOPMENT REGULATIONS

While regulation of residential development is necessary to uphold public health and safety, some view the control as excessive. Although some regulations have helped improve the quality of residential environments, others contributed to problems of housing affordability and to the reduction of personal freedom to make use of one's own property.

The rising cost of land and of site improvements is evidenced by comparing data provided by the National Association of Home Builders (NAHB). In 1949 land and improvements comprised 11 percent of the price of a new single-family home. By 1982 the percentage had increased to 24 percent (National Association of Home Builders, 1985). Finished lot costs continue to represent a significant percentage of the overall cost of single-family homes at 23.6 percent (National Association of Home Builders, 2003). NAHB elaborates on specific issues in the residential development process.

1. The process of rezoning is cumbersome and may take several months or years before approval is granted. Such time lags add to the developers' costs. Some communities and states use zoning as a means to control growth. By setting minimum lot and building sizes and limiting types of dwellings, growth can be encouraged or stymied. Central to growth management laws is the concept that local government should manage growth for the proper use of resources; however, some communities actually use zoning regulations or the permit process to prevent growth.

2. Low-density (large lot) developments result in inefficient use of public utilities. Roads, sewers, and drainage systems are expensive to build and maintain, and these costs are passed on to homebuyers. Low-density, single-use zoning results in sprawling development resulting in long commutes, traffic congestion, air pollution, and wasted energy.

3. Local governments continue to use outdated standards governing lot dimensions, building setbacks, and site orientation, although more creative land planning techniques are available.

4. Street design and construction standards can account for 30 percent or more of land development costs. In an earlier era cars were smaller and street maintenance costs were lower.

5. Provisions requiring dwelling units to meet minimum sizes have resulted in exclusionary zoning practices. These requirements lock out low- and moderate-income community residents who are unable to afford large homes (National Association of Home Builders, 1985).

Other problems with current planning include the lack of balanced growth, particularly in the suburbs where the "not in my backyard" (NIMBY) approach is used in many discussions (namely, growth is great, but not in my backyard, my neighborhood, or my town). As many communities face economic problems, the infrastructure has not been maintained or newly built. Communities across the country will find themselves in need of new water systems, new sewers, street paving, and other infrastructure in the near future. Without appropriate infrastructure, communities cannot be sustained. Another concern is the ability to maintain a quality environment. The impact of uncontrolled or inappropriate growth leads to quality-of-life issues. Housing affordability is a great concern among families.

PHYSICAL COMMUNITY DEVELOPMENT COMPROMISES

The planned unit development (PUD) creates residential neighborhoods that can produce more profits for the developer and builder, while simultaneously providing a better environment for the people who live there (De Chiara, Panero, & Zelnik, 1995). Planned unit developments are usually part of the zoning code. Using a PUD approach, the planning commission may waive technical requirements (such as setback distances and height restrictions) to allow dwellings to be built together in clusters. Furthermore, planning officials may grant bonuses of extra floor area to developers in return for worthy site plans. PUD advantages for the developer and builder include:

- less land use for street construction,
- more efficient utility runs,
- more dwelling units,
- varied house types to reach a wider market, and
- ability to include mixed uses such as commercial/retail property within the residential development.

Possible benefits for people living in a planned unit development are larger houses for less money, convenience of local retail shops, and more choice of house type. In addition, PUDs often include open space and common areas as part of the trade-off for higher density development. The following discussion elaborates on the advantages of PUDs.

Builder/Developer Advantages

Streets and Utilities.   Generally, developers must include streets, sewers, and storm drains when they develop residential neighborhoods. Because there may be as much as 30 percent less street area under the PUD scheme, substantial savings can be realized in both the street costs and the associated provisions or utilities (De Chiara et al., 1995).

Dwelling Units.   By saving on the amount of land devoted to streets, developers reap benefits by dedicating more property to housing construction. In addition, the relaxation of setback (yard) requirements also permits the building of larger houses than possible under conventional zoning regulations. Bonus provisions allowed under the PUD scheme may further benefit developers and builders by permitting more structures on a given piece of land.

While conventional land development strategies may cause builders to construct a limited variety of housing types in a narrow range of prices, a PUD allows the builder to attract a wider segment of the housing market by building anything from a large detached house to small garden apartments. In this way the builder is able to respond to changing demographics as well as to unstable market conditions.

Resident Advantages

More House for the Money.   The PUD scheme can create a larger house for less money compared to the same house under conventional land planning regulations, because a large portion of the house's purchase price goes toward land costs. When land costs can be minimized through increased density and reduced yard requirements, those savings can be passed on to the homeowner. Infrastructure costs are also less because the dwelling units are closer together, requiring shorter runs for water, sewer, and electrical lines.

More Choices.   Whereas conventional land planning strategies tend to create block after block of the same type of dwelling unit, PUD neighborhoods offer a variety of house types. A single subdivision might include detached houses, duplexes, townhouses, and garden apartments. This variety not only allows for a broader mix of residents within the neighborhood, but also allows households to move from one type or size of home without leaving the neighborhood.

NEIGHBORHOOD SATISFACTION

What constitutes a satisfying neighborhood? *Neighborhood satisfaction* is an important aspect of well-being. Measuring satisfaction, however, can be a challenge. The simplest approach is to ask residents how satisfied they are. However, because satisfaction and dissatisfaction can relate to many sources, a more comprehensive approach would be to ask a series of questions about many different aspects of a person's neighborhood. According to environmental psychologist Gifford (1997), neighborhood satisfaction is influenced by personal, physical, social, segregation, and safety factors.

Personal Factors

Researchers have found that neighborhood satisfaction is higher when (1) residents believe their current neighborhood is an improvement over their former one, (2) the neighborhood has an adequate level of stimulation, and (3) residents feel at home in their neighborhood (Gifford, 1997). Some residents express neighborhood satisfaction simply because it is theirs. They feel rooted and have taken ownership. Similarly, residents who own their homes tend to express more satisfaction with the neighborhood compared to those who rent. Finally, satisfaction is increased if the neighborhood fits the residents' life stage. In other words, families with small children tend to prefer a neighborhood where other families with small children reside. For elderly people, neighborhood satisfaction increases their overall home satisfaction.

Physical Factors

Physical neighborhood characteristics affect residents' satisfaction. They may be less satisfied if the neighborhood is noisy or divided by a major traffic route, and more satisfied if the area has lots of green space, is visually appealing, and has housing stock in good physical condition. Morris and Winter (1978) found housing satisfaction to be the most important predictor of neighborhood satisfaction.

The availability and quality of neighborhood services may influence a person's sense of well-being. Examples include childcare programs, schools, seniors' programs, medical care facilities, and convenient shopping.

Social Factors

Most residents want good neighbors. For some, this concept means residents who are quiet and respectful of each other's privacy. For others it means forming strong social ties with other residents. Neighbors may serve as important support systems for each other if they provide emotional support and assistance with tasks or make material goods available for others to borrow. Dense neighborhood social networks may facilitate people's looking out for each other and exchanging resources. This action is often referred to as the concept of *neighboring* (Schwarz, Mauksch, & Rawls, 1995). For residents who favor social ties at the neighborhood level, the presence or absence of such ties will strongly influence neighborhood satisfaction. However, residents who find social links beyond the neighborhood will be less influenced by the presence or absence of social ties in the neighborhood.

Neighborhood Segregation

One of the least understood issues regarding housing and community is residential segregation. Neighborhood separation of households based on ethnicity has been an ongoing area of study for several decades. While neighborhood segregation has existed for some time, controversy exists over whether or not such divisiveness is getting better or worse. Clark (2002) indicated that ethnic segregation has substantially declined since the 1960s. He further suggested that such trends will continue toward more integrated neighborhoods in the future. In opposition, scholars such as Ellen (2004), Ihlanfeldt and Scafidi (2002), and Stults (2004) identified housing segregation as a persistent problem in America.

Several complex causes of the residential segregation issue have been considered.

- Prejudice and discrimination in the housing and mortgage market (Yinger, 1995), where African Americans are treated less favorably than whites in housing acquisition.
- Socioeconomic status including income, occupation, education, and wealth (Ihlanfeldt & Scafidi, 2002), which point to an inability of African Americans to afford housing in areas primarily occupied by whites.
- Self-selection and group avoidance, where individuals indicate a preference for living with members of their own group (Armor & Clark, 1995).

If neighborhood integration has improved, the Civil Rights Act of 1964 and the Fair Housing Act that followed deserve some credit. The American government made a strong commitment to reducing residential segregation by making it illegal to discriminate in housing transactions on the basis of ethnicity and other protected classifications. However, with the recent and continued influx of Hispanics, Asians, and other immigrants, the incidence, causes, and consequences of residential segregation will require continued investigation.

Safety Factors

Typically people feel safest in their own homes. Beyond the unit itself, neighborhood safety is a concern for most residents, and some neighborhood designs help residents to feel safer than do others. For instance, good lighting of public areas facilitates feelings of safety. Perception of safety is an important factor. Residents will not feel safe if they perceive their neighborhood to be unsafe even if crime data suggest otherwise. Urbanist Jacobs (1992) suggested that a lively street contributes greatly to neighborhood safety. For a street to be lively there must be "stores and other public places sprinkled along the sidewalks" (p. 36). "The safety of the street works best . . . where people are using and most enjoying the city streets voluntarily and are least conscious, normally, that they are policing"

(p. 36). According to Jacobs, street activity results in people who act as street watchers and sidewalk guardians, discouraging potentially negative behavior and encouraging positive pursuits.

FURTHER EVOLUTION OF NEIGHBORHOODS AND COMMUNITIES

Some residents demand more of their neighborhoods in terms of safety and conservation. As a result, the intentional neighborhoods described in the following text have become more common.

Gentrification

Gentrification and disinvestment are opposite ends of neighborhood transition. Disinvestment occurs when buildings deteriorate, areas are abandoned, and graffiti abounds. The middle and upper classes then move to "more desirable areas." When new money is invested in a neighborhood the upper class moves back and gentrification occurs. Warehouses become condos, old store fronts become romantic restaurants, landscaping is added to parks, and the area attracts more investment and new residents, fueled by an easier commute to jobs, access to mass transit, more services and entertainment, and interesting architecture. Displacement of the lower class and some racial groups result as rents and housing prices are no longer affordable (Wetzel, 2004). Gentrification is found in nearly every U.S. city.

Gated Communities

Recently, some people have become concerned about neighborhood safety. The solution for some has been the development of gated communities: small neighborhoods enclosed with a fence and a restrictive neighborhood entrance. The neighborhood is often designated literally with the use of an entrance gate. Usually, visitors wishing to enter are met by a gatekeeper or they must contact the person they wish to visit via intercom or phone. Some gated communities are lifestyle communities that focus on recreation, others are prestige communities appealing to persons who value exclusivity and status, and some are intended to enhance secure feelings. According to Lang and Danielsen (1997, p. 869), "gated communities offer their residents the perception of a safe haven in the new, often chaotic metropolis."

Researchers have raised a number of points about gated communities that deserve attention. Some argue that residents of gated communities may be lulled into complacency regarding protection against crime, as gated communities certainly do reduce the nuisance intrusions of unexpected callers. Some studies suggest that residents in walled-neighborhoods develop a strong sense of community among themselves at the expense of the larger community. One example is where residents oppose or vote down public bond issues for community swimming pools because many residents have private pools and see no need to spend tax dollars on such community resources. It is clear that developers have found a market segment that is willing to purchase homes in gated communities, since 40 percent of new homes in California are constructed behind walls (Lang & Danielsen, 1997).

Conservation Communities

Conservation communities are neighborhoods that incorporate sustainable housing and neighborhood design. Generally, a conservation neighborhood is created on a large tract of land but the housing is clustered on just a fraction of the site, with the rest reserved for recreation, farming, and other activities that preserve the area's topography (Dotson, 1997). Conservation communities not only create a good environment for people, but also preserve the most outstanding features of the land.

Some features of conservation communities include a lake or stream to accommodate water run-off that provides recreation for the residents and a haven for wildlife; forested areas to act as a natural barrier from surrounding developments and as a wildlife shelter; garden plots to provide food for the residents; and a transit stop to allow residents to commute to urban areas without using their automobiles (Dotson, 1997).

Housing in conservation communities reflects the most current technology related to energy conservation. House design incorporates extra insulation and caulking, double-glazed low-E windows, water-conserving toilets and faucet aerators, and passive solar orientation to take advantage of the sun's energy to heat the home. In addition, recycling is encouraged; some homes are actually made of recycled materials.

New Urbanism

Some developers have looked back to more traditional neighborhood planning principles in creating what many perceive to be better neighborhood settings (Kunstler, 1996). These *new urbanists,* as they are sometimes called, promote neighborhoods that have a well-defined edge and a focused center. They recommend that neighborhood size should be no more than one half mile from one end to the other or the distance for about a 10-minute walk. Proponents of this neighborhood design argue that neighborhoods of this size result in a better human scale (Kunstler, 1996).

Dwellings in this new urbanist tradition should be varied to accommodate different family types, income levels, and lifestyles. Commerce should be integrated into the neighborhood to support residents' needs, and public transportation should be readily available (Kunstler, 1996).

Traditional Neighborhood Development

This traditional neighborhood approach uses a street pattern that creates a number of alternative routes from one part of the neighborhood to another. This network is more like a traditional grid of streets and sidewalks than the winding pattern of streets with cul-de-sacs that is found in many suburban neighborhoods today. However, the traditional neighborhood development incorporates parks, squares, diagonals, T-intersections, roundabouts, and other devices to counteract the monotony of a grid layout. Another traditional feature of these neighborhoods is the incorporation of alleyways that de-emphasize automobile use and provide less visible space for trash collection and other functional necessities (Kunstler, 1996).

CONCLUSION

Local housing policies regulate the circumstances under which new houses and neighborhoods are created. Housing producers are constrained by local regulations and by consumer wants, needs, and ability to pay. Sometimes, housing policies unnecessarily hinder the processes of meeting community housing needs, including the need for affordable housing. Policymakers are challenged to provide housing opportunities that are acceptable to those who will live in them and to the community at large. An understanding of satisfaction with housing, neighborhood, and community affords a foundation for crafting policies that presents a range of housing opportunities that enhance a community's vitality.

REFERENCES

Armor, D., & Clark, W. A. V. (1995). Housing segregation and school desegregation. In D. Armor (Ed.), *Forced justice: School desegregation and the law.* New York: Oxford University Press.

Auld, J. W. (1997). Houses in communities: Putting the home in context. *Canadian Home Economics Journal, 47*(4), 149–151.

Briggs, X. (1997). Moving up versus moving out: Neighborhood effects in housing mobility programs. *Housing Policy Debate, 8*(1), 195–234.

Bronfenbrenner, U. (1989). Ecological systems theory. In R. Vasta (Ed.), *Annals of child development—six theories of child development: Revised formulations and current issues.* Greenwich, CT: JM Press.

Cater, J., & Jones, T. (1989). *Social geography: An introduction to contemporary issues.* London: Edward Arnold Publishers.

Clark, W. A. V. (2002). Residential segregation trends. In A. Thernstrom & S. Thernstrom (Eds.), *Beyond the color line: New perspectives on race and ethnicity in America.* Stanford, CA: Hoover Press.

Connor, S., & Brink, S. (1999). *Understanding the early years community component. Community impacts on child development.* Ottawa, Canada: Applied Research Branch, Strategic Policy Human Resources Development Canada.

Coon, J. A., & Damsky, S. W. (1989). *All you ever wanted to know about zoning.* Albany, NY: New York Planning Federation.

Coon, J. A., et al. (n.d.). *Zoning board of appeals.* New York: Office of General Council, Local Government Technical Series.

De Chiara, J., Panero, J., & Zelnik, M. (Eds.). (1995). *Time-saver standards for housing and residential development.* New York: McGraw-Hill.

Dotson, H. (1997). The new ruralist. *Landscape Architecture, 87*(9), 66–68.

Ellen, I. G. (2004, October). *Neighborhood racial integration: A contemporary portrait.* Presented at the Annual Association of Public Analysis and Management Research Conference, Atlanta, GA.

Ellen, I. G., & Turner, M. A. (1997). Does neighborhood matter? Assessing recent evidence. *Housing Policy Debate, 8*(4), 833–866.

Furstenberg, F. F., & Hughes, M. E. (1997). The influence of neighborhoods on children's development: A theoretical perspective and a research agenda. In J. Brooks-Gunn, G. J. Duncan, & J. L. Aber (Eds.), *Neighborhood poverty: Vol II. Policy implications in studying neighborhoods.* New York: Russell Sage Foundation.

Galaty, F. W., Allaway, W. J., & Kyle, R. C. (1999). *Modern real estate practice.* Chicago: Real Estate Education Company.

Gans, H. (1962). *The urban villagers.* New York: Free Press.

Gephart, M. A., & Brooks-Gunn, J. (1997). Neighborhood poverty. In J. Brooks-Gunn, G. Duncan, & L. Aber (Eds.), *Neighborhood poverty: Vol. II. Policy implications in studying neighborhoods.* New York: Russell Sage Foundation.

Gifford, R. (1997). *Environmental psychology. Principles and practice* (3rd ed.). Boston: Allyn & Bacon.

Harrison, H. S. (2000). *Houses: The illustrated guide to construction, design, and systems.* Chicago: Real Estate Education Corporation.

Hillery, G. A. (1955). Definitions of community: Areas of agreement. *Rural Sociology, 20,* 111–123.

Hornburg, S. P., & Lang, R. E. (1997). Editors' introduction. Bringing neighborhood back in housing in a community context. *Housing Policy Debate, 8*(4), 697–701.

Ihlanfeldt, K. R., & Scafidi, B. P. (2002). An empirical analysis of the cause of neighborhood racial segregation. *Berkeley Program on Housing and Urban Policy, Seminar and Conference Papers* (Paper S00-003). Available: *http://repositiories.cdlib.org/iber/bphup/meeting._papersS00-003/.*

Jacobs, J. (1992). *The death and life of great American cities.* New York: Vintage Books.

Jencks, C., & Mayer, S. (1990). The social consequences of growing up in a poor neighborhood. In L. E. Lynn & M. F. H. McGeary (Eds.), *Inner-city poverty in the United States* (pp. 111–186). Washington, DC: National Academy Press.

Kohen, D. E., Hertzman, C., & Brooks-Gunn, J. (1998). *Neighborhood influences on children's school readiness.* Ottawa, Canada: Applied Research Branch, Human Resources Development Canada (#W-98-15E).

Kretzmann, J. P., & McKnight, J. L. (1993). *Building community from the inside out.* Evanston, IL: Institute for Policy Research.

Kunstler, J. H. (1996). *Home from nowhere.* New York: Simon & Schuster.

Lang, R. E., & Danielsen, K. A. (1997). Gated communities: Walling out the world? *Housing Policy Debate, 8*(4), 867–899.

Liebow, E. (1967). *Tally's corner.* Boston: Little, Brown.

Lynch, K. (1981). *A theory of good city form.* Cambridge, MA: MIT Press.

Macionis, J. J., & Parrillo, V. N. (1998). *Cities and urban life.* Upper Saddle River, NJ: Merrill/Prentice Hall.

Meeks, C. (1980). *Housing.* New York: Prentice Hall.

Morris, E., & Winter, M. (1978). *Housing, family, and society.* New York: John Wiley and Sons.

Mumford, L. (1961). *The city in history.* New York: Harcourt, Brace & World.

National Association of Home Builders. (2003). *Building a balance: Single-family home cost breakdown.* Retrieved September 26, 2003, from *www.nahb.org/generic.aspx?sectionID=128&genericContentID=368.*

National Association of Home Builders. (1985). *Housing America: The challenges ahead.* Washington, DC: NAHB.

Nenno, M. K. (1996). *Ending the stalemate: Moving housing and urban development into the mainstream of America's future.* Lanham, MD: University Press of America.

Park, R. E. (1967). The city: Suggestions for the investigation of human behavior in the urban environment. In R. E. Park & E. W. Burgess (Eds.), *The city.* Chicago: University of Chicago Press. (Original work published 1916.)

Park, R. E., & Burgess, E. W. (1967). *The city.* Chicago: University of Chicago Press. (Original work published in 1916.)

Roske, M. (1983). *Housing in transition.* New York: Holt, Rinehart, and Winston.

Schwarz, B., Mauksch, R., & Rawls, S. (1995). Housing and the environmental social sciences. In R. Brent & B. Schwarz (Eds.), *Popular American housing* (pp. 73–114). Westport, CT: Greenwood Press.

Stults, B. (2004). *Housing segregation persists in many parts of the nation, study shows.* Available: *www.eurekalert.org/pub_releases/2004-05/uof-hsp05604.php.*

Tyler, L. L. (1997). *Housing resource guide.* New York: State University College of Oneonta.

Tyler, L. L., & Earhart, C. C. (1997). Housing in the context of community development. *Housing and Society, 24*(3), 20–46.

Wetzel, T. (2004). *What is gentrification?* Available at: *www.uncanny.net/~wetzel/gentry.htm.*

Whyte, W. F. (1943). *Street corner society. The social structure of an Italian slum.* Chicago: University of Chicago Press.

Wirth, L. (1938). Urbanism as a way of life. *American Journal of Sociology, 44,* 1–24.

Yinger, J. (1995). *Closed doors, opportunities lost: The continuing costs of housing discrimination.* New York: Russell Sage Foundation.

Federal Government Housing Policies

Carol B. Roskey and Mary Sue Green

Carol B. (Meeks) Roskey is Professor and Mary Sue Green is a Graduate Student, Department of Human Development and Family Studies, Iowa State University, Ames, IA.

Although the U.S. government's interest in housing began in the late 1800s with concerns about poor living conditions, little action took place until the twentieth century. With the post-WWI housing shortage in 1918, the government became interested in housing again. But it was the 1930s' depression era that led to housing programs aimed at providing employment and stabilizing the banking industry. The U.S. Department of Housing and Urban Development (HUD) was created in 1965 to consolidate federal housing activities into a Cabinet level department.

This chapter reviews housing programs that were developed following the depression, with an emphasis on current programs. Programs are divided into five themes: (1) quality of housing, (2) homeownership, (3) renter assistance, (4) affordability, and (5) fair housing. Over the years, the goals of housing programs have changed to meet current political, social, and economic concerns. Government involvement in housing is dictated when private enterprise is unwilling or unable to meet shelter needs. Through time, homeownership has been viewed as a positive social good, and the quality of life flowing from housing and its environment has been seen as a necessity for occupants' health and safety.

THE HOUSING MARKET

In order to understand government's role in housing it is important to briefly review the economic model for housing markets, which serves as the basis for housing policy. Housing markets are constantly changing; prices determine who is eligible for homeownership. Economic theory assumes that the housing market is competitive, buyers and sellers are knowledgeable, products are all alike, and resources are mobile. However, housing is fixed, durable, and provides services such as warmth and comfort not only from the structure itself but also from the neighborhood's quality. Policy may lower housing prices to make them more affordable. Housing, although needed, accounts for a large share of the household budget; thus, the housing market varies considerably from the markets for other goods and from economic theoretical assumptions about markets.

Housing markets are local; there is no uniform national housing market. Each house, duplex, and apartment is different, even if only in its location, so federal housing policy must be general. The market area is affected by local economic conditions, population growth, housing demand, and price and availability of units.

The U.S. housing market has experienced an expansion over the past several years, spanning the mid-1990s into the 2000s (Joint Center for Housing Studies of Harvard University, 2000). This expansion was partially supported by underlying economic conditions, as housing inventories have been stable and inflation has been relatively low. In addition, improvements in mortgage lending over the past few years ensured that capital is available for homeownership. The mortgage market is fairly national today and not bound to any one community as in earlier times. Interest rates have been at record lows for current homebuyers. Refinancing is less costly for borrowers and has been streamlined, which further facilitates mortgage financing growth.

Low downpayment requirements, homeownership counseling, and lower borrowing costs have allowed more low-income households to buy homes. As affordability increases, demand for federal action declines. Renters, unlike homeowners, have not benefited during this time. The increase in homeownership and the rising cost of rent have halted the growth in renter households (Joint Center for Housing Studies of Harvard University, 2001). Likewise, low levels of apartment construction have kept supply and demand markets in balance; therefore, rental vacancy rates have not changed.

ROLE OF THE FEDERAL GOVERNMENT

Congress often establishes housing policies such as making homeownership more affordable. HUD then develops programs to meet the policies established. The federal government's extensive and complex role in housing deals with both the production and consumption sides of housing. Federal objectives for housing production include a strong and stable supply of housing and available mortgage money at an affordable cost, as well as economic support. Objectives for housing consumption include better quality and affordable housing, and assistance to at-risk groups such as the elderly, minorities, handicapped, or low- and moderate-income families. Quality and safety of the environment and neighborhood are also supported by housing programs. Accessibility to housing, meaning both physical accessibility and availability to all races and cultures, has also been added to housing policy in recent years. However, these priorities have changed over time and with the political parties in power.

Policy Tools

The government uses a variety of tools in its programs. A policy tool, described as a means that governments have to implement policies, can include regulations, subsidies, grants, and information. One often used tool, a subsidy, is a means of financial assistance. It may subsidize a variety of the housing components at varying stages. A subsidy changes the use of resources in the economy's private sector. For example, a program could subsidize developers for the production of housing, possibly through subsidized interest rates that would provide interest rates below market rates. It could subsidize mortgage loans for homebuyers through subsidized interest rates or low downpayment requirements. Another government tool consists of regulations that control or govern behavior. Government regulations that include zoning, building and housing codes, rent control, and labor and environmental regulations may determine the location, appearance, and level of safety of housing units. Another government tool is setting regulations that hope to improve the quality of housing by setting standards. Although housing units must meet these standards, a variety of strategies may be used to obtain a result.

THEME 1—QUALITY OF HOUSING

The 1949 Housing Act (Public Law 81-171) set the tone for U.S. housing policy with its famous statement "a decent home and a suitable living environment for every American family." The 1949 Housing Act was concerned with the structural quality of housing as well as its design, construction, and livability. The U.S. Census Bureau measures housing quality by such items as overcrowding and lack of plumbing. The American Housing Survey (AHS), conducted by the Census Bureau for HUD, defines quality in terms of adequacy based on physical problems in the housing unit (Table 6.1) (U.S. Department of Commerce, 2003).

Although housing quality has improved drastically since 1949, approximately 9.3 million households still live in overcrowded

Table 6.1   Housing Adequacy Based on Physical Problems

Problem	Severe Inadequacy	Moderate Inadequacy
Plumbing	Unavailability of flushing toilets, bathtub or shower, hot or cold piped water inside the structure	Flush toilets broken down for six hours or more at least three times during the past three months
Heating	Heating equipment that broke down last winter a minimum of three times for at least six hours, or being uncomfortably cold for 24 hours or more because of broken heating equipment	Primary heating equipment includes unvented gas, oil, or kerosene heaters
Electric	In the last 90 days, having three of the following: exposed wiring, a room with no working wall outlets and three blown fuses, tripped circuit breakers, or having no electricity at all	In the last 90 days, having three of the following: exposed wiring, a room with no working wall outlets and three blown fuses, tripped circuit breakers, or having no electricity at all
Upkeep	Water leaks from outside, plumbing leaks, holes in the floor, holes or open cracks in walls or ceilings, 8 × 11 inches of peeling or broken plaster, or signs of rats in the last 90 days (any five of the above)	Three or four of the problems listed under Severe Inadequacy
Kitchen	There is no sink, refrigerator, or cooking equipment for individual unit	There is no sink, refrigerator, or cooking equipment for individual unit
Hallways	Having all of the following problems: no working light fixtures, loose or missing steps, loose or missing railings, and no working elevator	Having three of the four following problems: no working light fixtures, loose or missing steps, loose or missing railings, and no working elevator

Source: (U.S. Census Bureau. (2003d). *American housing survey for the United States.* Retrieved June 27, 2005, from www.census.gov/hhes/www/housing/ahs/ahs01/appendixa.pdf)

units (more than one person per room) or units designated as physically inadequate (Table 6.1). About 3.7 million households face both (Joint Center for Housing Studies of Harvard University, 2003). Typically, quality is promoted through regulation. Several examples of regulations related to housing follow: the HUD Manufactured Housing Program, Minimum Property Standards, lead hazard control, Healthy Homes Initiative, and air quality. Rehabilitation and repair programs are direct means of improving housing quality.

HUD's Manufactured Housing Program

update ✳ Manufactured housing accounted for approximately one of every nine new single-family homes built in 2002, with nearly seven million units constructed since 1976. Manufactured housing, also referred to as mobile homes, represents a viable option for low- and moderate-income households. In 2003 an average manufactured home cost $34.00 per square foot compared to $73.07 per square foot for a site-built home (Manufactured Housing Institute, 2004). The Manufactured Housing Program (MHP), a national HUD program established in 1974 to protect the health and safety of manufactured homeowners, was necessary because standards varied by local communities even though manufactured homes could be transported to several communities from one production plant. The MHP standards have been applied to all manufactured homes produced after July 15, 1976. One goal of the MHP is reducing personal injuries and deaths of manufactured home residents. A second goal is reducing insurance costs and property damage resulting from accidents in and to manufactured homes, and a third goal is improving the quality and durability of manufactured homes (U.S. Department of Housing and Urban Development, 2003d, 2003e).

Through the MPH, the Secretary of HUD was required to develop a set of National Manufactured Home Construction and Safety Standards (MHCSS). All manufactured homes are inspected by an agency approved by HUD and each manufacturer has an approved quality control program for the production process. A HUD label is applied to each home section to indicate that the home meets the HUD Code (U.S. Department of Housing and Urban Development, 2001a).

Two issues currently under discussion are a manufactured housing dispute resolution program that allows the producer or retailer to settle disputes more easily and a manufactured housing installation program that contains standards, training, licensing, and inspection for individuals and firms that set up the homes on site (U.S. Department of Housing and Urban Development, 2003c, 2003d).

Minimum Property Standards

The Minimum Property Standards (MPS) establish certain minimum standards for buildings constructed under HUD housing programs, including new single-family homes, multi-family housing, and health care type facilities. Prior to the mid-1980s, different Minimum Property Standards governed the various structures. Currently, HUD accepts the model building codes as established by building and architectural professions and local building codes, instead of having a set of separate standards. In addition to the model building codes, HUD also requires a fulfillment of durability requirements, which include such items as the doors, windows, gutters, downspouts, painting, wall coverings, kitchen cabinets, and carpeting. The MPS includes minimum standards for these and other items to ensure that the value of an FHA-insured home is not reduced by the deterioration of these components (U.S. Department of Housing and Urban Development, 2003d).

Health and Safety

Since the early 1990s the federal government has enacted several programs to encourage healthy home environments. Environmental hazards in the home harm millions of household members every year, especially children. The Office of Lead Hazard Control (OLHC), created in December 1991, aimed to eliminate lead-based paint hazards and other house-related threats to children's health and safety in low-income privately owned homes. Lead poisoning can reduce IQ, cause learning disabilities, and impair hearing. Nearly one million of the nation's children under six years of age have blood lead levels high enough to impair the ability to think, concentrate, and learn (U.S. Department of Housing and Urban Development, 2002b). OLHC provides funds to state and local governments to develop cost-effective ways to reduce lead-based hazards.

The office also advises programs and field offices on other healthy home issues such as asthma, toxic mold, allergens, carbon monoxide, and other hazardous agents that may be found in the home environment. HUD estimated that 26 million fewer homes have lead-based paint in 2003 compared with 1990 (U.S. Department of Housing and Urban Development, 2003f). The Centers for Disease Control and Prevention reported that the average amount of lead in children's blood declined by 50 percent in that decade.

The Residential Lead-Based Paint Hazard Reduction Act of 1992 directed HUD and the Environmental Protection Agency (EPA) to require disclosure of known information on lead-based paint and lead-based paint hazards before the sale or lease of most housing built before 1978 (U.S. Department of Housing and Urban Development, 2003f). In 1978 lead-based paint was banned; therefore, the requirements only apply to housing built before then.

Public Law 105-276 requires that HUD "develop and implement a program of research and demonstration projects that would address multiple, housing-related problems affecting the health of children" (U.S. Department of Housing and Urban Development, 1999b, p. 9). This initiative called for a multi-action plan, rather than attacking one danger at a time. Implementation costs are lower for the multi-action plan. The initiative is nationwide and includes development of partnerships and interagency agreements with a wide variety of public and private organizations on all levels.

In 1999 Congress established the Healthy Home Initiative (HHI), administered by HUD's Office of Lead Hazard Control, to protect occupants from housing-related health and safety hazards. In September 1999 HUD (1999b) published a new regulation to protect young children from lead-based paint hazards in housing that is financially assisted by the federal government or being sold by the government. HUD estimated that about 2.8 million housing units would be affected in the first five years (U.S. Department of Housing and Urban Development, 2002c).

THEME 2—HOMEOWNERSHIP

Homeownership has always been highly valued in the United States. Although the earliest housing issues focused on quality, it was thought that promoting homeownership would increase pride in not only one's home but also one's community. Homeownership was viewed as a stabilizing force in a community since owner occupied homes were better cared for than homes owned by landlords and occupied by renters. Homeownership is believed to provide personal financial security, strengthen families and communities, and promote economic growth. Thus began the government's successful push to provide access to homeownership. In 1890 less than half of U.S. households owned their homes. Today, over two thirds of all households own their homes, as shown in Figure 6.1.

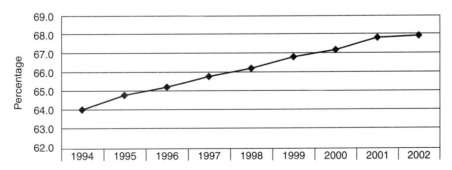

Figure 6.1   Increases in U.S. homeownership (*Source:* U.S. Census Bureau. (2002).
Housing vacancies and homeownership-annual 2002. Retrieved January 11, 2004, from
www.census.gov/hhes/www/housing/hvs/annual02/ann02t02.html)

14

Homeownership accounts for a large share of household wealth. Investments in buying homes amounted to $7.6 trillion in 2002, an increase of $405 billion from 2001. At the same time, households' stock portfolios lost $1.4 trillion in value. "In addition to its stabilizing role, home equity is more evenly distributed than stock wealth. . . . Home equity is an especially important source of wealth for those in the bottom fifth of the income distribution" (Joint Center for Housing Studies of Harvard University, 2003, pp. 6–7). One reason a wealth gap exists between whites and minorities is because minorities have lower homeownership rates (Joint Center for Housing Studies of Harvard University, 2003).

One of the more recent federal emphases has been the development of a National Homeownership Strategy to support homeownership (U.S. Department of Housing and Urban Development, 2005), which established a goal of 67.5 percent homeownership rate by the year 2000. This goal's achievement added an additional 8 million homeowners. By 2001 the rate of ownership was 67.8 percent and by 2002 it was 67.9 percent, which added another 1.1 million owners (Joint Center for Housing Studies of Harvard University, 2003). HUD developed several strategic themes including cutting the costs of homeownership, streamlining transaction costs, and opening and expanding opportunities in homeownership markets. For example, many prospective homebuyers have received counseling, and state and local governments have agreed on fast-track planning reviews for developers in order to speed up the building process.

Other factors contributing to the current growth in homeownership include historically low interest rates, increases in home values, changes in the mortgage finance system, and increasing household incomes. Although minority homeownership rates in the past few years have risen faster than those for whites, minority homeownership rates still fall behind those of whites with similar demographic characteristics such as age, income, and family composition, as shown in Figure 6.2.

In October 2002 President George W. Bush, in a White House Conference on Minority Ownership, pledged to reduce the homeownership gap between Hispanics, African Americans, and whites (U.S. Department of Housing and Urban Development, 2003g). As a result, he developed a Blueprint for the American Dream, which contains four key focus areas to increase minority ownership: "homeownership education and housing counseling; increasing the supply of affordable homes; giving families new options for upfront funds like the downpayment; and improving mortgage lending by increasing funds for affordable loans and redoubling efforts to root out illegal discrimination" (U.S. Department of Housing and Urban Development, 2003g).

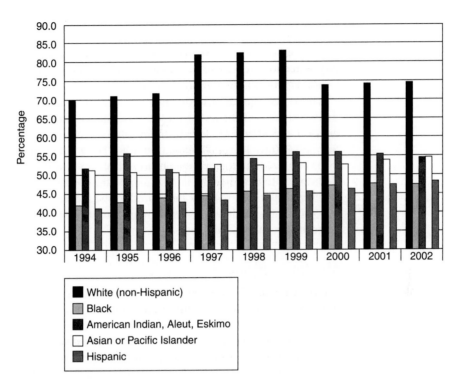

Figure 6.2   Homeownership rates by race of householder (*Source:* U.S. Census Bureau. (2002). Housing vacancies and homeownership-annual 2002. *Retrieved December 28, 2004, from* www.census.gov/hhes/www/housing/hvs/annual02/ann02t02.html)

Federal Tax Expenditures

The majority of federal government subsidies for U.S. housing are through tax expenditures. Tax expenditures are revenue losses attributable to provisions in the federal tax laws that allow special exclusions, exemptions, or deductions, or which provide a special credit, preferential tax rate, or deferred liability (Public Law 93-444). Tax expenditures for housing, which are subtracted from income before tax is paid to the federal government, include deductions from payment of federal income taxes for mortgage interest and property taxes, the deferral of capital gains (taxes on increased value of the house over the time of homeownership), the exclusion of capital gains on sales of the primary residence for homeowners over age 55, the exclusion of interest on state and local government bonds for housing, and the tax credit for construction or redevelopment of low-income housing. For 2003 these tax expenditures were estimated to total over $121.3 billion, with the largest expenditures for the mortgage interest deduction at $65.5 billion (Office of Management and Budget, 2003). This approach subsidizes homeownership to a much larger extent than any subsidy that exists in rental housing and may promote increased housing consumption.

These tax deductions currently favor the wealthy taxpayer and will do so even more in the future since the federal government increased the standard deduction in 2003 for married households from $7,850 to $9,500 (Public Law 108-27) (Internal Revenue Service, 2003). Many lower-income households will not have enough deductions to benefit from itemizing, and the mortgage interest paid and property taxes will not be related to the income taxes they will pay. More than half of the homeownership tax deduction benefits go to upper income groups.

Mortgage Finance

The use of mortgage assistance to support improved quality and quantity of housing purchased is a longstanding U.S. housing policy. Part of the 1931 White House Conference on Home Building and Homeownership recommendations included increasing the number of homeowners and strengthening the credit system for better protection of both homeowners and lending institutions. Mortgage assistance has taken a variety of forms including increasing access to mortgage funds by developing a national mortgage market, standardizing mortgage paperwork, subsidizing interest costs, and lowering downpayment requirements. In 2002 residential mortgage debt outstanding amounted to $6.97 trillion.

Loans

The government provides both loans and loan guarantees (in case homeowners do not repay their loans) through housing credit programs of the Departments of HUD, Agriculture (USDA), and Veterans Affairs (VA). In 2002 nearly 2 million households were supported by $200 billion in loan and loan guarantee commitments (Office of Management and Budget, 2003).

The Federal Housing Administration (FHA) operates one of the longest lived, most successful, and stable U.S. housing finance programs (Pennington–Cross & Yezer, 2000). FHA, which became part of HUD in 1965, provides mortgage insurance (a form of loan guarantee) for homebuyers who typically make small downpayments. Mortgage insurance will make the house payment in case the homeowner becomes disabled through injury. Although the federal government limits the value of housing that qualifies, there are no income requirements. Authorized in 1934 by the National Housing Act, FHA created the standard mortgage with which most U.S. homebuyers are familiar (Public Law No. 73-479). The standard mortgage has a set term and is fully paid off by the end of that term. In a balloon, short-term loan, you basically pay the interest monthly or yearly, with the entire balance due at the end of the loan period (Meeks, 1980).

In the 1940s FHA programs helped finance military housing as well as housing for returning WWII veterans and their families. From the 1950s to 1970s, FHA helped increase multi-family construction for the elderly, handicapped, and lower-income families by establishing special programs that targeted these groups. Today, the FHA focuses on assisting minority and first time homebuyers and provides mortgage insurance for manufactured housing loans, as well as site-built housing loans. In 2002, 79.5 percent of FHA loans went to first time homebuyers. Since 1934 FHA has insured almost 30 million mortgages and 38,000 multi-family mortgages representing 4.1 million multi-family units (U.S. Department of Housing and Urban Development, 2002a).

The Veterans Administration (VA) operates a loan guarantee program and provides direct loans when mortgage credit is not otherwise available. One group the VA offers special housing grants to is severely disabled veterans. A VA mortgage applicant is only eligible for assistance once in a lifetime and may not be required to make a downpayment.

The Rural Housing Service (RHS), called the Farmers Home Administration (FmHA) prior to 1994, operates rural non-farm as well as farm lending programs (Shadburn, 2003). RHS housing assistance includes support for mortgage loans to low- and very low-income borrowers, with interest rates as low as 1 percent. Very low-income homeowners can receive repair loans up to $15,000 and elderly homeowners can receive grants up to $5,000 for repairs, improvement, or removal of health and safety hazards. These funds can help make a home accessible for someone with disabilities (U.S. Department of Agriculture, 2003). The RHS is the lender of last resort, meaning that only borrowers who are unable to obtain financing from another source are eligible for RHS loans.

Secondary Mortgage Market

The financing activities and programs discussed previously apply to the primary mortgage market in which homebuyers interact with lenders to receive home financing. The secondary mortgage market in which lenders interact with the investment industry provides for the sales and purchases of mortgage loans from lenders, as well as the development of packages of loans for sale, as shown in the Fannie Mae example in Figure 6.3. The secondary market increases the funds available for housing, establishes a national mortgage market, and links local housing finance to broader capital mortgage markets.

Since the 1930s a strong secondary mortgage market has developed through the growth of two government-sponsored enterprises (GSEs): the Federal National Mortgage Association (Fannie Mae, FNMA) and the Federal Home Loan Mortgage Corporation (Freddie Mac, FHLMC). Both Fannie Mae and Freddie Mac, two of the world's largest financial institutions, are owned by investor-shareholders. The law requires that both entities purchase from local lenders a designated percentage of mortgages of low- and moderate-income homeowners, multifamily mortgages, and mortgages in underserved geographic locations such as central cities or rural areas.

As a policy tool, the government charters GSEs with special provisions that lower lending costs. Fannie Mae and Freddie Mac benefit in that the government attempts to protect holders of their obligations or Mortgage Backed Securities. However they are not guaranteed by the Federal government. The Congressional Budget Office has estimated that Fannie Mae and Freddie Mac activities reduce the interest rates that homebuyers pay (U.S. Department of Housing and Urban Development, 1996). In addition, both entities have helped standardize mortgage paperwork and increase innovation (use of technology) in the mortgage market. The federal government provides a line of credit to Fannie Mae and Freddie Mac, (specifically, the Secretary of the Treasury is authorized to purchase up to $2.25 billion of their debt if needed), exemption from registration with the Securities and Exchange Commission, and exemption from state and local income taxes (Federal National Mortgage Association, 2002).

A third secondary market entity is the Government National Mortgage Association (Ginnie Mae, GNMA), a wholly owned government corporation within HUD that supports mortgage market activities that cannot be economically carried out by the private market. Ginnie Mae facilitates secondary market activities for the FHA, VA, and RHS. However, Ginnie Mae does not issue, sell, or buy mortgage-backed securities, or purchase mortgage loans. It simply guarantees the timely payment of principal and interest from approved issuers like the Rural Housing Service (Government National Mortgage Association, 2003).

How Fannie Mae has provided $4 trillion to finance homes for over 45 million families since 1968.

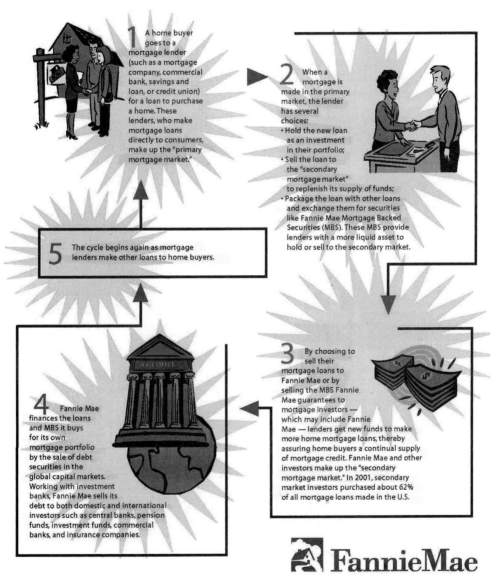

1 A home buyer goes to a mortgage lender (such as a mortgage company, commercial bank, savings and loan, or credit union) for a loan to purchase a home. These lenders, who make mortgage loans directly to consumers, make up the "primary mortgage market."

2 When a mortgage is made in the primary market, the lender has several choices:
• Hold the new loan as an investment in their portfolio;
• Sell the loan to the "secondary mortgage market" to replenish its supply of funds;
• Package the loan with other loans and exchange them for securities like Fannie Mae Mortgage Backed Securities (MBS). These MBS provide lenders with a more liquid asset to hold or sell to the secondary market.

5 The cycle begins again as mortgage lenders make other loans to home buyers.

3 By choosing to sell their mortgage loans to Fannie Mae or by selling the MBS Fannie Mae guarantees to mortgage investors — which may include Fannie Mae — lenders get new funds to make more home mortgage loans, thereby assuring home buyers a continual supply of mortgage credit. Fannie Mae and other investors make up the "secondary mortgage market." In 2001, secondary market investors purchased about 62% of all mortgage loans made in the U.S.

4 Fannie Mae finances the loans and MBS it buys for its own mortgage portfolio by the sale of debt securities in the global capital markets. Working with investment banks, Fannie Mae sells its debt to both domestic and international investors such as central banks, pension funds, investment funds, commercial banks, and insurance companies.

FannieMae

Figure 6.3 Secondary market flow chart (*Source:* Fannie Mae. (2003). Secondary mortgage market flow. Washington, DC: Fannie Mae)

THEME 3—RENTER ASSISTANCE

As previously noted, the high rate of homeownership is supported by tax expenditures. However, most housing assistance is targeted at rental housing. Three main types of rental assistance exist today: public housing (government owned housing units), project-based assistance (privately owned subsidized apartments), and tenant-based assistance (housing choice vouchers, also called Section 8 vouchers).

Public Housing

One of the earliest federal programs to provide low-income housing for families was part of the U.S. Housing Act of 1937 (Public Law 93-383). From its beginning as a jobs program in the 1930s, public housing developed into a major construction program and has continued to evolve over time (see example of the Chicago Housing Authority in Figure 6.4). Provisions are made to local public housing authorities through federal grants to assist with the development of housing for low-income households; currently 1.3 million households live in public housing (U.S. Department of Housing and Urban Development, 2000a, 2000b).

HUD, to determine eligibility for public housing, established income limits, which have changed over the years. Limits for households considered low income are set at 80 percent of the median income for the county or metropolitan area. Limits for very low-income households are set at 50 percent of the median income. In addition to an income requirement you must be elderly, a person with a disability or a family with children, and hold U.S. citizenship or eligible immigration status. However, housing authorities may deny admission to any applicant whose habits and practices may be detrimental to other residents or the property (such as using illegal drugs) (U.S. Department of Housing and Urban Development, 2000a). Preference may be given to households with the greatest housing needs.

As part of its legislative action in 1993 Congress authorized HOPE VI, Urban Revitalization Demonstration funding, aimed at rebuilding the most physically distressed public housing in the worst neighborhoods of the nation's largest cities. HOPE VI's goal was to eliminate dilapidated and dangerous structures, provide residents in these areas the opportunity to learn self-sufficiency skills, and increase community participation. Despite the progress made in replacing or repairing deteriorated units, the supply of public housing has continued to decline (Joint Center for Housing Studies of Harvard University, 2001). The waiting list nationwide is about 1 million, and in

Cabrini-Green High Rise on the North Side

The original Cabrini-Green development, built in 1942, consisted of low rises. But when the CHA extended the development in the 1950s it built a number of high rises, some as tall as 19 stories. As the years passed the project became synonymous with the widespread crime and violence that occurred there. As the surrounding neighborhood has gentrified, these high rises have become the focus of CHA demolition efforts.

The Robert Taylor Homes on the South Side

The Robert Taylor Homes comprise the largest public housing development in the United States. Originally consisting of 28 identical 16-story buildings, it was planned as a "city within a city," complete with businesses and schools. But this design, and the acres of land surrounding the project, only served to isolate its residents. And because it was built in the middle of a slum clearance site known as the "Black Belt," it almost guaranteed continued segregation of

Chicago's African Americans. At its peak Robert Taylor was home to 27,000 residents. Now many of the high rises have been torn down and their tenants relocated.

Westhaven Gardens, near the Henry Horner Homes

Orchard Park, near Cabrini-Green

Recognizing the inherent failure of warehousing hundreds of poor people in deteriorating high rises, the CHA is now constructing mixed income townhouses. The CHA hopes the redevelopment project at the Henry Horner Homes (left) will change the face of the entire development by reducing the density of the residents and ending their isolation from their surrounding community. The affordable townhouses near Cabrini-Green (right) are an example of the CHA actually building a new community for its tenants. The new development will include a town center, a commercial district with grocery and other shopping, new schools, a new police station, a community center, and a library. Some of the high rises have already been demolished, and residents have been relocated to the new townhouses.

Figure 6.4 Public housing in Chicago, Illinois (*Source:* Phoebe Hall; http://newmedia.medill.northwestern. edu/studentprojects/hall/projects/cha1.htm, retrieved January 31, 2005)

some areas households may be on the waiting list for 10 years or longer. In 2002 HUD modified its procedures to focus on smaller, more manageable grants to a wider range of public housing agencies (U.S. Department of Housing and Urban Development, 2000c). These programs are expected to improve success rates.

While the demand for publicly assisted housing may be high, federal funding for new public housing ceased in the 1994 fiscal year (U.S. Department of Housing and Urban Development, 2000d).

Rental Subsidies

In addition to the 1.3 million households in public housing, another 3.3 million households receive rental assistance. One subsidy type, known as project-based assistance, attaches rental assistance to specific units. The government provides funds directly to apartment owners who in return lower the rents for low-income tenants. Some apartments are designated for only the elderly or the disabled, and some are designated for families. A local public housing authority (PHA) can attach up to 20 percent of its rental assistance to specific units if the owner agrees to either rehabilitate or construct the units, or the owner agrees to set aside a share of units in an existing development. If a tenant moves from a project-based assisted unit, his or her assistance is terminated because the assistance remains with the unit.

In contrast, tenant-based assistance or housing choice vouchers are attached to the family, elderly person, or person with a disability, who can then choose and lease safe, decent, and affordable privately owned rental housing. Households assisted by this program, operated by the PHAs, must have income at or below 50 percent of the area median income (very low income). In addition, 75 percent of the households in any PHA's housing choice voucher program must be at or below 30 percent of the area median income. Households receiving a voucher are responsible for finding a unit with a reasonable rent as defined by the PHA which meets their needs and the housing quality standards evaluated by the PHA. The household is expected to pay at least 30 percent of its adjusted income for rent and utilities, and the PHA pays the remainder of the rent directly to the landlord. If the household moves, it may take the assistance with them to another unit (U.S. Department of Housing and Urban Development, 2001b).

A large unmet demand exists for affordable housing for very low-income households at 30 percent of area median income. Over 330,000 units of subsidized housing available to extremely low-income households were lost between 1991 and 1995 due to government funding cuts. Additionally, 65,000 households lost their federal direct subsidies for housing during the same time period (Joint Center for Housing Studies of Harvard University, 1999). This mismatch between demand and supply is expected to worsen. A robust economy alone will not solve the housing problems of families with limited incomes. Even families who work full-time for minimum wage find it difficult to afford decent quality housing in the private market (Joint Center for Housing Studies of Harvard University, 2001).

HUD planned to devote approximately 75 percent of its budget or $23 billion in 2004 for supporting the rental costs of low-income individuals and families (U.S. Department of Housing and Urban Development, 1999a). Currently, 3 million households live in housing that receives either tenant- or project-based assistance totaling close to $16 billion annually, making the project-based and tenant-based assistance (Section 8) the largest U.S. government program to provide housing assistance to low-income families (U.S. Department of Housing and Urban Development, 1999a). However, 9.7 million very low-income renters still need assistance, as shown in Figure 6.5. This need results in waiting lists for program assistance, many of which extend for several years before a household comes up for assistance consideration.

Other federal assistance programs have been targeted toward special groups. The HOPE IV program, established in 1993, is a government rental assistance initiative for very low-income, frail, elderly individuals who want to remain living independently. HOPE IV provides grants for Section 8 rental housing vouchers as well as for supportive services such as housekeeping, transportation, home-delivered meals, in-home health care, and counseling (U.S. Department of Housing and Urban Development, 2000c).

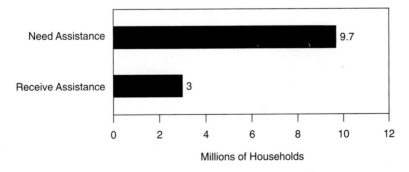

Figure 6.5   Rental assistance and need in millions of households (*Source:* U.S. Department of Housing and Urban Development. (1999a). Opting in: Renewing America's commitment to affordable housing)

The Family Unification Program, established in 1997, is meant to prevent family separation when the family is faced with a severe lack of housing. The program, funded through Section 8 voucher programs, targeted assistance for 16,000 families. A family may be entitled to Family Unification Program benefits if the child(ren) are in danger of being separated from the parent(s) and placed in out-of-home care because of a lack of adequate housing. For the purpose of this program, lack of adequate housing would be situations where the family is living in substandard housing or is in the process of being involuntarily displaced (U.S. Department of Housing and Urban Development, 2000b).

THEME 4—AFFORDABILITY

The definition of housing affordability has changed over time. Today, a household that spends more than 30 percent of its income for housing is said to have an affordability problem and is considered housing cost burdened. Households that spend more than 50 percent of their income for housing are said to have severe affordability problems and are considered severely housing cost burdened.

Housing affordability continues to remain a challenge for housing programs, as home prices and rents have risen faster than household incomes. Three in ten households have affordability problems (Joint Center for Housing Studies of Harvard University, 2003). More than 14.3 million households spend more than 50 percent of their incomes on housing and another 17.3 million spend between 30 percent and 50 percent of their incomes on housing, as shown in Figure 6.6.

Affordability problems remain for both homeowners and renters, particularly those in the lowest two quintiles of income (lowest 40 per-

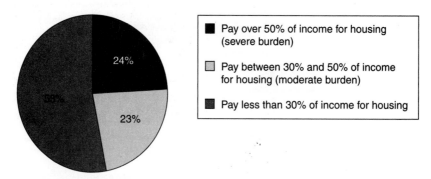

Figure 6.6 Subsidized renters' cost burden (*Source:* Joint Center for Housing Studies of Harvard University. (2003). State of the nation's housing: 2003)

cent). In 2001 and 2002, rising home prices were offset by lower mortgage interest rates. However, rising home prices have required more cash for downpayments, larger mortgages, or lower quality homes to be purchased than might otherwise have been the case (Joint Center for Housing Studies of Harvard University, 2003). In 2001 more than 7.3 million homeowners faced severe cost burdens, including 2.7 million who owned their homes free and clear. "This is the first time on record that homeowners have outnumbered renters with severe affordability problems" (Joint Center for Housing Studies of Harvard University, 2003, p. 25).

Since 1993 multi-family construction has barely kept up with the loss of rental units to demolition or destruction. New units are typically more expensive than the ones lost. Thus, typical renters spent about 26.9 percent of their incomes on housing in 2002 (Joint Center for Housing Studies of Harvard University, 2003). Four factors that negatively affect housing prices and rents include: (1) restrictions on the use of manufactured housing, (2) large lot developments, (3) infrastructure costs, and (4) land availability and regulations. Local community restrictions on the use of manufactured housing in developments and multi-family units limit the supply of low-cost housing. Figure 6.7 shows manufactured housing used successfully on a vacant lot in an existing neighborhood. Large lot developments

Manufactured housing used as in-fill housing in Wilkinsburg, PA, under the Urban Design Project sponsored by the Manufactured Housing Institute in conjunction with Susan Maxman and Partners.

WILKINSBURG, PA

Kelly & Mifflin Streets

2 or 3 Bedrooms
2 Baths
1447 sf

Figure 6.7 Manufactured housing in-fill project (*Source:* Manufactured Housing Institute; Photo from CD "Urban Design Project")

require a higher sales price than development with smaller lots. Infrastructure costs that are passed on to the developer save the community tax dollars, but increase the cost for the homebuyer or renter. Land availability and regulations restrict developers' choices and the lack of land increases demand, which therefore increases the cost of housing.

The cost of assisting all households with affordability problems exceeds the resources available. Even among subsidized renters, 24 percent have severe cost burdens in that they pay over 50 percent of their income for housing, and 23 percent have moderate cost burdens in that they pay between 30 percent and 50 percent of their income for housing (Joint Center for Housing Studies of Harvard University, 2003).

Homelessness

Homelessness is primarily caused by the lack of affordable housing, the limited availability of housing assistance, and the persistence of a low minimum wage. Psychological problems, lack of income, and an inability to deal with all of life's issues add to the causes of homelessness. The long waiting lists for housing assistance may force some individuals and families into homelessness, as shown in Figure 6.8. "Families with children are among the fastest growing segments of the homeless population" (National Low Income Housing Coalition, 2002, p. 1).

The Stewart B. McKinney Homeless Assistance Act (Public Law 100-77) is the only federal legislative response to homelessness. Prior to 1983 homelessness responses were primarily local. In 1983 a newly created federal task force on homelessness helped localities obtain surplus federal property. Advocates continued to push

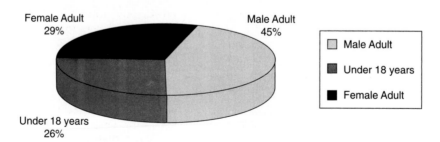

Figure 6.8   Homeless by sex and age (*Source:* Smith, A. C., & Smith, D. I. (2001). Emergency and transitional shelter population: 2000. U.S. Census Bureau, Census Special Reports, Series CENSR/01-2. Washington, DC: U.S. Government Printing Office)

for federal action, and in 1986 the Homeless Persons' Survival Act was introduced in Congress. Only a piece of this act survived in the Homeless Eligibility Clarification Act of 1986, which eliminated permanent address requirements and other barriers to existing programs such as Supplemental Security Income, Aid to Families with Dependent Children (now known as Temporary Assistance to Needy Families), Veterans Benefits, Food Stamps, and Medicaid. Also in 1986 the Homeless Housing Act created the Emergency Shelter Grant program and a transitional housing demonstration program (National Coalition for the Homeless, 1999). Congress passed legislation containing emergency relief provisions for food, shelter, mobile health care, and transitional housing in 1987 and renamed it the Stewart B. McKinney Homeless Assistance Act.

The McKinney Act has been amended four times, with each amendment expanding the scope and strength of the provisions in the original legislation. Modification of the distribution of funds and an expansion of eligible activities took place in 1988. The 1990 amendments added new programs to provide housing assistance to the homeless who have disabilities, mental illness, AIDS, and drug or alcohol addiction, and an outreach program was added for at-risk and homeless children. The 1990 amendments also required states to make grants to local educational agencies for the purpose of educating homeless children and youth. Title IV was expanded in 1992 to create low-cost shelter for persons who were unable or unwilling to participate in current supportive services. The Access to Community Care and Effective Services and Support (ACCESS) was created by the consolidation of mental health and alcohol and drug abuse treatment programs.

The most recent changes took place in 1994 and allowed local agencies to use closed military bases to assist homeless individuals. Amendments to the Education of Homeless Children and Youth program increased the flexibility of educational authorities, gave the parents of homeless children more power in choosing schools, and specified the rights of homeless preschoolers to a free and appropriate public preschool education. Educational authorities are now required to coordinate services with housing authorities (National Coalition for the Homeless, 1999).

Recently, a few McKinney Act programs have been repealed or restructured; in addition, funding has been declining. The McKinney Act's weakness is its reliance on emergency measures rather than dealing with root causes. Homelessness causes need to be addressed for it to end. The Bush Administration, however, has been targeting homeless assistance to those in chronic need, which accounts for only about 10 percent of all homeless persons.

Community Reinvestment Act

Additional legislation to address affordability included the Community Reinvestment Act (CRA) that was enacted by Congress in 1977 to encourage federally insured financial institutions to help meet the credit needs of the entire community in which they are chartered and conduct business. The act's main purpose is to revitalize and stabilize low- and moderate-income neighborhoods in order to attract businesses and increase retention of area residents. Institutions must keep track of the loans they make according to the geographic area. Also, local community groups often use the data from the institutions to determine if discriminatory patterns exist or if areas are being precluded from receiving loans.

THEME 5—FAIR HOUSING

A 40-year history exists of enacting legislation to prohibit housing discrimination. The Office of Fair Housing and Equal Opportunity (FHEO) enforces the Fair Housing Act and other civil rights laws to combat discrimination in the sale, rental, and financing of housing transactions and promotes equal housing opportunity without discrimination based on race, color, religion, sex, national origin, disability, or family status. Changes in the laws and regulations have taken place over time (U.S. Department of Housing and Urban Development, 2003a).

In the sale or rental of housing, the following are prohibited:

- denying or refusing to rent, negotiate, or sell housing;
- setting different terms, conditions, or privileges for the sale or rental of housing;
- falsely denying that housing is available; and
- denying access to or membership in a facility related to the sale or rental of housing (U.S. Department of Housing and Urban Development, 2003a).

In mortgage lending, the following actions based on the seven protected categories are prohibited:

- refusing to make a mortgage loan, provide information regarding loans, or purchase a loan;
- imposing different interest rates, points, or fees on a loan; and
- discriminating in appraising property.

When someone is exercising a fair housing right, it is illegal for anyone to threaten, coerce, intimidate, or interfere with that person.

It is also illegal to advertise a limitation or preference based on any discriminatory factor mentioned earlier. The landlord must make accommodations in rules, policies, practices, or services and necessary modifications to the dwelling or the common use areas in order for a person with disabilities to use the housing (U.S. Department of Housing and Urban Development, 2003a).

The Fair Housing Act covers most housing, but exempts three conditions: (1) owner occupied buildings with no more than four units, (2) single-family housing sold or rented without the use of a broker, and (3) housing operated by organizations and private clubs that limit occupancy to members. The Housing for Older Persons Act of 1995 (HOPA) also exempts properties restricted to those residents that are 55 years and older (U.S. Department of Housing and Urban Development, 2000c). These developments must have at least one household member who is 55 years of age or older living in 80 percent of their occupied units.

In addition to Congressional action, several Executive Orders are related to Fair Housing. An Executive Order is a "rule or order issued by an executive authority or regulatory agency of a government and having the force of law" (*Merriam-Webster's Collegiate Dictionary,* 2001). The Presidential Executive Orders regulating the Fair Housing Act focus on activities in which the federal government is involved through administration or ownership and operation of properties (U.S. Department of Housing and Urban Development, 2003b). Executive Order 12892 requires federal agencies to highlight fair housing in their programs and activities and created the President's Fair Housing Council. Other Executive Orders attempted to eliminate English proficiency as a barrier to program participation (Executive Order 13166) and improve the availability of community-based living arrangements for persons with disabilities (Executive Order 13217).

Home Mortgage Disclosure Act

Congress enacted the Home Mortgage Disclosure Act (HMDA) in 1975. During each calendar year, lending institutions must collect data regarding applications for home loans, home improvement loans, and home loan refinance. The data collected includes:

- identifying loan number and date of application,
- the type and purpose of loan,
- whether the loan application was approved or denied,
- the type of property,
- the amount of the loan,
- the date and type of action taken,

- the location of the property,
- the ethnicity, race, and sex of the applicant, and
- the gross annual income loan (Federal Financial Institutions Examination Council, 2003a).

These data are available to the public or advocacy groups, who use the data to identify any discriminatory lending patterns and to determine if institutions are meeting local housing needs. Lending institutions include banks, savings associations, credit unions, and other mortgage lending institutions (Federal Financial Institutions Examination Council, 2003b).

CONCLUSION

Housing policy is in a time of transition. Although the federal government continues to be the primary source of housing assistance to low-income households, state and local governments and nonprofit associations are currently playing a larger role in determining how federal funds are spent. The cost of housing makes it impossible to provide even minimal assistance to all who need assistance. Housing assistance vouchers are increasingly being used so that households might locate housing closer to job opportunities. Cost containment requirements at both the federal and state levels, however, are outweighing the needs of households.

U.S. housing policy will continue its primary focus on home-ownership through tax expenditures and mortgage market support (U.S. Department of Housing and Urban Development, 2005). Other strategies will include more partnerships with industry and local governments to reduce barriers to housing development like zoning and building codes. Housing counseling, higher FHA loan limits, and the creation of new Homeownership Zones to revitalize inner city neighborhoods are additional homeownership programs. Advocacy groups will continue to focus on whether discrimination exists in the lease, purchase, or mortgage markets.

The elderly have been defined as a special needs housing group. In the future as the number of elderly in the population rise, the government will focus more attention on programs to assist the elderly in affording and maintaining housing as well as services related to housing. Regulation of housing and housing development will continue and may even grow as communities seek to protect current residents.

In the short term particularly, low-income households will continue to have a difficult time finding housing they can afford in a location close to work and community services. U.S. policy is turning away from assisting those in need, whether it is housing need or income need. The philosophy of the government is aptly expressed by past HUD Secretary Cuomo, "The most powerful engine of economic growth in our nation is American business, and the most effective social program is a job" (U.S. Department of Housing and Urban Development, 1998, p. 1). Only the future will tell us whether this approach will provide the housing needed for all U.S. households and families.

REFERENCES

Federal Financial Institutions Examination Council. (2003a). *Home mortgage disclosure act: Regulation C.* Retrieved November 12, 2003, from www.ffiec.gov/hmda/RegC.htm.

Federal Financial Institutions Examination Council. (2003b). *Home mortgage disclosure act: Background & purpose.* Retrieved November 12, 2003, from www.ffiec.gov/hmda/history.htm.

Federal National Mortgage Association. (2002). *Annual information statement: 2002.* Retrieved November 19, 2003, from www.fanniemae.com/markets/debt/pfd/infostmtmar2002.pdf.

Government National Mortgage Association. (2003). *Ginnie Mae-Government National Mortgage Association GNMA.* Retrieved October 10, 2003, from www.investopedia.com/terms/g/ginniemae.asp.

Internal Revenue Service. (2003). *Tax law changes for individuals.* Retrieved October 7, 2003, from www.irs.gov/formspubs/article/0,,id+109876,00.html.

Joint Center for Housing Studies of Harvard University. (1999). *State of the nation's housing: 1999.* Cambridge, MA: Harvard University, Graduate School of Design, John F. Kennedy School of Government.

Joint Center for Housing Studies of Harvard University. (2000). *State of the nation's housing: 2000.* Cambridge, MA: Harvard University, Graduate School of Design, John F. Kennedy School of Government.

Joint Center for Housing Studies of Harvard University. (2001). *State of the nation's housing: 2001.* Cambridge, MA: Harvard University, Graduate School of Design, John F. Kennedy School of Government.

Joint Center for Housing Studies of Harvard University. (2003). *State of the nation's housing: 2003.* Cambridge, MA: Harvard University, Graduate School of Design, John F. Kennedy School of Government.

Manufactured Housing Institute. (2004). *Quick facts 2003–2004.* Arlington, VA: MHI.

Meeks, C. B. (1980). *Housing.* Englewood Cliffs, NJ: Prentice Hall.

Merriam-Webster's Collegiate Dictionary (10th ed.). (2001). Springfield, MA: Merriam-Webster, Incorporated.

National Coalition for the Homeless. (1999). *The McKinney act: NCH fact sheet #18.* Retrieved November 12, 2003, from www.nationalhomeless.org/mckinneyfacts.html.

National Low Income Housing Coalition. (2002). *Out of reach: Rental housing at what cost?* Retrieved November 11, 2003, from www.nlihc.org/index.html.

Office of Management and Budget. (2003). *Budget of the United States Government: Fiscal year 2004.* Washington, DC: U.S. Government Printing Office.

Pennington-Cross, A., & Yezer, A. (2000). The Federal Housing Administration in the new millennium. *Journal of Housing Research, 11*(2), 357–372.

Shadburn, J. (2003). *Congressional testimony.* Statement before the House Subcommittee on Government Management, Information and Technology Committee on Government Reform and Oversight, U.S.A. Retrieved October 7, 2003, from www.rurdev.usda.gov/rd/cong/1999/dcia.htm.

U.S. Department of Agriculture, Rural Housing Service. (2003). *Rural development online.* Retrieved October 29, 2003, from www.rurdev.usda.gov/rhs/sfh/indiv_sfh.htm.

U.S. Department of Commerce, Economics and Statistics Administration, U.S. Census Bureau. (2003). *The American Housing Survey.* Retrieved October 29, 2003, from www.census.gov/hhes/www/ahs.html.

U.S. Department of Housing and Urban Development. (1996, May). *Studies on privatizing Fannie Mae and Freddie Mac.* Washington, DC: U.S. Government Printing Office.

U.S. Department of Housing and Urban Development. (1998). *Cuomo says president's HUD budget seeks $1.8 billion increase to revitalize communities and create more jobs and housing* (HUD No. 93-32). Washington, DC: U.S. Government Printing Office.

U.S. Department of Housing and Urban Development. (1999a). *Opting in: Renewing America's commitment to affordable housing.* Retrieved November 3, 2003, from www.hud.gov/library/bookshelf18/pressrel/optingin.html.

U.S. Department of Housing and Urban Development. (1999b). *The healthy homes initiative: A preliminary plan.* Washington, DC: HUD.

U.S. Department of Housing and Urban Development. (2000a). *Family unification program.* Retrieved October 11, 2003, from www.hud.gov/progdesc/famuni8.html.

U.S. Department of Housing and Urban Development. (2000b). *Home investment partnership program (HOME).* Retrieved October 11, 2003, from www.hud.gov/progdesc/home1a.html.

U.S. Department of Housing and Urban Development. (2000c). *Hope for elderly independence (HOPE IV).* Retrieved October 11, 2003, from www.hud.gov/progdesc/hope4fin.html.

U.S. Department of Housing and Urban Development. (2000d). *Public housing development.* Retrieved October 11, 2003, from www.hud.gov/progdesc/pdev.cfm.

U.S. Department of Housing and Urban Development. (2001a). *Regulatory contact: What is HUD's role in the manufactured housing industry?* Retrieved October 23, 2003, from www.hud.gov/offices/hsg/sfh/mhs/prod04.cfm.

U.S. Department of Housing and Urban Development. (2001b). *Tenant based vouchers.* Retrieved November 11, 2003, from www.hud.gov/offices/pih/programs/hcv/tenant.cfm.

U.S. Department of Housing and Urban Development. (2002a). *About housing.* Retrieved October 23, 2003, from www.hud.gov/offices/hsg/hsgabout.cfm.

U.S. Department of Housing and Urban Development. (2002b). *Bush administration awards nearly $95 million to protect children and families from health and safety hazards in the home.* Retrieved November 19, 2003, from www.hud.gov/news/index.cfm.

U.S. Department of Housing and Urban Development. (2002c). *Rehab a home w/HUD's 203(k) rehab program.* Retrieved October 7, 2003, from www.hud.gov/offices/hsg/sfh/203k/203kabou.cfm.

U.S. Department of Housing and Urban Development. (2003a). *Fair housing—it's your right.* Retrieved November 12, 2003, from www.hud.gov/offices/fheo/FHLaws/yourrights.cfm.

U.S. Department of Housing and Urban Development. (2003b). *Fair housing laws and presidential executive orders.* Retrieved October 24, 2003, from www.hud.gov/offices/fheo/FHLaws/index.cfm.

U.S. Department of Housing and Urban Development. (2003c). Manufactured housing dispute resolution program: Advance notice of proposed rulemaking. *Federal Register, Part III, 68,* 11452–11454.

U.S. Department of Housing and Urban Development. (2003d). Manufactured housing installation program: Standards, training, licensing, and inspection: Advance notice of proposed rule making. *Federal Register, Part II, 68,* 11448–11449.

U.S. Department of Housing and Urban Development. (2003e). *Manufactured housing and standards.* Retrieved October 7, 2003, from www.hud.gov/offices/hsg/sfh/mhs/mhshome.cfm.

U.S. Department of Housing and Urban Development. (2003f). *The lead-based paint disclosure rule.* Retrieved October 23, 2003, from www.hud.gov/offices/lead/disclosurerule/index.cfm.

U.S. Department of Housing and Urban Development. (2003g, April 24). *White house conference on minority homeownership: Blueprint for the American dream.* Retrieved October 18, 2003, from www.hud.gov/initiatives/blueprint/index.cfm.

U.S. Department of Housing and Urban Development. (2005). *Bush administration announces record $1.4 billion to help hundreds of thousands of homeless individuals and families.* HUD News Release No. 05-007. Retrieved February 1, 2005, from www.hud.gov/news/release.cfm?content=pr05-007.cfm.

Interior Space Planning

Jean A. Memken and Starr Gobtop
Jean A. Memken is Associate Professor and Starr Gobtop is a Graduate
Student, Department of Family and Consumer Sciences, Illinois State
University, Normal, IL. Floor plans are by Jean A. Memken
and Starr Gobtop.

Interior space planning, a crucial aspect of the housing design process, was historically one of the more important housing topics taught to future professionals who worked with families and their housing. In their book *The House,* Agan and Luchsinger (1965) emphasized the importance of space planning in housing with the following statement:

> The house, whether it is designed to be built or chosen after having been built, should be arranged so as to facilitate these essential activities, foster harmonious family life, and minister to the privacy of the individuals living in it. It should fit the scale of living of the occupants. The criterion for judging the adequacy of the house is that the organization and provisions of space be such as to serve the functions of family life and the needs of each individual within the home. (pp. 75–76)

Successful housing evidences well-designed space planning and room arrangement, and thus enhances its occupants' quality of life. The philosophy of space planning has changed very little in the past four decades. However, because of the dramatic differences in family types and lifestyles that have come about in the last 20 years, fundamental space planning concepts are changing to accommodate contemporary lifestyles. According to architect and designer John Chrestia, "The first question that we ask a client is 'How do you want to live?' We have to consider the way we live in a space before we determine the space planning. . . ." (Lynch, 2003, p. 16).

In this chapter, you will learn how spaces within the housing unit accommodate the needs of a variety of household types and lifestyles. You will also learn how to apply space planning principles to create housing that provides an efficient living space as well as a supportive environment that contributes to overall quality of life.

CONCEPTUAL FRAMEWORKS

Two useful conceptual frameworks when considering space planning in the home come from White's (1986) work on space adjacency and Rapoport's (1987) ideas on the support of activities as a means of determining environmental quality. White (1986) perceived any design problem as an equation, and stated that the designer needs to examine the two sides of the space equation before creating a floor plan.

Figure 7.1 illustrates White's theoretical equation. One side is an analysis by which the problems, needs, floor plan, and opportunities to be capitalized upon are discovered and defined. The designer must work on this side of the equation to understand both the conditions (constraints and opportunities) imposed on the house or floor plan and its rooms, storage, and interior traffic. The other side of the equation features synthesis, where the designer/planner attempts to solve the problems, meet the needs, and capitalize upon the opportunities presented by the house and the individuals who will be living in it, using the decisions made about the space plan from the other side of the equation.

Housing is considered a dynamic process (Morris & Winter, 1978) rather than static; therefore, the needs of a young couple just starting their lives together will most likely be very different from those of an elderly couple who need accessible housing. However, a well-designed floor plan could satisfy some households for many years, perhaps even throughout an entire lifetime. As households change across the lifespan, so do their space requirements. Designers and consumers need to realize that a floor plan created for a present household will need to change as the household changes. Thus, flexible floor plans that are easily adapted to changing needs are

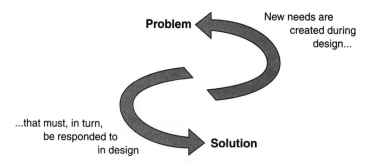

Figure 7.1 White's design equation as a theoretical basis for space planning (*Source:* Reprinted with permission by the Housing Education and Research Association.)

generally more desirable. Unfortunately, a floor plan design is rarely able to address every requirement of an individual household.

According to White (1986, p. 10), "analysis never really defines all the project requirements, and design synthesis never really solves all the problems or meets all the needs." In any floor plan or design there are always issues and requirements deemed more important than others. These concepts, when clearly identified and evaluated, constitute design priorities. Consequently, the true conceptual framework for a floor plan design is not really a linear equation but, rather, a cyclic one, as presented in Figure 7.2.

Rapoport (1987, p. 14) speculated that housing is a "system of settings in which particular systems of activities occur." Based on this definition, he theorized that housing quality can be described with a set of attributes, called an environmental quality profile, including the number and kinds of rooms and the configuration of those rooms into a floor plan. Because housing is culture-specific, one cannot assume that every householder will use spaces in the same way. This theory is especially important for U.S. designers, as most regions have an increasing multitude of ethnic backgrounds according to the U.S. Census Bureau. Rapoport (1987) believed that housing needs must be discovered and not assumed and that this

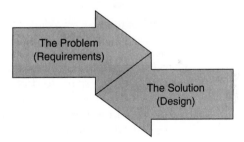

The problem includes the needs, issues, requirements, constraints, and opportunities of the individual for whom the floor plan is being designed.

The solution is the actual plan which responds to the needs, issues, requirements, constraints, and opportunities of the individuals residing in the home.

To understand and define the problem, we use our analysis tools (our minds, matrix diagrams, floor planning concepts, knowledge of client, and information sources)

To respond to the problem with a floor plan, we use our synthesis tools (design skills, creativity, planning, and insightfulness)

Figure 7.2 The cyclic relationship between the housing needs of the individual and the space planning solution that is implemented to address those needs (*Source:* Reprinted with permission by the Housing Education and Research Association)

discovery takes place as the designer considers the activity systems, lifestyles, and values of the household that will occupy the dwelling. Thorough client interviews and user-needs analyses become critical aspects of the predesign stage and thus the entire space planning process.

SPACE PLANNING CONCEPTS

Although many factors must be considered when selecting appropriate housing, the *floor plan*—the way the rooms are arranged and how the spaces within the house are used—is critical to the overall resultant satisfactions as well as dissatisfactions/dysfunctions of the residents as occupants experiencing the space over time. Floor plans can be evaluated in a number of ways. The following criteria, which are some of the most important issues to consider when evaluating the spaces and their arrangement within a home, apply to all housing forms, whether the residence is a manufactured home, townhouse, apartment, or single-family dwelling (Wedin, 1979).

Zoning

One of the first considerations in space planning is *zoning*. According to architects Cole and Prevost, home spaces should flow well from one another, but necessary separations between activities must exist (Lynch, 2003, p. 16). The three basic areas or interior zones within the home are:

1. The public zone, composed of spaces where non-family members are generally allowed.
2. The work zone, composed of areas where work activities that support the household's lifestyle take place.
3. The private zone, composed of rooms generally used exclusively by the household members for private activities.

Areas such as the foyer, the living room and dining room, and a powder room in larger homes are considered part of the public zone. In some households the public zone might also include the family room, the deck or enclosed porch, and the kitchen, depending on the household's lifestyle and the size and configuration of the rooms within the floor plan. If the household operates a home-based business that requires clients to come into the home for products and/or services, those rooms that house the business are part of the public zone.

The work zone includes the kitchen where food storage, preparation, serving, clean-up, and waste removal are priorities. Care of household clothing in the laundry space is a work zone function as well. Workspaces in the garage or other rooms could also be included. A home office or computer center might be considered part of the work zone depending on how that space is used.

Finally, the private zone of the house includes bedrooms and bathrooms. A den or family room might also be considered part of the private zone if the room is used exclusively by the family members (*House Planning Handbook,* 1988).

The interior zoning concept is based on three basic rules for a good floor plan. The first rule is that all three zones (public, work, and private) should be present in a floor plan. In the United States and most other countries, a residence would be considered substandard if one or more of the zones were not included in the floor plan. However, in a number of warm climates in Central America, Southeast Asia, the Middle East, Africa, and traditional Native American cultures, portions or all of the public and/or work zones are located in exterior spaces near to a hut, tent, cave, or other sleeping quarters.

Second, interior zones should not be split. Locating one bedroom on one side of the home while placing the rest of the bedrooms in the private zone on the other side of the home could maximize privacy in the one isolated bedroom, but it could also create a very confusing and unsuitable circulation pattern for many households. This is particularly important when young children are ill, when communication among teens and parents needs to be functional, and when aging occupants in poor health require assistance. There are exceptions to this rule, such as multigenerational families where two separate private areas may be warranted, or a couple that wants its bedroom separated from the guest bedrooms.

However, floor plans work best when work rooms are clustered together in one section of the house, public rooms and areas in another, and bedrooms and bathrooms in a third. In general, this principle provides for efficient traffic paths/circulation; convenient storage, technology, and other resources for tasks in the zone; effective communication among occupants; and other functions integral to a specific zone.

Rooms that might be considered part of more than one zone should be located between the two zones with which they are identified. For example, if a kitchen area is used for both work and entertaining, it should be located between the work and public zones. Likewise, a home office used to meet clients from the public should border both the work and public zones.

The third rule is that household members should not have to cross through the middle of one zone to get to another. Rooms need to be

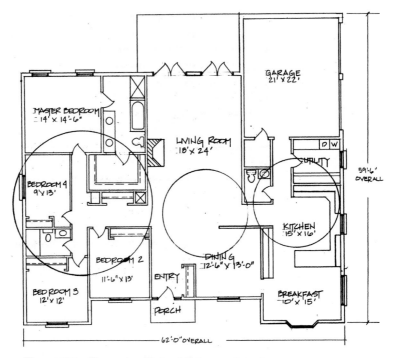

Figure 7.3   Floor plan that exhibits good zoning

arranged so that users can move from the work zone to the private zone without going directly through the middle of the public zone.

The floor plan in Figure 7.3 shows good zoning within the home. The home has been effectively divided into three separate zones: public, work, and private. By clustering all the similarly used rooms together, the space within the home is used efficiently and allows for a logical circulation pattern flow from one zone to the next without crossing the third. Because of the good zoning practices used in this home's design, little space in the floor plan is wasted for circulation, which is another cost effective aspect to consider when evaluating floor plans.

Circulation

Circulation paths within the housing unit should be as short and direct as possible (Kicklighter & Kicklighter, 1986). An efficient circulation pattern through the home utilizes minimal floor space, while long hallways and circulation paths that snake around, and sometimes through, rooms add significantly to the construction and operation costs (utilities, insurance, remodeling, cleaning, etc.) of the home

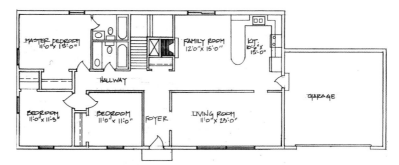

Figure 7.4　Functional circulation using a central hallway

without affording actual user-benefits or good, usable spaces. A central entryway and hallway often assist in the creation of a good circulation pattern in the home.

Zoning and circulation complement each other in house design. Usually, a floor plan that exhibits good zoning also will have excellent circulation, and vice versa. Figure 7.4 illustrates a floor plan with functional circulation. The central entryway in the home leads to a hallway that opens to each zone. The space devoted to this circulation path is only about 5 percent of the total square footage, an excellent circulation to usable space ratio. Moreover, it allows circulation from one zone to another without violating the third zone.

In addition to hallway placement, the designer must also think about the circulation within rooms. One trend in house design is open space planning where living, dining, and kitchen areas are all combined in one large area with no walls separating them. Therefore, the "rooms" within this open plan must accommodate circulation throughout the space as well as to the private zone without any separate hallways adjoining the rooms. A traffic pattern that cuts directly through a living room or family room is extremely undesirable.

Room entrances should be located so that traffic going through those rooms can move parallel to one wall. Furniture placement can help direct traffic flow in an open floor plan (Kilmer & Kilmer, 1992). Likewise, bedroom closets are best placed near the entryway to the bedroom, thus avoiding a circulation path that criss-crosses through the middle of the bedroom.

Figure 7.5 shows circulation paths through a home with open space planning. The advantages of open space design include:

1. reduced construction costs (fewer materials and labor costs);
2. reduced time for cleaning, maintenance, and upkeep of materials;

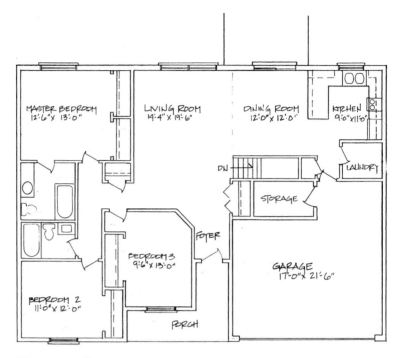

Figure 7.5   Open space plan

3. perception of larger spaces if partitions are omitted (fewer cubicles of space);
4. actual increase of space available (because wall thicknesses take up space);
5. flexibility of space use and furniture arrangement, and more potential for creativity and functions in space for special events, seasons, and stages of the life span; and
6. more effective transmission of air from heating and cooling ducts, and less pooling of cold and warm air in room.

Orientation

Orientation refers to the way a housing unit is situated on the lot. Often the home's orientation will affect the entire space plan's efficiency and arrangement. Figure 7.6 shows a single-family home site plan that features desirable orientation. Several aspects of orientation exist that should be considered when designing housing.

First, an east-west orientation is preferable to a north-south orientation in most U.S. locations. With an east-west orientation, which has the longer sides of the home facing north and south, windows

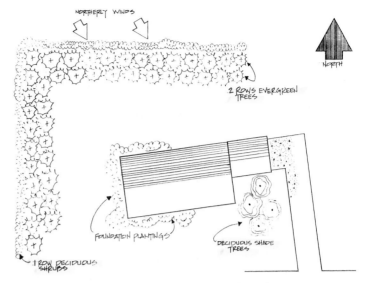

Figure 7.6 A house with advantageous orientation

can be placed on the home's south side to take advantage of the sun's position (low on the southern horizon) during the winter. These windows allow for passive solar heating during the winter months as well as natural lighting during the day. By putting few or no windows on the home's east and west sides, wintertime heat loss through glass (the surface with the highest heat transfer rate in the home) is minimized.

Also, summer's intense morning heat gain and light from the sun as it rises in the east and sets in the west can be avoided. The latter is a serious energy and cost of operation problem in that the early morning sun's heat is transmitted through the east windows prematurely (and to a lesser extent through east walls of the house), thus requiring cooling costs early in the day. Furthermore, afternoon sun directly heats west walls even hotter during the typically hottest part of the day although they are already warmed from calories of heat penetrating from exterior hot air throughout the day.

A second aspect of orientation is that windows should be positioned to take advantage of cross breezes, a sustainable behavior that can be employed instead of utilizing an air conditioner. Placing doors and windows so that prevailing summer winds can travel from one side of the home to another allows for natural cooling and ventilation, which is particularly helpful during the cooler evening hours.

Landscaping, a third important aspect of orientation, should be installed to act as a buffer to winter winds and as shade during the summer. Planting deciduous trees on the home's south side will provide shade for the south-facing windows in the summer, but will allow sunlight to penetrate through the windows during the winter. Coniferous trees and shrubs planted on the home's north and west sides can serve as a buffer for prevailing winter winds that come from the northwest in most parts of this country. In addition, the floor plan can be arranged so that the garage and utility areas are on the northwest corner of the home, further insulating the living spaces from cold winter winds and summer sun during afternoons (Kicklighter & Kicklighter, 1986). Figure 7.6 illustrates these three aspects of orientation.

A floor plan that incorporates many space planning concepts related to energy efficiency supports both environmental responsibility and household energy management, as shown in Figure 7.7. Rooms with heavier use are placed on the home's south side, while the garage and utility areas are on the north and west. In addition, closets and bathrooms serve as buffers to living areas, and the home features an airlock entry, a separate vestibule that keeps extreme cold or hot air from directly entering the home when the front door is opened.

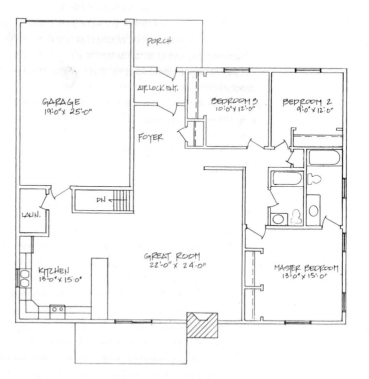

Figure 7.7 Floor plan supporting energy efficiency

Entryways

How a user enters and exits the home will have a direct impact on how the housing unit spaces should be arranged. Entryways should be easily accessible for household members and their guests, but they should also be secure and serve as a buffer between the exterior and the rest of the house. The following are some useful ideas for the design of home entrances.

A house's front entry should be somewhat separated from the remainder of the home's living areas. However, an entry closet near the front door to accommodate guests' coats is desirable (Wedin, 1979). Even a smaller townhouse apartment, like that shown in Figure 7.8, can have a separate entryway with storage for guests' and household members' coats, umbrellas, and other outerwear. In addition, a powder room for guests should be near the front entry and other public home areas. However, it should not be situated so that it is the first room a guest sees upon entering the home. An excellent design configuration for a public entryway into the home is evidenced in Figure 7.9.

The service entry, an additional entry to the residence, is oftentimes through an attached garage or on the side of the house nearest a detached garage. In many designs, this entrance is used most often by household members and others who provide home maintenance services. The service entry should be convenient to the kitchen so that household members can easily move groceries into their proper storage areas. It should also be convenient to the basement and garage for utility and repair service calls (Kicklighter & Kicklighter, 1986). In Figure 7.9, the garage opens into a utility/mud room that is close to the kitchen, which is an excellent configuration for the rooms adjacent to the service entrance.

The entryway to and from the back yard typically should be through the public zone. Having the only back door of the housing unit located in a master bedroom or through a kitchen work area can be disruptive to those family members seeking privacy in the bedroom or trying to work in the kitchen. However, the kitchen should have easy access to the back door so outdoor entertaining and dining can be easily accommodated (Allen, Jones, & Stimpson, 2004). Therefore, the position of the back entry should be convenient to both public and work areas. Figure 7.9 shows an excellent design configuration for a public entryway into the home.

A relatively new housing feature is having an entryway from the attached garage directly into the basement. This allows service professionals who work on plumbing or heating/cooling systems in the home direct access to the basement without entering any of the

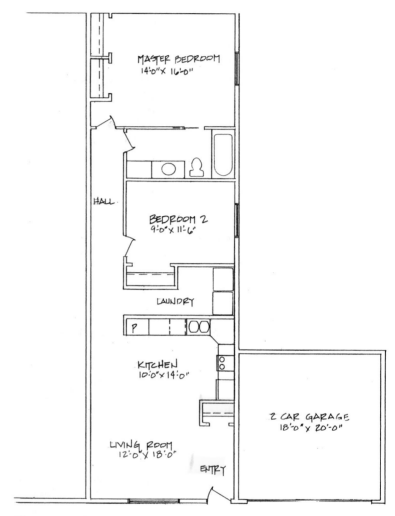

Figure 7.8 Entryway for a small townhouse

home's zones. If the garage door is kept open, it gives these skilled workers convenient access to where most of their work is done, and allows them to go into and out of the basement without having to enter the house from the front door (a possible home security benefit). A basement entry from the garage is also handy for family members who might have a basement work space, but need ready access to the garage where tools or other supplies might be stored. Children with basement play spaces also find a garage entry to the basement handy as they transition from playing indoors to outside.

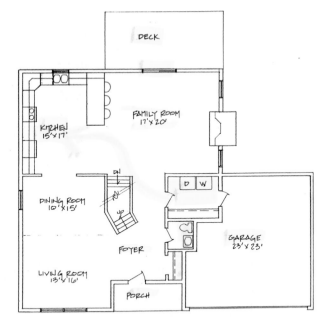

Figure 7.9a   Configuration for a public entryway [first floor]

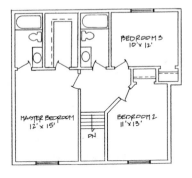

Figure 7.9b   Configuration for a public entryway [second floor]

Work Areas

The kitchen is often the home's primary work area. In recent years, the kitchen's design has changed a great deal to accommodate two or more cooks, an array of new household appliances, and a variety of activities that take place in this room in addition to meal preparation

(Building Research Council, 1993). There are four steps to planning an efficient kitchen.

The first step is to plan the kitchen location and arrangement so that it is a convenient work space and is easily accessible from the other home zones, as well as from the service entry. Second, decide on a kitchen configuration of the three basic work centers that include countertops, cabinet storage, appliances, and food preparation and clean-up resources. An effective work triangle will minimize traffic flow through the work area and provide adequate storage and work surfaces, but not include so much storage that the work triangle is inconveniently long and unnecessarily expensive.

Figure 7.10 shows four basic, modifiable kitchen configurations.

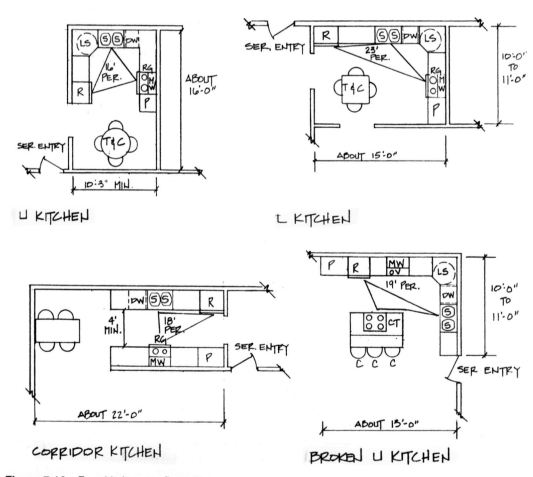

Figure 7.10 Four kitchen configurations

1. U-shaped
2. L-shaped
3. Corridor or two-wall
4. Broken U-shaped

The third step is to choose suitable space standards. Allow for adequate counter space for tasks and storage near major appliances and by the sink. Determine the unique needs of the kitchen space's users and plan the work areas in the kitchen accordingly. Finally, plan for efficient task operation in the kitchen. Locate the appliances, storage, and counters for convenience, safety, and other user needs. Evaluate the configuration in terms of efficiency and ease of maintenance (Building Research Council, 1993).

The efficiency of kitchen spaces is often evaluated by means of the work triangle, which is the circulation path that leads from the refrigerator to the sink and then to the range. Ideally, the work triangle perimeter should be no greater than 26 feet and no less than 12 feet (Cheever, 1996). A work triangle that is too large could indicate (1) excessive cabinet costs for the user, (2) a long traffic pattern, (3) inefficient work space with too much or wasted space between the parallel work centers, and (4) possibly too many doors to other rooms among the three basic work centers. A very small work triangle is an indication of inadequate counter and storage space with a likelihood of a crowded, overly compact kitchen.

Although the work triangle joins the three primary work centers in the kitchen—the food storage center, the food preparation center, and the cooking/baking center—two other centers have emerged in recent years that add to the kitchen's overall efficiency. The mixing center is a countertop at least 36 inches in length that can be used for a variety of cooking/baking activities (Cheever, 1996). Ideally, the mixing center should be located between the refrigerator and the sink, although it can be located anywhere in the kitchen that is convenient for the users.

The planning center, a more recent addition to the kitchen work area, includes a desk or writing surface where meals can be planned, bills paid, and correspondence written. Often, a computer and filing space is located in the planning center as well (*House Planning Handbook,* 1988). The planning center should not be included in the basic work triangle where spills would interfere with effective planning.

The laundry area has probably undergone the greatest number of changes since the turn of the century. What until recently has been delegated to a corner in the basement or garage (if, indeed, the home actually had laundry equipment) is now often a focal point in the home's work zone. A good placement of the laundry equipment is near the kitchen without actually being in the food preparation

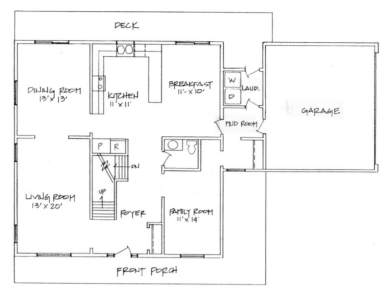

FIRST FLOOR

Figure 7.11a   Floor plan containing an efficiently located mud room [first floor]

area. This configuration facilitates work efficiency and the dovetailing of tasks without the risk of contaminating food preparation surfaces with soil from textiles to be laundered and the harmful chemicals found in laundry detergents, bleaches, and fabric softeners.

Laundry equipment and the water heater can be placed on a plumbing wall with the sink-dishwasher clean-up center placed on the backside of a plumbing wall or core for construction and energy operation efficiencies. The laundry equipment could then be placed in a small room between the service entry and the kitchen (a mud room as shown on Figure 7.11) or it could be located in a deep closet within the kitchen that is not too close to the actual food preparation area.

A recent housing trend is to locate the laundry area near the bedrooms where clean clothes are stored and most dirty clothing and linens originate, as shown in Figure 7.12. Having this work center in the private zone poses some advantages of storing laundered items and is suitable for some lifestyles. Having a laundry room near the bedrooms eliminates carrying baskets of clothing to and from the work zone to the private zone. Households that tend to do a load of laundry every day rather than just once or twice a week find this arrangement especially convenient. However, a disadvantage is the noise associated with the use of laundry equipment that could be considered disruptive in the private area. Laundry equipment and a water heater can be placed on or perpendicular to an adjacent

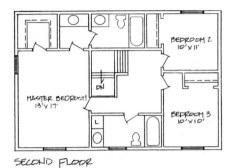

SECOND FLOOR

Figure 7.11b Floor plan containing an efficiently located mud room [second floor]

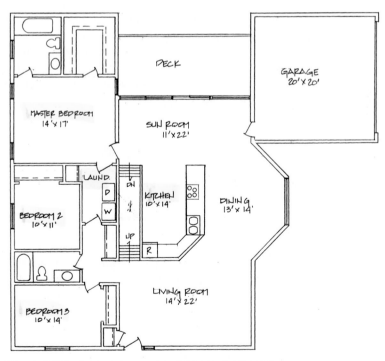

Figure 7.12 Laundry room located near bedrooms

plumbing wall for the bath to create a plumbing core for construction and energy operation efficiencies. A good option would be to locate the laundry area between the kitchen and bedrooms, if possible, so that it borders both the work and private areas.

Wherever the laundry area is located in the home, the most important consideration is that it be convenient for the user during normal routines. Today, the laundry room is not only a place where clothing and linens are laundered, but might also serve a variety of other activities such as ironing or sewing (Kilmer & Kilmer, 1992).

Storage

Storage space is an integral part of today's housing and should be effectively designed in every room. As previously mentioned, bedroom closets should be located near the bedroom entrance. Walk-in closets are popular features in modern floor plans; however, a large standard two-feet-deep wall closet can hold almost as many articles of clothing as a walk-in closet, and is considered a much more cost efficient use of space. More precisely, a $2' \times 6'$ closet provides 6' of rod length in 12 square feet of space while a $3' \times 6'$ walk-in closet also provides 6' rod length in 18 square feet.

Standard wall closets can also be situated to serve as sound buffers between the private zone and the other interior zones. For example, the closets have been arranged between the public and private zones in Figure 7.13. This arrangement could serve to filter noise from the home's public and work areas away from the private zone in order to respect household members trying to sleep or study in the private zone.

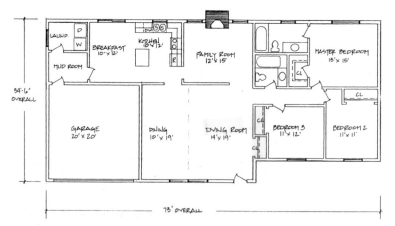

Figure 7.13   Closets arranged for buffering noise

Plumbing

In a multilevel home, plumbing should be concentrated by situating kitchens, laundry areas, and bathrooms next to each other or stacked above or below one another on various floors. In addition, these rooms need to be in close proximity to the water heater, often located below when there is a basement. Clustering rooms that contain plumbing requires less piping and transport of water throughout the housing unit, thus reducing water heating energy costs, wasted water when users flush and drain the hot water line of cold water that was once hot, and overall building costs (materials and labor). The house in Figure 7.14 provides a good example of centralized plumbing.

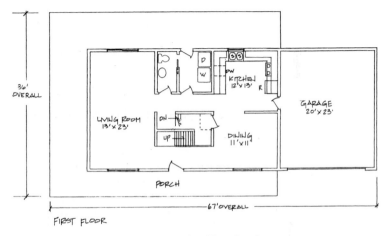

Figure 7.14a　Centralized plumbing [first floor]

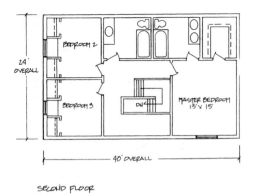

Figure 7.14b　Centralized plumbing [second floor]

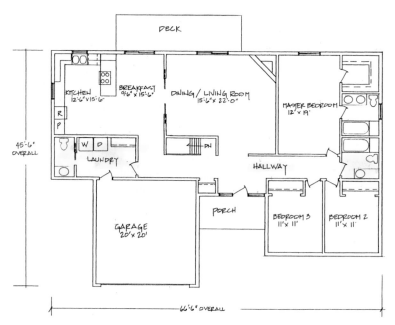

Figure 7.15   Placement of bedroom doors along a hallway

Privacy

In spite of today's more open floor plans, privacy is still a highly valued aspect of U.S. housing occupants. According to noted anthropologist Margaret Meade, privacy is the most variable of all human needs (Meade, 1979). In this country, our emphasis on the importance of the individual, as well as the need for autonomy, contribute to the desire for privacy. In addition, cultural norms still uphold the need for private spaces in the home to carry out selected activities. Almost all new housing construction today includes a private bath for the household head(s). A private den or study is much more prevalent in today's homes than in those built even 20 years ago. The great room concept where living rooms, family rooms, dining rooms, and sometimes even kitchens are combined into one space might have opened up the public and work areas of the home, but the private zone is still that—private.

The private zone needs to be secluded and be neither in direct sight nor sound transfer of the public area. Guests in the home should not be able to readily enter the private zone or even look into it. Often, the private zone includes a hallway that leads to each household member's bedroom and to the bathrooms. The entrance to a private bathroom or bedroom should not be situated at the end of that hallway. Because the hall is like a vista, the eye is automatically drawn to the end, and anyone visiting the home will quite likely gaze down to the end of the hallway. Therefore, it is a good idea to locate doors to private rooms along the sides of the halls so guests do not have a clear view of those rooms' interiors as seen in Figure 7.15.

CONCLUSION

Using a checklist like that shown in Table 7.1 to summarize the principles and information presented in this chapter can be valuable. Interior space planners and users can also use a checklist in the evaluation of floor plans. As previously mentioned, most floor plans do not meet all the criteria discussed in this chapter. However, a floor plan that includes most of these characteristics and accommodates the individual needs of the household should provide a functional plan that will provide a desirable living environment for the housing unit's residents.

Table 7.1   Floor Plan Evaluation Checklist

Floor Plan Evaluation Checklist	Yes	No
Zoning		
All zones present	____	____
Zones are split based on reason	____	____
Can move between zones without crossing a third zone	____	____
Circulation		
Position of front entry centralized	____	____
Short circulation paths	____	____
Dining room convenient to kitchen	____	____
Kitchen near garage or service entry	____	____
No room serving as a hallway	____	____
Organization of Space		
Front entryway set off from living area	____	____
Entry closet present	____	____

(Continued)

Table 7.1   (Continued)

Floor Plan Evaluation Checklist	Yes	No
Concentrated plumbing	____	____
Minimal hallway space	____	____
Laundry positioned conveniently	____	____
Closets positioned near bedroom doors	____	____
Storage space in each room	____	____
Kitchen work triangle undisturbed by traffic	____	____
All kitchen work centers present	____	____
Room sizes adequate for activities	____	____
Privacy		
Bath or bedroom not visible from public areas	____	____
Use of buffers in bedrooms	____	____

How well does this plan fit the household for which it was designed?

1. Poor
2. Acceptable
3. Fair
4. Good
5. Excellent

Total Score   (1 point for each *yes* plus the number
of the overall ranking)   _____

REFERENCES

Agan, T., & Luchsinger, E. (1965). *The house.* Philadelphia: J. B. Lippincott.

Allen, P. S., Jones, L. M., & Stimpson, M. F. (2004). *Beginnings of interior environments* (9th ed.). New York: Macmillan.

Building Research Council. (1993). *Kitchen planning standards.* Urbana, IL: University of Illinois College of Fine and Applied Arts.

Cheever, E. (1996). *Kitchen planning standards and safety criteria.* Hackstown, NJ: National Kitchen and Bath Association.

House Planning Handbook. (1988). Ames, IA: Midwest Plan Service, Iowa State University.

Kicklighter, C., & Kicklighter, J. C. (1986). *Residential housing and interiors.* South Holland, IL: Goodheart-Wilcox.

Kilmer, R., & Kilmer, W. O. (1992). *Designing interiors.* Orlando, FL: Harcourt, Brace, Javanovich.

Lynch, S. (2003). *77 habits of highly creative interior designers.* Gloucester, MA: Rockport.

Meade, M. (1979). Neighborhoods and human needs. In C. S. Wedin & L. G. Nygren (Eds.), *Housing perspectives.* Minneapolis, MN: Burgess.

Morris, E., & Winter, M. (1978). *Housing, family, and society.* New York: John Wiley and Sons.

Rapoport, A. (1987). Housing and culture. In L. Taylor (Ed.), *Housing: Symbol, structure, site.* New York: Cooper-Hewitt Museum.

Wedin, C. S. (1979). Floor plan evaluation. In C. S. Wedin & L. G. Nygren (Eds.), *Housing perspectives.* Minneapolis, MN: Burgess.

White, E. T. (1986). *Space adjacency analysis.* Tallahassee, FL: Architectural Media.

CHAPTER 8

Universal Design in Housing

Sandra C. Hartje, Kenneth R. Tremblay, Jr., and Craig Birdsong
Sandra C. Hartje is Associate Professor, Department of Family and
Consumer Sciences, Seattle Pacific University, Seattle, WA; Kenneth R.
Tremblay, Jr., and Craig Birdsong are Professors, Department of Design
and Merchandising, Colorado State University, Fort Collins, CO.

Universal design, which means good design for everyone, recognizes and accommodates the changes people experience over their lifespan, as shown in Figure 8.1. It seeks to design products and environments that are usable by all people, to the greatest extent possible, without the need for adaptation or specialized design (Mace, 1988). Universal design benefits people through all life stages including children, the elderly, and those inconvenienced at any time by a progressive condition or a temporary or permanent injury. Furthermore, universal design respects human diversity and promotes inclusion of all people in all life activities (Story, Mueller, & Mace, 1998).

To see the benefits of universal design, consider the following questions. Have you:

- been frustrated moving furniture into a house due to narrow doors and hallways?
- had difficulty opening a door while holding bags of groceries?
- had the flu and been too weak to climb stairs?
- observed a child struggling to see who is at the door because the peep hole was too high?
- been unable to invite a friend or family member to your home because its design did not accommodate him or her using a wheelchair?

If you answered yes to any of these questions, then you know that some design features limit the way people live. Houses can be designed to meet the needs of people at different ages, life cycle stages, and life circumstances through the incorporation of universal design.

Figure 8.1   Everyone can benefit from universal design *(Source:* Photodisc Collection/Photodisc Blue/Getty Images)

This chapter first addresses the importance of universal design in housing and traces its evolution, featuring a model that portrays similarities and differences among universal design and similar concepts. The principles of universal design are crucial to understand; thus, the discussion provides examples related to housing. We then consider universal design's benefits in housing: easy to use, convenient and safe, emotionally supportive, and facilitates full integration into the house's design. The chapter concludes with a discussion on the current status of universal design.

IMPORTANCE OF UNIVERSAL DESIGN IN HOUSING

The quality of our everyday lives is significantly affected by our housing, as shown in Figure 8.2. Not only do we spend a great deal of time in our homes, but they represent a major lifetime investment—

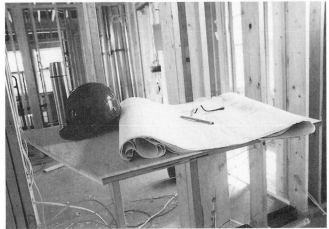

Figure 8.2 Older adults and children especially can benefit from universal design, whether it is in the form of a remodel or new home (*Source:* SW Productions/BrandXPictures/Getty Images. *Source:* Ryan McVay/PhotodiscGreen/Getty Images)

most likely, the largest single investment in a consumer product we will ever make. A house's lifespan can be over 100 years, and most people want to live in their homes as long as they can. Kochera (2002, p. 3) stated that "according to a 2000 AARP survey, more than 90% of persons age 65 and older would prefer to stay in their current residence as long as possible."

A home's architectural design features influence the quality of our lives and can either support or hinder our ability to live in our homes safely, comfortably, and conveniently. Traditionally designed homes—designed for an average person with average physical abilities such as a 20-year-old, nondisabled male—have been the norm for decades. Yet, no one is average throughout his or her life. Physical needs change as people age and move through the life cycle. Thus, most homes with built-in obstacles such as stairs and narrow doorways exclude people from visiting or living in them.

Although housing needs change over a person's lifetime, houses typically are neither designed nor built with the flexibility to adapt to residents' changing needs. Therefore, when a life event occurs such as an accident, disease, or condition that changes one's abilities, one must get by with current housing, modify the house to make it more supportive, or move. However, universal design features incorporated during the design phase and built in the original house will decrease or eliminate the need to extensively or expensively modify a home, get by with the features of the house currently lived in, or move at a later date to accommodate life changes.

Accessible, barrier-free, and *universal design* refer to housing or features in housing intended for people with disabilities and other special needs. Each term has a different meaning and purpose. While universal design encompasses accessible and barrier-free designs, accessible and barrier-free designs are not necessarily universal. Accessible generally means that the dwelling meets prescribed requirements for accessible housing; these vary widely and are often found in state, local, and model building codes as well as in agency regulations. Accessible features are often permanently fixed in place and noticeable. Accessible design requirements generally apply only to some types of buildings and are aimed at benefiting only some people, while universal design targets people of all ages, sizes, and abilities and is applied to all buildings, including housing. *Home modifications,* another frequently used term, refer to modifications made to existing dwellings for increased ease of use, safety, security, and independence. Sidebar 8.1 features home modifications for older adults.

Sidebar 8.1
Home Modifications for Older Adults

In our retirement years, most of us want to remain in our homes for as long as possible. We are familiar with the house and neighborhood, the interior and exterior reflect our personality, our furniture and accessories fit the home, and our home is a large part of our sense of independence. For those who decide to stay in their current homes, important questions to consider are:

- Will this house meet your needs in early and later retirement? Can you obtain in-home services such as delivered meals, home nursing, and housekeeping or take advantage of community services and government programs?
- Will you be able to handle the upkeep of the house and yard yourself or find someone to help?
- Is the home energy efficient or can energy-saving features be easily added?
- Is the home and surrounding neighborhood safe? What changes need to be made such as adding deadbolt locks, a door peep hole, exterior lighting, and smoke and carbon monoxide detectors?
- Does the home have a convenient physical layout for daily activities? Can major activities be clustered on one level of the home? Does it contain universal design features?
- Will the home remain affordable? Will you need to explore a home equity loan, a reverse equity mortgage, or renting out a portion of the home?

Additionally, individuals may want to consider home modifications, which are adaptations that can make your home more comfortable. Modifications may also make daily activities safer and easier. Depending on what changes are necessary, these modifications can be easy and essentially free, or relatively difficult and expensive. Fairly easy modifications include:

- Installing a distinguishing feature on the house front such as a mailbox or bright exterior color.
- Removing doormats or throw rugs, or securing them to the floor so they do not trip someone.
- Removing unnecessary furniture that reduces open space, especially low furniture such as coffee tables and footstools that someone may fall over.
- Making sure all furniture in the home is sturdy.
- Eliminating extension cords and keeping electrical cords out of the flow of traffic.
- Maintaining proper lighting. This is especially important to help those whose vision is reduced as they age.

(Continued)

Sidebar 8.1   Continued

- Keeping at least a 3 to 4 foot uncluttered path through each room.
- Placing the television in a location where it will not reflect a glare.
- Using contrasting colors to give important objects more visibility and cause them to stand out.
- Using devices that are low cost such as door knobs with levers that operate easily with a push, grab bars in the shower and by the toilet and tub, a handheld shower head with a flexible head, and adjustable rods in closets.

Numerous home modifications are more expensive. These should be considered carefully based on specific needs, and they include:

- Confining living quarters to one floor, or installing an electric chair or elevator.
- Changing the placement or content of kitchen and bathroom cabinets so you will not have to bend down to reach often-needed items. Add narrow shelves below upper cabinets for things that are used often so they can be accessed without reaching to a high shelf. Add a sink with motorized, adjustable height settings.
- Installing Lazy Susans, drawer dividers, storage organizers, sliding drawers, and shelves.
- Installing an intercom system, especially if someone in your home has limited mobility.
- Tinting windows, or installing awnings or window coverings, and installing more built-in lighting.
- Purchasing an electrically adjustable bed.
- Purchasing a stove with offset burners and front-mounted controls.
- Placing a heat-resistant surface on the counter adjacent to the stove.

In the long run it makes sense to design and build housing flexible enough to adapt to people's changing needs as they go through the normal stages of their lives. In the planning stage, builders and designers should bear in mind that they may not know who will eventually live in the home. The occupants' needs may change during the time they live in the property and if they move out, the next household is likely to have different needs. Therefore, a flexible approach to design appeals to a wider range of consumers.

EVOLUTION TO UNIVERSAL DESIGN

Universal design evolved from the changing demographics of age and disability, as well as the barrier-free design, assistive technology, and architectural accessibility movements, and also legislative activities in the late twentieth century.

Changing Demographics of Age and Disability

At the beginning of the twentieth century, older adults and people with disabilities were true minorities. The average human lifespan was only 47 years and people who received spinal cord injuries had only a 10 percent chance of survival. Most people with chronic conditions lived in nursing institutions (Story, Mueller, & Mace, 1998). In current times, science, medicine, and technology have succeeded in dramatically extending human lives. Never before have humans lived so long or survived illness and injury so much. In fact, the U.S. life expectancy in 2000 was 78 years, and 80 percent of people now live past 65 whereas only 1 out of 10 did throughout most of history. By 2010, 40 million people will be over 65; and by 2020 the Census Bureau estimates that 7 to 8 million people will be over age 85, while 214,000 will be over age 100. In contrast, only in 500 made it to age 100 at the end of World War II (Story, Mueller, & Mace, 1998).

In addition, more people are now living with disability. Two world wars created a large population of veterans with disabilities. Thanks to antibiotics and other medical advances, people are now able to survive accidents and illnesses which were previously fatal. Currently, 53.9 million Americans (20.6 percent of the population) are estimated to have some level of disability; 26 million have a severe disability. Among the population six years and over, 8.6 million people are estimated to have difficulty with one or more activities of daily living (ADLs), and 4.1 million need personal assistance of some kind.

The World Health Organization is moving toward a new classification system that emphasizes the functional status of all people. It assumes a continuum of relative degree of ability and acknowledges that many disabilities are not apparent but are based upon chronic health conditions that impact function such as arthritis, heart disease, and back problems. Ability is a dynamic contextual variable over time and circumstances. Even with general improvement in health status among elders, people are different physically, psychologically, and mentally as they age. These changing demographics of age and disability result in a population that is older and more disabled than many realize, and these trends will continue. The significant limitations imposed by products and environments designed and built without regard to the needs and rights of all American citizens are often unrecognized. Sidebar 8.2 highlights statistics regarding Americans with disabilities, based on the 2000 U.S. census.

12.

Sidebar 8.2

Americans with Disabilities, According to the Census Bureau's Public Information Office   49.7 million

Number of people age 5 and over in the civilian noninstitutionalized population with at least one disability. This is a ratio of nearly 1 in 5 U.S. residents, or 19 percent of the total population. Individuals are classified as having a disability if any of the following three conditions are true: (1) they are 5 years old and over and have a sensory, physical, mental, or self-care disability; (2) they are 16 years old and over and have difficulty going outside the home; or (3) they are 16 to 64 years old and have an employment disability. Forty-six percent of people with disabilities report more than one disability.
By age and sex:

- 7 percent of boys and 4 percent of girls ages 5 to 15 have disabilities.
- 20 percent of men and 18 percent of women ages 16 to 64 have disabilities.
- 43 percent of women and 40 percent of men 65 and over have disabilities.

9.3 million

The number of people age 5 and older with a sensory disability involving sight or hearing.

21.2 million

The number of people age 5 and older with a condition limiting basic physical activities, such as walking, climbing stairs, reaching, lifting, or carrying.

12.4 million

The number of people age 5 and older with a physical, mental, or emotional condition causing difficulty in learning, remembering, or concentrating.

6.8 million

Number of people age 5 and older with a physical, mental, or emotional condition causing difficulty in dressing, bathing, or getting around the home.

18.2 million

Number of people age 16 and older with a condition that makes it difficult to go outside the home to shop or visit a doctor.

21.3 million

Number of people ages 16 to 64 with a condition that affects their ability to work at a job or business.

Barrier-Free Design, Assistive Technology, Architectural Accessibility, and Supporting Legislation

Story, Mueller, and Mace (1998) explained that rehabilitation engineering and assistive technology emerged in the middle of the twentieth century. Universal design evolved out of the assistive technology, barrier-free design, and architectural accessibility movements of the 1950s. Efforts to improve prosthetics and orthotics intensified when thousands of disabled veterans returned from World War II in the 1940s. During the 1950s, the Veterans Administration and other federal organizations established engineering research centers to address technological problems of rehabilitation including communication, mobility, and transportation, and expanded these centers during the 1960s and 1970s. According to Story, Mueller, and Mace (1998, p. 10), "rehabilitation engineering became a specialty that applied scientific principles and engineering methodologies to these problems. The label *assistive technology* was applied to devices for personal use created specifically to enhance the physical, sensory, and cognitive abilities of people with disabilities and to help them function more independently in environments oblivious to their needs." They went on to state:

> Though coming from quite different histories and directions, the purpose of universal design and assistive technology is the same: to reduce the physical and attitudinal barriers between people with and without disabilities. Universal design strives to integrate people with disabilities into the mainstream and assistive technology attempts to meet the specific needs of individuals, but the two fields meet in the middle. In fact, the point at which they intersect is a gray zone in which products and environments are not clearly "universal" or "assistive," but have properties of each type of design. A number of products have enjoyed crossover success, often starting as assistive devices and becoming mainstream products, such as the kitchen utensils with thick grips popularized by Oxo International in the "Good Grips" line. A few products have moved the other way, typically conceived as high-tech devices for small markets that find new application in the rehabilitation arena, such as voice recognition software. (p. 11)

The 1950's barrier-free movement began a process of change in public policies and design practices. The movement was established in response to demands by disabled veterans and advocates for people with disabilities to create education and employment opportunities rather than institutionalized health care and maintenance. Physical environmental barriers were recognized as a significant hindrance to people with mobility limitations; barrier-free design helped remove those obstacles. In 1961 national standards were developed for *barrier-free* buildings. The American National Standards

Institute (ANSI) published the first accessibility standards, which were not enforceable until adopted by state or local legislative entities. A number of states responded by developing their own accessibility standards; by 1966, 30 states had passed accessibility legislation, and by 1973 that number increased to 49.

The Architectural Barriers Act of 1968 addressed the physical design of buildings and facilities used for employment and required all buildings designed, constructed, altered, or leased with federal funds to be made universally accessible. In addition, the civil rights movement of the 1960s and corresponding Civil Rights Act of 1968 inspired subsequent legislation to be passed in the 1970s, 1980s, and 1990s. Section 504 of the Rehabilitation Act of 1973, the first civil rights law for people with disabilities, made it illegal to discriminate on the basis of disability. This Act applied to federal agencies, public universities, federal contractors, and any other institution or activity receiving federal funds. By the 1970s legal standards used the term *accessible design*. These laws specified the responsibilities of designers, owners, and public agencies. However, almost exclusively, these accessible design requirements focused on the needs of people with mobility limitations and were applied to the built environment, but failed almost entirely to be applied to products.

The disability community became increasingly concerned about the evolving dichotomy of "us" versus "them," or "those" people, that rested on false assumptions that disability was a rare and static condition related largely to mobility and sensory limitations. They suggested that laws governing accessible design had reduced design to a set of minimum requirements. Although the laws offered invaluable protections, they had the unintended consequence of separating and stigmatizing the users. Advocates of both barrier-free and accessible design recognized that segregated accessible features were "special," often expensive, and usually unattractive.

Michael Bednar, an American architect, introduced the idea in the 1970s that removing environmental barriers enhanced functional capacity. He suggested that a broader, more universal concept beyond accessibility was needed (Bednar, 1977). The universal design movement emerged from the recognition that many features could be commonly provided and thereby rendered less expensive, but remain attractive and even marketable.

In 1987 a group of Irish designers succeeded in getting a resolution passed at the World Design Congress instructing designers everywhere to factor disability and aging into their work. In the United States, Ron Mace, an architect who had polio as a child and used a wheelchair and a ventilator, started using the term *universal design* and figuring out how to define it in relation to accessible design. Mace (1988) made the case that universal design was not a new science, a style, or unique in any way. It requires only an awareness of need and market and a commonsense approach to making everything we design and produce usable by everyone to the greatest extent possible. Mace realized that the term *universal* was not ideal because it could be interpreted to promise an impossible standard. No matter how committed the designer and how attentive to anticipating all users, there would always be a small number of people for whom an individual design just would not work. More accurately, universal design is a design approach in which designers strive to incorporate features that make each design more universally usable.

In 1988 the Fair Housing Amendments Act expanded the coverage of the Civil Rights Act of 1968 to include families with children and people with disabilities. The Act required accessible units in all new multi-family housing with four or more units, both public and private, not just those that received federal funds. The U.S. Department of Housing and Urban Development issued accessibility guidelines in 1991 to facilitate compliance.

In 1990 the Americans with Disabilities Act (ADA) awakened widespread public awareness of the civil rights of people with disabilities, and prohibited discrimination in employment, access to places of public accommodation, services, programs, public transportation, and telecommunications. Physical barriers that impede access must be removed wherever they exist. The ADA has a uniform nationwide mandate that ensures accessibility regardless of local attitudes.

Premises of Universal Design

The Adaptive Environments Center (2001) suggested that universal design is a way of conceptualizing design based on four premises. First, varying ability is not a special condition of the few but a common characteristic of being human. We change physically and intellectually throughout our lives. The old assumption about users that most fit within average norms, and a small and readily identifiable percentage have special needs, must no longer be used. Second, if a design works well for people with disabilities it works better for everyone. Third, usability and aesthetics are mutually compatible. And finally, at any point in our lives, personal self-esteem, identity, and well-being are deeply affected by our ability to function in our physical surroundings with a sense of comfort, independence, and control.

All people possess some level of ability. Design must accommodate these individual abilities with solutions that embrace every individual's needs. When a product cannot be used as intended, or

9

when a setting is hostile to a person's presence, it is the design's failure, not the individual's (Moore, 2001).

PRINCIPLES OF UNIVERSAL DESIGN

In the mid-1990s, the Center for Universal Design in collaboration with a consortium of universal design researchers and practitioners from across the United States developed the "principles of universal design," a set of seven principles created to guide a wide range of design disciplines. These seven principles may be applied to evaluate existing designs, guide the design process, and educate both designers and consumers about the characteristics of more usable products and environments. According to the Center, the principles of universal design address only universally usable design, while the practice of design involves more than consideration for usability. Designers must also incorporate other considerations such as economic, engineering, cultural, gender, and environmental concerns in their design processes. These principles offer designers guidance to better integrate features that meet the needs of as many users as possible.

The principles of universal design, presented in Figure 8.3, give the name of the principle as a concise and easily remembered statement

Principle One: Equitable Use
The design is useful and marketable to people with diverse abilities.

Principle Two: Flexibility in Use
The design accommodates a wide range of individual preferences and abilities.

Principle Three: Simple and Intuitive Use
Use of the design is easy to understand, regardless of the user's experience, knowledge, language skills, or current concentration level.

Principle Four: Perceptible Information
The design communicates necessary information effectively to the user, regardless of ambient conditions or the user's sensory abilities.

Principle Five: Tolerance for Error
The design minimizes hazards and the adverse consequences of accidental or unintended actions.

Principle Six: Low Physical Effort
The design can be used efficiently and comfortably and with a minimum of fatigue.

Principle Seven: Size and Space for Approach and Use
Appropriate size and space is provided for approach, reach, manipulation, and use regardless of user's body size, posture, or mobility.

Figure 8.3   Principles of universal design (*Source:* Center for Universal Design, Raleigh, NC)

of the principle's key concept and a definition of the principle as a brief description of the principle's primary directive for design. Two additional principles currently under review for potential inclusion are affordability and sustainability.

PRINCIPLES OF UNIVERSAL DESIGN APPLIED TO HOUSING

The principles of universal design apply to the design of products and environments, including housing. Examples of how the principles of universal design are applied to housing design features and products are provided in the following text. Many of the examples represent more than one principle.

Principle One: Equitable Use

The design is useful and marketable to any group of users, provides the same means of use for all users, avoids segregating or stigmatizing any users, and makes the design appealing to all users. Multiple height countertops, non-slip cutting surfaces, and wider interior doorways are examples of this principle in housing.

Principle Two: Flexibility in Use

A flexible approach to design means it will be more desirable to a wider range of consumers. The design accommodates a wide range of individual preferences and abilities, provides choice in methods of use, accommodates right- or left-handed access and use, facilitates the user's accuracy and precision, and is adaptable to the user's pace. Pull-out pantries and drawers, railings down both sides of the stairs, and a curbless shower are examples of this housing principle. An excellent example is an adjustable height, movable handheld shower head or 60″–72″ flexible hose that allows easy use by people of all heights. The shower head can be adjusted to the user's height; helps avoid getting hair, bandages, and casts wet; and can be used for back massage and rinsing hair.

Principle Three: Simple and Intuitive Use

The design is easy to understand regardless of the user's experience, knowledge, language skills, or current concentration level. The design eliminates unnecessary complexity, is consistent with user expectations and intuition, and accommodates a wide range of literacy and language skills. Housing design features that promote safety include stepless entrance and offset water controls in the shower and tub. Offset controls allow for easy access from outside the tub/shower, which reduces reaching and bending, without inconvenience when inside.

Principle Four: Perceptible Information

The design communicates necessary information effectively to the user regardless of ambient conditions or the user's sensory abilities. A housing example of this principle would be the use of a large dial on a thermostat or telephone.

Principle Five: Tolerance for Error

The design minimizes hazards and the adverse consequences of accidental or unintended actions. This means that the design arranges elements to minimize hazards and errors, provides warnings of hazards and errors, and provides fail-safe features. A housing example would be a crank or power-operated counter system. Lever handles can also be texturized to communicate to those with low vision that the door should not be opened.

Principle Six: Low Physical Effort

The design can be used efficiently and comfortably and with a minimum of fatigue. This means that the design allows users to maintain a neutral body position, uses reasonable operating forces, minimizes repetitive actions, and minimizes sustained physical effort. Housing design features that support comfort include the following.

- Lever door handles or loop handle pulls on drawers and cabinets that make it easier to operate with an elbow or knee if the hands are full and require little or no strength or twisting.
- Light switches at 44"–48" high, and thermostats 48" above the floor, that make it easier to reach with hands full (for example, with an elbow) and are more accessible to children.
- Electrical outlets placed at 18" minimum height that are easy to reach without bending and from a seated position. Users are also less likely to unplug appliances by pulling on the cord.
- Removable cabinet fronts at sink with insulated pipes improve access to these areas.
- Varied height counters that reduce bending and back strain.
- Front-loading washer and dryer with front controls that reduce the need to bend, stoop, or lean over to reach clothes.

Principle Seven: Size and Space for Approach and Use

The appropriate size and space are provided for approach, reach, manipulation, and use regardless of the user's body size, posture, or mobility. This means that a clear line of sight is provided to important elements, the reach to all components is comfortable for any user, the design accommodates variations in hand and grip size, and adequate space is provided. Examples of this principle include an entry door of 36″ minimum width, interior doors of 32″ clearance, and hallway width of a minimum 42″. Figure 8.4 shows applications of universal design principles.

UNIVERSAL DESIGN FEATURES AND PRODUCTS IN HOUSING

Universal design features and products are often presented by the room or space in which they are found and in the categories of structural or nonstructural elements. Structural elements are incorporated in new construction or major remodels. This is important because structural design elements are most cost effectively incorporated in the design phase of new construction. Nonstructural features are incorporated into a finished home. Lists of universal design features and products, available to housing consumers and professionals from the Center for Universal Design at North Carolina State University and from other organizations, include elements, features, ideas, and concepts that contribute to or can be components of universal design, and are intended as a guide. The features presented are those one might look for in universal housing, but not all features are expected to be included in any given home.

Also available for consumer use are guidelines and technical information for specific applications such as bathrooms, laundry rooms, and kitchens. The more universal design features or elements included in a home, the more usable the house is. Currently, there is not a single resource prioritizing design features, products, and materials in housing. A document entitled *Universal Design in Housing* (Center for Universal Design, 2003) provides the information presented in Figures 8.5 through 8.7. These are followed by a series of photographs, as shown in Figure 8.8 showing universally designed housing features, and a universally designed floor plan, as shown in Figure 8.9.

ч

Figure 8.4 Sketches of the universal design principles applied in housing (*Source:* Illustrated by Ying Ka)

(Continued)

Figure 8.4 *Continued*

BENEFITS OF UNIVERSAL DESIGN IN HOUSING

Universal design is not a particular house type or style. It is an approach to designing and building homes using a range of attitudinal, design, and construction refinements to create living spaces that benefit everyone now, yet are flexible enough to be adapted to specific needs as time and circumstance change people's lives. From the outside, a universally designed house will look the same as a traditionally designed house, and on the inside, many of the features and products are primarily seamless. Incorporating universal design features and products during the design and construction phase of housing results in easy-to-use, flexible, and safe housing that is emotionally supportive, integrated in design, and cost effective.

Easy to Use, Convenient, and Safe

Individuals who experience difficulty using their hands often find it difficult to do something as simple as turning the water on and off. Lever handles on faucets, an effective design solution as they can be operated with a closed fist, are readily available at home improvement centers and easily installed. Door handles also are available in a similar shape and have the added advantage of allowing one to open a door with an elbow or arm when the hands are full.

Feature	S* OR NS	Benefit(s)
1. Stepless entrances from exterior to interior • It is best to make all entrances stepless. More than one stepless entrance is preferred At least one stepless entrance is essential; if only one, do not place it through a garage or from a patio or raised deck.	S	Easier to move furniture and appliances in and out, to bring in groceries and packages, and to clear snow, ice, and leaves. Great for baby strollers and bicycles. Safer in wet or icy conditions. Easier than steps to repair and maintain.
2. Other entrance features:		
• One-half inch maximum rise at entrance and thresholds.	S	Reduces tripping hazards. Dollies hand-trucks move over easily.
• Minimum 5′ × 5′ level clear space inside and outside entry door.	S	Allows for maneuvering while opening or closing door.
• Weather protection such as a porch, stoop with a roof, awning, long roof overhang, and/or carport.	S	Provides sheltered space for people while unlocking the door, waiting for a carpool, making deliveries, and so forth.
• Built-in shelf, bench, or table with knee space below located outside the door.	NS	Provides a place to put packages while opening doors.
• Full-length sidelights, windows in doors, and/or windows nearby.	S	Allows all residents, including children and people using wheel chairs, to see who is at the door before opening it.
• Lighted doorbell at reachable height, intercom with portable telephone link, and/or hardwired intercom.	NS	Allows visitors to communicate with residents.
• Light outside entry door and motion detector controlled lights.	NS	Provides view of approaching visitors. Adds general illumination and sense of security. Illuminates lockset. Eliminates dark approaches to the home.
• House numbers should be large, high contrast, located in a prominent place.	NS	Easy for friends and emergency personnel to locate residence.

* S = Structural   NS = Nonstructural

Figure 8.5 Universal design features at entrances (*Source:* Center for Universal Design, Raleigh, NC)

Feature	S OR NS	Benefit(s)
Interior Circulation		
• An open floor plan design.	S	Minimizes hallways and doorways and maximizes sight lines.
• At least one bedroom and accessible bathroom located on an accessible ground floor entry level (same level as kitchen, living room, etc.).	S	
• Clear door opening width (32″ minimum, 34″–36″ wide doors), for all doorways.	S	Improves circulation, especially with many visitors, such as at parties. Also reduces damage to door jambs when moving large furniture or appliances, equipment, and ladders.
• Flush thresholds at all doorways.	S	Provides space to move out of the way of the door swing when pulling it open.
• Clear floor place (18″ minimum) beside door at pull side at latch jamb.		
• Circulation route 42″ minimum width.	S	Provides maneuvering room in the hallways and archways.
• Turning space in all rooms (5′ diameter).	S	
Vertical Circulation		
• All stairs should be appropriate width and have space at the bottom for later installation of a platform lift, if needed.	S	Easy access between floors.
If a two-story dwelling:		
• At least one set of stacked closets, pantries, or storage spaces with knock-out floor.	S	Becomes shaft for later elevator installation—at a great cost savings.
Or		
• A residential elevator with minimum 3′ × 4′ clear floor area installed at the time of initial construction.	S	
• Stair handrails to extend horizontally beyond top and bottom risers.	S	Steadies users at top and bottom of stairs.

Figure 8.6 Universal design features for circulation (*Source:* Center for Universal Design, Raleigh, NC)

Feature	S OR NS	Benefit(s)
Interior Circulation		
• Space between face of cabinets and cabinets and walls should be 48″ minimum.	S	
• Clear knee space (minimum 29″ high) under sink (must have pipe protection), counters, and cooktops. May be open knee space or achieved by means of removable base cabinets or fold-back or self-storing doors.	NS	Provides pen storage space for serving cart, trash can, recycle bins, and so forth. Permits sitting in a stool to work at the sink or cooktop.
• Variable height (28″–42″) work surfaces . such as countertops, sinks, and/or cooktops. May be mechanically adjustable in 2″ increments or be electrically powered through a continuous range.	S	Allows tall people to work without excessive bending by bringing work closer to user. More usable to children and shorter adults, so the whole family can help with meal preparation. Allows person to work while seated. Provides built-in desk in kitchen.
• Contrasting color border treatment on countertops.	NS	Makes it easier to detect the edge of counters and reduces likelihood of spills. Makes it easier to repair damaged edges without matching entire countertop.
• Stretches of continuous countertops, particularly between refrigerator, sink, and stove top.	S	Allows sliding of heavy items and easy, one-level food flow.
• Adjustable height shelves in wall cabinets.	NS	
• Full-extension, pull-out drawers, shelves, and racks in base cabinets.	NS	Easy reach to all storage space. Easier to maneuver large items in and out of cabinets.
• Full height pantry storage with easy access pull-out and/or adjustable height shelves.	S	Makes storage at all heights reachable. Provides maximum storage capacity.
• Front-mounted controls on all appliances.	NS	Facilitates easy reach. Eliminates dangerous reaching over hot burners, reducing the chance of burns and spills.
• Single-lever water controls at all plumbing fixtures and faucets.	NS	Easy to adjust water temperature and volume. Can operate with a single hand or elbow. Single-lever controls with fewer parts are less costly to repair, maintain, and clean.

Figure 8.7   Universal design features for kitchens (*Source:* Center for Universal Design, Raleigh NC)

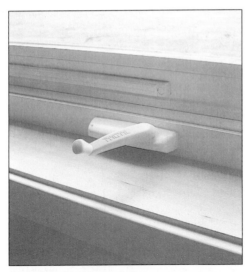

Crank hardware on window. (*Source: Photo courtesy of ADAptations Inc.®; Bellevue, WA*)

Lever hardware on doors. (*Source: Center for Universal Design; Raleigh, NC*)

Easy touch rocker switch, mounted 44″–48″ from floor. (*Source: Photograph courtesy of Experience Universal Design; Arlington, WA*)

Toilet paper holder for ease of use. (*Source: Photo courtesy of ADAptations Inc.®; Bellevue, WA*)

Figure 8.8   Photographs illustrating universally designed features in housing

Single-lever faucet, adjustable mirror hung over wall, lavatory, and electrical outlets 18″–24″ for easy reach. (*Source: Photograph courtesy of Experience Universal Design; Arlington, WA*)

Opening window latch using a closed fist. (*Source: Photograph courtesy of Experience Universal Design; Arlington, WA*)

Window for viewing the outdoors at 36″ maximum sill height. Seating accommodates multiple users including someone using mobility equipment. (*Source: Photograph courtesy of Experience Universal Design; Arlington, WA*)

Figure 8.8   Continued

Exterior front entrance. House numbers are large, high contrast, and located in a prominent place; covered porch provides weather protection while unlocking and opening door; level, clear space outside entry door; good general illumination; stepless entrance (threshold less than 1/2″) for ease of access; door is 42″ wide; side-light window; and illuminated doorbell and intercom at reachable height of 40″–44″. (*Source: Photo courtesy of ADAptations Inc.®; Bellevue, WA; same house as shown in floor plan*)

Interior front entrance. Clear floor space beside door on pull-side provides space to move out of door swing; side-light window (partial height at client's request); 5′ × 5′ level clear space inside and outside door; and lever door handle and loop pull hardware on closet door. (*Source: Photo courtesy of ADAptations Inc.®; Bellevue, WA; same house as shown in floor plan*)

General features of the kitchen include continuous countertop from refrigerator to stovetop to sink for easy sliding and one level food flow; drop-in range; full extension glides on drawers; 9″ × 6″ toe kick space for ease of cleaning; side-by-side refrigerator; 14″ space between countertop and upper cabinets; good natural light; task lights under upper wall cabinets; and loop pull hardware on cabinetry. (*Source: Photo courtesy of ADAptations Inc.®; Bellevue, WA; same house as shown in floor plan*)

Figure 8.8 Continued

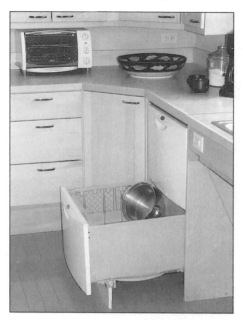

Cabinets with loop hardware and pull-out two-drawer dishwasher. It also has audible features, recessed toe kick, and racks that are within easy reach and require less bending. (*Source: Photo courtesy of ADAptations Inc.®; Bellevue, WA; same house as shown in floor plan*)

Pull-out surface supports refrigerator activities as well as provides additional seated work surface; side-by-side refrigerator allows for easy reach of items, particularly with pull-out shelves; and adjacent counter on right side of refrigerator supports freezer activities. (*Source: Photo courtesy of ADAptations Inc.®; Bellevue, WA; same house as shown in floor plan*)

Cooktop and oven have front-mounted controls that eliminate dangerous reaching over hot burners; drop-in range with smooth counter transition and high toe kick clearance; and easy access hood and light combination. (*Source: Photo courtesy of ADAptations Inc.®; Bellevue, WA; same house as shown in floor plan*)

Figure 8.8   Continued

Pull-out pantry. (*Source: Photo courtesy of ADAptations Inc.®; Bellevue, WA; same house as shown in floor plan*)

The kitchen's island work center as designed per client's preferences includes dual-height cabinets and countertops for multiple users; undercounter microwave with easy-to-read controls and no lip at front edge; Lazy Susan in corner cabinet; electrical outlets in multiple locations; pull-out drawers and pull-out work surface; side-hinged oven; and eating counter behind microwave area. (*Source: Photo courtesy of ADAptations Inc.®; Bellevue, WA; same house as shown in floor plan*)

Figure 8.8 Continued

Also in the laundry room there is a faucet with single-lever and integral hose; and shallow (6″) sink with offset rear drain that facilitates ample knee space under fixture. *(Source: Photo courtesy of ADAptations Inc.®; Bellevue, WA; same house as shown in floor plan)*

The laundry room has front-load washer with front controls; front-load dryer with front controls; loop cabinet hardware; and counter space that provides convenience for laundry activities. *(Source: Photo courtesy of ADAptations Inc.®; Bellevue, WA; same house as shown in floor plan)*

Figure 8.8   Continued

In the bathroom there is a curbless shower with all walls reinforced with I″ plywood for future grab bar application; offset valve for ease of access; and glide bar (40″) with adjustable hand-held shower unit and minimum 69″ hose. *(Source: Photo courtesy of ADAptations Inc.®; Bellevue, WA; same house as shown in floor plan)*

Toilet has clearance adjacent to it for ease of maneuvering and access; counter-mount lavatory with rear drain and single-lever faucet. *(Source: Photograph is courtesy of Experience Universal Design; Arlington, WA)*

Figure 8.8　Continued

Universal design minimizes the possibility of accidents because the home's design is easy to understand regardless of the user's experience, knowledge, language skill, or concentration level. The National Safety and Health Council records nearly six times the number of accidental deaths in the home than in the workplace. Safety is of utmost concern in utilizing universal design features and products. For example:

Leaning over to plug in a lamp or other electrical equipment into a traditional height wall outlet is difficult for many individuals and awkward, if not hazardous, for some, such as people with balance problems or who use walkers. Electricians install baseboard outlets at the height they do out of habit. Installing outlets a little higher—18 inches is recommended—makes them easier to reach from a

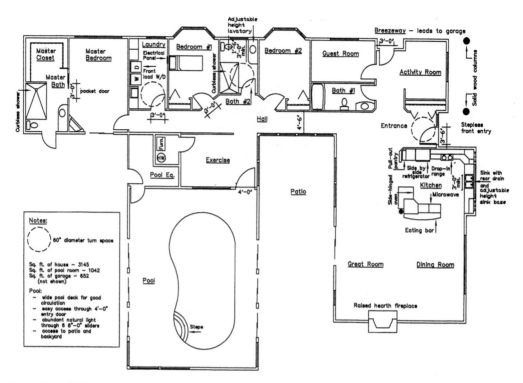

Figure 8.9 This house was custom designed for a young client to be both accessible and universal; built on a half acre in Tacoma, Washington, in 2002 (*Source:* Floor plan courtesy of ADAptations, Inc.®; Bellevue, WA)

seated or standing position. Similarly, wall switches, thermostats, intercoms and other wall-mounted controls are often installed out of habit at a height that is too high for seated individuals to easily operate. These controls can be lowered to make them more usable by everyone. (Connell, 2001)

Emotionally Supportive

Universal design eliminates potential emotional headaches by creating homes everyone can use. Remaining in a home should be the residents' option; they should not be a prisoner in their own home or be forced to move from their house when it no longer accommodates their needs. Young and Pace (2001) suggested universal design may minimize and even eliminate the traumatic experience of older adults being forced to leave the comfort and security of familiar surroundings and a community of friends just because they are no longer able to climb the stairs in their own home. Further, a sense of security and comfort develops in knowing you can stay in the familiar surroundings of your home, neighborhood, and community.

Integrated into Overall Design of House

Universal design features and products integrated into the house during the design and building phase result in an integrated design that is both functional and aesthetically pleasing. In contrast, features and products added in a renovation or remodel often look like add-ons and give the house an institutional or "special" look. The design features stand out rather than being integrated into the environment. For example, navigating steps is often difficult and unsafe for individuals who experience problems walking. A solution is to berm the entrance—grade the yard to create a gently sloping walk to one or more entries to the home. A bermed entry can be incorporated into new construction or accomplished as a renovation to existing housing. Unlike ramped entries, bermed entries do not have a stigmatizing appearance. They do not look temporary or added on and can be landscaped as an attractive entry to the home. When incorporated into homes of younger families, bermed entries make entering and exiting with strollers, moving furniture, and similar activities easier and safer.

Cost Effective

Designing and building a house with universal design features and products may not cost any more than building a conventional house, and will save money over time. Nonetheless, some design features may be slightly more expensive than their standard counterparts, depending somewhat on the site and the floor plan. Young and Pace (2001) reported that there are only slightly increased costs of incorporating universally designed features during initial home construction and these, too, may decrease. As universal design features and products become the design and construction standard in the housing industry, costs will decrease as products become more available and professionals in the construction industry become more knowledgeable and skilled.

The cost differential between universal design/construction and traditional design/construction is about 2 percent to 3 percent according to the Universal Design Housing Network (2003). The Queensland Government Department of Housing (2003) agreed, stating that "a recent study showed that the cost of modifications of an existing detached house to AS4299 without prior adaptive features could be as high as $24,600. The cost to provide the same

3

features, if incorporated in the design stage, is estimated to be $4,400." Cost savings estimates vary and will become more accurate as more projects are completed. Whether the cost is slightly more or not may be irrelevant, given the fact that the house will last a lifetime.

Additionally, costs are saved by reducing the need to retrofit at a later date, delaying moves to residential care facilities, reducing the need for temporary residential care, and saving home health care costs. The cost of incorporating universal design features and products into new home construction is always less than the cost to retrofit later. Altering an existing home to accommodate changing abilities or lifestyles can cost up to three times more than the same inclusions during the initial design and build stage. Furthermore, because features in a universally designed house have more than one function or can be easily adapted later, costly renovation often may be avoided.

CURRENT STATUS OF UNIVERSAL DESIGN

Although the application of universal design features and products in housing is expanding, challenges do still exist. A lack of awareness of universal design remains among housing consumers and professionals. Comprehensive and concise guidelines for universal design features and products are not currently available in a single format. In addition, single-family or other forms of private housing are not required to be accessible, let alone universal.

Another difficulty lies in the confusion of universal design with related terminology. While there is significant overlap in the concept of universal design with the intent of concepts such as accessible design, adaptable design, and barrier-free design, they are not synonymous. A study by Deardorff and Birdsong (2003) surveyed experts in the field of universal design to clarify the definitions and relationships of universal design, adaptable design, accessible design, barrier-free design, lifespan design, and transgenerational design—terms commonly found in the literature and often used interchangeably. The experts represented three groups: leadership from prominent universal design organizations, authors referenced in the literature, and current and former members of the National Advisory Council (NAC) for the Center for Universal Design. Data from 23 experts were collected, analyzed, and resulted in the accepted definitions shown in Table 8.1.

To visually clarify universal design terms, the model developed at the Center for Universal Design was revised based upon experts' comments with proposed and existing definitions, and is displayed

Table 8.1   These terms and definitions reflect the combined views of 23 universal design experts. (Deardorff & Birdsong, 2003)

Term	Definition	Source
Universal design	Design of products and environments to be usable by all people, to the greatest extent possible, without the need for adaptation or specialized design.	Center for Universal Design, 1997
Accessible design	Products and environments that are easy to approach, reach, enter, or use.	Deardorff & Birdsong, 2003
Adaptable design	Flexible features that can be adjusted for the personal needs of specific users in a short time by unskilled labor without involving structural or finish material changes.	Mace, 1990; Story, 1998
Barrier-free design	Eliminating obstacles in a space or product, thereby accommodating persons with disabilities.	Wilkoff & Abed, 1994
Lifespan design	Products and environments that consider the needs of children through older persons.	Deardorff & Birdsong, 2003

Source: Reprinted with permission by the Housing Education and Research Association.

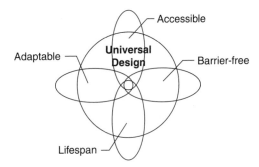

Figure 8.10   Model of the relationships among accessible, adaptable, barrier-free, lifespan, and universal design (Deardorff & Birdsong, 2003)
(Source: Reprinted with permission by the Housing Education and Research Association)

in Figure 8.10. All written comments from the experts suggested a degree of overlap between universal design and accessible design, adaptable design, barrier-free design, and lifespan design. The model demonstrates how the terms often overlap one another depending on the specific example. However, there are always exceptions where a design solution may be one but not the other. Hence the terms do not overlap each other entirely. All of the terms fall within the definition of universal design but, again, there are exceptions where a design solution may be accessible for one population but not for another, putting it outside the boundary of universal design.

In the 1990s several state and local governments began considering ways to encourage various accessibility features in single-family homes. An article in *Housing and Society* summarized state and local jurisdictions methods to promote accessibility features in new single-family homes (Hartje, 2004). The four categories of existing state and local policy that address accessibility in single-family homes include the following.

Category #1: Builder Requirements for Housing Built with a Public Subsidy

Universal design features at the most basic level are represented by the concept of *visitability*. Visitability, or basic accessibility, ensures people who use mobility equipment have access into their neighbors' homes. Concrete Change (2003), an international effort to make all homes visitable, requires three essential features for visitability—one zero-step entrance; all main floor interior doors, including bathrooms, with 32″ of clear passage space; and at least a half bath on the main floor. Visitability ordinances generally require, at a minimum, four or five features on the main level of the home. These features include a zero-step entrance, wider interior doorways (32″ clear opening) and hallways (42″), basic access to a bathroom, raised electrical outlets and lowered switches, and wall reinforcements in the bathrooms. Visitability represents a limited set of features, minimum standards for access, and is an important but small component of universal design. Cities that have this category of ordinances include Atlanta, Georgia (1992); Austin, Texas (1998); and Urbana, Illinois (2000).

Category #2: Builder Requirements for Incentives for Unsubsidized Housing

Vermont was the first state to establish a set of visitability features for almost all housing, even privately financed housing, representing the second category. As of 2002 the Vermont law required any speculatively built single-family or multi-family housing unit to adhere to a number of construction standards that closely follow the visitability legislation. The EasyLiving^{cm} Home certificate program in Georgia provides another example of the second category.

Category #3: Tax or Fee Incentives to the Consumer

A third approach is a consumer-based strategy that includes tax and fee incentives for the consumer. In Freehold Borough, New Jersey, consumers can reduce building permit fees when construction includes accessibility features. Most recently in Escanaba, Michigan, consumers are eligible to receive a $150 cash rebate from the city after a compliance inspection. The ordinance offers a financial incentive for voluntarily meeting a long list of visitability features.

Category #4: Consumer Awareness Campaigns

The fourth and final category consists of consumer awareness campaigns. A noteworthy example is the program in Irvine, California, whereby consumers can select and pay for the universal design features of their choice, whereas other features are included at no additional cost. Features range from lever door hardware, a standard feature at no cost, to 32″ wide interior doors and a curbless shower in lieu of standard tub or shower, as optional features for additional costs.

CONCLUSION

At the time this chapter was written, universal design language was being incorporated in government documents for housing design and construction. For example, the City of Seattle, Washington, 2002 Housing Levy included language stating that "applicants are strongly encouraged, to the maximum extent financially feasible, to incorporate universal design principles in all housing units developed under the rental production and neighborhood opportunity programs." A current Seattle Housing Authority project also contains universal design language.

As more people experience the benefits of universal design, it will expand into all housing markets. Most likely, universal design's expansion in housing will take place through programs that both require and encourage it. The goal is to transform the housing market into one where universal design features and products in housing are the standard for design and construction, rather than the exception.

Once students and professionals are clear and consistent in the use of universal design, their work can move beyond the sterile appearance associated with ADA/accessibility mandates and into more aesthetically pleasing design solutions. Consumers, in turn, may come to expect every environment to be pleasant as well as usable to the greatest extent possible without need for adaptation. Hopefully, all of us will see the day that universal design is nothing more than good design.

REFERENCES

Adaptive Environments Center, Inc. (2001). *Adaptive environments & universal design.* Available: www.adaptenv.org.

Bednar, M. J. (Ed.). (1977). *Barrier-free environments.* Stroudsburg, PA: Dowden, Hutchinson & Ross.

Center for Universal Design. (1997). *The principles of universal design.* Raleigh, NC: Center for Universal Design, North Carolina State University.

Center for Universal Design. (2003). *Universal design in housing.* Raleigh, NC: Center for Universal Design, North Carolina State University.

Center for Universal Design. (2004). *A brief history of universal design.* Available: www.design.ncsu.edu/cud.

Concrete Change. (2003). *Visitability defined.* Retrieved June 28, 2005, from www.concretechange.org/definition_of_visitability.htm.

Connell, B. (2001). *Universal design in housing.* Available: www.asaging.org.

Deardorff, C., & Birdsong, C. (2003). Universal design: Clarifying a common vocabulary. *Housing and Society, 30*(2), 119–137.

Hartje, S. C. (2004). Developing an incentive program for universal design in new, single-family housing. *Housing and Society, 31*(2), 195–212.

Kochera, A. (2002). *Accessibility and visitability features in single-family homes: A review of state and local activity.* Washington, DC: AARP.

Mace, R. (1988). *Universal design: Housing for the lifespan of all people.* Washington, DC: U.S. Department of Housing and Urban Development.

Mace, R. (1990). *Definitions: Accessible, adaptable, and universal design.* Raleigh, NC: Center for Universal Design, North Carolina State University, Fact sheet number 6.

Moore, P. (2001). *Universal accessibility is the reason for design.* Available: www.asaging.org.

Queensland Government Department of Housing. (2003). *Universal housing design booklet—A realistic approach to the future.* Available: *www.housing.qld. gov.au.*

Story, M. (1998). Maximizing usability: The principles of universal design. *Assistive Technology, 10*(1), 4–12.

Story, M., Mueller, J., & Mace, R. (1998). *The universal design file: Designing for people of all ages and abilities.* Raleigh, NC: Center for Universal Design, North Carolina State University.

Universal Design Housing Network. (2003). *Building with universal design assures lifetime use of your home.* Available: www.udhn.org.

Wilkoff, W., & Abed, L. (1994). *Practicing universal design: An interpretation of the ADA.* New York: Van Nostrand Reinhold.

Young, L., & Pace, R. (2001). The next-generation universal home. In W. Prsider & E. Ostroff (Eds.), *Universal design handbook* (pp. 34.3–34.21). New Yrork: McGraw-Hill.

Housing Affordability

Christine C. Cook, Carmen D. Steggell, Andrea Suarez, and Becky L. Yust
Christine C. Cook is Associate Professor, Department of Human
Development and Family Studies, Iowa State University, Ames, IA;
Carmen D. Steggell is Associate Professor, Department of Apparel,
Interiors, Housing, and Merchandising, Oregon State University,
Corvallis, OR; Andrea Suarez is Community Development Planner,
Greenville County Redevelopment Authority, Greenville, SC; and
Becky L. Yust is Associate Professor and Head, Department of Design,
Housing, and Apparel, University of Minnesota, Minneapolis, MN.

Community planners, housing professionals, and human service providers understand that the lack of affordable housing is a crisis for both communities and individual households. For communities, affordable housing contributes to economic growth and is a necessary component in attracting and keeping employment opportunities, and can also be a community revitalization tool. Quality neighborhoods and job opportunities are threatened when decent affordable housing is unavailable (Millennial Housing Commission, 2002). For families, affordable housing fosters self-sufficiency, brings stability to families, and improves life outcomes for children (Millennial Housing Commission, 2002).

Despite the importance of affordable housing, not everyone agrees that a mix of low- and moderate-cost housing is needed in our communities. One of the major challenges facing policymakers and community advocates who sponsor affordable housing programs is "how to build a constituency for addressing housing needs" (Dolbeare, 2001, p. 111). This chapter's goal is to provide information necessary for people to become affordable housing advocates. We begin the chapter by defining affordable housing and examining spiraling housing costs that affect both owners and renters. Next, we consider explanations for escalating costs and affordable housing shortages. In addition, we illustrate the particular housing affordability dilemma for low-income households whether they are homeowners or renters.

Since affordable housing shortages stem from issues related to both the supply of and demand for housing, the chapter ends with strategies to reduce housing costs and to increase the resources of low- and moderate-income households. These households need a coordinated effort to increase the housing supply. However, it will take more than social service advocates' and housing professionals'

21

efforts to thwart the rise in housing costs-it will take the education of community leaders and local citizens as well.

WHEN IS HOUSING AFFORDABLE?

The definition of *affordability* has varied over time, and remains vague. The U.S. Department of Housing and Urban Development (HUD) standard is that a household should spend no more than 30 percent of its total income on housing costs, including mortgage or rent payments and utilities. Federal government housing programs also use the 30 percent rule to identify populations in need of affordable housing. Households who spend more than 30 percent of their income on housing are considered to be "housing cost burdened," and those paying more than 50 percent of their income on housing are "severely housing cost burdened."

According to the *Encyclopedia of Housing* (van Vliet, 1998), several indices have been developed to measure housing affordability on national and regional scales. These indices allow comparisons across jurisdictions and are frequently used to formulate and evaluate local housing policies. Sidebar 9.1 spotlights some affordable housing indices.

Sidebar 9.1
Affordable Housing Indices

A number of housing affordability indices have been developed to compare the status of housing affordability across jurisdictions.

Housing Opportunity Index (HOI)

Developed by the National Association of Home Builders, the HOI ranks 169 metropolitan areas by the relative ease with which a family of median income can purchase a home. This index is based on median household income, as estimated by HUD, and on the prices of new and existing housing units. Using an allowable-purchase multiplier derived from interest rates, the index measures the percentage share of homes on the market that a median income household can afford. The higher the index value, the greater the degree of affordability on the market.

The National Low Income Coalition Rental Housing Index (RHI)

The RHI measures the affordability of rental housing using HUD's Fair Market Rent data. Assuming an affordable monthly rent set at 30 percent of household income, the index calculates the income necessary to rent housing in each metropolitan area.

National Association of Realtors (NAR) Affordability Index

The NAR index is the ratio of the median income to the minimum income required to qualify for a conventional loan covering 80 percent of the median price of existing single-family homes. An index value of 110 means that a family earning the median family income of an area has 110 percent of the income necessary to qualify for the 80 percent loan. Twenty-two metropolitan areas are covered by the index.

Price Index of New One-Family Houses Sold

This price index was designated by the U.S. Census Bureau to measure changes over time in the sale price of new single-family houses with the same characteristics. Index scores are derived from five separate price models, four of them for detached houses in each census region (Northeast, South, West, and Midwest) and one for attached houses throughout the United States. Seven components are included in all five price models: geographic division within region, location in relation to a metropolitan statistical area, floor area, number of fireplaces, number of bathrooms, type of parking facilities, and type of foundation. The sale price used in the index covers not only cost of labor and materials but also land cost, direct and indirect selling expenses, and seller's profit.

Source: C. Nagel. (1998). *Affordable housing indices*

Most of the affordability indices tend to underestimate affordability problems for large- and/or low-income households.

> To illustrate, a family earning $42,000 annually might pay 30% of its income or $1050 per month; it would, however, be more difficult for a comparable household with only $12,000 annual income to pay 30% of its income ($300 per month) because the lower-income family would have less discretionary income remaining for food, clothing, health care and other basic needs. Also, a family of five or six would need more nonhousing goods and services than would a family of two or three. (Jensen, 1998, pp. 11–12)

These shortcomings led Stone (1993) to develop an affordability measure that related both household size and income level. Using this calculation with 1991 U.S. Census Bureau data, he concluded that one in three households were "shelter poor" because they were paying more than they could afford for shelter costs, leaving them without enough money to purchase the minimum necessary non-shelter items such as food and clothing.

update ←

In addition to family size, geographic variation in housing costs and income affects housing affordability. The median U.S. household income in 2002 was $56,500, but it varied greatly depending on location. For U.S. metropolitan areas the median income was $60,300, and for nonmetropolitan areas, $45,000 (U.S. Department of Housing and Urban Development, 2003a). Nonmetropolitan areas of Mississippi had one of the lowest median incomes in the country ($36,500), and metropolitan areas of Connecticut had one of the country's highest median incomes ($75,900). Because of this variability, affordability is tied to a particular geographic area's median household income. In short, an affordable housing unit in rural Monona County in Iowa, where the median household income is $46,600, and San Jose, California, where the median household income is $105,500, may be quite different. Of course if a household in San Jose earns only $45,000, this presents that household with serious affordability problems that may not exist for a household in Iowa. Housing costs also vary greatly across the country.

update ←

For example, in 2002 the median cost of existing single-family homes varied from $215,400 in the West to $136,000 in the Midwest (U.S. Department of Housing and Urban Development, 2003c). Figure 9.1 compares real estate listings from California and Iowa.

Daly City, CA 94015 [San Francisco]
MLS ID#: 290565

$750,000
4 Bed, 2.5 Bath
1,320 Sq. Ft.

Single Family Property, Area: St. Francis Heights, County: San Mateo, Year Built: 1960, City view, View, Two story, Garage, Basement, Fireplace(s), Dining room

Photo by George Cusing,
RE/MAX Westlake Investments.

Estimated payment:
$3,352 Per Month

Des Moines, IA 50310
MLS ID#: 62150661

$168,900
4 Bed, 2 Bath
1,770 Sq.

Ft.
Single-Family Property, Area: Des Moines East, County: Polk, Approximately 0.49 acre(s), Lot is 21,200 sq. ft, Year Built: 1950, Garage, Central air conditioning, Fireplace(s), Dining room, Hardwood floors

Estimated payment:
$755 Per Month

Photo by Bill Eisenlauer, RE/MAX Real Estate Group

Figure 9.1   2005 Comparison of real estate listings between California and Iowa. *(Source: Original listings http://remax.realtor.com/FindHome)*

HOUSEHOLDS AND HOUSING COSTS

The spiraling cost of housing is well documented (Millennial Housing Commission, 2002). However, "the difficulty every student of housing has in investigating questions of housing cost and affordability is that of separating rhetoric from reality. One must differentiate between cost increases due to our greater consumption of housing compared to real changes in cost" (Bourne, 1981, p. 185). Comparing housing prices over time is complex because multifaceted explanations exist for the rise in housing costs. In the United States in 1982, the median cost of a new single-family home was $69,300. Twenty years later, in 2002, the median cost of a new home was $187,500, an increase of 170 percent (U.S. Department of Housing and Urban Development, 2003c). Existing single-family homes are generally less expensive to purchase than a new home. The median sales price of an existing U.S. home in 2002 was $158,300.

update

In part, rising housing costs are simply due to inflation; that is, the continuous and accelerating rise in prices due to increases in wages and costs. However, housing costs have risen faster than inflation (U.S. Department of Housing and Urban Development, 2003c). Increases in the cost of materials and labor also help explain why it is difficult to deliver new, affordable housing. Land values have increased and the escalating price of land is passed on to homeowners and renters. Municipal land use and building code regulations and development charges have resulted in higher priced housing. Last, but certainly not least, the rise in housing costs can be attributed to changes in households' demands for more space of a higher quality, particularly for bedrooms, bathrooms, and garages.

Homeowners and renters both have housing affordability issues; 13.4 million renter households and 14.5 million owner households have housing affordability problems (Millennial Housing Commission, 2002). Spending more than 30 percent of income is an especially significant hardship for low-income households because it prevents them from meeting other basic needs or saving and investing for the future. For cost-burdened renters, the struggle is to pay rent and utilities. For cost-burdened owners, the problem is keeping up with property maintenance as well as holding onto home equity. Elderly and disabled owners, for example, may be unable to keep their homes in good repair.

19

Homeownership and Affordability

To garner a picture of homeownership affordability nationwide, HUD produces an "affordability index," which shows the relationship between the median income in the area and the median income required to qualify for a mortgage. Table 9.1 lists the U.S. index for selected years since 1972. An affordability index value of 100 indicates that households with median income could purchase the median priced home. The ability of a median income household to purchase a median priced home improves as the affordability index value rises above 100.

Table 9.1 shows that the mortgage rate has a significant effect on affordability. During the early 1980s, a household's ability to purchase a home was very low, as shown by affordability indices of less than 70. At that time average interest rates were more than 15 percent. During the 1990s, the affordability index rose, though it remained below the affordability of the 1970s. Increasing rates of homeownership closely correlate with the rising affordability index.

Almost 70 percent of U.S. households owned their home in 2002 (Joint Center for Housing Studies, 2003). However, not all segments of the U.S. population have shared equally in this increase. The Millennial Housing Commission (2002, p. 15) reported that: "Not all households that want to buy homes and are capable of managing the responsibilities of homeownership have been able to do so." Homeownership rates differ significantly when one examines the characteristics of households by age, race, household type, and income.

Younger families are less likely to be homeowners than their older counterparts. For example, 23 percent of households with a head of household under the age of 25 owned a home, while 39 percent of those aged 25 to 29 years owned a home (U.S. Department

Table 9.1   Housing Affordability Index: 1972, 1982, 1992, and 2002

Period	Median Existing Price	Mortgage Rate	Median Family Income	Income to Qualify	Affordability Index
1972	$26,700	7.52	$11,116	$7,183	154.8
1982	$67,800	15.38	$23,433	$33,713	69.5
1992	$103,700	8.11	$36,812	$29,523	124.7
2002	$158,300	6.55	$52,692	$38,640	136.4

The Federal Housing Finance Board's monthly effective rate (points are amortized over 10 years) combines fixed-rate and adjustable-rate loans.
Source: U.S. Department of Housing and Urban Development, 2003c

[handwritten margin notes: "Student loan burden?", "update →", "discrimin- ation }", "Updates to: 1983, 1993, 2003, 2004, 2005, 2006, 2007, 2010, 2009"]

of Housing and Urban Development, 2003c). These percentages have remained fairly stable for the last 20 years. Finding affordable housing remains a challenge for first-time homebuyers since their earnings are relatively low and they have not had much time to accrue downpayment money.

Once households own a home, they are less likely to move; thus, the older the householder is, the more likely he or she is to own a home. Over 50 percent of households with the householder aged 30 and above owned their homes (U.S. Department of Housing and Urban Development, 2003c). However, over 80 percent of households in which the head of household was 55 years of age and older owned their homes in 2002.

Discriminatory practices in our society continue to be constraining factors in homeownership rates for minorities. Historically poor quality educational opportunities and systemic discrimination in employment result in minorities earning less income; thus, they may not be able to qualify for mortgages (Joint Center for Housing Studies, 2004). Additionally, discriminatory marketplace practices (e.g., steering individuals away from particular neighborhoods, lack of support in the mortgage application process, etc.) affect access to affordable rental and ownership opportunities (Urban Institute, 2002).

Table 9.2 lists homeownership rates for selected years between 1983 and 2002 among different race and ethnic groups. Hispanics

Table 9.2 Change in Homeownership Percentage Rates by Race and Ethnicity: 1983, 1993–2002

	Non-Hispanic			
Period	White	Black	Other	Hispanic
1983	69.1	45.6	53.3	41.2
1993	70.2	42.0	50.6	39.4
1994	70.0	42.5	50.8	41.2
1995	70.9	42.9	51.5	42.0
1996	71.7	44.5	51.5	42.8
1997	72.0	45.4	53.3	43.3
1998	72.6	46.1	53.7	44.7
1999	73.2	46.7	54.1	45.5
2000	73.8	47.6	53.9	46.3
2001	74.3	48.4	54.7	47.3
2002	74.5	47.9	55.1	48.2

Source: U.S. Department of Housing and Urban Development, 2003c

[handwritten: 17]

have experienced the greatest increase in ownership rates since 1983, with a 7 percentage point increase (41.2 percent to 48.2 percent). However, their homeownership rate, like that of African Americans, is still less than 50 percent. White households have the highest rates of homeownership; between 1983 and 2002, homeownership rates for whites increased 5.4 percentage points.

Homeownership rates also differ by household type. In 2002 married couples with or without children had the highest rates of ownership with 78.9 percent and 86.8 percent, respectively. This is partially due to having two wage earners in the household able to contribute to the housing costs. Single-parent households with children have the lowest homeownership rate of any household type, as only 43.6 percent are homeowners (U.S. Department of Housing and Urban Development, 2003c).

"Rising home values and falling interest rates gave the housing sector a boost in 2002" (Joint Center for Housing Studies, 2003, p. 1), but there has been a dramatic jump in the number of homeowners spending half their incomes on housing. The most vulnerable homeowners are those with low and extremely low incomes; that is, households with incomes 50 percent to 80 percent, and below 30 percent of an area's median income, respectively. In 2001 about 7.3 million homeowners reported spending more than half of their incomes on housing, up from 5.8 million in 1997 (Joint Center for Housing Studies, 2003). Table 9.3 illustrates homeowners' ability to pay housing costs, as a percent of household income. It "shows the monthly median housing costs for renters, owners, and then all households across the income spectrum" (Millennial Housing Commission, 2002, p. 16). The table shows that 9 percent of owners have extremely low incomes and on average pay half of their income for housing.

Renting and Affordability

Renter households make up about one third of U.S. households, which equates to nearly 36 million households. Federal and state programs help lower-income households to acquire below-market interest rate mortgages and reduced downpayments in order to purchase homes. The remaining households who rent often have significantly lower incomes; for them, finding affordable rental housing is especially difficult. In fact, it is generally agreed that the shortage of low-cost rental units means that poor households that rent suffer the most severe housing cost burdens (Joint Center for Housing Studies, 2003; Millennial Housing Commission, 2002). As shown in Table 9.3, extremely low-income and very low-income renters have average housing cost burdens that are higher than owners in the same income categories (58 percent and 35 percent compared to 50 percent and 25 percent, respectively).

Table 9.3 Housing Costs Far Exceed Lower-Income Households' Ability to Pay

Households				Monthly Housing Costs		Cost as % of Income
	Number (Millions)	Share	Median Reported Income	Affordable	Actual	
OWNERS						
Extremely low income	6.4	9%	$6,500	$163	$300	50
Very low income	7.1	10%	$15,613	$390	$324	25
Low income	10.7	16%	$27,000	$675	$453	21
Moderate income	14.3	21%	$41,200	$1,030	$633	17
High income	30.3	44%	$81,000	$2,025	$908	13
All	68.8	100%	$45,000	$1,135	$617	17
RENTERS						
Extremely low income	8.5	25%	$7,000	$175	$426	58
Very low income	6.2	18%	$17,000	$425	$509	35
Low income	7.3	22%	$26,541	$664	$565	25
Moderate income	6.6	19%	$40,000	$1,000	$643	19
High income	5.3	16%	$68,000	$1,700	$736	12
All	33.9	100%	$24,400	$610	$560	25

Source: Extracted from data in the Millennial Housing Commission Report, 2002, p. 15 (Figure 5)

The supply of low-cost rental housing units has not been suffi-cient for the demand, particularly for renters with extremely low in-comes. Comparisons of renter households by income and the stock of units they can afford show a critical shortage of affordable apart-ments for extremely low-income households. In addition, a sub-stantial portion of affordable rental housing for lower-income households is old and located in neighborhoods with little access to jobs or adequate facilities and services (Millennial Housing Commission, 2002). Making matters worse, higher-income house-holds outbid lower-income households for rental units in an effort to limit their housing expenses, sharply reducing the number of af-fordable units for others. There is nothing to prohibit higher-income households from renting low-cost units. In fact, higher-income households are estimated to occupy 2.7 million of the 7.9 million lowest cost rental units, thus reducing the supply of low-cost units even more (Joint Center for Housing Studies, 2003). The mismatch between the supply of low-cost rental housing and its demand is illustrated in Figure 9.2. The figure also shows the affordable housing supply (labeled as "available to the income group") that is inhabited by wealthier, higher-income households.

In sum, low-income renters experience the worst housing affordability problems (Housing Assistance Council, 1997; Joint Center for Housing Studies, 2003, 2004; Millennial Housing Commission, 2002; *Out of Reach,* 2002; Stone, 1993). The average rent for one- and two-bedroom apartments varies widely around the country, and even within states. For example, in California the average Fair Market Rent (FMR) is $1,024, but the FMR in San Francisco is $1,940. In Iowa, the FMR on a two-bedroom apartment is $518 and in Des Moines, its largest city, the FMR is $649 on a comparable unit. In order to afford a two-bedroom home at the nationally weighted Fair Market Rent, a renter would have to earn $14.66 per hour, nearly three times the federal minimum wage (*Out of Reach,* 2002). The National Low Income Housing Coalition estimates that a person needs to work 69 hours a week, year round at the minimum wage, to rent an average one-bedroom apartment in the United States. For an average two-bedroom apartment, a person would need to work 86 hours a

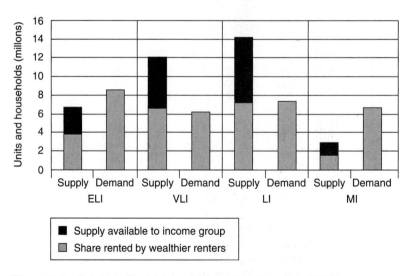

Figure 9.2 Existing affordable rental housing mismatch (1999)

Includes vacant and occupied units. Demand defined as number of households that fall under Area Median Income (AMI) cutoffs; supply defined as number of units priced at under 30 percent of income. ELI = Extremely low income; VLI = Very low income; LI = Low income; MI = Middle income. (*Source:* Millennial Housing Commission, 2002)

> **Sidebar 9.2**
> **The National Low Income Housing Coalition**
>
> The National Low Income Housing Coalition—a national organization dedicated solely to ending America's affordable housing crisis—is committed to educating, organizing, and advocating to ensure decent, affordable housing within healthy neighborhoods for everyone.
>
> As part of this commitment, the NLIHC annually publishes *Out of Reach,* a rental housing cost analysis that is targeted to all low-income households.
>
> *Out of Reach* contains income and rental housing cost data for the 50 states and the District of Columbia by state, metropolitan area, nonmetropolitan area, and county as well as a Housing Wage for each of these localities. The concept of the Housing Wage was developed by NLIHC to demonstrate what a full-time worker must earn per hour in order to afford rental housing at HUD's Fair Market Rent.
>
> *Source: Priced Out,* 2002. The full report is available at *www.nlihc.org*

week. There is no U.S. region where the minimum wage is adequate to afford the two-bedroom Fair Market Rent if a household should not spend more than 30 percent of total household income on housing costs (*Out of Reach,* 2002). Sidebar 9.2 discusses The National Low Income Housing Coalition and its publication, *Out of Reach*.

Federal and sometimes state and local governments provide housing assistance to low-income renters. Public housing is one option for extremely low-income households, those whose earnings do not exceed 30 percent of the area median income with adjustments for household size. Public housing was established to provide decent and safe rental housing for eligible low-income families, the elderly, and persons with disabilities. Public housing comes in all sizes and types, from scattered-site, single-family houses to high-rise apartments. Approximately 1.3 million households live in public housing units, managed by about 3,300 housing agencies (Millennial Housing Commission, 2002).

Other options to serve low-income households are programs that target the renter and those that target the housing structure or development. Section 8 vouchers (also called Housing Choice Vouchers) allow households to find housing in the open market that meets quality and affordability standards, after which the government pays the difference between the units rental rate and 30 percent of the household's income. Almost 1.6 million households are served through tenant-based programs. Finally, private developers, including not-for-profit organizations, build and manage housing for low-income households with federal assistance. Project-based assistance accounts for just over 1.9 million units nationwide. All federal rental assistance programs account for over 4.8 million units (Millennial Housing Commission, 2002).

UNDERSTANDING THE SHORTAGE IN AFFORDABLE HOUSING

Various factors impact affordability by affecting the cost of home building and housing development, including: (1) demands for space and amenities, (2) restrictive local government regulations, and (3) failure to preserve existing affordable housing. When these factors raise the cost of the housing supply in a community, the proportion of affordable housing shrinks.

Increasing the Cost of Housing: Additional Space and Amenities

A major contributor to housing costs is that the housing built today is not comparable to housing built 20 or even 10 years ago. Table 9.4 illustrates just a few of the changes during the most recent decade. Homes have increased more than 10 percent in overall size, and additional square footage requires additional materials. Labor costs and regulatory costs have also increased. The current median price per square foot to construct a house in the United States is about $64, up from $57 per square foot in 1995 (U.S. Census Bureau, 2000). Land is also a major component of new housing prices. As shown in Table 9.4 actual lot sizes have decreased in 10 years

Table 9.4   Select Characteristics of New Single-Family Homes Built in the United States

Characteristic	1992	2002	Percentage Change
Median square footage of house	1,920 sq. ft	2,114 sq. ft	10.1%
Houses with 4 bedrooms or more	29%	36%	24.1%
Houses with 2$^1/_2$ baths or more	47%	55%	17.0%
Houses with 2-car garages or more	75%	82%	9.3%
Median square footage of lot	17,865 sq. ft	16,454 sq. ft	−7.9%

Source: National Association of Home Builders, 2003b. Reprinted by permission from Builder-Books. Please visit www.builderbooks.com for books, booklets, brochures, and other products of interest to the building industry

by almost 8 percent. Therefore, households are buying additional space and features in the home, but the density of the housing units per acre is increasing as a strategy to keep the overall price from increasing even more.

About 20 percent of new housing units are in multi-family buildings. Characteristics in these new structures have also contributed to higher prices. Table 9.5 illustrates that the overall size of new units within multi-family structures has increased. However, as the number of bedrooms and bathrooms in these units increases, they also more easily accommodate households with children. Units in multi-family buildings are generally more affordable than single-family homes.

Increasing the Cost of Housing: The Role of Local Government Regulations

When land is in short supply, values rise and housing costs increase. Balancing land use restrictions that protect natural resources, farmlands, and environmental quality with the demand for development is difficult. The National Association of Home Builders (2003a) argued that local government regulations are responsible for the lack of affordable housing. Several empirical studies support this argument, finding that increased government regulation leads to higher housing costs and decreased amounts of new construction (Feldman, 2002; Fischel, 1990; Somerville & Mayer, 2003). The main types of local government regulations that are blamed for housing affordability problems are: (1) impact fees, (2) code restrictions, (3) growth restrictions, and (4) exclusionary zoning tactics.

Impact Fees.   In many communities the rapid pace of growth has strained local infrastructure, and the existing revenue source is not able to meet the needs of the growing community. Impact fees, also

Table 9.5   Select Characteristics of Units Completed in New Multi-Family Buildings

Characteristic	1991	2001	Percentage Change
Median square footage of unit	980 sq. ft	1,104 sq. ft	12.7%
Units with 3 bedrooms or more	12%	21%	75.0%
Units with 2 baths or more	43%	58%	34.9%

Source: National Association of Home Builders, 2003c. Reprinted by permission from Builder-Books. Please visit www.builderbooks.com for books, booklets, brochures, and other products of interest to the building industry.

known as System Development Charges (SDCs), are placed on developers by local governments as a way of funding infrastructure improvements associated with the development (such as sewage, streets, public parks, and schools). These impact fees are often passed on from developers to homebuyers, increasing the price of a home (Weitz, 1985). Impact fees have the potential to increase housing prices across an entire market (Delaney & Smith, 2001). Furthermore, impact fees constrain the supply of new housing, increasing the probability that currently affordable units will become unaffordable through a "filtering" process (Somerville & Mayer, 2003).

Code Restrictions.   Builders argue that code restrictions further constrain the new affordable housing supply by continually raising the standard of housing and by creating additional bureaucratic steps that increase development costs. Andres Duany (2001), founder of the New Urbanism movement, reflected on the role of code restrictions in the affordable housing shortage:

> In the past, people would build for themselves. . . . But there are now myriad regulations that, in the name of eliminating bad housing, have inadvertently eliminated the supply of inexpensive housing. Today, only licensed professionals can design, permit, and build housing. Bureaucratic friction thus makes housing for the poor available only with artificial supports. (p. 40)

Increasingly high standards mandated through local building codes result in safer housing, but by creating regulations that eliminate substandard housing, housing costs rise (Feldman, 2002).

Growth Restrictions.   When local residents and policymakers begin to worry that their community is growing too quickly or in a manner that they do not think is appropriate, they sometimes implement growth-slowing policies. Urban growth boundaries are helpful in combating urban sprawl. They slow the pace of expanding road systems, water supply systems, waste disposal systems, and other infrastructure as well as protect farmlands. However, in limiting the amount of land available for housing, land costs are driven up.

Exclusionary Zoning.   The supply of affordable housing is further limited through zoning (the practice of restricting the uses of land by forming special districts in which only certain land uses are permitted). By restricting the amount of land available to build new developments, zoning is partially responsible for raising housing costs. In addition, many municipalities use exclusionary zoning tactics that seek to exclude low-cost housing from the municipality (Katz, 2000; Mieszkowski & Mills, 1993). Municipalities use several basic tactics to zone out families with low incomes—creating minimum lot sizes, imposing minimum square footage, and reducing the amount of land zoned for multi-family units or manufactured homes. Imposing design standards that substantially increase the cost of development is another tactic to reduce the amount of affordable housing (Span, 2001). For instance, many municipalities prohibit the use of vinyl siding as a building material or require the use of expensive building materials, such as brick.

Increasing the Cost of Housing: Failure to Preserve Existing Affordable Housing

Another contributor to the affordable housing shortage is the loss of affordable units to gentrification or to a lack of repairs. According to Bailey and Robertson (1997), gentrification describes the process by which members of the "professional/managerial" class move to previously decayed inner-city neighborhoods, renovating the housing stock. Due to gentrification, many low-income families can no longer afford their homes' property taxes, and landlords no longer find it profitable to rent to low-income families. Thus, many low-income families are displaced from their formerly affordable housing.

Code restrictions mandating that renovated buildings must meet current code standards also affect the ability to preserve affordable housing. The expense of rehabilitating older buildings is greatly increased by requiring that houses meet codes that were not in place at the time of original construction. Because of the high costs associated with bringing a house up to current code, the housing unit may be lost to decay or demolition (Duany, 2001).

CHALLENGES FOR LOW-INCOME HOUSEHOLDS

Given this chapter's discussion, it may already seem obvious that obtaining affordable housing is a challenge for low-income households. However, like the term *housing affordability,* the term *low income* means different things to different people. In the language of HUD, a family is designated as low income based on its size, its income, and where it resides. If a family's income falls below 80 percent of the area median income, it is considered low income. It is considered very low income if its income is below 50 percent of the area median. A new category, extremely low income, consists of households earning below 30 percent of the area median (Joint Center for Housing Studies, 2003, 2004; Millennial Housing Commission, 2002; *Out of Reach,* 2002).

Some individuals and families are more likely to need affordable housing including welfare recipients, single-parent families, minority households, the elderly (particularly the very old and those living alone), rural households, and individuals with physical or cognitive disabilities. Individuals or families that fall into more than one of these groups have an increased likelihood of paying too much for poor quality housing. One example of a multiple risk household would be a rural, African American, single mother receiving welfare benefits. Some reference already has been made in this chapter to the conditions faced by these individuals and families; however, only a cursory examination of the challenges facing low-income people is possible.

Welfare reform, enacted in 1996 as the Personal Responsibility and Work Opportunity Reconciliation Act (PRWORA), has led to increasing discussion on the housing problems for those receiving or newly terminated from welfare benefits. Since economic self-sufficiency is one of the mainstays of welfare reform, the role of housing and housing assistance has been identified as critical to recipients' economic success (Kingsley, 1997; Newman, 1999). Approximately 25 percent of the nation's 7.6 million welfare recipients receive direct housing subsidies through public and assisted housing programs (U.S. Department of Housing and Urban Development, 2001). Data indicate that the majority of welfare recipients who are not receiving government housing assistance spend more than half their incomes on housing (U.S. Department of Housing and Urban Development, 1998).

Single mothers and female headed households often struggle to make ends meet. Precarious housing quality and the affordability are constant concerns (Cook & Bruin, 1994; Mulroy, 1988, 1996). A recent series of policy reports, *Unlocking the Door—Keys to Women's Housing* (2000), highlight the housing problems of women, specifically single mothers. "Women head 59% of the 5.3 million families with 'worst case' housing needs" (Couch, 2000, p. 1). About 30 percent of female-headed families are poor. They have the highest poverty rate of any family type and comprise the majority of poor families (U.S. Census Bureau, 1999). For women, the ability to earn a sufficient wage to afford housing is compromised by a persistent wage gap (Thomas, 2000). It has been argued, too, that conventional housing's design is not appropriate for many women because its size, location, and cost do not respond to single mothers' childcare, transportation, or employment needs.

Racial minorities also experience labor and housing market inequities. Furthermore, reports on discrimination against racial minorities suggest that finding housing, whether categorized as affordable or not, is more difficult because of unfair treatment as they search for rental and owner housing opportunities. "The greatest share of discrimination for Hispanic and African American home seekers can still be attributed to being told units are unavailable when they are available to non-Hispanic whites and being shown and told about fewer units than a comparable non-minority" (U.S. Department of Housing and Urban Development, 2000, p. 1). According to a recent HUD report on discrimination in metropolitan housing markets, housing discrimination, though generally down since 1989, still exists at unacceptable levels (U.S. Department of Housing and Urban Development, 2000).

An upward trend in discrimination continues in the area of geographic steering for African Americans. Furthermore, Hispanics, compared to non-Hispanics, receive less help from agents when obtaining financing. Hispanics were more likely in 2000 than in 1989 to be quoted a higher rent than their white counterparts for the same unit, and Hispanic renters were more likely to experience discrimination in their housing search than African American renters. Prospective owners and renters who are Asian and Pacific Islanders also experienced consistent adverse treatment relative to whites with similar income and credit history (U.S. Department of Housing and Urban Development, 2000).

Special housing affordability challenges also face millions of low-income rural residents (Housing Assistance Council, 1997). Though rural housing data are often difficult to locate, HUD reported that the overall number of units with rents below $300 is shrinking, declining by 13 percent between 1996 and 1998 alone (U.S. Department of Housing and Urban Development, 1999). Neither income from low-wage employment or welfare is sufficient to afford to own or rent available housing in many rural communities. Though housing costs are substantially lower in rural communities than in the metropolis, "more than four of every ten rural poverty-level households pay over 50% of their meager incomes for housing" (Housing Assistance Council, 1997, p. 2). Poor rural households also must often choose between housing that is affordable and housing that is structurally sound. Rural households are more likely than urban dwellers to live in *inadequate housing*—housing with severe structural defects, lead paint problems, and vermin infestation (Housing Assistance Council, 1997).

Whether living in cities or in isolated rural locations, the elderly are especially vulnerable to shortages of affordable housing. Though their needs deserve more attention than is possible in this chapter, suffice it to say that limited and fixed incomes affect aging adults generally and certain subgroups of elderly particularly. People most likely to live in poor quality housing that would benefit from affordable housing are those 85 years of age or older; minority groups, especially African Americans and Hispanics; single persons, as opposed to married households; rural dwellers; and the very low-income elderly (Golant, 1992). However, moderate-income elderly may be the most disadvantaged when examining the availability of affordable housing options. This occurs because the poorest elderly can qualify for many government-sponsored housing and service programs. Those who have incomes just above the poverty level do not qualify for these programs, nor can they afford the options offered in the private sector such as retirement and assisted living communities (Golant, 1992).

Individuals with cognitive or physical disabilities may or may not be elderly but share some of the same housing concerns with them. According to a recent report, "people with disabilities are priced out of every housing market area in the United States" (O'Hara & Cooper, 2003, p. 1). Supplemental Security Income (SSI) benefits, income provided to people with disabilities, does not adequately meet the cost of rental housing, and this gap between benefits and housing costs continues to widen. It is likely that the need for affordable housing for people with disabilities is underestimated because many live "invisibly" in institutions, nursing homes, or extended families' homes until suitable housing is available. Finding affordable housing that meets the special design requirements of individuals with cognitive or physical disabilities may be especially challenging. Housing designed for individuals with disabilities may require costly adaptations such as ramped access, wider doors, and kitchen and bathroom modifications. Although fair housing laws dictate modest accommodations in renter-occupied housing for those with disabilities, no regulations affect privately developed, owner-occupied housing, whether newly developed or existing.

By prohibiting or limiting the number of group homes in a community, zoning regulations can thwart the provision of affordable housing options for people with disabilities. In some communities the development of group homes requires a special use permit, and scrutiny of and approval by a governing body of the municipality. Furthermore, the municipality may place a limit on the number of group homes and/or limit the number of unrelated adults that may live together, which can limit the housing options of people with disabilities (Advocacy Incorporated, 2003).

HOMELESSNESS

For some families, a failure to find affordable housing leads to homelessness. Most housing experts and social service advocates agree that multifarious and complex reasons exist for homelessness, including a lack of affordable housing. Although homelessness is sometimes characterized as an individual and family problem rather than a housing issue, substantial evidence exists that escalating housing costs, the loss of low-cost rental and owner housing stock through demolition and gentrification, and a steady decline in rental assistance since the 1980s have added to the homelessness crisis (American Planning Association, 2003).

As with other social issues, there is often debate about the homeless population's size and composition. By law, the "literally" homeless are those in shelters or "in a public or private place not designed for, or ordinarily used as, a regular sleeping accommodation for human beings" such as automobiles, parks, under bridges, and on the street (American Planning Association, 2003, p. 2). As many as 800,000 Americans may be homeless each night, and some argue that the figure is much higher (American Planning Association, 2003). A broader definition of homeless individuals and families would certainly increase the total substantially. An inestimable number of individuals and families may be living with relatives or friends (often called doubled-up) in overcrowded conditions, or living in substandard or otherwise uninhabitable buildings. These households are often described as the "hidden homeless." It seems likely that the homeless population in rural communities is largely hidden since there are fewer shelters or housing alternatives compared to their urban counterparts.

Families with children are one of the fastest growing segments of the homeless population. Estimates suggest that more than one third of the homeless are families with children and that, in rural areas, families and single mothers are the largest group of homeless people (American Planning Association, 2003; U.S. Department of Agriculture, 1996).

Homeless children are particularly vulnerable to poor educational experiences that can have lifelong impacts. They are more likely to miss school than children living in more stable situations and are, as a result, susceptible to developmental and learning delays. The homeless population, however, is not a homogeneous group. More than half of the homeless are single adults, most often men between the ages of 30 and 50. Though estimates differ, as many as one fourth of the homeless may experience serious, ongoing mental illness, and about half of the single adult homeless struggle with a history of substance abuse (Burt & Cohen, 1989; National Coalition for the Homeless, 2002).

Affordable housing opportunities are one of the critical social support services needed by the homeless. Transitionally homeless individuals and families are those who generally move quickly through the homeless assistance system once they are able to access it. The transitionally homeless are especially in need of affordable housing because they tend to be families that work in entry level and/or low-paying jobs or are on fixed incomes like the elderly or those persons with disabilities. Income supports and rental assistance is needed to keep these individuals and families housed. Earning a sufficient wage to meet the basic needs of a worker and his or her dependents without reliance on public or private subsidies, called a "living wage," is also important. Furthermore, programs are needed that support low-cost homeownership opportunities and promote community shelters. The chronically homeless, those individuals that experience long-term homelessness, often have health or substance abuse problems in addition to extreme poverty. They need permanent supportive housing that combines social services and affordable housing.

SOLVING THE AFFORDABILITY PROBLEM

With rising housing costs and stagnant income levels among lower-income households, millions of Americans struggle to afford decent housing. This is not a new problem; in fact, the U.S. federal government has had programs to provide housing for low-income people since 1937 (Mitchell, 1993). However, using a variety of programs and a number of approaches, "the number of [housing] assisted households peaked at 5 million in the mid-1990s and has been dropping ever since" (Dolbeare, 2001, p. 111). Today, fewer than 34 percent of renters in the bottom fifth of the U.S. income distribution receive housing assistance (Joint Center for Housing Studies, 2003) and nearly 28 million American households spend more than 30 percent of their income on housing (National Association of Home Builders, 2002).

How can we solve the problem? Although many programs already exist, there is still not enough affordable housing. To garner the support needed to solve the affordability problem, the public must become aware of the critical need for affordable housing and be willing to provide the support needed.

Already 59 percent of Americans say that the federal government should address the availability of affordable homes and 65 percent say that local government should do something to make affordable homes available (Hart, 2002). However, public perceptions of subsidized housing and housing-assisted households are negative and NIMBYism (not in my back yard) is rampant (National Low Income Housing Coalition, 2003). The first step in solving the affordability problem must be to correct misperceptions of housing programs and replace them with more positive images. Finding ways to do this are critical and should be considered in all housing policy discussions (Dolbeare, 2001). Only then will we be able to solve the problem.

When the public embraces the need for affordable housing and is willing to provide the necessary support, the question becomes how best to meet the needs. As discussed earlier, an imbalance exists between the cost of housing and the resources of low- and moderate-income households. It follows then that solutions could address either reducing housing costs or increasing the resources households can access to fulfill their housing needs. Some of these strategies help builders and developers (both for-profit and not-for-profit) as they provide housing, while others target housing consumers directly. Some of the existing programs and some new ideas from both approaches are shown in Table 9.6 and discussed in the following pages.

REDUCING THE COST OF HOUSING

Land Use Strategies

One land use strategy to address affordability is promoting higher density and mixed-use development. When land prices are high, building more housing units on the available land reduces the cost of each unit. If the housing units are built above an income-producing business, housing costs may drop even more (National Association of Home Builders, 2002). Municipalities that wish to increase housing affordability could consider reducing minimum lot sizes. This would allow for greater housing density.

Increasing affordable housing opportunities can also be accomplished by reducing other land use regulations that drive up housing costs such as costly design standards and minimum square footage requirements. State or federal legislation requiring that communities have "sufficient" amounts of land zoned for multi-family housing or manufactured housing also has the potential to improve the number of affordable housing options in a community.

Zoning restrictions often reduce affordable housing, but zoning may also be used to add to the affordable housing stock. Communities can create inclusionary zoning which requires developers of multi-unit rental housing or even single-family homes to make a certain percentage of the units affordable to households making less than the area median income. Inclusionary zoning may employ incentives such as density bonuses. Developers who build more affordable units than the required minimum can be given a density

4

Table 9.6   Solving the Housing Affordability Problem

	Possible Solutions	
Problem	**Strategies to Reduce Costs**	**Strategies to Increase Resources**
High Cost of Land	• Relax land use restrictions • Increase housing density • Use inclusionary zoning • Promote mixed-use development • Establish Community Land Trusts	
Rising Building and Management Costs	• Streamline building methods and use standardized components • Utilize factory-built housing • Donate materials and labor • Utilize "self-help" strategies • Reduce impact fees	
Costs of Financing	• Provide low interest loans for builders/developers • Sustain Low Income Housing Tax Credits • Increase level of funding for HOME and CDBG programs	• Provide no and low interest mortgages for homebuyers • Provide homebuyer education
Low Wages		• Provide financial management education • Provide "livable wage" • Establish match savings plans • Expand Section 8 (Housing Choice Vouchers) rental assistance • Improve Public Housing • Expand Earned Income Tax Credit

bonus allowing more units in the development. In effect, the affordable housing units are built on "free" lots (Katz, 2000).

A unique strategy to decrease housing costs by controlling land costs is known as a Community Land Trust (CLT). Typically, a low-income homebuyer purchases a home in a CLT, while a nonprofit organization holds the land itself in a trust. In that way, the buyer's cost is for the house only. If the buyer ever chooses to sell, the buyer and the CLT share in any appreciated equity, the home is sold to another low-income buyer, and the property remains affordable. Figure 9.3 shows a CLT example in Burlington, Vermont.

The Burlington Community Land Trust (BCLT) is a nonprofit, member-based organization in Burlington, Vermont. Our mission is to ensure access to affordable homes and vital communities for all people through the democratic stewardship of land.

BCLT was the first municipally funded community land trust and today is the largest community land trust in the United States, with over 2,500 members. BCLT has become a national model of locally controlled affordable housing and community revitalization.

BCLT provides a wide range of housing opportunities. BCLT properties include over 270 rental apartments and 370 shared-appreciation single-family homes and condominiums. Through its land stewardship, BCLT ensures that these properties will remain affordable.

Steps for buying a home through BCLT:

- You must be a customer of the NeighborWorks® Homeownership Center of Vermont. This means that you have:
  - Attended an Orientation Meeting.
  - Completed the 8-hour Homeownership Workshop.
  - Met with a Housing Specialist for a one-on-one meeting.
- You must become a member of BCLT. This means that you join BCLT (membership dues of at least $1).
- You must purchase a home in Chittenden, Franklin, or Grand Isle County.

Click to enlarge

Purchase Price:
$147,000

(minus BCLT grant of
$35,430)

Your Mortgage:
$111,570

Lyman Meadows Condominium Hinesburg

UNDER DEPOSIT

2-bedroom, $1\frac{1}{2}$ bath end unit condominium in Hinesburg. Quiet village neighborhood is close to schools, stores, and Rt. 116. Exterior features include extensive landscaping with well-maintained grounds, front porch, back deck, and storage closet. Heat is energy-efficient gas fired hot water. Unit comes with water softener, gas stove, dishwasher and refrigerator. Association dues include all outside maintenance, snow and trash removal. Cats and dogs allowed.

Figure 9.3 Burlington Community Land Trust (*Sources:* Burlington Community Land Trust, 2005. Used with permission. Information about Burlington Community Land Trust found at www.bclt.net/aboutbclt.shtml. Listing of Land Trust Home for Sale found at www.getahome.org/homes_for_sale.htm. Retrieved January 21, 2005)

Building and Management Costs

When considering the cost of building a house, the cost of materials and labor must be considered first. However, saving money by using inferior building materials simply adds to the long-term housing problem. The home building industry is unique in that it has resisted assembly-line construction. Still, streamlined building methods and standardized components may reduce some costs.

Factory-built housing, including manufactured and modular housing, offers economies in the manufacturing process that can significantly reduce costs. Manufactured housing may reduce costs in another way. Site-built homes, particularly those built in urban areas, often suffer from vandalism and theft of materials while under construction. With manufactured housing the home can be closed-in quickly after delivery, making it less vulnerable to vandalism and theft.

Unfortunately, manufactured homes suffer an image problem that has followed the industry from the days of the "mobile home" before the HUD Code was implemented. The negative image may even contribute to NIMBYism. In addition, while replacing skilled craftsmen with low-wage factory jobs decreases building costs, the low-wage workers may then need housing assistance themselves.

One way to decrease building costs is by using donated labor and materials. This strategy is used by many faith-based organizations. In this plan, community members donate their labor to build modest homes for selected low-income households.

Resident labor, another form of donated labor, is used in urban homesteading programs and self-help housing. These strategies allow people to reduce costs by building or rehabilitating their own homes, often referred to as earning "sweat equity." Some self-help programs require that several households work together to create homes for all involved. No household can move in until all the housing units are completed. Some organizations with experience in using self-help and volunteer labor include ACORN Housing Corporation, Habitat for Humanity, and the Housing Assistance Council (U.S. Department of Housing and Urban Development, 2003b). Figure 9.4 shows a "typical" U.S. Habitat for Humanity house.

"Self-help housing" also applies to rental housing. Tenant management has been used in public housing and in privately owned buildings. Costs are reduced when occupants make repairs, maintain essential services, and secure the premises (Kolodny, 1986).

Finance Costs

The cost of money is an important component of house prices. Money for construction and ultimate purchase (whether by landlord or homebuyer) is usually borrowed at an interest rate that is factored

Some of the design criteria for a "simple, decent" house include the following:

• Living space of about 1,000 square feet (exact size depends on number of bedrooms)

• One bathroom

• Covered primary entrance

• Three-foot doorways and three-foot, four-inch hallways to allow wheelchair access

While all U.S. Habitat houses share similarities, the differences in climate and construction techniques ensure ample individuality. Plus, homeowners are given opportunities to customize their homes when possible. Average house cost: $46,600 (U.S. dollars).

Figure 9.4 The "typical" U.S. Habitat for Humanity house (*Source:* Information found on www.habitat.org/how/naexamples.html, retrieved January 19, 2005. Reprinted with permission)

into the housing unit's cost. Low-interest loans for constructing or rehabilitating affordable housing can reduce the price of each housing unit. Once the housing has been built or rehabilitated, low interest loans can be used by potential landlords and homebuyers to reduce overall housing costs.

The federal government also supports the development of affordable rental housing through the Low Income Housing Tax Credit. This tool is used by housing developers, and is not a direct subsidy for low-income consumers. In this program, those who build or rehabilitate affordable housing may use federal and state tax credits to obtain a dollar-for-dollar reduction in income tax liability for up to 10 years. The tax credit reduces the developers' business costs and acts as an incentive to build or rehabilitate affordable housing.

The HOME Investment Partnership grant can also be used for the production of new affordable housing units, and the Community Development Block Grant (CDBG) can be used for a wide variety of housing activities. These programs allocate funds by formula in a "block" to states, urban counties, cities, and other jurisdictions, and have been responsible for the development of a great deal of affordable housing. Local officials have the authority to choose how to spend housing dollars to meet local needs.

Increasing Resources for Housing

Some argue that the most direct strategy for affordable housing is on the resource side. More money—either to produce affordable housing or directly into the consumer's pocket—is the most obvious answer to affordability. Literally hundreds of programs address the resource side of affordable housing; some are directed toward affordable homeownership while others promote rental housing.

As a matter of public policy, the U.S. federal government encourages homeownership. Home purchase assistance to low- and moderate-income homebuyers includes grants and no-interest loans for downpayment and closing costs, and special low mortgage interest programs. Special savings programs also exist in which low-income households' savings are matched by a nonprofit organization. The account (Individual Development Account) is tied to financial literacy training. Funds can be used only for specific purposes, but include home buying.

Educated buyers are generally considered to have a lower risk of default than others, so in most parts of the country first-time homebuyers with a low or moderate income can qualify for lower-cost loan terms by completing a homebuyer education course. Some faith-based organizations even offer no-interest loans for low-income buyers. This strategy greatly reduces the cost of a house, but requires the sustained financial support of donors.

Two federal housing programs, Public Housing and Section 8 Vouchers, provide affordable housing through subsidizing rents. Most housing advocates believe that these two programs should be continued and expanded because it is likely there will always be a shortage of affordable housing for the poorest of the poor that simply cannot and will never be provided by the private sector. Unfortunately, instead of increased federal funding these programs have experienced deep cuts beginning in the 1980s. In fact, federal funding for assisted housing dropped from $71.2 billion in 1978 to $16.8 billion in 1997 (*Home Sweet Home,* 2001). In 1997 the number of new federal housing subsidies was one seventh the number of subsidies provided in 1977. According to a study by the Center on Budget and Policy Priorities, if the government maintained the level of commitment to housing subsidies that it had in the 1970s, the housing shortage would be dramatically smaller, with 3 million additional renters receiving assistance (Daskal, 1998). In addition to the decrease in subsidies available, a growing movement exists to allow individuals with higher incomes to live in government-subsidized housing units in order to create a mix of incomes, thereby decreasing the number of units available to very low-income renters (Daskal, 1998).

CONCLUSION

Housing's importance is greater than the sum of individual housing units. As the largest component of most household budgets and the largest financial asset of many American families, affordable housing is indispensable to them, their children, and their communities. Increasingly it takes two incomes to afford housing, particularly among low- and moderate-income households. As we have shown, households earning minimum wage must work upwards of 65 to 70 hours a week to afford shelter in many U.S. communities. Former Secretary of HUD Andrew Cuomo observed, "There are many good $6 an hour jobs in today's economy, but not much $6 an hour housing" (*Home Sweet Home,* 2001, p. 11).

As we have seen, there are many approaches to the affordable housing problem and varied strategies to reduce housing's cost. Programs have come and gone throughout U.S. history, but it is clear that there will always be a population segment that the market does not or cannot serve. Many argue that some government-supported production will always be needed for purposes of neighborhood stabilization, helping people with special needs, and cushioning low-income housing from inflationary price pressures.

Surveys show that Americans are increasingly concerned about the availability of affordable housing, and yet housing tends to be low on most policy agendas (Nelson, 2003). In addition, those who need affordable housing often are characterized as needing government handouts. Affordable housing (meant to be affordable housing for the masses) continues to be characterized as the subsidized high-rise projects of old. "Often overlooked are the housing needs of productive individuals or families whose life-cycle situation or income, or both limit their housing options" (Nelson, 2003, p. 4).

Surprisingly, in some communities, school teachers, police officers, and other valuable community positions pay less than the area median income and the people holding these positions have difficulty finding affordable housing. Perhaps it will require a call to action by citizens if the affordable housing crisis is to be acknowledged and the shortage rectified. Future housing losses and gains need our attention. Comprehensive housing assessments should be a part of every community's future plan so that a dialogue to meet future housing needs can occur, protecting all citizens' interests.

REFERENCES

Advocacy Incorporated. (2003). Overcoming barriers to opening group homes for people with disabilities. Retrieved September 16, 2003, from www.advocacyinc.org/HS2_print.htm.

American Planning Association. (2003). *Policy guide on homelessness.* Washington, DC: American Planning Association. Retrieved April 18, 2003, from www.planning.org/ policyguides/homelessness.htm.

Bailey, N., & Robertson, D. (1997). Housing renewal, urban policy and gentrification. *Urban Studies, 34*(4), 561–578.

Bourne, L. S. (1981). *The geography of housing.* New York: John Wiley & Sons.

Burt, M., & Cohen, B. (1989). *America's homeless: Numbers, characteristics, and the programs that serve them.* Washington, DC: Urban Institute.

Cook, C., & Bruin, M. J. (1994). Determinants of housing quality: A comparison of White, African-American and Hispanic single-parent women. *Journal of Family and Economic Issues, 15*(4), 329–348.

Couch, L. (2000). Women and rental housing. In *Unlocking the door—Keys to women's housing.* Silver Springs, MD: McAuley Institute.

Daskal, J. (1998). *In search of shelter: The growing shortage of affordable rental housing.* Center on Budget and Policy Priorities. Retrieved September 16, 2003, from www.cbpp.org/615hous.htm.

Delaney, C. J., & Smith, M. T. (2001). Pricing implications of development exactions on existing housing stock. *Growth and Change, 32*(1), 1–12.

Dolbeare, C. N. (2001). Housing affordability: Challenge and context. *Cityscape: A Journal of Policy Development and Research, 5*(2), 111–130.

Duany, A. (2001). Three cheers for gentrification. *American Enterprise, 12*(3), 36–40.

Feldman, R. (2002). The affordable housing shortage: Considering the problem, causes and solutions. *Region* (Federal Reserve Bank of Minneapolis), *16*(3), 7–14.

Fischel, W. (1990). *Do growth controls matter? A review of the empirical evidence on the effectiveness and efficiency of local government land-use regulation.* Cambridge, MA: Lincoln Institute of Land Policy.

Golant, S. M. (1992). *Housing America's elderly.* Newbury Park, CA: Sage Publications.

Hart, P. D. (2002). *Results of the Fannie Mae Foundation affordable housing survey.* Washington, DC: Fannie Mae Foundation.

Home sweet home: Why America needs a national housing trust fund. (2001). Center for Community Change. Retrieved September 16, 2003, from www.communitychange.org/index2.htm#2.

Housing Assistance Council. (1997). *Rural housing and welfare reform: HAC's 1997 report on the state of the nation's rural housing.* Washington, DC: Housing Assistance Council.

Jensen, M. E. (1998). Affordability indicators. In W. van Vliet (Ed.), *The encyclopedia of housing* (pp. 11–12). Thousand Oaks, CA: Sage Publications.

Joint Center for Housing Studies. (2003). *The state of the nation's housing.* Cambridge, MA: Joint Center for Housing Studies of Harvard University.

Joint Center for Housing Studies. (2004). *The state of the nation's housing.* Cambridge, MA: Joint Center for Housing Studies of Harvard University.

Katz, B. (2000). *The need to connect smart growth and affordable housing.* Speech before the Vermont Affordable Housing Conference, November 29, 2000.

Kingsley, T. (1997). *Federal housing assistance and welfare reform: Uncharted territory.* Available: Urban Institute, http://newfederalism.urban.org/html/anf19.html.

Kolodny, R. (1986). The emergence of self-help as a housing strategy for the urban poor. In R. Bratt, C. Hartman, & A. Meyerson (Eds.), *Critical perspectives on housing* (pp. 447–462). Philadelphia, PA: Temple University Press.

Mieszkowski, P., & Mills, E. (1993). The causes of metropolitan suburbanization. *Journal of Economic Perspectives, 7,* 135–146.

Millennial Housing Commission. (2002). *Meeting our nation's housing challenges: Report of the bi-partisan Millennial Housing Commission.* Retrieved August 15, 2003, from www.mhc.gov.

Mitchell, J. P. (1993). Historical overview of direct federal housing assistance. In J. Mitchell (Ed.), *Federal housing policy and programs past and present* (pp. 187–206). New Brunswick, NJ: Rutgers University.

Mulroy, E. A. (1988). *Women as single parents.* Westport, CT: Auburn House.

Mulroy, E. A. (1996). Affordable housing: A basic need and a social issue. *Social Work, 41*(3), 245–249.

National Association of Home Builders. (2002). *America is facing a silent housing affordability crisis.* Washington, DC: National Association of Home Builders.

National Association of Home Builders. (2003a). *Barriers to affordable housing.* Retrieved August 19, 2003, from www.nahb.org/generic.aspx? genericContentID=3516&sectionID=207&print=true.

National Association of Home Builders. (2003b). *Characteristics of new single-family homes (1987–2002).* Retrieved August 23, 2003, from www.nahb.org/generic.aspx? sectionID=130&genericContentID=374.

National Association of Home Builders. (2003c). *Characteristics of units completed in multifamily buildings (1985–2002).* Retrieved August 23, 2003, from www.nahb.org/generic.aspx?sectionID=130&genericContentID=375.

National Coalition for the Homeless. (2002). *Who is homeless?* (NCH Fact Sheet #3). Retrieved September 17, 2003, from www.nationalhomeless.org.

National Low Income Housing Coalition. (2003). *The NIMBY report.* Washington, DC: National Low Income Housing Coalition. Retrieved September 15, 2003, from www.nlihc.org.

Nelson, A. C. (2003). Top ten state and local strategies to increase affordable housing supply. *Housing Facts & Findings, 5*(1), 1, 4–7.

Newman, S. J. (Ed.). (1999). *The home front: Implications of welfare reform for housing policy.* Washington, DC: Urban Institute Press.

O'Hara, A., & Cooper, E. (2003). *Priced out in 2002.* Washington, DC: Consortium for Citizens with Disabilities Housing Task Force.

Out of reach: The gap between housing costs and income of poor people in the United States. (2002). Washington, DC: National Low Income Housing Coalition.

Somerville, C. T., & Mayer, C. J. (2003). Government regulation and changes in the affordable housing stock. *Federal Reserve Bank of New York Economic Policy Review, 9*(2), 45–62.

Span, H. (2001). How the Courts should fight exclusionary zoning. *Seton Hall Law Review, 32,* 1–60.

Stone, M. (1993). *Shelter poverty.* Philadelphia, PA: Temple University Press.

Thomas, L. (2000). Women, pay equity and housing. In *Unlocking the door—Keys to women's housing.* Silver Springs, MD: McAuley Institute.

Unlocking the door—Keys to women's housing. (2000). Silver Springs, MD: McAuley Institute. Retrieved August 26, 2003, from www.mcauley.org/bhconline/voice-tools.htm#UTD.

The Urban Institute, Metropolitan Housing and Communities Policy Center. (2002). *Discrimination in metropolitan housing markets: National results from phase 1, phase 2, and phase 3 of the Housing Discrimination Study (HDS).* Washington, DC: U.S. Department of Housing and Urban Development. Retrieved January 11, 2005, from www.huduser.org/publications/hsgfin/hds.html.

U.S. Census Bureau. (1999). *Current population reports. Money income in the United States, 1998 P60–206.* Washington, DC: U.S. Department of Commerce.

U.S. Census Bureau. (2000). *Current construction reports—Characteristics of new housing: 1999, C25/99-A.* Washington, DC: U.S. Department of Commerce. Retrieved September 6, 2003, from www.census.gov/prod/2000pubs/c25-99a.pdf.

U.S. Department of Agriculture. (1996). *Rural homelessness: Focusing on the needs of the rural homeless.* Washington, DC: U.S. Department of Agriculture.

U.S. Department of Housing and Urban Development. (1998). *Rental housing assistance—The crisis continues: The 1997 report to Congress on worst case housing needs.* Washington, DC: U.S. Government Printing Office.

U.S. Department of Housing and Urban Development. (1999). *Waiting in vain: An update on America's rental housing crisis.* Washington, DC: U.S. Government Printing Office.

U.S. Department of Housing and Urban Development. (2000). *Discrimination in metropolitan housing markets: National results from phase 1 and phase 2 of the Housing Discrimination Study.* Retrieved August 23, 2003, from www.huduser.org/publications/hsgfin/hds.html.

U.S. Department of Housing and Urban Development. (2001). *Welfare reform.* Retrieved February 1, 2003, from www.hud.gov/wlfrefrm.cfm.

U.S. Department of Housing and Urban Development. (2003a, February). *FY2003 HUD income limits briefing material.* Retrieved August 23, 2003, from www.huduser.org/datasets/il/fmr03/index.html.

U.S. Department of Housing and Urban Development. (2003b). *Self-help homeownership opportunity program.* Retrieved September 16, 2003, from www.hud.gov/offices/cpd/affordablehousing/programs/shop/index.cfm.

U.S. Department of Housing and Urban Development. (2003c, May). *U.S. housing market conditions.* Retrieved August 23, 2003, from www.huduser.org/periodicals/ushmc/spring03/.

van Vliet, W. (1998). *The encyclopedia of housing.* Thousand Oaks, CA: Sage Publications.

Wallace, J. E. (1995). Financing affordable housing in the United States. *Housing Policy Debate, 6*(4), 785–814.

Weitz, S. (1985). Who pays infrastructure benefit charges: The builder or the home buyer? In J. C. Nicholas (Ed.), *The changing structure of infrastructure finance* (pp. 79–98). Cambridge, MA: Lincoln Institute of Land Policy.

Homeownership

Sue R. Crull, Marilyn J. Bruin, and Thessalenuere Hinnant-Bernard
Sue R. Crull is Associate Professor, Department of Human Development
and Family Studies, Iowa State University, Ames, IA; Marilyn J. Bruin is
Associate Professor, Department of Design, Housing, and Apparel,
University of Minnesota, Minneapolis, MN; and Thessalenuere Hinnant-
Bernard is Assistant Professor, Department of Human Environment and
Family Sciences, North Carolina A & T State University, Greensboro, NC.

Individuals, families, and other types of households decide how to house themselves based on many factors. In the United States, financial resources and available housing options play an important role in consumer decisions and the consumption of housing. The financial ramifications of housing the nation's population are enormous with over 120 million housing units. The majority of U.S. households own their housing units—in the second quarter in 2004, 69.2 percent (or over 73 million) of the occupied housing units were owner-occupied (U.S. Department of Housing and Urban Development, 2004).

Housing cost is often the largest component of a household budget. The median monthly housing cost for U.S. renters and owners was $648 and $757, respectively, in 2003. Monthly housing cost for renters includes rent, property insurance, and utilities. In contrast, the monthly housing cost for owners includes mortgage payments, property insurance, real estate taxes, routine maintenance, utilities, and association fees where appropriate. Median ratios of housing costs to income (the proportion of income spent on housing) for U.S. households indicate that on average renters pay 27.5 percent of their incomes for housing expenditures and owners pay 18.0 percent. Although renters pay less than owners in dollar amounts, housing costs are higher as a percentage of income for renters than for owners. The figures for owners, however, are somewhat misleading because 40 percent of homeowners had no mortgage payments (U.S. Department of Housing and Urban Development, 2004).

Because purchasing a home is a large investment, knowledge of the financial aspects of housing consumption is paramount in optimizing housing decisions (*Kiplinger's,* 2002). These decisions have implications for families' financial stability and well-being. Based on the assumption that informed consumers make better or more satisfying decisions, this chapter's purpose is to familiarize you with the basic concepts of housing finance and the processes of buying and maintaining a home.

HOUSING CHOICE

Homeownership has long been part of the "American Dream," which translates into a privately owned house and lot, and is connected to the Jeffersonian and rural ideal. In the mid-1700s Thomas Jefferson proposed that each colonist should reside in his or her own home and plot of land. This rural ideal concept was supported in the Homestead Act of the 1800s and continues to be supported by public policy. Homeownership is equated with "family virtue, political stability, and civic responsibility" (Kelly, 1993, p. 149). The enthusiasm for homeownership is both financial and psychological. Generally, homeownership is a good financial investment providing tax breaks, building wealth, and reflecting status. Psychologically, homeownership provides personal control and privacy, a sense of security and pride, and freedom of individual expression (*Kiplinger's,* 2002). Sidebar 10.1 describes the ideal of the "American Dream."

Sidebar 10.1
New Immigrants and the American Dream

Recent studies suggest that, like native-born citizens, U.S. immigrants pursue the "American Dream" of homeownership. However, important differences exist in their ownership experiences. When compared to native-born homebuyers, immigrants buy higher-priced homes and make larger downpayments. Because of these larger downpayments, they hold higher equity values in their homes than comparable native-born homeowners (Drew, 2002).

Immigrant homeowners also tend to devote a larger proportion of their income toward mortgage payments and related housing costs. "Among all recent (since 1997) homebuyers, 39 percent of immigrants are paying at least 39 percent of their income in monthly housing costs, compared to 28 percent of native first-time homebuyers" (Drew, 2002, p. 5). In comparison, the median housing cost burden for the overall population of homeowners with a mortgage was 21.7 percent in 2000 (Bonnette, 2003). It follows that immigrant homeowners are more vulnerable for financial problems including foreclosure during an economic downturn.

Immigrant homebuyers are concentrated in high-priced, metropolitan markets and clustered in suburban, single-family units built before 1985. They tend to have larger households in smaller homes than comparable native-born homeowners (Drew, 2002). The housing needs and preferences of U.S. immigrants since 1997 increasingly shape the demand for owned housing units in metropolitan markets (Drew, 2002).

Because people place such a strong emphasis on homeownership, renting is often thought of as a less desirable housing choice. However, for many individuals, families, and other types of households renting may be the best choice. In actuality, some housing experts are concerned that too much emphasis is placed on homeownership because the incentives in U.S. housing policy are much greater for homeownership than renting (Lindamood & Hanna, 1979; Shinn & Gillespie, 1994). Figure 10.1 shows an example of single-family homes.

Advantages and Disadvantages of Homeownership

One important advantage of homeownership is that households can control several aspects of their housing environment. If they wish to change things, they can decorate and remodel to their preferences. Three main financial advantages exist for homeownership: (1) equity, (2) income tax deductions, and (3) control over housing expenses. Equity is the property's value less the property's loan. Therefore, homeownership is a form of built-in savings as equity accumulates over the years as the mortgage is paid. Homeowners can deduct

Figure 10.1   "American Dream" of tree-lined street of single-family homes

mortgage interest and property taxes from their income taxes. The U.S. tax code subsidizes homeownership and makes ownership more attractive than renting for many households. Also, owners can decide if and when they want to make repairs, improvements, or change the décor in their homes, while renters may be denied requests for changes due to landlord policies that control modifications, and may also be susceptible to periodic increases in rent.

A disadvantage of homeownership is that home equity is not a liquid asset and you cannot easily withdraw money from your investment. However, with the current use of home equity credit lines this concern is diminished. Home maintenance may be a disadvantage if household members do not like to do routine repairs or pay others to do them. A home purchase is usually a long-term (15 to 30 years) commitment and the investment is not risk free; a home may depreciate rather than appreciate and the household could lose money over time. For some households, homeownership is a stressful event due to the complexity of the home buying process and the financial ramifications associated with the decision. Most households feel that the advantages of homeownership outweigh the disadvantages. History has shown that, over the years, most homes appreciate in value and homeowners benefit financially from owning their own homes (Zielenbach, 2004).

The Housing Market

The U.S. housing market has been economically strong during the past several years. The decrease from the double-digit mortgage interest rates of the 1980s, as shown in Table 10.1, fostered a housing market boom during the 1990s. The housing affordability index, which has been over 100 since 1986 and reached an all time high of 140.5 in 2003, indicates the relationship between household median income and the median priced house. Values over 100 mean that the median income household has more than sufficient income to purchase a median priced house (U.S. Department of Housing and Urban Development, 2004).

Although interest rates and the affordability index shown in Table 10.1 tend to show changes, the homeownership rate has remained well over 60 percent. Stability in the homeownership rate is based on the fact that households either own units outright, or are established in a mortgage arrangement and do not move in and out of ownership as the market changes. When interest rates drop and the affordability index increases, homeowners often refinance mortgages to lower rates or sell their homes and purchase ones of higher value. However, these procedures do not affect the homeownership

Table 10.1 Homeownership Rates, Average Mortgage Interest Rates, and Affordability Index

| Year | Homeownership (% households) | Interest Rate | | Affordability Index |
		30-Year Fixed	15-Year Fixed	
1982	64.8	16.09	NA	69.5
1983	64.6	13.23	NA	83.2
1984	64.5	13.87	NA	89.1
1985	63.9	12.42	NA	94.8
1986	63.8	10.18	NA	108.9
1987	64.0	10.20	NA	114.2
1988	63.8	10.33	NA	113.5
1989	63.9	10.32	NA	108.1
1990	63.9	10.13	NA	109.5
1991	64.1	9.25	NA	112.9
1992	64.1	8.40	7.96	124.7
1993	64.0	7.33	6.83	133.3
1994	64.0	8.35	7.86	131.8
1995	64.7	7.95	7.49	129.3
1996	65.4	7.81	7.32	133.3
1997	65.7	7.59	7.13	133.9
1998	66.3	6.95	6.59	141.1
1999	66.8	7.44	7.06	139.1
2000	67.4	8.05	7.72	129.2
2001	67.8	6.97	6.50	135.7
2002	67.9	6.54	5.98	135.0
2003	68.3	5.83	5.17	140.5

Source: www.huduser.org/periodicals/, U.S. Housing Market Conditions, August 2004, Table 11, Table 14, and Table 28

rate directly because homeowners are just changing mortgages or homes, not ownership status. The increase in the U.S. homeownership rate in the past 10 years is due to a favorable housing market that allowed renters to move into homeownership. Sidebar 10.2 shows how homeownership impacts families.

Sidebar 10.2
The Impact of Homeownership on Families

Encouraging family homeownership is a federal policy priority (Colton, 2003). In recent years innovative programs have increased home-ownership opportunities for low-income, single-parent, and minority families (Retsinas & Belsky, 2002). Although relatively little is known about the relationship between homeownership and resident families, an emerging body of research measures the impacts of ownership tenure (Belsky & Duda, 2001; Haurin, Parcel, & Haurin, 2002; Rohe, Van Zandt, & McCarthy, 2001; Rossi & Weber, 1996). Several re-searchers suggest positive causal relationships between homeown-ership and life satisfaction, self-esteem, and self-efficacy (Clark, 1997; Rohe & Basolo, 1997; Rohe & Stegman, 1994a, 1994b). In another re-cent study, researchers suggest that homeownership increases ac-cess to opportunity; however, homeowners and their family members need to possess psychosocial characteristics, such as self-esteem and motivation, in order to make the best use of available opportuni-ties (Rohe, Van Zandt, & McCarthy, 2002).

Researchers also explore the impact on children of growing up in an owned home; children reared in owned homes have higher quality housing, higher cognitive scores, and fewer behavior problems when compared to children reared in rented homes. Children of homeown-ers are more likely to finish high school and avoid teenage pregnancy; as adults they complete more education and earn higher wages than individuals reared in rental housing (Boehm & Schlottman, 1999; Green & White, 1997; Harkness & Newman, 2002; Haurin, Parcel, & Haurin, 2002). Green and White's (1997) study on homeownership's influence on positive outcomes such as education and delayed child-bearing is particularly relevant for low-income families.

HOME BUYING BASICS

Prequalifying for Homeownership

Once a household chooses to buy a home, it must estimate how much it can afford to spend for a house, often using "rule of thumb" guidelines based on income multiplier guidelines. For example, the income multiplier guidelines suggest a household can afford to pur-chase a home priced at two and one half times its combined annual gross income (Fannie Mae, 1996) or can qualify for a loan up to twice its combined annual gross income (*Kiplinger's*, 2002). Based on these guidelines, if the annual gross income is $45,000, the house-hold can afford to buy a house priced up to $112,500 or finance a home with a loan up to $90,000.

Some financial advisers believe the income multiplier guidelines are too simple and do not consider important factors such as loan interest rates, the loan's term, the downpayment amount, and the household's indebtedness. For example, assume a household will pay one fourth of its income for a loan. A variation in one factor, the interest rate, has a significant impact on the amount of loan that this household can afford and, therefore, what price it can pay for a home. In Table 10.2, based on a household with $45,000 annual income, $10,000 downpayment, and a 30-year fixed mortgage, the borrower can afford to buy a home priced at $166,400 with a loan at a 6 percent interest rate, compared to a home purchase of $116,800 with a loan at a 10 percent interest rate. For the income multiplier guidelines to accurately predict that a household with $45,000 annual income can buy a home priced at two and one half times its income ($112,500) or can qualify for a loan up to twice its income ($90,000), the interest rate would need to be in the 11 percent to 12 percent range. Table 10.2 illustrates the effect of interest rates on home price and loan amount rule of thumb guidelines.

A more accurate approach to determine how much homebuyers can afford to spend for a house is to calculate the amount they can spend for housing each month based on their combined monthly gross incomes and monthly debt loads if they add housing payments to their current debt obligations. The most common prequalifying guidelines include:

1. No more than 28 percent of monthly gross income should be used to cover house payments, which include mortgage principal and interest, property taxes and homeowner's insurance, and mortgage insurance if applicable. This is called the *front-end ratio*.
2. No more than 36 percent of monthly income should be used to cover total debt payments including credit card obligations, car payments, and student loans, as well as the proposed home mortgage payment. This is called the *back-end ratio*.
3. The difference between the two ratios is 8 percent of the monthly income; therefore, the amount of debt allowed other than the house payment is relatively small.

The process of calculating qualifying ratios—the front-end ratio (28 percent) and the back-end ratio (36 percent)—is part of the process called prequalification.

Most U.S. households use a mortgage loan to purchase a home, although there are other methods used such as cash or contract. If a mortgage is used, the amount of house a household can buy with 28 percent of its monthly income is dependent on the amount that household has for a downpayment, the term (length of time) of the

19

Table 10.2   Loan Amount and Home Price Comparison with Various Interest Rates

Interest Rate	Loan Amount	Downpayment	Home Price
6%	$156,400	$10,000	$166,400
7%	140,900	10,000	150,900
8%	127,700	10,000	137,700
9%	116,500	10,000	126,500
10%	106,800	10,000	116,800
11%	98,400	10,000	108,400
12%	91,100	10,000	101,800
13%	84,700	10,000	94,700
14%	79,100	10,000	89,100

A household has an annual gross income of $45,000. It will spend 25 percent of its income for the housing mortgage payment plus an additional 3 percent for property taxes and insurance. The household has $10,000 for a downpayment and wants a 30-year fixed mortgage.

Loan amounts were generated by using the "How Much House Can You Afford?" calculator on www.homepath.com.

mortgage, and current interest rates. Several Internet mortgage calculators use the 28 percent and 36 percent ratios and provide estimates of maximum home purchase price based on entering information about downpayment, term, and interest rate. Table 10.3 provides examples of the maximum home purchase price a household with $50,000 annual income can buy using the 28 percent ratio and a 5 percent downpayment, with three different interest rates and 30-versus 15-year mortgage terms. Using the 28 percent housing cost ratio, the monthly payment is always the same in Table 10.3. However, purchase price, loan amount, and downpayment amount change a great deal due to the mortgage term and interest rate.

Buyers usually must meet both ratios to qualify for a mortgage. The qualifying ratios are often raised a few percentage points if the mortgage-granting institution believes a household will substantially increase its income in the near future or can document a record of timely rental payments equal to or more than the proposed mortgage payment. Also, if the household is considering a FHA, VA, or a specialized loan such as a first-time homebuyer product, more flexible qualifying ratios may apply.

Through the prequalification analysis, the household learns more about its financial situation and can determine the price range of homes that it can afford. The household also learns if its financial situation is appropriate for serious consideration of a mortgage

Table 10.3   Housing Costs Comparisons Based on 28 Percent of Monthly Income

	Interest Rate	Purchase Price	Loan Amount	Down-Payment	Monthly Payment
30-Year Mortgage	5%	$228,832	$217,391	$11,441	$1,167
	6%	204,890	194,645	10,245	1,167
	7%	184,641	175,409	9,232	1,167
15-Year Mortgage	5%	$155,340	$147,573	$ 7,767	$1,167
	6%	145,572	138,294	7,278	1,167
	7%	136,669	129,836	6,833	1,167

A household has $50,000 in annual gross income and 28 percent of its monthly income is $1,167.00. It can pay a 5 percent downpayment. The household's debts other than housing are 8 percent of monthly income ($333).

Calculations were generated by using the "How Much House Can You Afford?" calculator on www.homepath.com.

application. It is not uncommon to find that households meet the front-end ratio but cannot qualify for a mortgage because their debt load is too high and they do not meet the back-end ratio. Many times this situation is remedied by paying off credit card debts, or by selling an expensive car and replacing it with a more economical model. Also, homebuyers can purchase a less expensive house that puts their house payment below the 28 percent, and that allows for more than 8 percent of their monthly income for other debt.

Mortgage Financing

The mortgage portion, the principal and interest (PI), of the monthly housing payment is influenced by five interrelated factors:

- purchase price of the home,
- downpayment,
- term (or length) of the mortgage,
- interest rate for the mortgage, and
- type of mortgage.

The amount of money the household initially puts toward a house purchase is considered the downpayment, and it influences the amount of the mortgage loan. Therefore, the amount a household needs to borrow (the mortgage) to buy a specific house is the purchase price minus the downpayment. A larger downpayment results in a smaller mortgage which, in turn, requires smaller monthly housing payments.

Most lenders consider 20 percent down necessary for a conventional mortgage and require private mortgage insurance if the household makes less than a 20 percent downpayment. Mortgage insurance is paid by the buyer and provides the lender insurance. If the household defaults on the loan, the lender will not lose money if the home's value has decreased when the lender repossesses the property.

The term and type of the mortgage influences the interest rate charged for the loan. Table 10.4 represents the type of information often placed in local newspapers listing current mortgage rates for lenders. If the fixed rate mortgage is for 15 years rather than for 30 years, the interest rate is usually a little lower (for example, 8.25 percent instead of 8.50 percent). Interest rates also vary by type of mortgage, lender, and if a mortgage origination fee (Org) is charged (usually one point) or discount points (Dis) are offered to get a lower rate. It pays to shop around for a mortgage loan in order to get the most favorable financial terms, as terms are likely to vary by lending institution.

The household spends less on total interest cost with a 15-year loan due to the short duration of the loan contract compared to the 30-year loan, as shown in Table 10.5. Because the loan is spread over a 15-year term rather than 30 years, the household likely will be paying a larger monthly payment with the shorter-term mortgage because they make 180 monthly payments rather than 360 monthly payments to repay the loan. The mortgage term influences both the interest rate (Table 10.4) and the size of the monthly payment

Table 10.4   Mortgage Rates for Two Lenders

Lender	30-Year Fixed		15-Year Fixed		1 Year ARM				5/25	
	Rate	Org/Dis	Rate	Org/Dis	Rate	Org/Dis	A/L Cap	Margin	Rate	Org/Dis
First Bank	8.500	0/0	8.250	0/0	7.625	0/0	1.5/4.5	3.000	8.375	0/0
X Credit U	8.375	1/0	8.175	1/0	7.500	0/0	2/6	2.750	8.500	0/0

Table 10.5   Mortgage Costs Vary by Interest Rate, Term, and Downpayment

Interest Rate	Term Years	Down-payment	Loan Amount	Monthly Payment	Total Loan Cost	Total Interest
8%	30	10%	$90,000	$660.39	$237,740	$147,740
7%	30	10%	90,000	598.77	215,557	125,557
7%	15	10%	90,000	808.95	145,611	55,611
7%	30	20%	80,000	532.24	191,606	111,606

The fixed mortgage is based on a home with a $100,000 purchase price.
Monthly payments were generated using the "Mortgage Payment Calculator" on www.realtor.com

(Table 10.5), which in turn determines the total loan cost of buying a home with a mortgage. In Table 10.5, the total loan cost was estimated by multiplying the monthly payment by the number of months in the term. The total interest was then estimated by subtracting the loan amount from the total loan cost. The amount of the downpayment that determines the amount of the loan also influences the total loan cost of buying a home. Table 10.5 also shows that a lower interest rate and a shorter term substantially reduce the total interest paid.

The interest rate is mainly determined by the U.S. prime lending interest rate, which in turn is influenced by the national economy. When mortgage interest rates drop, a flurry of home buying usually takes place because the lower rates translate into lower monthly housing costs. Therefore, the option of home buying becomes available to more households because more households can afford the lower monthly payments. Also, a decline in interest rates motivates households who desire larger and/or better homes to sell their existing homes and purchase homes of higher value. Monthly payments on a larger mortgage now fit into more budgets because lower interest rates translate into lower monthly payments for more expensive homes. Conversely, when mortgage interest rates increase, home buying activity tends to decrease because the higher interest rates translate into higher monthly payments or a lower-priced home for the same payment.

The Fixed Rate Mortgage

The monthly housing payment is determined in part by the type of mortgage the household uses to finance the home. Although there are several mortgage variations, only the two basic types will be emphasized here—fixed and adjustable rate mortgages. A household with a fixed rate mortgage will have less fluctuation in the monthly payment for the mortgage's duration. Two components of the monthly payment (the principal and the interest) are stable during the life of a fixed rate mortgage and an amortization schedule shows how the monthly payment is distributed to principal and interest each month. A household with an adjustable rate mortgage (ARM) can expect the monthly payment to change periodically due to fluctuations in the U.S. prime interest rate.

Factors affecting the amount of the monthly housing payment are often referred to as "PITI," which consists of the following items:

1. Principal (P), which is the amount paid on the loan;
2. Interest (I), which is the amount charged by the lender for giving the mortgage loan; and

3. Property taxes (T) and homeowner's/hazard insurance cost
   (I), which go into an escrow account that the lender uses
   to pay the taxes and insurance for the homebuyer.

In the graph shown in Figure 10.2, the first 15 bars show the payment for the first month of each year of a 15-year fixed rate mortgage obtained in February of 2001. The 16th bar represents the payment in the final month. The graph illustrates how the principal and the interest portions (PI) of the payment amortization schedule change over the life of a $108,000 loan at an 8 percent interest rate with a 10 percent downpayment. In the first mortgage payment, the interest is $720; the principal is $312. In the final payment in February of 2016, the interest is $7 and the principal is $1,025. The total amount of the principal and interest to be paid each month is always the same amount ($1,032) in a fixed mortgage; however, the P and I amounts going to each category change over the loan's duration.

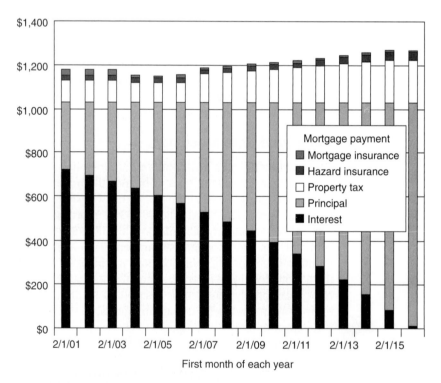

Figure 10.2 Monthly mortgage payments for the first month of each year (fixed 15-year mortgage starting 2/1/00, 8 percent rate, 10 percent down, $108,000)

Most lenders require 20 percent of the purchase price as a down-payment on a conventional mortgage, which yields a loan for 80 percent of the purchase price (loan to value ratio). Buyers with a smaller downpayment are usually required to purchase mortgage insurance, which protects the lender in case the homeowner defaults on the mortgage. Because the downpayment in Figure 10.2 is less than 20 percent, mortgage insurance is required for the first three years until the balance owed on the principal reaches 80 percent of the home's value. Also, the payment includes escrow for property taxes and homeowner's/hazard insurance (TI) that increases over the term of the loan because the cost of insurance and property taxes increases over time due to inflation. Although an escrow account for taxes and insurance is not required on all loans, most lenders today encourage the homebuyer to set up an escrow account.

The Adjustable Rate Mortgage

An adjustable rate mortgage (ARM) allows for changes in interest rates over the loan's term. Initially, the interest rate for an ARM is lower than the rate for a fixed mortgage. An adjustment schedule is included in the ARM terms and designates when the interest rate will be adjusted. If the adjustment period is yearly, then the interest rate can change annually to reflect the current market interest rate. The ARM is tied to an index, such as the average rate of Treasury securities, which is listed in the mortgage and is used to regulate the mortgage interest rate. The ARM also contains an adjustment margin, which is a percentage amount the lender adds to the index rate when calculating the mortgage rate.

Most ARMs also include two types of "caps" which influence the amount the interest rate can fluctuate. The lifetime cap limits the amount that the interest rate can change over the term of the mortgage. If the initial interest rate is 7 percent and the lifetime cap is 6 percent, the interest rate can never exceed 13 percent. A periodic cap, often specified as $1^1/_2$ percent to 2 percent, limits the amount the interest rate can change in one adjustment period. However, if the rate increases more than the periodic cap, the rate can increase again at the next adjustment period to make up for the difference in the periodic cap and the index in the previous adjustment period even if the index has not changed. For example, if the index plus margin calls for an increase of two percentage points and the periodic cap is one and one half percentage points, the rate increases by one and one half points in the adjustment period and then an additional half percentage point in the following adjustment period. Sometimes caps also apply to interest rate reductions.

Other Mortgage Alternatives

Several other types of mortgages are on the market, but most are some combination of the two basic types previously presented. For example, a step-rate or two-step mortgage combines aspects of the fixed and adjustable rate mortgages. This type of mortgage allows the borrower to pay fixed payments for the first few years, usually five to seven, and then reset the rate based on an index for the loan's remaining years. This provides the fixed rate stability but also allows for later market adjustments. Sometimes a lender will offer a first-step rate that is slightly lower than a 30-year term fixed rate to entice the borrower into a contract. However, both the borrower and the lender are aware that the interest rate will be adjusted to market rate at the second step. If the interest rate increases greatly during the first step, the household will have a large increase in the monthly housing payment for the second step and may end up paying more interest than if it had originally financed a 30-year fixed mortgage. It is always difficult to predict the future. If a household expects to sell the home during the first step (five to seven years), the two-step mortgage may be an excellent choice.

Some mortgages are written with balloon payments due at the end of the term. In some cases the lender will help the borrower refinance the amount due and in other cases the borrower is expected to pay the lump sum when the balloon payment comes due. Balloon payments are a common tactic used in predatory lending, which is discussed later in the chapter.

Insurance

When purchasing a home, the homebuyer can be approached to buy three different types of insurance: homeowner's/hazard insurance, mortgage insurance, and credit life insurance. Hazard insurance, which is required by the lender, is sold as part of a homeowner's insurance policy and protects the lender and the homeowner against property losses or damages due to fire, tornado, and so forth. The homeowner's policy usually includes a feature that reimburses the homeowner for losses or damages to personal property such as furniture and clothing. Also included in most homeowner's policies is a liability component that provides protection for personal liability, medical payments for injuries to others, and damage to others' property.

The second type of insurance, mortgage insurance, is only required if the homebuyer does not have a 20 percent downpayment and is needed only as long as the loan-to-value ratio stays under 80 percent. Mortgage insurance protects the lender, although the homebuyer pays for it. In the event that the homebuyer defaults on the loan and the property's value has depreciated, the lender is protected against loss.

The third type of insurance is credit life insurance that would pay off the mortgage in the event of the homebuyer's death. The main problem with credit life insurance is that the beneficiary is the lender, not the homebuyer's family, and paying off the loan at the time of death may not be in the family's best interest. Purchasing a life insurance policy independent of the mortgage may be a better choice in providing the family with both resources and choices in the event of the homebuyer's death.

Equity

Equity, the financial value the homeowner accumulates in the process of owning the home, is figured by subtracting the money owed for the home from the market value. The market value is established when the home is sold or by an appraisal if the home is not being sold. Equity usually includes the dollar amount of the initial down-payment, the dollar amount the household has paid in principal on the mortgage, and the dollar amount the home has appreciated in value since the household acquired the home. Equity is often considered a form of built-in savings. Through the process of buying the home and paying the monthly payments, the household builds equity or savings that become available when it sells the home.

Equity can also help establish a line of credit or loan which allows the household to use its "equity savings" to finance current expenditures. Home equity is often used to finance remodeling projects, automobile purchases, or vacations. However, caution should be used when using home equity for a credit line or loan because the household is obligating its home in an additional debt commitment. The home equity loan is considered a debt just like any other loan and the household must pay back the loan plus interest. Therefore, the household with an equity loan has two monthly payments—the mortgage payment and the equity loan payment.

Home equity can also be used to provide a reverse mortgage, which allows older homeowners to live in their homes and draw on equity to meet living expenses. The Federal Housing Administration (FHA) provides government-backed insurance to lenders who make reverse mortgages to homeowners over the age of 55. With FHA-insured reverse mortgages, homeowners never owe more than the values of their homes. They cannot be forced to sell or move if their loans exceed the homes' values. The pooled funds collected from FHA insurance premiums compensate lenders when reverse mortgage loans exceed the homes' values. With a reverse mortgage, the equity can be drawn out in a lump sum, in monthly installments, or through periodic withdrawals. Typically, a reverse mortgage is repaid with interest when the home is sold or upon the homeowner's death when his or her estate is settled (*Kiplinger's,* 2002).

Income Tax Deductions

One of the major advantages of homeownership is the income tax deduction. Homeowners can deduct property taxes and interest payments (mortgage and equity loan) in personal income tax calculations. During a mortgage's early years, the interest payments are high and the deduction can be substantial. However, over time, as the mortgage is paid the interest portion of the monthly payment declines. Therefore, the tax advantage also declines. In 1998 the capital gains tax regulations on personal homes was changed. Under the new regulations households selling homes after owning them for at least two years and living in them for the two most recent years do not pay taxes on capital gains up to $250,000 if a single homeowner and $500,000 if a married couple (*Kiplinger's,* 2002).

Types of Ownership

Most single-family detached homes and their surrounding yards are owned by individuals or couples. A single adult usually buys a house in his or her own name. Married couples usually own their homes through joint tenancy with the right of survivorship. Under joint tenancy when one spouse dies, the other spouse is the home's sole owner. When homes are purchased by adults who are not legally married, they may choose to hold the property in joint tenancy, tenancy in common, or form a legal partnership. Although the latter two ownership types do not include right of survivorship, the property may be transferred to the other adult through a will. Ownership arrangements may vary if the home is located in a community-property state (Arizona, California, Idaho, Louisiana, Nevada, New Mexico, Texas, Washington, and Wisconsin).

Condominium ownership includes an individual dwelling (either detached from or attached to other units) and an undivided proportional interest in common areas such as yards, elevators, hallways, and recreational areas, as shown in Figure 10.3. Condominium ownership usually includes fees for maintenance and routine costs such as yard care. Condominium owners have the same mortgage arrangements and tax regulations as owners of single-family detached homes.

Cooperative ownership, however, differs from ownership of a single-family or condominium unit. In a cooperative, the owner actually buys a share in a corporation, which allows the householder to live in a particular unit as a tenant-stockholder. Usually, the corporation holds the mortgage on all of the units and common space, pays the taxes,

Figure 10.3   Condominium-owned housing in multi-unit building

and supervises maintenance and routine care. If the cooperative meets specified requirements of the Internal Revenue Code, the tenant-stockholder receives tax deductions similar to owners of single-family detached homes or condominiums (*Kiplinger's,* 2002).

THE PROCESS OF PURCHASING A HOME

After potential homeowners complete self-evaluations of renting versus buying and determine that their prequalification status is favorable for purchasing a home, they are ready to continue the process. Securing financing, searching for a house in a desired neighborhood, making an offer, and closing on a home can be intimidating, especially for first-time homebuyers, because of the vocabulary and regulations surrounding home finance. Therefore, most homebuyers work with several professionals who are knowledgeable of the process. This section details additional information about the process, professionals, and vocabulary of purchasing a home, as outlined in Figure 10.4.

Mortgage Preapproval

When a household decides that it definitely wants to pursue homeownership, it can work with a mortgage lender to secure preapproval, often in the form of a commitment letter that confirms a mortgage

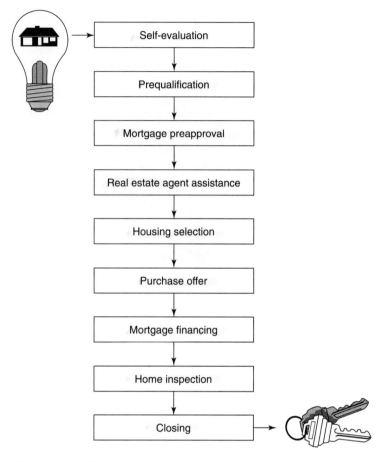

Figure 10.4   The process of purchasing a home

institution has approved the buyer. The lender will back the buyer in securing a mortgage quickly for a property that falls within the preapproved amount. Although preapproval is not for a specific house, it is for a specific loan amount. The preapproval process helps a householder target its search to a very specific price range. A preapproval letter also strengthens the buyer's negotiating position in a tight housing market. Most mortgage lenders charge a fee for processing information and documenting the credit history before issuing a preapproval letter, which is based on a current credit history and verified income, and expires after a specified time period.

Credit Check

Householders with stable employment and spotless credit histories typically qualify for a prime rate mortgage, which has the best terms and is offered to borrowers who are considered low risk. Prospective homebuyers should always apply for a prime rate mortgage.

Under a federal law, the Equal Credit Opportunity Act, lenders are prohibited from denying mortgage financing based on an applicant's race, color, religion, national origin, age, sex, marital status, or participation in a public assistance program. If an applicant is denied a mortgage, the Equal Credit Opportunity Act requires the lender to acknowledge the reasons for the denial in a letter. The law also requires the lender to consider the loan based on the applicant's financial criteria, not the criteria of the location or neighborhood of the dwelling to be purchased. The law's intent is to discourage discrimination.

If potential borrowers are denied a loan because they lack the necessary downpayment, they need to work on saving additional funds. If a poor credit history is the reason, they need to maintain an excellent record of repayment for a longer period of time. One of the most important determinants of getting a mortgage is the applicant's credit score; most mortgages have a minimum acceptable score. Applicants who meet the qualifying ratios and have an "A" credit rating, no late payments, and no bankruptcies will typically qualify for a prime mortgage.

Borrowers denied a prime mortgage may also explore the option of subprime financing. Good subprime lending is intended to make mortgage funds available to borrowers with impaired credit history. Because the mortgage lenders assume a greater risk, subprime mortgages are offered at higher interest rates than prime mortgages and are therefore more expensive for the homebuyer. Table 10.6 shows the effects of credit scores on interest rates, which in turn affect monthly payments and total interest cost for a mortgage. Many homebuyers with a subprime mortgage can refinance and receive a lower interest rate in a few years if they maintain a good credit history.

Assistance from a Real Estate Professional

State governments license real estate agents or associates, who are supervised by, and share commissions with, a broker, an agent who has met additional licensing and experience requirements. Most communities have several agents. In larger communities, agents may specialize by neighborhood or type of housing. One way for a prospective homebuyer to find an agent is to drive through desired neighborhoods noting which listing agents have houses advertised. Most agents will belong to a Multiple Listing Service, which means that they can show and sell houses listed by other agents in the Multiple Listing Service. It is important for homebuyers to find an agent they are comfortable with, one who listens to their needs. However, homebuyers need to understand that agents earn commissions based on a house's selling price. Some communities have buyer's

Table 10.6 Credit Scores' Influence on Mortgage Rates

FICO Score	Interest Rate	Monthly Payment	Total Interest
720–850	5.488%	$567	$104,133
700–719	5.613	575	106,964
675–699	6.151	609	119,345
620–674	7.301	686	146,830
560–619	8.531	771	177,600
500–559	9.289	826	197,181

The table above is based on a 30-year fixed loan for $100,000.
Calculations were generated by using the "Loan Savings Calculator" on
www.myfico.com on March 17, 2004.

Figure 10.5   House for sale advertised by real estate agent

representatives, who help prospective homebuyers find a home for
a set fee rather than a commission based on the house's price
(Thomsett, 1996). Figure 10.5 shows a house for sale by a real estate agent.

Housing Selection

Viewing houses on the market can be exciting, but it can also be
frustrating. In 1995 the average homebuyer looked at 15 houses during a five-month period before completing the purchase (Razzi, 1997).

After viewing several houses in an afternoon, it is difficult to remember which one has new carpeting and which one has the beautiful tree in the backyard. Prospective homeowners are encouraged to devise a system of note taking to make comparisons. Prospective homeowners need to be critical. Almost no one finds everything he or she wants in one home, so a buyer must decide the most important features and which can be sacrificed.

Once a desired unit is located, homebuyers should conduct additional research. They can check insurance rates and utility statements, and review neighborhood crime statistics and city records on the property. They can drive by the location at various times of the day to check neighborhood activity, noise levels, and traffic congestion. If applicable, they can also visit local schools, parks, and churches.

Purchase Offer

A purchase offer is a legally binding contract the homebuyer uses to make an offer on a desired property. Homebuyers need to read the offer carefully and ask questions about any parts they do not understand. When a seller accepts a purchase offer, both parties enter into a commitment called a purchase agreement. Earnest money, typically an amount between 1 percent and 3 percent of the house's purchase price, accompanies the offer. Earnest money is held in escrow until the transaction closes; at closing earnest money is considered part of the downpayment. Acceptance of the purchase offer begins the escrow period, when the property is off the market and the paperwork for closing is completed. If the buyer backs out of the sale, the earnest money is typically forfeited to the seller.

A purchase offer should clearly state what is included in the house's sale (window treatments, appliances, etc.), as well as set dates for a final walk-through inspection of the empty property, a closing date, and a date for possession. It should also include contingencies—clauses defining conditions that void the purchase offer. The buyer will typically include a contingency for an inspection and appraisal, and final approval by the lender. For example, if the property appraisal, which is conducted by a professional, is lower than the home's purchase price, the homebuyer has the opportunity to void the purchase offer.

Mortgage Financing

As discussed earlier in this chapter, most real estate purchases are financed with a mortgage, a long-term loan on real property, which serves as collateral on the loan. A mortgage is also a legal document that allows the lender to retain title or place a lien or claim on the title, and gives the lender the right to demand full payment if the borrower fails to make payments. Many lenders will demand full payment after a second missed payment. If a borrower defaults on a mortgage, the lender can foreclose on the property, sell it, and use the proceeds to pay off the loan. Any proceeds that remain after the mortgage, liens, and foreclosure costs are paid to the borrower. A mortgage also lists the borrower's responsibility for payment of taxes, homeowner's/hazard insurance, and maintenance to ensure the lender's investment in the property.

Homebuyers must provide many documents for the lender's inspection during the approval process. Soon after the closing, the lender will typically sell the mortgage on the secondary mortgage market. A loan officer and the loan committee at the lending institution compare applications with underwriting guidelines to estimate a mortgage's worth on the secondary market. Securing a mortgage involves decisions about the downpayment amount, mortgage type, loan term, and interest rate. Interest rates vary slightly between mortgage institutions and also vary because some institutions request additional fees "up-front" in return for lower interest rates. A common word in the mortgage process is "points," which refers to a one-time sum of money that is paid to the lender when the loan is secured. One point is equal to 1 percent of the loan.

In Table 10.4, X Credit Union lists one point under the origination column, which means that the credit union charges 1 percent of the loan amount in return for a lower rate. An origination fee is not the application fee, which covers the costs of processing a loan application. For example, the application fee includes costs to collect credit reports, complete paperwork for mortgage insurance, and put together appraisals. However, an origination fee is a form of prepaid interest that is calculated as a percentage, usually 1 percent, of the loan amount. Loans with an origination fee should have a lower rate than a loan without an origination fee because the origination fee prepays a portion of the interest (*Kiplinger's,* 2002).

Sometimes a lender also offers discount points to lower the interest rate, which are paid to the lender at the time of closing. In essence, the homebuyer pays additional charges up-front in the form of points to get a loan at a lower interest rate. If there is a choice about number of points, consumers need to think carefully about paying several points to get a lower rate because the money might be better spent by increasing the downpayment and therefore decreasing the loan amount.

For a fee, mortgage brokers will take applications and search for a loan for prospective homebuyers. Some mortgage brokers identify lenders with relaxed underwriting or approval guidelines for individuals who have been denied a prime mortgage. A mortgage broker may provide a valuable service for consumers who do not have the time or expertise to search for a subprime loan. However, predatory lending practices have become more common in the past 10 years. Predatory lending involves subprime loans with extremely high interest rates, large loan fees, and loan procedures unfavorable to the homeowner. Potential homebuyers need to investigate mortgage brokers carefully and proceed with caution.

According to Reichel (1998) the following documents are needed for a mortgage application:

- Account numbers for all banking, credit, and investment accounts.
- Addresses for all financial institutions.
- Checking and savings account statements for the previous two to three months.
- Recent tax return and pay stubs.
- Divorce settlement if anyone involved is divorced.
- Payments, repayment schedule, and balance information on all debts.
- Balance sheets and tax returns from businesses if self-employed.
- Verification of gifts if gifts are used for the downpayment or to qualify.

Home Inspection

A home inspection is a wise expenditure when considering such a large purchase. The inspection serves two purposes. One, it assures the buyer of the housing unit's structural integrity. Second, it helps the homebuyer maintain the dwelling. Therefore, it is important for the homebuyer to walk through the house with the inspector and receive an estimate of the life of major components and systems such as the roof and heating system. The home inspector can also offer advice on operation and maintenance. If the home inspector identifies major concerns, the homebuyer who included an inspection contingency in the purchase offer can renegotiate the purchase offer.

Closing

At the closing or settlement meeting, the final step in the home buying process, checks are written to pay for a variety of fees and cover the downpayment, a multitude of papers are signed, the deed is recorded with the new owner's name, and the homebuyer receives the home's keys. Homebuyers must plan to cover many fees in addition to the downpayment. Who pays which fees varies across the country. Typically buyers pay the costs associated with obtaining a mortgage such as fees for a credit report, a survey, termite inspection, an appraisal, loan processing fees, and notary charges, as well as the lender's inspection. In some states the buyer also pays for the title search and insurance as well as fees to transfer and record the sale of property with the local tax assessor or recorder.

In the last quarter of 1999, "The mean costs paid by borrowers were $4,385 or 5.0% of the sales price" (U.S. Department of Housing and Urban Development, May, 2000, p. 5). At the closing the borrowers must provide proof of homeowner's/hazard insurance and prepay the interest on the first month of the mortgage. Closers or settlement agents are required by federal law to provide an itemized list of charges, called a HUD-1 Settlement Statement, to the borrower at least 48 hours before the closing. Borrowers should review the statement; they may wish to consult an attorney, especially when making a first purchase or moving to a different state since real estate law is state specific. Homebuyers should not assume that what was true with a purchase in one state will apply to a purchase in another state. Nor should longtime homeowners assume that fees and regulations that were common in the past apply to current home purchases.

DIFFICULTIES WITHIN THE PROCESS

Discrimination

In 1968 the Federal Fair Housing Act became law, prohibiting discrimination in housing because of race, color, religion, sex, and national origin. The Act has been amended over the years to include familial status and disability as additional protected characteristics. The Act's goal is to end discrimination in a home's sale or rental on the basis of the seven protected household characteristics. For example, a landlord cannot refuse to rent to a household that is of a certain race. States and communities can add additional characteristics to the federal list but cannot delete any of the federally mandated characteristics.

The federal Fair Housing Act also prohibits real estate professionals from "steering" potential homebuyers, which refers to the practice of only showing individuals properties in neighborhoods populated by households with specific characteristics. Another discriminatory practice is redlining, which denies credit to specific neighborhoods and communities on the basis of racial, ethnic, and economic makeup. Financial institutions actually used to draw a red line around selected areas on maps designating where they would not grant loans.

The term *fair housing* refers to several consumer laws or acts prohibiting discrimination. The protections included under the Equal Credit Opportunities Act were previously discussed in the section on preapproval. For example, a lender cannot legally refuse to make a mortgage loan to a qualified buyer if the applicant is female; or a lender cannot vary the interest rate, points, or fees if the applicant is disabled or Jewish. The U.S. Department of Housing and Urban Development will help consumers who feel their housing rights have been violated: *www.hud.gov/offices/fheo/FHLaws/FairHousingJan2002.pdf*

Subprime and Predatory Lending

Over the past several years mortgage lenders have been originating subprime lending, which provides loans to borrowers who do not meet prime borrowers' standards. Borrowers of subprime loans have lending patterns that indicate a high risk of default. Therefore, these loans are linked to an applicant's credit history. Subprime borrowers typically are referred to as "B/C" credit customers, as distinguished from "A" or prime borrowers.

Subprime lending has provided opportunities to a multitude of low- and moderate-income minority borrowers who a decade earlier might not have qualified (Gale, 2001). Credit-impaired borrowers have benefited from the subprime market. Legitimate subprime lending serves a very useful function and "clearly the increased availability of credit for higher risk borrowers has played an important role in increasing home ownership opportunities" (National Housing Conference, 2001, p. 5).

Subprime lending's popularity was shown by its growth from 1993–1998. Nationally, in 1993 subprime lenders made only 100,000 home purchases or refinance loans. By 1999 over one million home purchases or refinance loans were made by subprime lenders (U.S. Department of Housing and Urban Development, April, 2000). Legitimate subprime lenders make loans that are appropriately priced to compensate for the risk of lending to those with less than good credit. However, it has been suggested that subprime loans are often given to borrowers with good credit, which is unethical and considered to be a predatory practice (Community Reinvestment Association of North Carolina, 2000).

Predatory lending, a combination of unfair or abusive loan terms, unscrupulous and misleading marketing, and high-pressure sales tactics that limit information or choices available to consumers (Davis, 2000), has become a serious problem for homeowners and potential homeowners. This lending type is commonly used to strip away home equity and place homeowners in compromised situations that can cause serious harm. A disconcerting effect of predatory lending is the rapid turnover of property and ultimately an increase in vacant housing structures.

Predatory lending is often used synonymously with subprime lending. However, predatory lending is more accurately characterized as an extension of subprime lending involving extreme fees and/or terms. Although all predatory lending is subprime, not all subprime lending is predatory. Many explanations exist for the growth of subprime and predatory lending. Some of these explanations include an increase in homeownership among the less experienced, the use of information technology to target specific homeowners, and less attention to fair lending in refinance and home equity lending.

Predatory lending involves a number of predatory practices. Some of these practices are:

- **Steering:** deliberately turn/steer borrowers to high interest rates.
- **Deceptive marketing:** flooding of phone calls, door-to-door solicitations, mailings, and so forth.
- **Bait and switch:** offering one set of terms, but presenting worse terms at closing.
- **Asset-based lending:** lending without regard to ability to repay.
- **Flipping:** successive repeated refinancing.
- **Balloon payment:** loan in which most of the principal is still owed at the end.
- **High interest rate:** extraordinary rates well above the subprime rate.

While many of these practices may not be predatory as separate entities, the lender's failure to fully disclose the risk or cost associated with each individual term to the borrower can make the loan problematic. Sidebar 10.3 shows examples of predatory lending.

Sidebar 10.3
Examples of Predatory Lending

Joan T.'s sole income is $600 a month from Social Security. When she needed to fix a leaky roof, the loan she got had hidden fees and unneeded life insurance. Now, after paying her loan each month, she's left with only $55 for food and utilities.

(Continued)

Sidebar 10.3 *Continued*

Adela G. was paying off her home when a salesman talked her into a 12 percent home equity loan to pay off her credit cards. He said she could reduce her monthly payments from $500 to $250. He did not tell her about the large balloon payment that was due in three years. Adela lost her home to foreclosure.

Dave J. wanted to give his wife the kitchen of her dreams. The contractor never finished the job—but Dave still has to pay the loan every month.

Anne D. knew her credit rating was not the best but she needed to pay medical bills. She thought the 16 percent home loan offered by "the helpful man who called on the phone" was the best she could get. She could have gotten a better rate by shopping around.

Source: Reprinted with permission from AARP.

North Carolina was hit fastest and hardest by predatory lending. Estimates state that $1 billion in equity would be stripped from North Carolina homeowners through predatory practices (Center for Responsible Lending, 2002). North Carolina acknowledged the problem and has attempted to combat predatory lending by enacting the Mortgage Lending Act (2001). It was the first of its kind and has saved consumers at least $100 million in predatory loans without drying up the availability of subprime loans for borrowers in the state (*How Is It Working?*, 2002).

Predatory lending, also known as reverse redlining, refers to the targeting of neighborhoods with residents who have had limited access to financial services and have traditionally found it difficult to obtain financing, with the intention of extending predatory loans. Predatory lending violates the Fair Housing Act of 1968 and the Equal Credit Opportunity Act of 1972. Each act requires equal treatment of applicants based on their protected classes; therefore, targeting specific groups is a violation.

Reverse redlining takes place most often in communities where predatory lenders face no competition. Its victims are often the same victims of redlining. The same neighborhoods which were once denied financial opportunities are targeted with overpriced products. They purposely take advantage of residents by pushing high cost loans and soliciting aggressively over the phone, through the mail, or in face-to-face interaction. Many reverse redlining loans are so bad that the recipients would be better off not receiving a loan at all (U.S. Senate Committee on Banking, Housing, and Urban Affairs, 2001).

Just as neighborhoods were once identified as African American or white, they are now being identified as prime or subprime, with the latter especially vulnerable to predatory lending.

> Increasingly, sub-prime lending is becoming the only option of all too many low-income and minority borrowers. This reality sadly documents the continued existence of the race line in America and the continued existence of the dual lending market in the United States. Whereas before, African Americans were openly denied access to credit, today the "race tax" is more sophisticated, more costly— and equally exploitative. Where once redlining undermined communities, today "reverse redlining" has become the norm and threatens to undermine our communities' economies, social services, and tax base. Sadly, an analogy to racial profiling is appropriate here. We have all become familiar with the term "Driving While Black." Sub-prime predatory lending has become the equivalent of "Borrowing While Black" (U.S. Senate Committee on Banking, Housing, and Urban Affairs, 2001).

POSTPURCHASE CONCERNS

Homeownership is generally a wise investment. Rapid property appreciation between 1995 and 2001 helped many households build wealth in the form of home equity (Guerrero, 2003). Home equity loans and refinancing opportunities allow households to access that wealth. "Home equity provides families with the resources to finance their children's education, trade up to better homes, build financial resources for retirement, and purchase major goods and services" (Joint Center for Housing Studies, 2003, p. 10). However, many decisions influence a home's equity value. This section reviews issues that influence households' ability to build and protect their home equities.

Maintenance and Repairs

Deferred maintenance, or neglecting to make timely repairs that prevent additional damage, detracts from a home's value. Examples of deferred maintenance include cracked or peeling paint, crumbling masonry, and broken fixtures. The goal of regular preventative maintenance is to avoid an expensive crisis such as a leaky roof, and to extend the life of expensive items such as the heating, ventilation, and air conditioning systems.

Maintenance and replacement of housing components are not generally spread out evenly over time. For example, appliances have a life expectancy of approximately 10 years. By year 10, it is not uncommon for a homeowner to replace several appliances. Wise homeowners plan for the expense of routine maintenance as well as the replacement of expensive items. Conventional wisdom suggests that maintenance costs increase with the home's age. For example, the owners of a brand new $150,000 home should budget about $1,000 each year for routine maintenance. Owners of a 30-year-old, $150,000 home should budget about $4,000 per year. Households may want to establish a separate bank account for maintenance into which they put these estimated repair and replacement funds each month. The accumulated maintenance fund will allow the homeowner to replace a roof or a heating and cooling system (two of the more costly repairs) without financial trauma.

Remodeling and Improvements

The rapid recent increase in home equity due to inflating housing costs has helped many homeowners, especially middle-income households, finance large home remodeling projects (Guerrero, 2003). Data from the 2001 Consumer Practice Survey estimates the average remodeling project cost $5,121 (Guerrero, 2003). However, homeowners need to make informed decisions when investing money in home remodeling and improvement projects. They also need to carefully decide when and how to choose contractors. Poor workmanship by the homeowner or a contractor can diminish a home's value. Homeowners need to realistically decide if and when they can competently complete a project before hiring a contractor.

Refinancing

With low interest rates on mortgages and rising home values, many homeowners refinance their mortgages to lower payments or to liquefy equities; 47 percent of homeowners with mortgages refinanced at least once in 1999 (Brady, Canner, & Maki, 2000). There are many considerations regarding refinancing options for a new mortgage, a home equity loan, or a line of credit. Decision points include the interest rate on current mortgage, current available interest rates, expectations for interest rates in the near future, fees and closing costs, length of time the homeowner expects to own the property, and differences in tax advantages (Brady et al., 2000; Canner, Dynan, & Passmore, 2002).

Foreclosure Prevention

Mortgage agreements allow lenders to foreclose on or take back property if mortgage payments become delinquent. Borrowers with a history of timely payments and an expectation of bringing the mortgage current within six months may be able to work out an agreement if they experience an unexpected financial hardship, such as temporary loss of employment or medical expenses. A variety of loss mitigation tools are available to prevent a mortgage foreclosure. Loss mitigation tools are used to work out a solution that keeps the homeowner in the house and at the same time helps the lender work to recover the balance of the mortgage. Loss mitigation tools include the following:

1. A special forbearance that reduces or suspends monthly payments.
2. A partial release that requires payment of the principal; however, the interest rate is reduced or suspended.
3. A loan modification, which changes one or more of the mortgage terms.

With any loss mitigation tool, the past due amount may be added to the end of the loan (Fannie Mae, 1993).

If it is not financially possible for the homeowner to become current on the mortgage, another solution is to sell the property and pay off the mortgage. The lender or mortgage insurer may agree to a short sale, in which the lender and mortgage insurer agree to accept proceeds from the sale to pay off the mortgage even if the proceeds are less than the mortgage balance.

CONCLUSION

Financial choices about housing are some of the most important decisions individuals, families, and households ever make. Not only is the cost of housing one of the largest expenditures in their budgets, but the way the housing is financed, either rented or purchased, involves many options and legal ramifications. Hopefully, this chapter has informed and prepared you to be a better consumer of housing. Actually, the material presented in this chapter is just the beginning. If this topic interests you explore the Internet, the library, or your favorite bookstore for additional information, as an abundance of information is waiting for you. Be sure to study the housing real estate rules in the state in which a purchase is anticipated since real estate law, except where specified by federal law, is unique to each state.

REFERENCES

Belsky, E. S., & Duda, M. (2001). Anatomy of the low-income homeownership boom in the 1990s. In N. P. Retsinas & E. S. Belsky (Eds.), *Low-income homeownership* (pp. 15–63). Washington, DC: The Brookings Institute.

Boehm, T. P., & Schlottman, A. (1999). *Does home ownership by parents have an economic impact on their children?* Paper presented at the Mid-Year Meeting of the American Real Estate and Urban Economics Association, New York.

Bonnette, R. (2003, September). *Housing costs of homeowners: 2000 Census brief* (Report No. CrKBR27). Available: www.census.gov/prod/2003pubs/c2kbr-27.pdf.

Brady, P. J., Canner, G. B., & Maki, D. M. (2000). *The effects of recent mortgage refinancing.* Retrieved November 4, 2003, from www.federalreserve.gov/pubs/bulletin/2000/0700lead.pdf.

Canner, G., Dynan, K., & Passmore, W. (2002). *Mortgage refinancing in 2001 and early 2002.* Retrieved November 4, 2003, from www.federalreserve.gov/pubs/bulletin/2002/1202lead.pdf.

Center for Responsible Lending. (2002, October). *The case for predatory lending reform* (CRL Policy Paper #2). Retrieved May 27, 2003, from www.responsiblelending.org/lending_basics/reform.cfm.

Clark, H. (1997). *A structural equation model of the effects of homeownership, self-esteem, political involvement and community involvement in African–Americans.* Arlington, TX: University of Texas at Arlington, School of Social Work.

Colton, K. W. (2003). *Housing in the twenty-first century.* Cambridge, MA: Harvard University.

Community Reinvestment Association of North Carolina. (2000). *Community guide to predatory lending research.* Retrieved November 27, 2002, from www.cranc.org/research.

Davis, C. K. (2000). *Predatory lending: What is FDIC doing?* Paper presented at the Annual Meeting of the Iowa Homeownership Education Project, Ames, IA.

Drew, R. B. (2002, August). *New Americans, new homeowners: The role and relevance of foreign-born first-time homebuyers in the U.S. housing market* (N02-2.). Cambridge, MA: Harvard University, Joint Center for Housing Studies.

Fannie Mae. (1993). *Foreclosure prevention: Controlling default* (2nd ed.). Washington, DC: Fannie Mae.

Fannie Mae. (1996). *A guide to homeownership.* Washington, DC: Fannie Mae, National Housing Impact Division.

Gale, D. E. (2001). *Subprime and predatory mortgage refinancing: Information, technology, credit scoring, and vulnerable borrowers* (Program on Housing and Urban Policy Conference Paper Series C01-001). Berkeley, CA: University of California, Institute of Business and Economic Research.

Green, R., & White, M. (1997). Measuring the benefits of homeowning: Effects on children. *Journal of Urban Economics, 41,* 441–461.

Guerrero, A. M. (2003, October). *Home improvement finance: Evidence from the 2001 consumer practices survey* (N03-1.). Cambridge, MA: Harvard University, Joint Center for Housing Studies.

Harkness, J., & Newman, S. J. (2002). Homeownership for the poor in distressed neighborhoods: Does this make sense? *Housing Policy Debate, 13*(3), 597–630.

Haurin, D. R., Parcel, T., & Haurin, R. J. (2002). Impact of home ownership on child outcomes. In N. P. Retsinas & E. S. Belsky (Eds.), *Low-income homeownership* (pp. 427–446). Washington, DC: The Brookings Institute.

How is it working? (2002). Retrieved May 27, 2003, from *www.resposnsiblelending.org/nc_lawhowits_working.cfm.*

Joint Center for Housing Studies. (2003). *The state of the nation's housing.* Cambridge, MA: Harvard University, Joint Center for Housing Studies.

Kelly, B. M. (1993). *Expanding the American dream: Building and rebuilding Levittown.* New York: State University of New York Press.

Kiplinger's. (2002). *Buying and selling a home.* Washington, DC: Kiplinger Books, The Kiplinger Washington Editors, Inc.

Lindamood, S., & Hanna, S. D. (1979). *Housing, society and consumers.* New York: West Publishing Company.

Mortgage Lending Act. (2001). *North Carolina Mortgage Lending Act.* Retrieved July 5, 2005, from www.e-prmi.com/northcarolina/ mortgage.act.htm.

National Housing Conference. (2001, April). Expanding the dream of homeownership. *National Affordable Housing Policy Review, 1*(1).

Razzi, E. (1997). Buying a home in a buyer's market. *Kiplinger's Personal Finance Magazine, 50*(4), 64–70.

Reichel, C. H. (1998). *Navigating the affordable mortgage maze.* Baton Rouge, LA: Louisiana State University Agricultural Center.

Retsinas, N. P., & Belsky, E. S. (2002). *Low-income homeownership.* Washington, DC: The Brookings Institute.

Rohe, W. M., & Basolo, V. (1997). Long-term effects of homeownership on the self-perceptions and social interaction of low-income people. *Environment and Behavior, 29*(6), 793–819.

Rohe, W. M., & Stegman, M. (1994a). The impact of home ownership on the self-esteem, perceived control and life satisfaction of low-income people. *Journal of the American Planning Association, 60*(2), 173–184.

Rohe, W. M., & Stegman, M. (1994b). The impact of home ownership on the social and political involvement of low-income people. *Urban Affairs Quarterly, 30*(3), 152–172.

Rohe, W. M., Van Zandt, S., & McCarthy, G. (2001). *The social benefits and costs of homeownership* (Working Paper LIHO.01-12). Cambridge, MA: Harvard University, Joint Center for Housing Studies.

Rohe, W. M., Van Zandt, S., & McCarthy, G. (2002). Home ownership and access to opportunity. *Housing Studies, 17*(1), 51–62.

Rossi, P. H., & Weber, E. (1996). The social benefits of homeownership: Empirical evidence from national surveys. *Housing Policy Debate, 7*(1), 1–35.

Shinn, M., & Gillespie, C. (1994). The roles of housing and poverty in the origins of homelessness. *American Behavioral Scientist, 37,* 505–521.

Thomsett, M. C. (1996). *How to buy a house, condo, or co-op* (2nd ed.). Yonkers, NY: Consumers Union.

U.S. Department of Housing and Urban Development. (2000, April). *Unequal burden in Atlanta: Income and racial disparities in subprime lending.* Retrieved November 27, 2002, from www.hud.gov/library/bookshelf18/pressrel/subpratl.pdf.

U.S. Department of Housing and Urban Development. (2000, May). *Housing needs report shows crisis worsening.* Washington DC: Office of Policy Development and Research.

U.S. Department of Housing and Urban Development. (2004, August). *U.S. housing market conditions* (Second Quarter). Washington, DC: Office of Policy Development and Research.

U.S. Senate Committee on Banking, Housing, and Urban Affairs. (2001). *Hearing on predatory lending: The problem, impact, and responses.* [Second hearing in a series, testimony by David Berenbaum.] Retrieved November 29, 2002, from www.senate.gov./~banking/01_07hrg/072701/berenbaurm.htm.

Zielenbach, S. (2004). Affordable housing: A critical analysis of low-income homeownership strategies. *Journal of Affordable Housing and Community Development Law, 13*(4), 446–457.

Sustainable Buildings and Communities

Leona K. Hawks, Kerry F. Case, and Jane D. Reagor
Leona K. Hawks is Extension Housing and Environment Specialist,
College of Natural Resources, Utah State University, Logan, UT; Kerry F.
Case is Utah House Program Coordinator, Utah State University, Logan,
UT; and Jane D. Reagor is Associate Professor, Department of Human
Ecology, University of Tennessee, Chattanooga, TN.

This chapter examines an increasingly important topic in recent years. The concept of sustainability can be traced back to President Theodore Roosevelt, who said in 1910 "I recognize the right and duty of this generation to develop and use the natural resources of our land; but I do not recognize the right to waste them, or to rob, by wasteful use, the generations that come after us" (Roosevelt, 1910). Later in 1987 the United Nations World Commission on Environment and Development defined *sustainable development* as that which "meets the needs of the present without compromising the ability of future generations to meet their own needs" (Joint Center for Sustainable Communities, 2003). Sustainable development places equal and integrated emphasis on three main elements: economic prosperity, environmental quality, and community well-being.

You might ask, "Why is sustainable building important?" In order to save precious resources for future generations and to ensure equitable distribution of those resources, we must implement resource-efficient measures in all areas of human activity. Because buildings and the ways they are designed use a great deal of resources, they contribute to the natural environment's deterioration. Buildings (commercial and residential) account for 36.4 percent of total U.S. primary energy consumption, and 30 percent of the total greenhouse gas emissions (carbon dioxide) that lead to air pollution, acid rain, and global climate change (U.S. Department of Energy, Energy Information Administration, 2000). Buildings also consume 25 percent of all harvested wood and 17 percent of the fresh water supply (US-ICLEI Cities for Climate Protection Campaign & Renew America, 1998). More than 53 percent of the wetlands were lost in the lower 48 states between the late 1700s and the mid-1980s due to development (U.S. Environmental Protection Agency, 1994).

Deforestation, one of the major causes of the greenhouse effect, is a major cause of plant and animal habitat destruction and results in the extermination or endangerment of thousands of species. Right now in the United States, 511 animal species and 736 plant species are listed as endangered or threatened under the Federal Endangered Species Act. An additional 82 animal and 144 plant species are candidate species for the listing (U.S. Department of the Interior, Bureau of Land Management, Idaho, 2004). This does not account for the thousands of animal and plant species that have already become extinct because of loss of habitat.

More than 76 million residential buildings and nearly 5 million commercial buildings are in the United States, and according to the U.S. Department of Energy (2003), buildings account for one third of all U.S. energy consumption. By 2010, 38 million new buildings will be added to the existing stock. The challenge will be to build these buildings using smart, energy efficient, and sustainable design so that they use a minimum of nonrenewable energy and produce a minimum of pollution (Smart Communities Network, 2004). This chapter will review concepts of sustainable building and strategies for implementation.

WHAT IS A SUSTAINABLE BUILDING?

The U.S. Department of Energy (2003) defined *sustainable buildings* as structures that use resources (energy, water, materials, and land) efficiently, minimize waste in construction, conserve the natural environment, and are healthy for existing and future generations. Sustainability is truly a "whole house" approach to building design and construction, and the end product is a better built residential building or commercial structure (Gillman, 1990).

To conserve resources, sustainable buildings often set new standards for design, construction, energy efficiency, and water conservation. Just by employing sustainable building practices, it is possible to reduce energy consumption by as much as 70 percent to 90 percent (Barnett & Browning, 1999), water use by 35 percent or more (Rocky Mountain Institute, 2004), and building material use by 30 percent (U.S. Department of Energy, Building America Program, 2001).

In many cases, sustainable buildings cost about the same as conventional buildings to construct, and their improved comfort and performance translate into lower utility and maintenance costs. Sustainable buildings are less expensive to heat, cool, and light because of their energy efficiency. In addition, when it comes time to sell, they tend to have a high resale value (Building Environmental Science and Technology—Howard Associates, 1997).

Power plants (often for coal) produce the energy (electricity) used in buildings, and cause air quality problems, and contribute to climate change. By reducing the energy consumption of buildings, less demand is put upon power plants to produce electricity, which reduces air pollution. The energy used in building operation accounts for 49 percent of sulfur dioxide emissions, 25 percent of nitrous oxide emissions, and 10 percent of particulate emissions, all of which negatively impact air quality. In addition, buildings produce 33 percent of the country's carbon dioxide emissions—the chief pollutant blamed for climate change (Smart Communities Network: Creating Energy Smart Communities, 2004; U.S. Department of Energy, Energy Efficiency and Renewable Energy Network, 2004).

SUSTAINABLE BUILDINGS MAXIMIZE SITE PLANNING

A sustainable building includes more than just the design of the building itself. Effective siting and landscaping are also essential for sustainable design. Careful attention to the building site is necessary when determining the building's placement. It should be positioned to take advantage of solar access, view, natural breezes, slope, vegetation, and water bodies if present, as shown in Figure 11.1. In the plan, building and outdoor activity areas should be placed in proper relationship to climatic and other natural factors on the site. If the

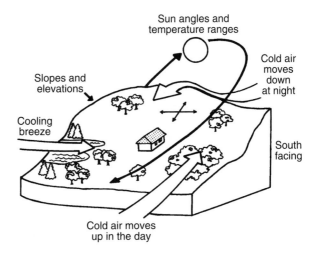

Figure 11.1   Selecting the building site

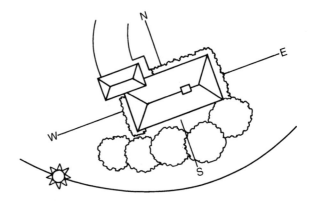

Figure 11.2   Orientation of building

building is oriented correctly, sunlight will provide solar heating gain in the winter and minimize overheating from east and west summer sunlight, as shown in Figure 11.2. Proper site planning of a building reduces the amount of energy required to heat and cool the building. If an active solar panel is included in the design and construction, the building must be appropriately oriented toward the sun's angles for solar collectors to operate efficiently.

Sustainable Buildings Protect the Site

When the site and construction plans are designed, the landscape plan should be included. According to Philips (2004), the landscape plan must be regenerative; that is, it must accommodate natural systems. When done correctly, the building's site plan minimizes vegetation disturbance, earth grading, water path alterations, and destruction of animal species. Precautions are taken to protect the site's trees, vegetation, and native grasses, and consideration is given to erosion control in order to preserve the site and its water quality. Additionally, dust and airborne pollutants are contained or minimized.

To protect the site, areas are often identified for construction, parking, waste disposal, cleanup efforts, and to stockpile materials such as topsoil and recyclables. As part of the bid document for a sustainable building, contractors are often required to describe how demolition, construction, and installation will be managed to minimize site damage. Individuals who want to preserve the site during construction often require contractors to sign compliance agreements that post dollar values on trees, bushes, and grasses, and requires compensation if any of the listed items are damaged.

ENVIRONMENTALLY FRIENDLY MATERIALS AND DESIGNS

Sustainable design considers the full environmental cost of everything that goes into a building including all the resources consumed in extraction, transportation, manufacturing, and the eventual disposal of construction products and materials. For example, compare the true environmental costs of using straw bale or wood in the wall construction of a Utah house. Both are natural, renewable materials, but wood has a much higher total embodied energy than straw, or a higher environmental cost. Wood consumes more resources and produces greater levels of pollution because it requires more processing (milling) and transportation (very little wood is grown and harvested in some states) than straw bale (a readily available by-product of local agriculture). Since transportation helps determine the full environmental cost, the location of construction may impact the comparative sustainability of individual materials or products.

A number of sustainable alternatives to standard construction methods and materials are available in the United States today, such as using straw bales, insulated concrete forms (ICFs), structural insulated panels (SIPs), rammed and poured earth, and even old tires and soda cans. Each of these choices has advantages and disadvantages when compared to traditional building methods, but many of them use fewer resources and produce less waste. Straw bales are being used to insulate and support the roof. ICFs, concrete-filled polystyrene or polyurethane boards or blocks filled with rebar and concrete, are used in wall construction. SIPs are polystyrene or polyurethane panels sandwiched between oriented strand boards (OSBs). Rammed earth is made by mixing earth with concrete and compacting it between forms to create walls.

In his book *The Natural House,* Daniel Chiras (2000) offered a helpful list of "criteria for evaluating green building products" that can be used to evaluate various construction and interior materials. The list of criteria includes:

1. low embodied energy,
2. efficient use of resources,
3. little or no pollution production,
4. readily recyclable materials when useful life is over,
5. products made from recycled or natural materials,
6. products produced by socially and environmentally responsible companies,
7. products produced from sustainable harvested materials,
8. products produced or manufactured locally,
9. nontoxic materials,

10. durable materials,
11. low life cycle,
12. aesthetically appealing,
13. meets building requirements, and
14. competitively priced.

Low embodied energy refers to the total energy used to create a product including the energy used in mining, harvesting, processing, fabricating, and transporting the product. *Life cycle cost* is the cost of buying, operating, maintaining, and disposing of a system, equipment, product, or facility over its expected useful life.

Sustainable Buildings Use Durable Materials and Products

A sustainable building is designed to last a long time. Selecting durable building materials and products can reduce environmental impacts. For example, metal roofs last four times longer than 15-year asphalt roofs, and they can be recycled when they need to be replaced.

Sustainable Buildings Use Recycled and Reused Materials

One way to increase a house's overall sustainability is to incorporate recycled materials. Recycled alternatives include cellulose and mineral fiber insulation, engineered lumber, steel "stud" framing, manufactured and structural wood products, sheathing for building exteriors, carpeting, plastic decking, and counter tops. Also, some fiberglass manufacturers are using portions of recycled glass in their insulation (*Environmental Building News*, 1995).

Use of salvaged products is another approach to boosting sustainability. Many communities have for-profit and nonprofit groups that deconstruct buildings and sell the salvaged items to the public. It is possible to purchase used large timbers, moldings, cabinets, appliances, light fixtures, tubs, bricks, windows, and just about anything found in old buildings.

Sustainable Buildings Reduce Waste

Waste can occur at many different points in the construction process, and is caused by the inefficient use of resources and/or the inappropriate disposal of materials. Fortunately, a number of groups have devised innovative programs and technologies for reducing the amount of resources consumed and waste produced in construction. The U.S. Department of Energy's Building America Program has developed an advanced framing system which reduces housing costs by eliminating unnecessary studs, top plates, and headers. Using 2" × 6" studs placed 24 inches apart, instead of more closely spaced 2" × 4" studs 16 inches apart, improves energy efficiency, saves construction time, and reduces the total amount of lumber needed to build a building. Also, designing and building a house using standard dimensions (wall lengths in multiples of 2 feet or 4 feet and ceilings at 8 feet) saves money by reducing cut-off waste and the cost of taking that waste to the landfill (Stover, 1997). Pieces of materials can be stored in an enclosure rather than a dumpster, so workers can see what can be salvaged instead of cutting full pieces.

Appropriate waste disposal is an important consideration for any sustainable construction project. According to the World Watch Institute, waste from building construction accounts for 40 percent of landfill space (Barnett & Case, 1997), and much of this can be recycled. Strategies include:

- recycling cardboard, plastic packaging, steel scrap, and drywall;
- storing and reusing lumber cutoffs;
- chipping up drywall scraps for use as a soil amendment; and
- chipping wood for landscape mulch.

Getting rid of construction waste is expensive and can be a significant part of the total budget. Reducing the amount of waste being hauled to the landfill can save hundreds of dollars per building and reduce the need for communities to increase landfill space.

Sustainable Buildings Use Renewable Resources

Renewable resources can replenish themselves naturally, like trees grown in sustainable forests or energy from sunlight or wind. Look for the sustainable wood certification stamped on the wood. Greater use of renewable technologies can reduce the rate at which fossil fuel resources are being depleted. Furthermore, renewables can assist local communities in meeting energy needs as they continue to grow.

The most common renewable energy source is solar energy. Energy from sunlight (solar) is often grouped into two categories: passive solar and active solar. Use of solar systems can provide electricity, space heating, and domestic hot water.

Passive Solar Design.   Passive solar design allows winter sunlight into the building but blocks summer sunlight with overhangs, awnings, and/or deciduous trees, as shown in Figure 11.3. Passive design does not require any mechanical methods to capture the sun's energy. It simply allows the sun's heat and light into the building,

Figure 11.3   Passive designed house

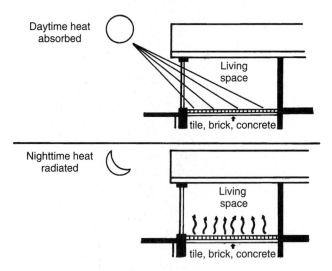

Figure 11.4   Thermal mass

usually through large south-facing windows. Stone, concrete, or ceramic walls or tile floors will take advantage of that passive energy by acting as a "thermal mass" that absorbs the sun's heat during the day and radiates it back into the building at night, as shown in Figure 11.4.

When possible, the residential building's long axis should run in an east-west direction in colder climates so that the largest amount of wall surface and windows face south, taking advantage of the low-angle winter sunlight. The most used rooms and outdoor activity areas should be located on the south side to take advantage of

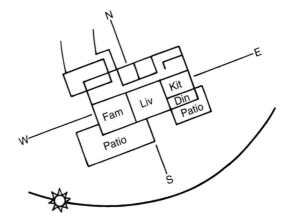

Figure 11.5   Most used rooms on south

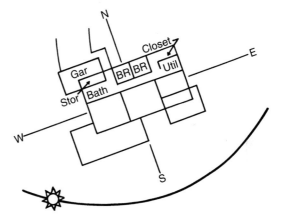

Figure 11.6   Rooms used less on north

the heat from winter sunlight, as shown in Figure 11.5. Garages, utility rooms, storage areas, and less frequently used rooms should be located on the north to act as buffers against cold winter winds, as shown in Figure 11.6.

In warmer climates such as the southern United States, residential buildings should be designed to reduce heat loads. The most used rooms and outdoor activity areas are on the north or east sides of the building. Garages, utility rooms, storage areas, and less frequently used rooms are located on the south side to act as buffers against the summer heat.

Additionally, window placement and size are critical. Windows should be designed to admit winter solar heat (if wanted), utilize day lighting, and avoid heat gain from the hot summer sun. Roof overhangs must be wide enough to be effective. If correctly designed, overhangs provide shade on walls and windows from high-angle summer sun, but let in low-angle winter sun, as shown in Figure 11.7.

Solar day lighting, another form of passive design, brings natural daylight into the building in order to reduce the use of artificial lighting. Day lighting is important not only from an energy savings perspective, but also from emotional and psychological perspectives. Although medical science has not yet agreed on the exact cause of Seasonal Affective Disorder (SAD), it seems to be brought on by a chemical imbalance in the brain resulting from the lack of natural light, called *malillumination*, during the winter months. People suffering from malillumination or SAD experience feeling down, have less energy, experience weight gain, have difficulty getting up in the morning, and are unable to function normally. The treatment for this disorder is natural or full spectrum light (SciART, 2004).

Active Solar Design.   Active solar design differs from passive design because energy is harvested from the sun by mechanical means such as electrically driven equipment. Examples include photovoltaics (PV), solar domestic hot water heaters, and solar outdoor lights. Because of the increased use of renewables, these new technologies are becoming more cost effective and competitive with conventional technologies.

Over the next 10 years the costs associated with photovoltaic systems are expected to fall to the cost level of available power as more consumers start using these technologies (U.S. Department of Energy, Energy Efficiency and Renewable Energy, 2004). Photovoltaics, or solar cells, use semiconductor materials to convert sunlight directly into electricity through the photovoltaic process, as shown

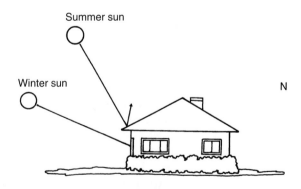

Figure 11.7   Overhangs shade windows

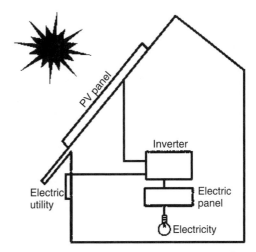

Figure 11.8   PV panel converts sunlight

Figure 11.9   Photovoltaics solar roof

in Figure 11.8. They can be placed on the roof, wall, or ground. PV systems no longer require batteries for storage; they can be connected directly to the utility grid, as shown in Figure 11.9. If the system generates more electricity than the building consumes, the extra energy is sold back to the utility company or the customer receives credit. Many state governments require local utilities to purchase the energy back from the PV system. However, the utilities often pay a lower amount per kilowatt hour (kWh) than they charge consumers. These grid-tied systems are becoming more common because they do not require the maintenance associated with batteries used to store solar energy. However, when the DC current is converted to the AC electrical current used in the building, some energy is lost in the conversion. As a result, not all the electricity generated by the PV can be used to power the building.

PV systems are also being used to power outdoor lighting. Some outdoor lights have their own individual solar cells and others are wired to a central PV panel with battery storage. Solar outdoor lights are available at local building centers, and can be used for pathways and accent lighting or motion-activated security lighting.

Solar domestic hot water heating systems are used in more than 1.5 million U.S. homes and businesses, and over 94 percent of these customers consider this method of heating water a good investment (U.S. Department of Energy, 2004). Solar water heaters—mounted on a roof, wall, or ground—use the sunlight to heat water. Performance varies depending on the system and how much solar energy is available at the site. After the water is heated it is stored in a tank similar to a conventional gas or electric water heater tank, as shown in Figure 11.10. In many areas building codes require a conventional water heater as a backup just in case there is no sunlight.

Ground source geothermal heating and cooling heat pumps are another example of renewable energy. However, ground source geothermal heat pumps should not be confused with air heat pumps. Ground source geothermal heating and cooling is a renewable resource because it utilizes the heat from beneath the earth's surface. Ground source has been used for more than half a century for heating in Scandinavian countries and for cooling in the southern United States. Still, it is one of the least recognized renewables, perhaps because the system components are much less visible than wind rotors or solar panels. The heat exchanger is usually hidden in the basement, and the loop that delivers the energy is completely buried using different configurations.

The earth itself is an enormous solar collector, storing almost half the sun's radiation in rocks, soil, and water. In climates that swing between hot summers and cold winters, this stored heat can be

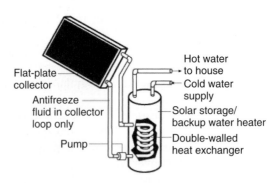

Figure 11.10   Solar water heater

extracted from the ground to provide heating, cooling, and in some cases domestic hot water. According to the U.S. Department of Energy, Federal Technology Alerts (1995), ground source heat pumps are one of the most efficient ways to heat and cool a building. Most of these new ground source geothermal heating and cooling systems are closed looped systems and do not extract water from the earth. Thermal energy is transferred from the earth to the fluid in the pipe and is upgraded by passing to a heat exchanger. Ground source heating and cooling circulates a solution through a buried plastic pipe, absorbing a small amount of heat from the surrounding soil. When this warmed fluid returns to the building and passes through the unit's compressor and exchanger, the solar heat is released and circulated either as warm air in ducts or as warm water in coils. In the summer the circulation is reversed to take the heat from the room, defuse the heat into the ground, and return cooled air from the ground to rooms.

Wind power, another commonly used renewable energy, is the world's fastest growing energy technology, as shown in Figure 11.11. Today, the United States has more than 6,300 megawatts of wind-generating capacity. However, wind power is not always feasible. Zoning codes prohibit wind turbine placement within the community in many areas. However, small wind turbines have emerged as

Figure 11.11 Wind turbine (*Source:*
Bergey Windpower)

an attractive and viable method of generating electricity for residential buildings. In order to be cost effective, most rotors require a constant wind velocity of at least 7 miles per hour (Green Culture, 2004).

People often ask how wind turbines work. Generally, wind turbines are installed on top of a tall tower because they are most efficient when placed off the ground, in open fields, and away from buildings. They collect kinetic energy from the wind and convert it to electricity that is compatible with a building's electrical system using an inverter. Since the wind does not always blow, the house is usually served simultaneously by the wind turbine and a local utility. If wind speeds are below 7 mph, then there is no electricity generated by the wind turbine and the utility purchases all of the needed power. As wind speeds increase, turbine output increases and the amount of power purchased from the utility is proportionately decreased. When the turbine produces more power than the home needs, the extra electricity is sold to the utility. In this type of system, no batteries are used for energy storage. All of this is done automatically.

Sustainable Buildings Are Energy Efficient

America's 81 million buildings (residential and commercial) annually consume roughly $220 billion worth of energy. As mentioned previously, U.S. buildings consume over 40 percent of the energy used in the United States, including 60 percent of the electricity, and contribute almost 35 percent of the country's carbon dioxide (CO_2) emissions (Smart Communities Network, 2004). By reducing local energy consumption, efficient buildings can also reduce air pollution and improve local environments. In a traditional stick-built house, a 50 percent energy use reduction is relatively easy to achieve and a 70 percent to 90 percent reduction is possible with good design and efficient appliances and equipment (Barnett & Browning, 1999). Just saving one unit of electricity eliminates the need to burn three or four units of fuel at a power plant. In addition, reducing the average residential building's energy use by 80 percent will reduce its CO_2 emissions by almost 90,000 pounds over a 30-year period (Barnett & Browning, 1999). As already discussed, sustainable, energy efficient homes often use renewable technologies, passive and active solar design, and additional methods to make them energy efficient.

Minimize Air Leakage.   Energy efficient buildings are designed and built to minimize air leakage. Infiltration occurs when air leaks into the building and exfiltration occurs when air leaks from the inside of the house to the outside. Leaks can occur through the walls, where windows and doors are framed, where brick or siding overlaps the foundation wall, inside the basement, where the sill rests on the foundation, around any penetrations of the outside wall (faucets, electrical outlets, and water pipes), and where the outside chimney or other masonry joins outside walls, as shown in Figure 11.12. Air leakage can also occur through the attic where insulation is inadequate or not installed properly. These areas must be sealed to reduce infiltration and exfiltration, and make the building energy efficient. Heating and cooling ducts can also be an area of air leakage. Ducts need to be sealed properly using special mastic that seals and joins two pieces of material together and remains flexible over time.

Heating and Cooling Systems Placed in the Proper Location. The Consortium for Advanced Residential Buildings has tested and designed residential buildings around the mechanical system in order to increase efficiency and reduce waste. In their designs, the heating or cooling system is in the building's center, which places the furnace/air handler closer to the rooms. This technique allows for shorter distances to heat or cool rooms, less ducting, and smaller ducts, which result in fewer air leaks (Stover, 1997). According to scientists (Xu, Bechu, Carrie, Dickerhoff, Fish, Kristiansen, Levinson, McWillians, Wang, & Modera, 1999) at the Lawrence Berkeley National Laboratory, leakage of conditioned air from broken or disconnected ducts accounts for 20 percent to 40 percent of a building's energy loss. The technique of locating heating and cooling equipment close to where it will be used can also be applied to water heaters, which can save on energy costs and materials usage.

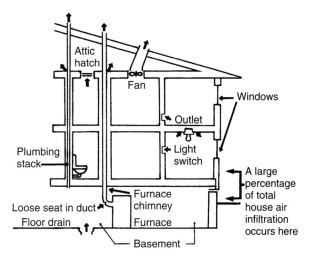

Figure 11.12 Air leakage in house

High Levels of Insulation.   An energy efficient home has higher levels of insulation than the standard residential building. This means that the insulation levels exceed the American Council of American Building Official's Model Energy Code (MEC), which has been adopted by most states (State Legislative Report, 1997). These buildings usually have five characteristics: higher levels of insulation, high-performance windows and doors, wraps and vapor barriers that reduce infiltration, controlled mechanical ventilation with heat recovery, and low energy use through energy efficiency.

High-performance Windows.   Low-performance windows can increase energy costs by as much as 10 percent because of conduction and air leakage between frames and rough openings, as shown in Figure 11.13. Depending on the climate, leaky windows and doors can bring dry air or moist air into the residential building. The performance of any given window can be evaluated by the U-value, Low "E" glazing found in the window, Solar Heat Gain Coefficient (SHGC) measure, Visible Transmittance (VT) measure, Air Leakage (AL) rating, Condensation Resistance (CR) measure, Energy Star® logo, and possibly the voluntary National Fenestration Rating label.

U-value measures how well a window conducts heat. The rate of heat loss is indicated in terms of the U-factor that generally falls between 0.20 and 1.20. Lower U-values provide more insulation and are more energy efficient, as shown in Figure 11.14.

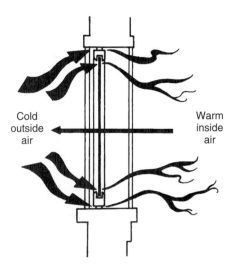

Cold outside air

Warm inside air

Figure 11.13   Window conduction and air leakage

	R-Values	U-Values
Single glazing	.98	1.02
Double glazing (1/2″ air space)	2.04	.49
Triple glazing (1/2″ air space)	2.92	.39

Figure 11.14   Window R-values and U-values

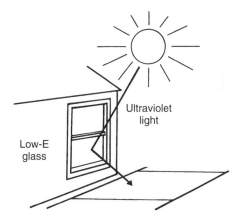

Figure 11.15   Low-E reflects UV light

Low E window glazing is a thin, transparent, heat-reflective coating applied during manufacturing, which may vary depending on the climate. The low E coating allows light through the glazing but restricts ultraviolet light transmittance that can fade interior furnishings, carpets, curtains, and so forth, as shown in Figure 11.15. In addition, low E glazing reflects heat inside the building back into the room, acting as a mirror to keep the heat inside the building, as shown in Figure 11.16.

Windows are also measured by the Solar Heat Gain Coefficient (SHGC). The SHGC, also called a shading coefficient, measures how well a window absorbs or reflects heat from sunlight. SHGC is expressed between 0 and 1; the lower the coefficient, the better the window is at blocking the sun's heat (U.S. Department of Energy, Energy Efficiency and Renewable Energy, 2004). In contrast, the higher the coefficient, the better the window is at letting in the sun's heat. Windows in hot or temperate climates should have a low SHGC; and in cold climates, it should have a high SHGC coefficient.

Figure 11.16   Low-E reflects heat

Window performance can also be determined by Visible Transmittance (VT) measures, an optical property which measures how much light comes through the window, indicating the amount of visible light transmitted. It is expressed between 0 and 1; the higher the VT, the more light transmitted.

Air Leakage (AL), another measure of window performance, is expressed as the equivalent cubic feet of air through a square foot of window area and measures the heat loss and gain by infiltration through the window assembly. The lower the AL measure, the less air that is passing through cracks in the window assembly. To prevent air infiltration and heat loss due to conduction, frames should have thermal breaks—an air space or insulation added to the inside of the window frame, as shown in Figure 11.17. Without these breaks, there can be a good deal of heat loss. Operable windows such as casement windows tend to have lower air infiltration ratings than most sliding or double-hung windows because of the tighter seal, making them more efficient.

Another measure of window performance is Condensation Resistance (CR), which measures a product's ability to resist condensation formation of that product's interior surface and is expressed between 1 and 100. The higher the CR rating, the better that product is at resisting condensation formation.

Most of these window performance measures are found on the National Fenestration Council (NFRC) sticker, as shown in Figure 11.18. NFRC performs a voluntary, third-party testing of the whole window performance that allows consumers to compare different windows. Not all windows have this sticker. However, just because a window has the NFRC sticker does not mean that the window is energy efficient. The NFRC sticker will display on a tested window the

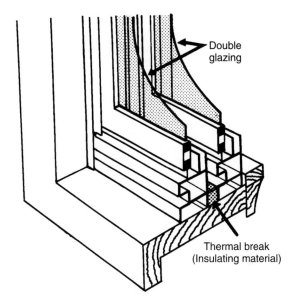

Figure 11.17   Energy efficient windows

Figure 11.18 National
fenestration label *(Source:*
National Fenestration Rating
Council, Inc)

U-value, SHGC, and VT, and may include AL and CR. Depending on the area of the country, different values will be selected for different performance features.

High-performance Doors.   An energy efficient building has energy efficient doors. Pre-hung, foam core, metal insulated entry doors generally provide better thermal performance than wooden solid-core doors. These pre-hung doors are usually better insulated and the weather-stripping is made to better fit the door. Local codes should be checked to determine door requirements.

Energy Efficient Appliances and Equipment.   An energy efficient house has energy efficient appliances, heating and cooling systems, and other equipment. The easiest way to determine the efficiency of appliances and other equipment is to read and compare energy information found on labels and ratings. Labels and ratings that can be used to indicate energy performance are the Energy Guide labels and Energy Star® logo, as well as the AFUE, SEER, EER, and HSPF ratings.

The yellow Energy Guide label required by the government for most appliances is a useful tool for comparing the annual energy costs of similar products, as shown in Figure 11.19. The Energy Star program was developed by the U.S. Environmental Protection Agency and the U.S. Department of Energy. Use of the Energy Star logo certifies that the product (thermostats, computers, furnaces, heat-pumps, clothes washers, dishwashers, refrigerators, and many others) exceeds government standards for energy efficiency (U.S. Department of Energy, 1997).

AFUE, EER, SEER, and HSPF are nationally accepted measures of energy efficiency; in all cases, the higher the number the more efficient the equipment, as shown in Figure 11.20.

- The Annual Fuel Utilization Efficiency (AFUE) rating is found on furnaces and indicates how well a furnace converts energy into usable heat. The rating is expressed as a percentage of the annual output of heat to the annual energy input to the furnace. For example, a 90 percent AFUE rating means that for every British thermal unit (BTU) of gas used, the system will provide 0.9 BTU of heat. A higher AFUE rating indicates a more efficient system.
- The Energy Efficiency Ratio (EER) is a measure of how efficiently a cooling system will operate when the outdoor temperature is at a specific level (usually 95 degrees). In more technical terms, it is the ratio of an air conditioner's cooling capacity, in BTUs per hour, to the total electrical input in watts under test conditions specified by the Air-Conditioning and Refrigeration Institute. The higher the EER ratio, the more efficient the cooling system.
- The Seasonal Energy Efficiency Ratio (SEER) is a measure of a central air conditioner's total cooling output in BTUs during its normal usage period, divided by the total electrical energy input in watt-hours during the same period. The test procedure is determined by the Air-Conditioning and

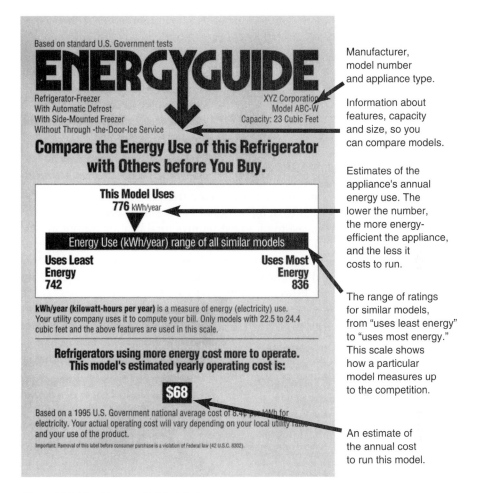

Figure 11.19 Energy Guide label (*Source:* U.S. Department of Energy, Office of Energy Efficiency and Renewable Energy)

ENERGY EFFICIENCY RATINGS

Ratings	Efficient
AFUE (annual fuel utilization efficiency)	90 or above
EER (energy efficiency ratio)	10 or above
SEER (seasonal energy efficiency ratio)	12 or above
HSPE (heating seasonal performance factor)	7 or above

Figure 11.20 Energy efficient ratings

Refrigeration Institute. As with the other rating systems, a higher SEER reflects a more efficient cooling system. A SEER rating of 14 is very energy efficient. In addition to selecting a high SEER rating, air conditioning needs to be properly sized, correctly installed, properly operated, and correctly maintained. In high humidity climates the Sensible Heat Ratio (SHR) is also important. For example, in Florida a SHR of 0.70 is recommended. The SHR is almost as important as the SEER ratio because removing moisture is just as critical as cooling the air. In this case, 70 percent of the air conditioner's energy goes into cooling and 30 percent goes into removing moisture from the air.

- The Heating Seasonal Performance Factor (HSPF) is a measure of a heat pump's total heating output in BTUs during its normal usage period, divided by the total electrical energy input in watt-hours during the same period. A high HSPF equates to a more efficient heating system (City, Light & Power, Energy Services Offices, 2003).

Energy Efficient Lighting.   Energy efficient homes will also use energy efficient lighting such as compact fluorescent lighting (CFL), dimmers, occupancy sensors, and smart residential building technologies to control lighting along with security, heating, and cooling. Compact fluorescent lighting, the best choice for energy efficiency, comes in a variety of sizes and shapes, as shown in Figure 11.21, including reflector floodlights. They can also replace other lamps in regular light sockets, usually incandesce. (In the lighting industry, the term *lamp* is used instead of bulbs) CFLs can last up to 10,000 hours or 10 times longer than a standard incandescent lamp, and consume 75 percent less electricity. CFLs produce three

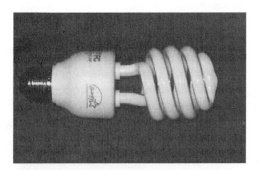

Figure 11.21   Compact fluorescent light
(*Source:* Energy Star, U.S. Environmental Protection Agency and U.S. Department of Energy)

to four times more light per watt than incandescent lamps. For example, a 40-watt fluorescent lamp produces more light than a 150-watt incandescent lamp. CFLs also produce less "waste heat," reducing air conditioning loads in the summer in warmer climates (U.S. Department of Energy and National Renewable Energy Laboratory, 1995).

The new electronic ballasts on CFLs last longer and do not flicker as much as the magnetic ballasts. In addition, some compact fluorescent lights can now be dimmed, but only if they are labeled as "dimmable" and have the appropriate dimming switches. A light can be adjusted from bright for reading to a gentle glow for watching TV or dining. Dimmers set lower than maximum reduce energy consumption and heat production.

Occupancy or motion sensors are often used in rooms where people forget to turn off the lights, like in bathrooms or the lights outside. Occupancy sensors provide automatic on/off switching of lighting loads for convenience, security, and long-term energy savings. The way they control light may be infrared, ultrasonic, or both. The Passive Infrared (PIR) units respond to changes in the infrared background by turning lights on when people enter space being monitored, and off when the space is unoccupied. The Ultrasonic (US) units transmit an ultrasound signal and monitor changes in the signal's return time to detect occupancy (Leviton, 2004).

Energy efficient residential buildings use smart thermostats and smart building technologies. Smart thermostats can be programmed to adjust temperature settings automatically. They also maximize energy savings because they are more dependable than humans in changing temperatures. Smart thermostats include a microprocessor and thermistor sensors. The microprocessor, the heart of any computer, is fabricated on a single chip. Thermistors are special solid temperature sensors that behave like temperature-sensitive resistors; hence their name is a contraction of *thermal* and *resistor*. Thermistors typically work over a relatively small temperature range, compared to other temperature sensors, and can be accurate and precise within that range. Thermistors perform one or more of the following energy control functions: (1) store and repeat multiple daily settings (which can be manually changed without affecting the rest of the daily or weekly program), (2) store six or more temperature settings a day, and (3) adjust heating or air conditioning turn-on time as the outside temperature changes. Most have liquid crystal temperature displays, and some have back-up battery packs that eliminate the need to reprogram in case of a power failure. The new smart thermostats can be programmed to accommodate any lifestyle.

Smart residential building technologies do much more than smart thermostats, as they control the whole building rather than just the temperature. These technologies can control many aspects of a building: heating, cooling, lights, security, hot tubs, music, window shades, telephones, and appliances. Smart building technologies use a microprocessor that is programmed with each housing system's schedule.

Energy Efficient Buildings Meet Certain Performance Standards.
New buildings are more energy efficient than houses built 20 years ago. With the new construction technologies and emphasis on the Model Energy Code, residential building Energy Rating Systems (HERS), Energy Star, and LEED building guidelines, buildings can be even more efficient than the standard home being built today. New residential buildings should meet energy efficiency levels specified in the Council of American Building Officials Model Energy Code/1995 (CABO-MEC), or standard 90.2-1993 "Energy Efficient Design of New Low-Rise Residential Buildings" of the American Society of Heating, Refrigeration and Air Conditioning Engineers (ASHRAE). Both CABO-MEC and ASHRAE work with the U.S. Department of Energy to make sure the energy standards for building codes are up-to-date (Building Environmental Science and Technology—Howard Associates, 1997). These codes are only a starting point, and buildings that are sustainable often exceed these standards.

Energy efficient homes are often validated by building energy ratings or certifications. The most prominent are HERS (Home Energy Rating Systems) and the LEED (Leadership in Energy and Environmental Design). HERS provides a standardized evaluation of a building's energy efficiency and expected energy costs. This nationally recognized rating system was jointly developed by the U.S. Department of Energy and Energy Rated Homes™ of America. Raters evaluate building plans and building specifications; estimate annual utility costs; test the building for air leaks; test ducts for leakage; and visually inspect insulation levels, windows, doors, heating and cooling systems, water heaters, solar gain, lighting, and appliances. Then they make recommendations for other resource efficient measures. Buildings receive scores between 0–100; the higher the better. This rating shows a building's estimated annual energy use, compared to a reference building of the same square footage, number of bedrooms, and so forth, and built to comply with the national Model Energy Code. The MEC building is assigned a score of 80–100. For every 5 percent reduction in energy use compared to the MEC building, the HERS score increases by one point. Thus, a building with a HERS score of 86 would be 30 percent more efficient and a building that scores 90 would be 50 percent more efficient (Fannie Mae, 2000).

LEED, a rating system developed by the U.S. Green Building Council (USGBC), is used to evaluate building systems in terms of their sustainability efforts. LEED is different from other rating systems because it is based on a "green credit" system. For example, 5 percent of a building's materials must be from salvaged materials in order to earn a point for the salvaged materials credit. According to the USGBC (2004), LEED certification is the most important tool for sustainable building practices in existence today. However, LEED certification can be somewhat expensive for residential buildings.

Qualify for Energy Efficient Mortgages.   Because of energy efficiency, residential buildings may qualify for special mortgages. The Energy Efficient Mortgage (EEM) is designed to provide homebuyers an incentive to purchase more resource efficient buildings. Some EEMs offer zero downpayments and add projected utility savings to an income for the purpose of mortgage qualification (thus giving greater buying power). To qualify, the house must meet certain energy efficiency requirements and be inspected and rated by a certified energy auditor or rater.

Some homes are constructed by certified builders who have received specialized training and are required to meet tough standards to be certified. These builders may market their residential buildings using the Energy Star® Home logo. Energy Star® residential buildings and builders can be found by looking for advertisements featuring the Energy Star® label. To find a local Energy Star® Home builder, contact the Energy Star® Homes program hotline at 1-888-STAR-YES or visit the U.S. Environmental Protection Agency's Web site for a list of building partners.

Sustainable Buildings Use Water Efficiently Inside and Outside

Buildings use hundreds of gallons of water each day, and much of this water waste can be reduced or reused. Just by incorporating simple and low-cost measures in new construction, water use could be reduced by about one half when compared to buildings constructed in the 1980s. Fresh water resources are being rapidly depleted by shrinking reservoirs, dropping aquifer depths, and by development (Building Environmental Science and Technology—Howard Associates, 1997), making water conservation an important consideration. Water savings correspond with energy savings. Reduced water usage also means a decrease in the transportation, treatment, and heating of water.

Gray-water and Rain-water Collection Systems.   In many areas of the country, gray-water and rain-water collection systems are being used to reduce domestic water demand. These systems are being used to flush toilets and irrigate landscapes. Gray-water, water that has come into human contact, is collected from sinks, showers, and tubs. It is stored and then used to flush toilets and irrigate landscapes. As shown in Figure 11.22, rain-water and snowmelt systems collect water off the roof using gutters and downspouts, store it in a cistern, and deliver it to the point of use with gravity or by using a sump pump. Because this water has never come into human contact, there may be fewer restrictions placed on its use by the Department of Health and local governments.

Water-conserving Fixtures and Appliances.   Low-flush toilets, smaller diameter water piping, low-flow shower heads and faucets, small tubs, and water-saving dishwashers and clothes washers all help lower residential building water use. The water heater's location is also important in reducing water use. People often waste water by running the tap a long time to get hot water. Moving hot water closer to the point of use saves water and energy. Sustainable builders plan plumbing so the shortest possible length of pipe runs from the water heater to areas where hot water is used. Instantaneous "tank less" water heaters—located at the point of hot water use— can limit the need to let a faucet or shower run while waiting for hot water to travel from the tank.

Water-wise Landscaping.   In some communities, especially in the western states, more than 67 percent of residential water use is used outdoors, primarily to irrigate the landscape (Envision Utah, Urban Planning Tools for Quality Growth, 2002). A water-wise landscape, also known as a *xeriscape*, can greatly impact overall water consumption. A water-wise landscape is one that fits with existing and/or natural water patterns present on the site. This includes respecting natural drainage patterns and limits set by the region's

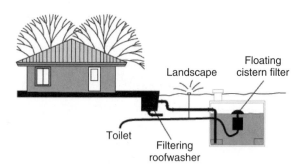

Figure 11.22   Rain-water and snowmelt harvesting

annual precipitation. While plant selection and irrigation methods are essential parts of designing a water-wise landscape, modification of the owner's watering habits is probably the most fundamental part of reducing water consumption. In designing a water-wise landscape, careful attention should be paid to the following.

- **Plant selection:** Use plants that are well-suited to the location's natural water regime. Native plants may be preferable because they are well-adapted to the region and often support native fauna.
- **Plant placement:** Group plants with similar water, light, and nutrient needs together in hydrazones, which are planting areas consisting of plants that require similar amounts of water and an irrigation system that provides the correct level of water for those plants. Also make sure plants will receive an appropriate amount of sunlight; placing shade plants in full sun will lead to increased water demand.
- **Irrigation:** Develop a thorough irrigation plan that takes into account the landscape's various needs. Subsurface irrigation will reduce water loss through evaporation. Drip systems can be designed to deliver water at the base of individual plants, eliminating excess water being wasted on the space between plantings. Installing a shut-off device triggered by precipitation levels eliminates unnecessary watering.
- **Mulch:** Mulch is a protective covering spread on the ground that helps prevent water loss through evaporation. It can also reduce herbicide application by helping to control weeds.
- **Storm water and run-off management:** Hard, nonpermeable surfaces like driveways and paths can cause run-off problems. Alternatively, permeable surfaces like pavers or gravel walkways will allow water that falls on the site to seep into the ground. This filters out pollutants like pesticides and fertilizers, and helps keep water on the site rather than sending it down the storm drain. Storm water can also be caught as it comes off the roof and reserved for use on the landscape during dry periods.

Sustainable Buildings Use Resource-Efficient Landscaping

In order to create a truly sustainable living space, you must consider the surrounding landscape and its interaction with the building. It makes little sense to spend time and money constructing a sustainable home, just to place it in a water- and energy-hungry landscape. But what does a sustainable landscape look like? It depends on how you plan to use it: as storage, an entertainment area, a play area for pets or children, a garden, an area to attract wildlife, or simply for aesthetic pleasure. It also depends on the natural parameters set by the local bioregion. A sustainable landscape in Portland, Oregon (with an average annual precipitation of approximately 40 inches), may look very different from one in Salt Lake City, Utah (with an average annual precipitation of approximately 16 inches). While the specific eco-region in which a building is constructed will dictate much of what constitutes that setting's sustainable landscape, some basic guiding principles apply across most settings. Sustainable landscapes increase energy efficiency, conserve water, promote biodiversity, and help filter pollutants from air and water. They can also offer a place to process and hold waste and produce food. Studies indicate that sustainable landscaping can reduce building heating costs by 30 percent, building cooling costs by 50 percent, and outdoor water consumption by 80 percent (Moffat & Schiler, 1994).

Reduction in a building's heating and cooling loads can be accomplished through the creation of wind breaks, and placement of trees to control sunlight, as shown in Figure 11.23. On the north and west sides of the house, evergreen trees, shrubs, vines, fences, or earth berms can be used to create buffers from winter wind. Earth berms and fences can channel winds away from the building and provide insulating features. Placing shrubs and trees next to the house can also provide protection by creating an insulating space next to the walls.

Proper tree placement is important for controlling sunlight coming into the house and can reduce solar heat entering the building in the summer. Heat from summer sunlight can be reduced by

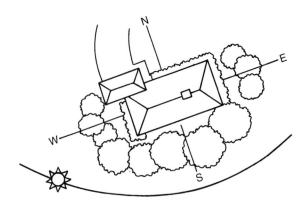

Figure 11.23   Sustainable landscape

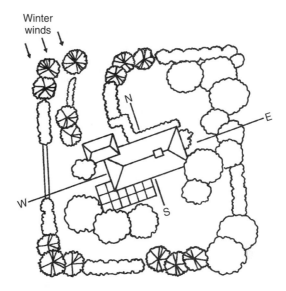

Figure 11.24   Use of trees and shrubs to reduce heat gains

planting deciduous trees and shrubs along the building's east, west, and south sides, as shown in Figure 11.24. Both placement and expected height at maturity need to be considered when selecting shade trees. If deciduous trees are tall enough they will not only shade the walls, but also the roof. However, if the building has a roof-mounted solar system, trees should not shade the solar system. The east and west sides should have shorter deciduous trees or medium-to-tall shrubs to create shade from the hot morning and afternoon sunlight. Because their leaves drop in late fall, deciduous trees allow sunlight onto south walls and windows in the winter. However, if deciduous trees are planted too close to the house and in front of windows, some of the heat gain through the windows in the winter can be blocked by the bare branches. Keep trees a minimum of 10 feet from paved surfaces as roots can damage hardscapes. If utilizing a septic tank, tree placement is also extremely important.

Attention should be paid to reducing maintenance when creating an energy efficient landscape. Group plants in beds rather than dispersed throughout the lawn area. Appropriate plant selection and landscape design can reduce mowing and weed removal demands and make human-powered (as opposed to gas or electric) lawn equipment more viable. Remove thin strips of grass (lawns should be at least one half as wide as they are long) and group plants in beds rather than dispersing them throughout the lawn area. Solar power can also be used for outdoor lights, hot tubs, and swimming pools. New solar-powered lawn mowers are making their way onto the market as well.

In 2000 (the most recent year for which data were available), food and yard waste together made up over 23 percent of the total household waste generated in the United States (U.S. Environmental Protection Agency, 2002). Much of that waste can be processed right in the household landscape through composting. Residential compost systems allow owners to turn yard waste and kitchen scraps into a nutrient-rich soil addition instead of sending it to the landfill or incinerator. This saves landfill space, reduces pollution associated with waste incineration, and decreases the total resources required to collect and transport household waste.

Most of the food produced in the United States is grown and processed far from where it is consumed. As the distance increases between where food is consumed and where it grows, so do the environmental costs of obtaining food. By devoting even a small part of the landscape for a garden, a family or individual can reduce the pollution and resource consumption involved in obtaining the food they need.

Sustainable Buildings Provide Healthy Indoor Environments

A sustainable building is healthy. According to the American Lung Association (2004), elements within our homes and workplaces have been increasingly recognized as a threat to human health. According to the U.S. Environmental Protection Agency, indoor air pollution is almost always worse than outdoor air pollution, even in large industrialized cities (U.S. Environmental Protection Agency and U.S. Consumer Product Safety Commission, 1995). Since most Americans spend 90 percent of their time in an enclosed environment, they are exposed to polluted air on a regular basis. Therefore, it should be no surprise that indoor air quality has become a major U.S. concern considering the increased number of respiratory illnesses, allergic irritations, and asthma, especially in children (Chandra, Beal, & Downing, 1997).

Creating a healthy building includes careful consideration of all indoor environmental quality issues. Indoor pollutants, unpleasant smells, inadequate lighting, excessive noise, humming lights or appliances, and inadequate ventilation can lead to irritation, poor health, and reduced productivity. In extreme cases these unhealthy conditions can lead to injury and even death. Because modern residential buildings are usually built to be more airtight, they have greater potential of trapping indoor air quality contaminants, especially if not properly ventilated. When a tight house is coupled with interior products and materials that generate indoor pollutants, occupants may develop serious health problems.

Sustainable Buildings Are Designed for the Life Cycle

If all houses could be built using universal design principles, then aging adults, accident victims, and people suffering from diseases would no longer have to unwillingly change residences. People with temporary or chronic physical ailments often must move because of an inability to conduct daily activities such as bathing, cooking, sleeping, or using the bathroom in a standard home. Designing a residential building for the entire life cycle means creating a home where residents can age in place. Universal design simplifies life by making a residential building more usable for people of all ages, sizes, and abilities. Universal design essentials include accessible routes in and around the building, a no-step entrance, wider hallways and doorways, no thresholds in the showers, lever handles for doors and sink faucets, environmental controls (light switches, electrical outlets, thermostats, etc.) in reachable locations, reinforced bathroom walls for grab bars, and usable bathrooms and kitchens. In this sense, usable means any person can fully utilize all aspects of the bathroom and kitchen and not encounter any barriers.

Right now most residential buildings are not built using universal design concepts; therefore, people with disabilities are excluded from being invited to dinner or other social events because of the barriers found in many homes. If all residential buildings had just a few basic universal design concepts incorporated into their designs, people with disabilities would have more choices in where they can visit and live.

WHAT IS A SUSTAINABLE COMMUNITY?

In order to understand sustainable buildings, it is essential to better understand sustainable communities because one impacts the other. A sustainable community is one in which people work together to create places where natural and historic resources are preserved, jobs are available, sprawl is contained, neighborhoods are secure, education is lifelong, transportation and health care are accessible, and all citizens have opportunities to improve the quality of their lives (President's Council on Sustainable Development, 1996). Sustainable communities address infrastructure issues such as transportation, housing, utilities, rural/urban land use, economic development, information systems, urban sprawl, accessibility, and promotion of local products and services. Sustainable businesses and households make efficient use of land, energy, and other resources, allowing them to achieve a high quality of life with minimal waste and environmental damage. These communities are healthy and secure, and they provide people with clean air to breathe and safe water to drink.

In many communities, decisions about development, transportation, housing, services, and other issues are made in a piecemeal fashion. Most communities are not planned, but instead develop haphazardly. Today many communities are looking at the concept of sustainability and smart growth, and finding ways of incorporating it into their long-range plans. Sustainable communities do not just happen; they require dedicated local governments and citizens who understand sustainability and what it means to their communities. Specific characteristics of sustainable communities include the following.

- **Sustainable communities are well-designed.** People can sense when they enter a well-designed community. Although well-designed communities may differ in style or location, they are all durable, integrated into their natural settings, and efficient in meeting community needs. People live, work, and play in their own community. The principles of sustainable design are reflected in the choices made by local governments and citizens and a community's physical infrastructure. Building codes shape how much energy, water, and materials a building consumes in its construction and operation, while zoning ordinances influence decisions on building design and siting, as well as development layouts. Efficient land use protects vulnerable environmental areas that provide recreational benefits to humans and habitat for plants and wildlife.
- **Sustainable communities control growth.** While some growth may be necessary, uncontrolled growth can have a devastating effect on communities. Sustainable communities manage growth in order to decrease sprawl, conserve open space, respect nature's carrying capacity, and provide protection from natural hazards such as floods or landslides.
- **Sustainable communities respect the natural environment.** Sustainable communities recognize that they are part of the larger natural environment. They are aware of the greater community of flora and fauna, natural and native habitats, indigenous animals and plants, wetlands, and streams. Good planning minimizes areas of vegetation disturbance, earth grading, and water channel alterations. It recognizes the

importance of native or natural habitat, and strives to reestablish diverse natural systems.

- **Sustainable communities are pedestrian friendly.** Communities are discovering the benefits of pedestrian friendly design. Planning areas for compact development promote walking to obtain goods and services and can result in decreased automobile use, traffic, and air pollution.
- **Sustainable communities respect historic characteristics and local building styles.** According to Francesa Lyman (1997), author of "Twelve Gates to the City," historic buildings have an undeniable appeal, partly because they are often built to last and they use materials and styles appropriate to the regional climate. Historical structures give society an important sense of connection, tradition, and education about the past.
- **Sustainable communities have public spaces.** Another casualty of modern community planning has been the traditional public spaces such as town squares, open markets, and plazas (Lyman, 1997). Historically, people congregated in public spaces, which provided a way to connect people to the place. These have been displaced by shopping malls, private clubs, parking lots, and gated communities.
- **Sustainable communities preserve open spaces.** When considering open land for residential or industrial development, an awareness and appreciation of natural systems is essential. Visionary planner Frederick Law Olmsted, who has long been acknowledged as the founder of American landscape architecture, described urban parks as the lungs of a city (Rybcazynski, 1999). The flora and fauna clean the city's air and give breathing room away from the city's congestion. Olmsted was one of the landscape planners for Central Park in New York City, and became famous for creating natural wilderness landscapes in parks. Urban parks are just one example of open space. Forests, farmland, mountains, plains, deserts, and wetlands also give communities and regions vital breathing room.
- **Sustainable communities allow for mixed uses.** Zoning that allows for more efficient and more sustainable design promotes mixed-use development such as having a store, apartment building, and school on the same block. Zoning ordinances that promote mixed-use development can give people easy access to a full range of facilities and services without driving long distances (Lyman, 1997).
- **Sustainable communities promote economic development, jobs, and education.** A strong local economy is at the core of a sustainable community because economic development

and the jobs it creates are essential vehicles for meeting human needs. Before anything else, people must be able to provide basic necessities for themselves and their families. Communities that prosper will be those that develop strategies to create resilient local economies by using the unique strengths of their people and places. Sustainable communities need a flexible, well-educated workforce.

- **Sustainable communities encourage sustainable buildings.** It is very difficult to review sustainable housing without understanding communities and their impacts on buildings. Through master plans, approved developments, building codes, and zoning ordinances, communities dictate how areas are developed and how buildings are constructed.

CONCLUSION

In this chapter, sustainable buildings and communities were explored in order to provide information about strategies, methods, and materials used to construct sustainable homes and create sustainable communities. Hopefully, this information will change behaviors, attitudes, and decisions about sustainability. Ultimately, human choices will lead society away from unsustainable consumption patterns and hopefully reduce the negative impacts people are having on the environment. Society can rise to the challenge, or continue unsustainable consumption of natural resources and the degradation of the environment until there is little left for future generations.

REFERENCES

American Lung Association. (2004). The problem with our residential building environments. In *Healthy house—raising the standard home environments.* Available: www.lungusa.org.

Barnett, D. L., & Browning, W. D. (1999). *A primer on sustainable building* (2nd ed.). Snowmass, CO: Rocky Mountain Institute.

Barnett, S., & Case, S. (1997). Green specifying: Why not? *The Construction Specifier, 50*(1) 16–25.

Building Environmental Science and Technology—Howard Associates. (1997). *Good for the environment, good for the economy.* Available: www.nrg.builder.com.

Chandra, S., Beal, D., & Downing, A. (1997, November). *Allergy resistant housing—principles and practice.* Paper presented at the Environmental and Economic Balance: The 21st Century Outlook Conference, Miami, FL.

Chiras, D. D. (2000). *The natural house: A complete guide to healthy, energy-efficient, environmental homes.* White River Junction, VT: Chelsea Green Publishing.

City, Light & Power, Energy Services Office. (2003). *Efficiency ratings.* Available: www.cwlp.com/Energy_services/efficiency-ratings.htm.

Environmental Building News. (1995). *Insulation materials: Environmental comparisons.* Available: www.buildinggreen.com/features/ins/insulation.cfm.

Envision Utah, Urban Planning Tools for Quality Growth. (2002). *Water conservation.* Salt Lake City, UT: Envision Utah.

Fannie Mae. (2000). *Home performance power: Fannie Mae's guide to buying and maintaining a green home.* Washington, DC: Fannie Mae.

Gillman, R. (1990). *Sustainability: The state of the movement.* Available: www.context.org/ICLIB/IC25/Gilman.htm.

Green Culture. (2004). *Wind power.* Available: www.solargoods.com/docs/windpow_info_faq.shtml.

Joint Center for Sustainable Communities. (2003). *Joint center report.* Retrieved July 6, 2005, from www.usmayors.org/uscm/sustainable.

Leviton. (2004). *Leviton: Building a connected world.* Available: www.levitron.com/sections/prodinfo/sesor/seframe2.htm.

Lyman, F. (1997). Twelve gates to the city. *Sierra Magazine, 82* (May/June), 29–35.

Moffat, A., & Schiler, M. (1994). *Energy-efficient and environmental landscaping.* South Newfane, VT: Appropriate Solutions Press.

Philips, A. (2004, May). The value of green landscape and architecture. *The Construction Specifier,* 28–38.

President's Council on Sustainable Development. (1996, February). *Sustainable America: A new consensus for prosperity, opportunity, and a healthy environment for the future.* Washington, DC: President's Council on Sustainable Development.

Rocky Mountain Institute. (2004). *Household water efficiency.* Available: www.rmi.org/sitepages/pid123.php.

Roosevelt, T. (1910). *The new nationalism.* Available: www.usinfo.state.gov/usa/infousa/facts/democra/31.htm.

Rybcazynski, W. (1999). *A clearing in the distance: Frederick Law Olmsted and America in the nineteenth century.* New York: Simon & Schuster.

SciART. (2004). *Seasonal affective disorder (SAD) and light therapy.* Available: www.kaliszincolor.com/light-therapy/A_sad.htm.

Smart Communities Network: Creating Energy Smart Communities. (2004). *Green buildings introduction.* Available: www.sustainable.doe.gov/buildingsgbintro.shtml.

State Legislative Report. (1997). *The Model Energy Code for residential buildings.* Available: www.ncsl.org/programs/esnr/modelec.htm.

Stover, D. (1997). Reengineering the American home. *Popular Science Magazine,* (May), 62–65.

US-ICLEI Cities for Climate Protection Campaign & Renew America. (1998). *Global warming: Local solutions renew America's national town meeting.* Washington, DC: New America.

U.S. Department of Energy, Building America Program, Office of Building Technology, State and Community Programs, Energy Efficiency and Renewable Energy. (2001, January). *Whole-house building approach benefits builders, buyers, and the environment* (NREL/BR-55027745). Golden, CO: U.S. Department of Energy.

U.S. Department of Energy, Energy Efficiency and Renewable Energy. (2004, March). *Solar history timeline: The future.* Available: www.eere.energy.gov/solar/solar_time_future.html.

U.S. Department of Energy, Energy Information Administration. (2000). *Monthly energy review—March.* Washington, DC: U.S. Department of Energy.

U.S. Department of Energy, Federal Technology Alerts. (1995). *Ground-source heat pumps applied to commercial facilities.* Available: www.pnl.gov/fta/2_ground.htm.

U.S. Department of Energy, National Renewable Energy Laboratory, Energy Efficiency and Renewable Energy Clearinghouse. (1995, December). *Energy-efficient lighting* (DOE/GO-10095-056, FS 141). Washington, DC: U.S. Department of Energy.

U.S. Department of Energy, Office of Energy Efficiency Renewable Energy Network, Smart Communities Network. (2003). *Creating energy smart communities. Green buildings introduction.* Available: www.sustainable.doe.gov/buildings/gdinto.shtml.

U.S. Department of the Interior, Bureau of Land Management, Idaho. (2004). *Endangered, threatened, and special status plants and animals.* Available: www.id.blm.gov/whatwedo/spec_status.htm.

U.S. Environmental Protection Agency. (1994). *Our built and natural environments—status and trends of wetlands in the coterminous United States.* Washington, DC: U.S. Environmental Protection Agency.

U.S. Environmental Protection Agency. (2002). *Municipal solid waste in the United States: 2000 facts and figures.* Available: www.epa.gov/espaoswer/non-hw/muncpl/msw99.htm.

U.S. Environmental Protection Agency and U.S. Consumer Product Safety Commission. (1995, April). *The inside story: A guide to indoor air quality* (EPA 402-K-93-007). Washington: DC: U.S. Environmental Protection Agency and U.S. Consumer Product Safety Commission.

U.S. Environmental Protection Agency and U.S. Department of Energy. (1997, May). *Saving with Energy Star, saving the earth, saving your money* (EPA 430-F-97-054). Washington, DC: U.S. Environmental Protection Agency and U.S. Department of Energy.

U.S. Green Building Council. (2004). *LEED Green Building System*™. Available: www.usgbc.org/AboutUs/programs.asp.

Xu, T., Bechu, O., Carrie, R., Dickerhoff, D., Fish, W., Kristiansen, O., Levinson, R., McWilliams, J., Wang, D., & Modera, M. (1999). *Commercial thermal distribution systems* (Final Report for CIEE/CEC Indoor Environment Department). Berkeley, CA: Lawrence Berkeley National Laboratory.

CHAPTER 12

Housing Challenges for the Twenty-first Century

Andrew T. Carswell, John L. Merrill, Anne L. Sweaney, and Kenneth R. Tremblay, Jr.
Andrew T. Carswell is Assistant Professor, Department of Housing and Consumer Economics, University of Georgia, Athens, GA; John L. Merrill is Professor Emeritus, School of Human Ecology, University of Wisconsin, Madison, WI; Anne L. Sweaney is Professor and Head, Department of Housing and Consumer Economics, University of Georgia, Athens, GA; and Kenneth R. Tremblay, Jr., is Professor, Department of Design and Merchandising, Colorado State University, Fort Collins, CO.

This concluding chapter addresses a number of challenges that our society faces in providing safe and affordable housing to its population. While many of the challenges introduced throughout this book were discussed as distinct areas, many of them are actually interrelated, which makes the task of addressing them even more daunting.

HOUSING AFFORDABILITY

The growing lack of affordable housing is one of the most critical housing challenges facing our society. Working families often have difficulty finding decent, affordable housing, and communities are increasingly recognizing that they need additional affordable housing units to attract new businesses. The term *affordable housing* is now often replaced by the term *workforce housing* since important service workers such as teachers, firefighters, nurses, and police officers are often among those who cannot afford housing in the communities in which they work.

One of the major reasons for the housing affordability challenge is that housing prices have increased much faster than income for low- and moderate-income households. As discussed in Chapter 6, the U.S. government considers housing unaffordable if a household pays more than 30 percent of its gross income to obtain it. In fact, the average American household pays approximately 25 percent of its income for housing. However, many households with incomes of less than 50 percent of the median (about $28,250) pay 50 percent or more of their income for housing (U.S. Department of Housing and Urban Development, 2003). While more often true of renter households who tend to have lower incomes, it is also true of very low-income homeowners. Although the supply of low-cost units is declining, government-subsidized housing programs have not expanded to meet demand.

When households pay such a high percentage of their incomes for housing they are often unable to pay for other necessities such as health care and food. These households have difficulty paying for home maintenance and repair, and are also at great risk of becoming homeless when emergencies arise or their incomes are disrupted, since they typically are unable to accumulate any savings.

The housing affordability problem for very low-income households requires that either incomes be raised or the supply of affordable housing units be increased. The National Low Income Housing Coalition (NLIHC) has devised a figure it calls the housing wage and has developed a side-by-side comparison of wages and rents for every county and state, called *Out of Reach* (National Low Income Housing Coalition, 2005a). The report calculates the amount of income a household must earn to afford various sizes of rental units (0, 1, 2, 3, and 4 bedrooms). For example, the wage that a person must earn to afford a moderately priced two-bedroom rental unit in Puerto Rico in 2004 was $7.22 per hour, in Georgia it was $14.12, and in the District of Columbia the wage was $22.83 per hour (National Low Income Housing Coalition, 2005b). This is well above the wage that many workers earn. A household with two wage earners makes the rent more manageable, but for single parents with no second worker the income proportion is excessive. The housing wage is even higher for families that need more than two bedrooms.

Unfortunately, while the average household income continues to rise, it has increased much more slowly at the lower end of the income scale. Between 1989 and 1999 incomes for the bottom 20 percent of households increased 1 percent while those in the top 20 percent increased 15 percent. Even the middle fifth of families saw only a 2 percent increase in income during this period (Bernstein, McNichol, Mishel, & Zahradnik, 2000). The challenges facing potential homeowners were discussed in Chapter 10.

In the meantime, developing or even maintaining the supply of housing affordable to people with low incomes has become increasingly difficult, as noted in Chapter 9. Surveys report that Americans recognize the lack of affordable housing for working people as one of the most serious problems facing their communities (Nelson, 2003).

However, when it comes to supporting specific housing developments for low-income households in their own neighborhoods, Americans are likely to say "Not in My Back Yard" (NIMBY). Local resistance to working family housing, referred to as NIMBYism, frequently slows down development as the developers negotiate with local residents, which drives up costs. In other cases it results in development plans being dropped.

Even with full local support, developing affordable housing for working families is a challenge. Affordable housing developers have to compete with developers of higher-end housing for land and financing. In many cases the only way that developers can produce affordable housing is to compete for government subsidies. Low-income housing developers often must pull together subsidies from a variety of sources. While this may be necessary, it delays projects and reduces the number of units that are built. Many developers do not get involved in lower-end projects because of governmental red tape and a lack of incentives, and the perception that they will lose money on the project. State finance agencies and financial institutions need to be proactive in making the process more user friendly or the programs designed to help those in need will be underutilized.

INDUSTRY CHALLENGES

The U.S. housing industry has been one of the least progressive industries, as discussed in Chapter 4. Unlike other countries such as Sweden and Japan, the majority of U.S. houses continue to be stick built on the site as opposed to being built in a factory and transported to the site. This tradition is beginning to change as more home components are built in factories. However, as mentioned in Chapter 2, any housing construction process changes must be viewed in the context of prevailing American housing norms.

The creation of large production builders and the increasing lack of skilled labor have helped to move the industry along. Because of the limited availability of land and labor the industry is now being encouraged to accept some new technologies and create more efficient building techniques. This is the current mission of the U.S. Department of Housing and Urban Development's PATH (Partnership for Advancing Technology in Housing) program. In the future, manufactured housing and stick-built housing will meet somewhere in the middle. Stick builders are using more factory-built components and manufactured producers are getting more involved in installation and making certain the units are properly sited and secured.

LAND USE AND SPACE CONCERNS

Many arguments related to the lack of affordable housing can be tied to the lack of developable land in many metropolitan areas. As urban areas become fully developed, land prices escalate to the point where it is out of reach for many people. As households move further away from the urban center, suburban households soon feel the same growth pressures that their urban counterparts have experienced. As the suburbs become more densely developed a new phenomenon occurs—the development of "exurbs," or suburbs of the suburbs. This growth exerts increasing pressure on the natural environment as trees and green spaces are cleared to make way for development. According to the American Farmland Trust study, "Farming on the Edge: Sprawling Development Threatens America's Best Farmland," "Every single minute of every day, America loses two acres of farmland" (American Farmland Trust, 2005, p. 1). Texas leads the nation in farmland loss, followed by Ohio, Georgia, North Carolina, and Illinois.

As discussed in Chapter 5, municipal services are strained by this outward and often inefficient growth pattern. Miles of roads and streets need to be built to accommodate the community needs of the exurban residents, and other utility needs, such as electricity, sewer, and water, must be met as well. These needs create pressure on municipal budgets and resources in order to meet increased demand. While excessive growth has traditionally been a matter of some concern for citizens, there is some evidence that combating sprawl is no longer the highest priority for many Americans (Brookings Institution, 2001; Romero & Liserio, 2002). As sprawl becomes more common, people may feel it is inevitable, be desensitized to it as a problem, or feel that the immediate benefits outweigh the short- and long-term costs.

One way that urban planners are addressing some of the aspects of low-density suburban development is New Urbanism (Katz, 1994), which advocates higher density developments including various types of housing along with stores and offices. Celebration and Seaside, Florida, are examples of this movement. New Urbanists believe that front porches along with narrow streets, back-alley garages, shallow setbacks, and trees lining the streets may promote the small town neighborliness found in the 1920s (Brown, Burton, & Sweaney, 1998). The goal is to create communities where residents not only live but also shop and work, and therefore have less need for their automobiles. Such communities make mass transit much more practical. Additionally, these communities can foster socially cohesive communities where residents know each other (Fulton, 1996). Some research has suggested that homebuyers have become tired of sprawl-type communities and see New Urbanism as a healthier alternative, and will thus pay a premium for the privilege of living in such a neighborhood (Eppli & Tu, 1999).

A number of state and local legislatures have addressed policies that attempt to combat sprawl through enticing citizens back to urban areas. Maryland initiated a "smart growth" program in the mid-1990s which sought to not only redevelop residential communities in urban areas, but also to protect rural areas from overdevelopment. This program established a job creation tax credit and a program which encouraged workers to live near their places of employment. While initial reviews of smart growth programs were mixed (Cohen, 2002), other jurisdictions have followed suit in implementing their own versions of smart growth.

AGING IN PLACE: HOUSING DESIGN FOR OLDER ADULTS

Statistical projections released by the U.S. Census Bureau show that almost 28 million Americans will be 65 years and older by the year 2025, while those 85 years and older will number slightly over 7 million. This will represent an 89.4 percent increase in the number of persons 65 and over and a 452 percent increase in the number of persons 85 and over from 2001 levels. By comparison, the total U.S. population is projected to increase by 21.6 percent during this period (U.S. Census Bureau, 2000).

Reaching age 65 does not automatically mean that a person will have health limitations. Many Americans lead active independent lives well into their 80s. However, as people age the chances increase that they will experience some physical or mental challenges with living independently. Only about 45 percent of all persons over 65 years of age report any disability, with 8 percent experiencing a disability so severe that they need assistance. However, 75 percent of persons over 80 report some type of disability and 34 percent report a disability severe enough that they require assistance (Administration on Aging, 2003). Physical and mental disabilities such as increased forgetfulness not only make it more difficult for older persons to care for themselves and their homes, but can also lead to isolation, depression, and other problems.

The increase in the number of older persons has led to a rapid increase in housing targeted specifically to older households. However, producing housing for older people who seek retirement housing but cannot afford market prices is a challenge. Another challenge is providing housing with supportive services at affordable prices for those persons who need some assistance but are not ready for the level of care provided by nursing homes, and who can actually benefit by retaining as much independence as possible.

The majority of older Americans report wanting to stay in the same homes they lived in when they were younger and to age in place. As they are familiar with their environment and know the neighborhood, the desire to stay put is understandable. However, some older people stay in their homes long after they would have benefited from a more supportive environment. Their bathrooms do not accommodate walkers, and entering the home itself requires climbing steps. A variety of home modifications as well as good space planning, as reviewed in Chapter 7, can help older adults live independently. Additionally, wider acceptance of universal design and design for visitability by both builders and consumers, as discussed in Chapter 8, would potentially provide for all Americans to age in place if that is their preference.

LOSS OF COMMUNITY

An acute awareness exists within the social science community that the traditional residential neighborhood and the sense of community that emanates from within that neighborhood is disappearing. Sociologist Robert Putnam's research on the decline of community shows a shockingly high degree of social disengagement in many aspects of everyday life, but none more disturbing than within the structure of the residential neighborhood itself. In his critically acclaimed book *Bowling Alone,* Putnam (2000) provided empirical data that the level of "neighboring," which signifies the maintenance of close contact with one's neighbors on a weekly basis, has been sharply declining for several decades, and there is no real reason to believe that the trend will reverse itself over time. This is partly due to the increased time pressures experienced by many families, as often all adults in the house work outside the home and their children have complicated schedules of after-school activities.

The loss of community also results from the flight to the suburbs and beyond. This low-density development usually means that no services are within walking distance so that when family members leave home it is usually in an automobile, dramatically reducing opportunities for neighbor-to-neighbor contact. The flight out of urban areas also makes it more difficult for communities to preserve the historically significant houses presented in Chapter 1. While no overwhelming evidence exists that Americans preferred the communities of yesteryear over modern ones, Putnam's work seems to suggest that the disconnection in these social networks is not a progressive trend that should be welcomed.

One trend that may be countering this devolution of community is the increase in the number of homeowners' associations that are sprouting up in new developments all over the country. According to the Community Association Institute, the growth in homeowners' and neighborhood associations since 1970 has been phenomenal. In 1970, 10,000 communities had organizations and by 2004 the number grew to 260,000. These association-governed communities include homeowners' associations, condominiums, cooperatives, and other planned neighborhoods. "More than 50 million Americans live in association-governed communities. Some 1.25 million people serve on community association boards, with another 300,000-plus serving as committee members" (Community Association Institute, 2005, p. 1). The advantages of homeowners' and neighborhood associations often mentioned in the literature are that they help to protect home values, serve as a social network, and assist in meeting the increased demand for the provision of services.

NATURAL RESOURCE ALLOCATION

A major future challenge will be the sustainable use of our natural recourses, as reviewed in Chapter 11. Many Americans have said that our next war may be over water. In a number of communities the major new construction barrier is lack of available water. Americans have changed the way they view this resource. One can take a quick tour through the grocery store and see how the shelf space has increased for bottled water from a decade ago. Soft drink companies have added signature bottled water brands to their product lines and sell it at the same price as the colas. As water is an integral part of our lives, it is even more crucial that water be conserved as the population continues to increase. Water-efficient landscaping, as discussed in Chapters 3 and 11, can certainly help in conservation efforts.

Many newly built homes are far more energy efficient than those built just a decade ago. This is partially due to the presence of local building codes and regulations, many of which are considered to be the most stringent in the world. Still, the United States cannot rely totally on the traditional oil, natural gas, and electricity-based energy resources that have predominated in houses for over a century. Many alternative energy sources abound including solar and wind energy. These types of power sources become much more attractive alternatives as the price of oil increases.

Most energy efficiency efforts are rooted in the need for more consumer education and offer innovative solutions to achieve that end. Effective programs should educate households on both improving the energy efficiency of older homes through insulation, and note the proactive steps households can take to reduce unnecessary energy costs within their homes. While increasing energy efficiency, according to Chapter 3 it is also important for households to maintain good indoor air quality and adequate moisture control.

One of the innovative ways that the lending community has addressed energy use is through the introduction of energy efficient mortgages (EEMs). While largely ignored for many years, EEMs are now offered by many lending institutions. New homebuyers who take out an EEM are essentially rewarded for purchasing an energy efficient house (identified by an Energy Star rating program). Because the new homebuyer is projected to save considerable dollars through lower heating and cooling costs over the house's lifetime, the lender reasons that the borrower will be able to assume a higher mortgage than would typically be allowed under normal underwriting circumstances. While these programs are more readily available in the United States, a large number of lenders still do not originate EEMs out of fear that the mortgage is too risky, in that borrowers may simply choose to match higher energy efficiency with increased wasteful energy consumption over time.

CONCLUSION

While it is difficult to predict the future, all indicators suggest that housing affordability, industry challenges, land use and space concerns, housing for older adults, loss of community, and resource allocation will be the greatest housing challenges in the twenty-first century. How we as housing consumers and future homeowners address these challenges will partially determine the quality of life for us and our descendants. In addition, it is extremely important for community stakeholders and leaders to be aware of these challenges and address them before a further housing crisis is created through unintended consequences. You could be part of the solution by making wise housing decisions and perhaps by entering one of the many housing professions yourself.

REFERENCES

Administration on Aging. (2003). *A profile of older Americans—2003.* Washington, DC: U.S. Department of Health and Human Services.

American Farmland Trust. (2005). *Farming on the edge: Sprawling development threatens America's best farmland.* Retrieved February 12, 2005, from www.farmland.org/farmingontheedge/major_findings.htm.

Bernstein, J., McNichol, E., Mishel, L., & Zahradnik, R. (2000). *Pulling apart: A state-by-state analysis of income trends.* Available from the Economic Policy Institute: www.epinet.org.

Brookings Institution. (2001). *Growth at the ballot box: Electing the shape of communities in November 2000.* Washington, DC: Brookings Institution.

Brown, B. B., Burton, J. R., & Sweaney, A. L. (1998). Neighbors, households, and front porches: New urbanist community tool or mere nostalgia? *Environment and Behavior, 30*(5), 579–600.

Cohen, J. (2002). Maryland's "smart growth": Using incentives to combat sprawl. In G. Squires (Ed.), *Urban sprawl: Causes, consequences and policy responses.* Washington, DC: Urban Institute Press.

Community Association Institute. (2005). *Data on U.S. community associations.* Retrieved February 12, 2005, from www.caionline.org.

Eppli, M., & Tu, C. (1999). *Valuing the new urbanism: A report on the impact of the new urbanism on single-family home prices.* Washington, DC: Urban Land Institute.

Fulton, W. (1996). *The new urbanism: Hope or hype for American communities?* Cambridge, MA: Lincoln Land Institute.

Katz, P. (Ed.). (1994). *The new urbanism: Toward an architecture of community.* New York: McGraw-Hill.

National Low Income Housing Coalition. (2005a). *Out of reach.* Retrieved February 12, 2005, from www.nlihc.org/oor2004/.

National Low Income Housing Coalition. (2005b). *Out of reach.* Retrieved February 12, 2005, from www.nlihc.org/oor2004/table9.htm.

Nelson, A. C. (2003). Top ten state and local strategies to increase affordable housing supply. *Housing Facts & Findings, 5*(1), 1, 4–7.

Putnam, R. D. (2000). *Bowling alone: The collapse and revival of American community.* New York: Simon & Schuster.

Romero, F., & Liserio, A. (2002). Saving open spaces: Determinants of 1998 and 1999 "anti-sprawl" ballot measures. *Social Science Quarterly, 83*(1), 341–352.

U.S. Census Bureau. (2000). *Tables NP-T3-B and NP-T3-F.* Washington, DC: Population Programs, Population Division.

U.S. Department of Housing and Urban Development. (2003, February). *FY2003 HUD income limits briefing material.* Retrieved August 23, 2003, from www.huduser.org/datasets/il/fmr03/index.html.

Index

'b' indicates boxed material;
'i' indicates an illustration;
't' indicates a table

A

Abandoned dumps, 61
Access to Community Care
    and Effective Services
    and Support
    (ACCESS), 159
Accessibility, 222–223
Accessible, barrier-free
    design, 194
Accessible design
    definition of, 221i, 221t
    legal standard, 200
ACORN Housing Assistance
    Corporation, 248
Active solar design, 300–304,
    301i, 302i, 303i
Activity support, 168
Adaptable design, 221i, 221t
Adaptive Environments
    Center, 201–202
Adjustable rate mortgage
    (ARM), 267, 269
Adults, with disabilities, 198b
Aerosol containers, 75i
Affordable housing
    challenge of, 327–329
    crisis in, 229
    factors of, 236–239

Age
    and home ownership,
        230–231
    and housing choice, 31
Aging in place, 104
Air cleaners, 72
Air freshners, 84
Air leakage, energy
    efficiency,
        304–305, 305i
Air Leakage (AL), windows,
    308, 309i
Air movement, 59
Air temperature, 59
    and moisture, 69
Allergies, 57
Amenities, 41, 43
American Council of
    American Building
    Official's Model Code
    (MEC), 306
"American Dream," 39, 258,
    258b, 259i
American Farmland
    Trust, 330
American Housing Survey
    (AHS), 31, 141
American Lung
    Association, 320
American National Standards
    Institute (ANSI), 199–200
American Society of Heating,
    Refrigeration and Air

Conditioning Engineers
    (ASHRAR), 314
Americans with Disabilities
    Act (1990), 202
Annual Fuel Utilization
    Efficiency (AFUE), 310, 311i
Antimicrobial finishes, 71
Apartment, 14
Appliances, water-
    conserving, 316
Appliances/equipment, 310, 311i
Application phase, mortgage
    lending, 98
Appraisal, 101–102
Appraisal Institute, 102
Approach/use, 202i, 205
Architectural
    accessibility, 199
Architectural Barriers Act
    (1968), 200
Asbestos, 43, 57, 65i, 85
Asset-based lending, 282
Assistive technology, 199
Attached garage entrance,
    177–178
Automated valuation models
    (AVMs), 102
Automotive waste, 62

B

Baby boomers, 31, 38, 39t,
    88, 104

Baby bust generation, 37
Back door, 177, 179i
Back drafting, 68
Bait and switch practices, 282
Balloon payments, 282
Banks, and mortgage
  lending, 99–100
Barrier-free design
  definition of, 221i, 221t
  universal design, 199–200
Basement, 86
Bathrooms
  indoor air control, 84
  universal design features,
    205, 212i, 217i
  ventilation fans, 66–67
Bednar, Michael, 200
Bedroom, indoor air
  control, 85
Bedroom standard, 41
Book of Modern Homes, 21
Bowling Alone, 332
Broken U-shaped kitchen,
  180i, 181
Brokerage firm, 94
Brown fields, 60
Builders, accessibility
  requirements, 222
Building codes, 88, 91–92
Building costs, 246b, 248
Building materials, 64
Building permit, 91
Building products, criteria
  for, 295–296
Building site
  and home health, 59–62
  orientation, 293–294, 294i
Built environment, 26
Bungalow style, 14–17
Burlington Community Land
  Trust, 246, 247i

C

Cabrini-Green development,
  Chicago, 153i

Cape Code style, 2, 4–5
Carpets, 82
Cast iron stove, 11
Center for International
  Design, 202i, 202–203
Center for Universal Design,
  205, 220–221
Chicago public housing
  projects, 153i
Children
  with disabilities, 198b
  homeless families, 243
Chimneys, 3, 17
Chiras, Daniel, 295
Chrestia, John, 167
Circulation
  floor plan checklist, 187t
  interior space, 172–174, 173i
  universal design features,
    209i–210i
City, definition, 116
Civil Rights Act (1968),
  200, 201
Climate variables, and home
  health, 58–59
Closing phase
  home purchase process,
    279–280
  mortgage lending, 99
Code restrictions, 238
Collective socialization, 117
Colonial homes, 4
Combustion gases, 57, 65i
Commercial buildings,
  number of, 292
Communities
  conservation, 133
  gated, 132–133
Community, definition, 114
Community amenities, 49–50
Community Association
  Institute, 333
Community building
  movement, 116
Community development, 115

Community Development
  Corporations (CDC), 106
Community Development
  Block Grants (CDBG), 250
Community Land Trust (CLT),
  246, 247i
Community Reinvestment Act
  (CRA), 160
Compact Fluorescent Lighting
  (CFL), 312i, 312–313
Comprehensive plan,
  community development,
  118–119
Condensation, 69
Condensation Resistance
  (CR), 308
Condominium ownership,
  272, 273i
Condominiums, 42
Conservation communities, 133
Consortium for Advanced
  Residential Buildings, 305
Construction age, 64
Construction draws, 91
Consumer awareness
  campaigns, 223
Contract builders, 93
Cooking/baking center, 181
Cooling systems, 305
Cooperative ownership,
  272–273
Cornice, 7
Corridor kitchen, 180i, 181
Cost, universal design, 219–220
Cost approach, appraisal,
  101–102
Council of American Builders
  Official's Model Energy
  Code (CABO-MEC), 314
Country Cottages, 8
Covenants, 124–125, 125i–126i
Craftsman style, 15
Credit check, 274i,
  274–275, 276t
Credit life insurance, 279, 280

Credit lines, 271
Credit unions, 100
Cross gables, 17
Crowding, 47
Cultural orientation, 36–37
Cuomo, Andrew, 251
Custom builders, 92–93

D

Defensible space, 48
Deforestation, 292
Department of Energy, 292
Design terms, universal design, 220–221, 221i, 221t
Dew point, 69, 70
Disabled
  demographic changes, 197, 198b
  housing affordability, 242
Discrimination
  home purchase, 280
  housing affordability, 231, 241
Doors
  energy efficiency, 309–310
  universal design features, 211i
Dormers, 8
Dosage, 57
Double-hung windows, 6
Downing, Andrew Jackson, 8, 12
Downpayment, 265–266, 266t, 269
Draperies, 83
Dry cleaned goods, 85
Duany, Andres, 238
Durability requirements, HUD, 144
Dust mites, 79, 84
Dutch Colonial style, 17

E

Eastlake style, 12
Echo boomer generation, 31, 37

Eclectic styles, 17–20
Ecological model, 25, 26, 113, 116
Education, and housing choice, 34
Education of Homeless Children and Youth program, 159
Elderly. *See* Older adults
Emergency Shelter Grant program, 159
Encyclopedia of Housing, affordability indices, 226
Energy, building consumption, 291, 304
Energy efficiency, 175, 176
Energy Efficiency Ratio (EER), 310, 311i
Energy Efficient Mortgage (EEM), 315, 334
Energy Guide Label, 310, 311i
Energy Star®, 310, 315
Entryways
  interior space, 177–178, 178i, 179i
  universal design features, 208i, 213i
Environment, and sustainable buildings, 291–292
Environment-behavior, and housing, 44–45
Environment-health interaction
  building materials, 64
  building site, 59–62
  climate variables, 58–69
  furnishings, 74–77
  indoor air quality, 71–72, 82–86
  lifestyle, 77–80
  moisture, 68–71
  risks, 56b
  storm run-off, 62–63
  understanding, 56–58

ventilation, 64, 66–68
water systems, 72–74
Environmental Protection Agency, 320
Environmental tobacco smoke (ETS), 77–78
Equal Credit Opportunity Act
  home purchase, 275
  predatory lending, 282–284
Equitable use, 202i, 203
Error tolerance, 202i, 204
Ethnography, 115
Evaporation, 69
Exclusionary zoning, 238–239
Executive order, definition, 161
Exposure, home environment, 57

F

Face-to-face seating, 46
Factory-built housing, 20–22, 106, 109i. *See also* Manufactured
Fair housing, definition of, 281
Fair Housing Act, 160, 161
Fair Housing Amendment Act, 201
Family life cycle, 32
Family type, and housing choice, 31–32
Family Unification Program, 156
Fans
  negative pressure, 68
  replacement air, 67–68
  size, 67
  types, 66–67
Farm land, loss of, 330
Farmers Home Administration (FmHA), 149
Faucet, 212i
Federal Endangered Species Act, 292
Federal Energy Alerts, heat pumps, 303

Federal Fair Housing Act
  home purchase, 280
  predatory lending, 283–284
Federal Home Loan Mortgage
  Corporation (FHLMC,
  Freddie Mac), 150
Federal government
  housing affordability factor,
   236, 237
  housing policies, 140–141
Federal Housing
  Administration (FHA)
  housing finance, 148–149
  reverse mortgages, 271–272
Federal National Mortgage
  Corporation (FNMA,
  Fannie Mae), 150
Feedlots, 61
Fertilizers, 62, 86
Fiberboard, 65i
Field Guide to American
  Homes, 1
Financing costs, 246b,
  248–250
Fireplace, 83
First-time homebuyers, 40
Fixed rate mortgage,
  267–269, 268i
Flexibility, design principle,
  202i, 203
Flipping, 282
Floor plan
  circulation, 173
  interior design, 168i,
   168–169
  universal design, 205, 218i
  zoning rules, 171–172, 172i
Floor plan evaluation
  checklist, 187t–188t
Floor tiles, indoor air
  control, 83
Food preparation center, 181
Food storage center, 181
Foreclosure prevention, 286
Formaldehyde, 65i, 75i, 82

Front entrance, 177, 179i
Front gable, 3
Functional neighborhoods, 114
Furnishings
  and home health, 74–77
  indoor air control, 82

G

Gambrel roof, 3
Garage, 86
Gated communities, 132–133
Gen X, 37, 39t
Generational differences,
  housing choice, 37–38
Gentrification, 132, 239
Georgian style, 5–6
Good Faith Estimate, 98
Gothic revival style, 8–9
Government National
  Mortgage Association
  (GNMA, Ginnie Mae), 150
Government-sponsored
  enterprises (GSEs), 150
Grandfathering, 121
Gray-water collection system,
  315–316
Greek revival style, 6–8
Greenhouse effect, 292
Group homes, 242
Growth restrictions, 238

H

Habitat for Humanity,
  248, 249i
Hall and Parlor homes, 2–5
Hazard insurance, 279
Hazardous chemicals
  control, 76b
  description of, 75, 75i
  storage and disposal, 76–77
Healthy home environment,
  56, 144–145. *See also*
  Environment-health
  interaction

Healthy Home Initiative
  (HHI), 145
Healthy Indoor Air for
  America's Homes,
  guidelines, 82–86
Heating Seasonal
  Performance Factor
  (HSPF), 310, 311i, 312
Heating systems, 305
"Hidden homeless," 243
Hierarchy of human needs, 27
High-rise apartment
  structures, 20
Hipped roof, 3, 16
Home, purchasing process,
  273–280
Home building, 90–94
Home Energy Rating Systems
  (HERS), 314
Home equity, 271, 284
Home improvements, 103
Home inspection, 279
HOME Investment
  Partnership, 250
Home modification, definition,
  194, 195b–196b, 196
Home Mortgage Disclosure
  Act (HMDA), 161–162
Home product hazards,
  75i, 76b
Homeless, legal definition, 243
Homeless Eligibility
  Clarification Act
  (1986), 159
Homeless Persons' Survival
  Act, 159
Homelessness, 158–159,
  242–244
Homeowners Associations, 333
Homeownership
  affordability problems,
   156–157
  disadvantages of, 260
  family impact, 262b
  financial benefits, 259–260

and housing affordability,
229, 230–232, 230t,
231t, 233t
and housing choice,
258–259, 259i
housing costs, 257
housing market,140,
260–261, 261t
housing norms, 145–150
increase in, 145i
manufactured housing, 107
median monthly costs, 257
mortgage financing,
265–267
prequalifying for, 262–265,
264t, 265t, 273–274, 274i
promotion of, 250
and race, 147i
tenure, 40
types of, 272–273
Homestead Act, 258
HOPE VI, 152, 155
House, The, 167
Household
characteristics of, 30–33
definition, 31
and homeownership, 232
types, 29
Housing adequacy, U.S.
Census Bureau, 142t
Housing
dynamic process, 168–169,
169i
industry, 329
market, 139–140,
260–261, 261t
median cost of, 257
needs, 27–29
norms, 29, 38–44, 50
quality of, 141–145
rising costs of, 229
selection, 276–277
space/amenities, 236t,
236–237, 237t
system of settings, 169–170

universal design
benefits, 207
universal design general
principles, 203–205,
206i–207i
values, 29, 35
Housing Act (1937), 152
Housing affordability
crisis in, 225, 227–228
description of, 156–158
and geographic location,
228, 228i
indices of, 226, 226b–227b,
230t, 231t
solutions for, 245–246, 246b
Housing and Society, 222
Housing and Urban
Development
accessibility guidelines, 201
affordability index, 230t, 231t
creation of, 139
Fair Market Rental data, 226b
healthy and safety, 144–145
housing affordability, 226
housing policies, 140
low income families, 239
manufactured homes, 107
manufactured housing
program, 142
minimum property
standards, 142–144
mortgage assistance, 150
PATH program, 329
and public housing, 152
rental assistance, 155
web site, 281
Housing Assistance
Council, 248
Housing challenges
affordability, 327–329
housing industry
practices, 329
land use, 330–331
loss of community,
332–333

natural resource allocation,
333–334
older adults, 331–332
Housing choice
factor identification, 29
and homeownership,
258–259
and life cycle, 31–33
and lifestyle, 29–30,
35–38, 50
as self symbol, 49
and social class, 33–34
Housing for Older Persons
Act of 1995 (HOPA), 161
Housing Opportunity Index
(HOI), 226b, 230t
Housing projects, 116. *See
also* Public housing
Housing start, 90, 91i
HUD-1 Settlement
Statement, 280
Human ecology model, 26, 28

I

Immigrants, home
ownership, 258b
Impact fees, 91, 237–238
Income
and housing choice, 34
and housing costs, 232–236,
233t, 234i, 327–328
medium monthly costs, 257
Income approach,
appraisal, 102
Income tax, homeownership
deduction, 272
Indoor air quality
control of, 76b, 82–86
and home health, 43, 71–72
In-fill housing, 157i
Insulation, energy
efficiency, 306
Insurance, 106, 279
Interaction distance, 46

Interest rates
  mortgage factor, 265,
    266t, 267
  and mortgage lending,
    96–97
  predatory
    practices, 282
Interior space
  circulation, 172–174, 187t
  conceptual framework,
    168–170
  entryways, 177–178,
    178i, 179i
  housing design, 167
  orientation, 174–176, 175i,
    176i
  plumbing, 185, 185i
  privacy, 186i,
    186–187, 188t
  storage, 184
  work areas, 179–182, 182i,
    183i, 184
  zoning, 170–172, 172i, 187t
International Building
    Code, 91
Intimate space, 45
Investment, real
    estate, 89
Irrigation, landscaping, 317

J
Joint tenancy, 272

K
Kaiser Committee, 87
Kitchens
  indoor air control, 84
  planning rules, 180i,
    180–181
  universal design features,
    205, 213i–215i
  ventilation fans, 66
  work area, 179–180

L
L-shaped kitchen, 180i, 181
Lamp, term, 312
Land subdivision regulations,
    88–89
Land use strategies,
    affordable housing, 245
Landfills, 61
Landscape plan, 294
Landscaping
  and home health, 63
  and orientation, 175–176
  resource-efficient, 317–320,
    318i, 319i
  water-wise, 316–317
Large lot development, 157–158
Laundry rooms
  universal design features,
    205, 216i
  work area, 181–182, 182i,
    183i, 184
Lawrence Berkeley National
    Laboratory, 305
Lead-based paint, 43, 57, 65i,
    83, 144, 145
Leadership in Energy and
    Environmental Design
    (LEED), 314–315
"Leapfrog" development, 94
Life cycle
  current patterns, 33
  description of, 30
  and housing choices, 32–33
  stages of, 32
  and sustainable building
    design, 321
Lifespan design, definition of,
    221i, 221t
Lifestyle, and home health,
    77–80
Living areas, 82–84
"Living wage," 244
Loan package assembly, 98
Loss mitigation tools, 286

Low embodied energy, 296
Low income family
  HUD determination, 239
  special populations, 240–242
Low Income Housing Tax
    Credit, 249
Low-income homeowners, 42
Low-income housing
  federal support, 152,
    162–163, 250–251
  rental assistance,
    154–155, 250
Lustron Home, 21, 22
Lyman, Francesca, 323

M
Mace, Ron, 200–201
Maintenance/repairs, 285
Male householder families, 31
Managed growth, 94
Management costs, 246b, 248
Mansard roof, 3
Manufactured Home
    Construction and Safety
    Standards (MHCSS), 143
Manufactured housing. See
    also Factory-built
  and affordability, 157
  HUD standards, 143
  and housing structure, 42
  industry, 106–110
Manufactured Housing
    Institute (MHI), 107
Manufactured Housing
    Program (MHP), HUD, 143
Manufactured Housing
    Research Alliance
    (MHRA), 107, 108
Married-couple families, 31, 34
Maslow, Abraham, 27
Material Safety Data Sheets
    (MSDS), 75, 77
Mechanical filtration, 72
Mechanical ventilation, 66

Microclimate, 59–60
Millennial generation, 31, 37, 39t
Millennial Housing Commission, home ownership, 230
Minimum Property Standards (MPS), HUD, 142–144
Minimum wage, 235
Minorities, and remodeling industry, 104
Mixed income townhouses, 153i
Mixing center, 181
Mobile homes, 248
Modern architecture, 1–2
Modular homes, 22, 106
Moisture
    and home health, 68–71
    indoor air pollution control, 83
    and mold, 70
    prevention of, 70–71
Molds, 57, 65i, 70, 71
Mortgage(s)
    application documents, 99, 279
    brokers, 278–279
    companies, 99
    financing of, 148, 277–279
    five financing factors, 265–267
    insurance, 96, 106, 279–280
    interest rates, 97i
    lending practices, 96–101
    origination process, 98
    payments, 267–268, 268i
    preapproval/prequalification, 98, 273–274, 274i
    processing stage, 98–99
    purchase price factor, 265, 267

terms, 265, 266t, 266–267, types, 265, 266, 266t, 267–270
Mortgage Bankers Association of America (MBAA), 100, 101
Mortgage Lending Act (2001), 283
Mortise and tenon-timber framing, 10
Moth repellents, indoor air control, 85
Mud room, 182i, 183i
Mulch, landscaping, 317
Multifamily home
    builders, 93
    characteristics of, 237
    structures, 13–14, 42
Multipaned windows, 17
Multiple Listing Service (MLS), 95, 275
Municipal water system, 72–73
Mutual savings bank, 100

N

National Association of Home Builders (NAHB)
    building industry, 92, 126, 127
    on government regulation, 237–238
    HOI, 226b
    land-site improvement costs, 126–127
    Remodeling Council, 103, 104
National Association of the Realtors (NAR), 95, 227b
National Association of the Remodeling Industry (NARI), 103
National Association of Residential Property Managers (NARPM), 105

National Fenestration Council (FRC), rating label, 306, 308, 309i
National Homeownership Strategy, 146
National Housing Act (1949), 42, 141
National Low Income Coalition Rental Housing Index (RHI), 226b-227b
National Low Income Housing Coalition (NLIHC)
    description of, 235b
    housing costs, 234–235
    housing wage, 328
National Manufactured Housing Construction and Safety Standards Act, 107
Natural environment, 26
Natural House, The, 295
Natural resources, allocation challenges, 333–334
Neighborhood(s)
    definition, 114
    integration, 131
    planning, 127
    resource theory, 117
    safety, 131–132
    satisfaction, 129–132
    statistical, 114
    study of, 115
    traditional, 134
Neighborhood Crime Watch programs, 48
Neighboring
    concept of, 130
    decline of, 332
New urbanism, 133–134, 330–331
"New Urbanist," 94
Nonconforming uses, 121
Nonfamily household, 32

Norm, definition, 38
"Not in my backyard,"
    (NIMBY), 127, 329

O

Occupancy sensors, 313
Occupation, and housing
    choice, 34
Office of Fair Housing and
    Equal Opportunity
    (FHEO), 160
Office of Lead Hazard
    Control (OLHC), 144
Older adults. *See also* Seniors
    demographic change, 197
    home modification, 194,
        195b–196b, 196
    housing affordability,
        241–242
    housing needs, 162
    number of, 331
    and universal design,
        218–219
Older home hazards, 65i
Olmstead, Frederick Law, 323
Open space design,
    173–174, 174i
Orientation
    interior space, 174–176,
        175i, 176i
    site planning, 293–294, 294i
Origination fee, 278
Out of Reach, 235b, 328
Overcrowding, 41

P

Palladian windows, 8
Panelized homes, 22, 107
Passive Infrared (PIR)
    units, 313
Passive solar design,
    297–300, 298i, 299i, 300i

Pattern books, 8
Perceptible information,
    202i, 204
Personal Responsibility and
    Work Opportunity
    Reconciliation Act
    (PRWORA), 240
Personal/personalized space,
    45, 49
Pesticides, 57, 61, 62, 75i, 86
Pests, 69, 78–79
Pets, 79–80, 84
Photovoltaics (PV),
    300–302, 301i
Physical community
    development
    compromises, 128
    critique, 126–127
    process 118–119
    tools, 119–125
Physical effect, 202i, 204
"PITI" costs, 267–268
Planned unit development
    (PUD)
    builder advantages,
        128–129
    description, 128
    resident advantages, 129
Planning
    housing approaches,
        113–114
    kitchen center, 181
Planning commissions, 118
Plants, 317, 319
Plumbing, 185, 185i
Policy tools, federal, 141
Porches, 8
Possessions, 49
Post and beam framing, 10
Prairie style, 16
Precipitation, 59
Predatory lending, 281–284,
    282b–283b
Prequalification phase, 98

Preservation rules, 88
Pressed-wood, 82, 84
Pressure-treated lumber, 65i
Price Index of New One-
    Family Houses Sold, 227b
Privacy
    floor plan checklist, 188t
    interior space, 186i,
        186–187
    spatial relationships, 46–47
Private mortgage insurance
    (PMI), 96
Private water source, 72–73
Private zone, 170, 171
Production builders, 93
Project-based assistance
    housing units, 236
    rent, 154
Property manager,
    functions, 105b
Property value
    assessment, 102
Proximics, 45
Pruitt-Igoe housing, St. Louis,
    20, 116
Public housing
    affordable housing
        solutions, 250
    and low-income renters,
        235
    renter assistance, 52–154
Public housing authority
    (PHA), 154
Public space, 45, 46
Public zone, 170
Purchase offer, 277
Purchase price, 265, 267
Putnam, Robert, 332, 333

Q

Quality, housing norm,
    42–43
Queen Anne style, 12–13

Queensland Government Department of Housing, 219–220

R

Race, homeownership, 231t, 231–232
Racial minorities, housing affordability, 240–241
Radon gas, 43, 57, 65i, 86
Railroads, impact of, 11
Rain-water, 315–316, 316i
Ranch style, 18–19, 20
Real estate agent/broker home purchase process, 275–276, 276i
    role of, 94–96
Real estate development, 88–90
Real estate licenses, 95
Real Estate Settlement Procedure Act (RESPA), 95
REALTORS®, 95, 96
Redlining, 280–281
Refinancing, 285–286
Regent Park, Toronto, 116
Regulations, federal policy tool, 141, 142
Rehabilitation Act (1973), 200
Relative deprivation theory, 117
Relative humidity, 69
Remodeling, 103–104, 285
Rental housing
    cost of, 234i, 234–235
    history of, 20
    renter population, 40
    supply of, 235–236
Rental assistance/subsidies, 152–156
Renters
    affordability problems, 156–157

housing affordability, 229, 232–236, 233t, 234i
    median monthly costs, 257
Residential buildings, number of, 292
Residential Lead-Based Paint Hazard Reduction Act (1992), 144
Residential lending, 97, 98i
Residential property management (RPM), 104–105
Residential segregation, 130–131
Reverse mortgages, 271–272
Reverse redlining, 283, 284
Roaches, 78–79
Robert Taylor Homes, Chicago, 116, 153i
Roof drainage, and home health, 63
Roosevelt, Theodore, 291
Rural Housing Service (RHS), 149, 150
Rural residents, housing affordability, 241

S

Safety, neighborhood, 131–132
Sales, appraisal approaches, 101
Savings and loan associations (S&L), mortgage lending, 99–100
Seasonable Energy Efficiency Ratio (SEER), energy efficiency, 310, 311i, 312
Sears, Roebuck and Company, 21
Seating, 46
Seattle Housing Authority, 223

Secondary mortgage market, 149–150
Section 8 voucher program, 155, 156, 235, 250
Self
    home as symbol of, 49
    in human ecology model, 26–27
"Self-help housing," 248
Semi-custom builders, 93
Senior housing builders, 93
Seniors. See also Older adults
    and housing choice, 38, 39t.
    and remodeling, 104
Sensible Heat Ratio (SHR), 312
Septic systems, 57
Service entry, 177, 179i
Shelter, 27
Shingle and Stick style, 12
Side gable, 3
Silent generation, 38
Simple/intuitive use, 202i, 203–204
Single-family homes
    characteristics of, 236t
    construction activities, 93b
    early apartments, 14
    housing starts, 90
Single-parent families, 32, 34
Site planning, 293i, 293–294
Site-built homes, 106
Size, family, 32
Sleeping room, sharing, 41
Smart thermostats, 313
Smoke detectors, 85
Social class, and housing choices, 33–34
Social contagion, 117
Social-cultural environment, 26
Socioeconomic status, 33
Solar day lighting, 300

Solar energy designs,
  297–304, 298i, 299i, 300i
Solar Heat Gain Coefficient
  (SHGC), 307
Solar quanity and quality, 59
Space adjacency, 168i,
  168–169
Space(s)
  housing norm, 40–41
  social, 45
  sociofugal, 47–48
  sociopetal, 47–48
Space/size, universal design
  principle, 202i, 205
Spatial relationships, 45–49
Special (zoning) permits, 124
Standard of Normative
  Need, 41
Statistical
  neighborhoods, 114
"Steering," 280, 282
Steward B. McKinney
  Homeless Assistance Act,
  158, 159
Storage, interior space,
  184, 184i
Storm run-off, 62–63
Storm water, 317
Structure, housing
  norm, 42
Stud wall framing, 10–11
Subdivision regulations, 124
Subprime lending, 281, 282
Subprime rates, 100, 101
Subsidized housing, 222
Subsidy
  federal policy, 141,
  250–251
  tax deductions as, 147–
  148, 249
Suburbs, 332–333
Supplemental Security
  Income (SSI), 242
Susceptibility, home
  environment, 58

Sustainable building(s)
  appliances/equipment,
  310, 311i
  building products, 295–296
  definition of, 292
  energy efficiency, 304–310,
  305i, 306i, 307i, 308i, 309i
  indoor environments,
  320–321
  lighting, 312i, 312–314
  life cycle design, 321
  performance standards,
  314–315
  renewable resources,
  297–304, 298i, 299i, 300i
  site planning, 293
  site protection, 294
  value of, 291–293
  waste reduction, 296–297
  water resources, 315–317
Sustainable communities
  characteristics of, 322–324
  description of, 321–322
Sustainable development,
  definition of, 291
Switch, design
  features, 211i
System Development Charges
  (SDC), 237–238

T

Tax expenditures, housing,
  147–148
Tenancy in common, 272
Tenant-based assistance, 154
Tenements, 13
Tenure, housing norm, 39–40
Territoriality, 48
Thermistors, 313
Thermostats, 313
Title insurance, 106
Toilet paper holder, 211i
Toilets, 13
ToolBase Services, 94

Topography, and building
  site, 60
Townhomes, 41
Toxicity, home
  environment, 57
Tradition
  architecture, 1, 2
  neighborhood
  development, 134
Trailer homes, 22
Tree/shrub placement,
  318–319, 318i
Truth-in-Lending
  disclosure, 98
Tudor style, 17
"Twelve Gates to the City," 323
Two-wall kitchen, 180i, 181

U

U-shaped kitchen, 180i, 181
Underground storage tanks,
  61, 65i
Underwriting, mortgage
  lending, 99
United Nations World
  Commission on
  Environment and
  Development, 291
United States, economy and
  housing, 87
United States Department of
  Housing and Urban
  Development (HUD). *See*
  Housing and Urban
  Development (HUD)
United States Green
  Building Council
  (USGBC), 314–315
Universal design
  current status, 220–223,
  221i, 221t
  definition of, 194, 221t
  evolution to, 196–197,
  198b, 199–201

features/products, 205, 208i–210i,
general benefits of, 191–192, 192i, 193i, 194
general principles of, 202i, 202–203
housing benefits, 207, 217–220
housing principles of, 203–205
premises of, 201–202
Universal Design Housing Network, 219
Universal Design in Housing, 205, 208i–217i
Unlocking the Door-Keys to Women's Housing, 240
Urban housing, 13
Urban Land Institute (ULI), 89–90
Urban neighborhoods, 115
Urban theory, 116
Urbanism, 116
Utility room, indoor air control, 85

V

Vapor retarder material, 71
Vernacular architecture, 1
Ventilation, 64, 66–68, 72
Veterans Administration (VA)
housing finance, 149
rehabilitation technology, 199
Victorian style, 11–14
Visible Transmittance (VT), windows, 308

Volatile organic compounds (VOCs), 57, 65i, 71, 75i, 76

W

Wages, housing affordability, 246b
Water
contamination, 57, 65i, 74
control, 51b
pollution and storm run-off, 62, 317
systems, 72–74
testing, 73
treatment, 74
wells, 73–74
Water heaters, solar, 302i, 302–303
Water systems, and home health, 72–74
Water vapor, 69
Welfare recipients, 240
Wells, 73–74
White House Conference on Home Building and Homeownership (1931), 148
White House Conference on Minoirity Ownership (2002), 146
Whole house approach, 292
Whole-house fans, 67
Whole-house ventilation systems, 68
Wind power, 303i, 303–304
Windows
energy efficiency, 306–309, 306i, 307i, 308i

orientation, 175
universal design features, 211i, 212i
Women
householder families, 31
housing affordability, 240
Wood stove, indoor air control, 83
Work areas, interior space, 179–182
Work triangle, kitchen space, 180i, 181
Work zone, 170, 171
Workforce housing, 327
World Design Congress, 200
World Health Organization, 197
Wright, Frank Lloyd, 16

Y

Yard and garden waste, 63

Z

Zoning
affordable housing, 245–246, 246b
exclusionary policies, 238–239
floor plan checklist, 187t
interior space, 170–172
sustainable communities, 323
Zoning ordinances, 88, 119–122, 120i
Zoning requirements, 121i
Zoning Board of Appeals (ZBA), process, 122–124